THE

LIVES AND TIMES

OF

THE CHIEF JUSTICES

OF THE

Supreme Court of the United States.

BY

HENRY FLANDERS.

SECOND SERIES.

WILLIAM CUSHING — OLIVER ELLSWORTH — JOHN MARSHALL.

PHILADELPHIA:
J. B. LIPPINCOTT & CO.
LONDON: TRÜBNER & CO.
1858.

STEREOTYPED BY J. FAGAN.

PREFACE.

THE Chief Justices of the United States, with a single exception, were prominently engaged in the leading events of our history as a nation. They participated actively in the scenes of the Revolution, and assisted to lay the foundations of our government. Necessarily, therefore, the narrative of their lives must comprehend a wide compass of political and historical information. We have endeavored, however, to intermingle no more of such matter than would serve to illustrate the character and services of the men whose lives we have written, and the times in which they acted.

In preparing the present volume for the press, we have received material assistance from various sources, which has lightened our labours, and contributed much to whatever is valuable in their result.

The life of Cushing, from his entire devotion to the duties belonging to his station in the judiciary, and his consequent withdrawal from politics, furnished but scanty materials for the purposes of biography. Much interesting information, however, which public documents could not supply, was courteously placed in our hands by Mr. Charles C. Paine, of Boston. To the venerable Dr. James Kendall, of Plymouth, Massachusetts, we are indebted for several interesting reminiscences, and to the Honorable Josiah Quincy, Sr., for a portraiture of his moral and intellectual characteristics. We are also under particular obligations to Mr. William S. Russell, the Recording Secretary of the Pilgrim Society at Plymouth.

The life of Ellsworth contains a number of his letters, hitherto unpublished, written while a member of the Continental Congress, and during his stay in England after the conclusion of his mission to France. They were placed at my disposal by the late Mr. Joseph Wood, of New Haven, a son-in-law of Chief Justice Ellsworth, who had prepared a biography of him on a very extensive plan, and which comprehends, it is believed, all of his correspondence that is now in existence. The reader will perceive that we are also indebted to Mr. Wood for several interesting facts and anecdotes.

Marshall's letters respecting his biography of Washington, were politely submitted to my use by Mr. James H. Castle, of the Philadelphia bar, who has preserved with praiseworthy care the extensive correspondence of Judges Washington and Marshall, relating to the publication of that work.

To Mr. Winthrop Sargent, who is well known to the public by his graceful history of Braddock's Expedition, and to his friends by his liberal culture and genial disposition, we are especially indebted for various information and many valuable suggestions.

PHILADELPHIA, Sept. 1, 1857.

CONTENTS.

THE LIFE OF WILLIAM CUSHING.

CHAPTER I.

CHAPTER II.

1732 — 1771.

CHAPTER III.

1771 — 1775.

CHAPTER IV.

1775 — 1789.

CHAPTER V.

1689 — 1796.

CHAPTER VI.

1796 — 1810.

CHAPTER VII.

LIFE OF OLIVER ELLSWORTH.

CHAPTER I.

CHAPTER II.

1745 — 1771.

CHAPTER III.

1771 — 1784.

CHAPTER IV.

1775—1781.

CHAPTER V.

1781—1783.

CHAPTER VI.

1780—1784.

CHAPTER VII.

1784—1789.

CHAPTER VIII.

1787.

CHAPTER IX.

1788.

CHAPTER X.

1789—1796.

CHAPTER XI.

1796 — 1800.

CHAPTER XII.

1799 — 1800.

CHAPTER XIII.

1799 — 1800.

CHAPTER XIV.

1800—1801.

CHAPTER XV.

1801—1807.

CHAPTER XVI.

1807.

LIFE OF JOHN MARSHALL.

CHAPTER I.

CHAPTER II.

CHAPTER III.

1775 — 1780.

CHAPTER IV.

1781 — 1799.

CHAPTER V.

1782 — 1788.

CHAPTER VI.

1788.

CHAPTER VII.

1788—1797.

CHAPTER VIII.

1797—1798.

CHAPTER IX.

1799—1800.

CHAPTER X.

1800—1801.

CHAPTER XI.

1801—1835.

CHAPTER XII.

1800—1806.

CHAPTER XIII.

1829.

CHAPTER XIV.

1829 — 1835.

THE LIFE

OF

WILLIAM CUSHING.

THE

LIFE OF WILLIAM CUSHING.

CHAPTER I.

HIS ANCESTRY.

LATE in the summer of 1638, the good ship Diligent arrived at Boston, in Massachusetts, after a passage of nearly four months, from Gravesend, England. Among her passengers was Matthew Cushing, with his wife, Nazareth Pitcher, and five children. He had come from the old country, to unite his fortunes with the pious colonists of the new. He was a God-fearing man, as may be inferred from the names of his children; two of his sons being called Daniel and Jeremiah, and two others, Matthew and John. His only daughter was named Deborah.

Matthew Cushing settled at Hingham, where he purchased lands, and resided until his death, which occurred in the year 1660, at the age of seventy-two.

His youngest son, John, was born in 1627. He married a daughter of Nicholas Jacob, of Hingham, and subsequently removed to Scituate. He appears to have been a man of character, enjoying the confidence and respect of his fellow-citizens. He was an assistant of the colony government of Plymouth, and for several years a deputy to the colony court. He died in 1708, at the advanced age of eighty-one.

His eldest son, John, was born in 1662. He rose to distinction in the colony, and filled several important offices. He was Chief Justice of the Inferior Court of Plymouth, Counsellor of Massachusetts, and for several years a Judge of the Superior Court. He died January 19th, 1738. 'He was a gentleman,' says his contemporary, the Rev. Josiah Cotton, of Plymouth, 'well versed in law; the life and soul of our Court while he continued in it; a man, in the main, of justice and integrity. He was above seventy years old when he died, and retained his faculties tolerably well to his last sickness. When the aged and honorable are taken away, we ought to be sensibly affected, and earnestly pray that others may be raised up in their stead, that may do well and worthily in their day.'[1]

By his wife, Deborah Loring, of Hull, whom he married in 1688, Judge Cushing had several children; and among the number, a son, who was born July 17th, 1695, and called John.

He was bred to the bar; and, with abilities, learning, and genial manners, readily achieved the honors of his profession. He represented his native town several years in the General Court, was a Judge of Probate, a member of the Governor's Council, and a Judge of the Superior Court. This latter position he resigned in 1771. 'He had been on the Bench for twenty-five years, and sat at the hearing of the great question of Writs of Assistance in 1760, and at the trial of Captain Preston, and the British soldiers, for the massacre of

[1] Cotton's Annals, p. 259; an unpublished manuscript. The extract in the text is taken from the 'New England Historical and Genealogical Register,' for January, 1854, p. 42.

the 5th March, 1770. By the appointment of Chief Justice Hutchinson to be Governor, and the resignation of Judge Lynde, he had become senior judge, and the office of Chief Justice was tendered him; but he determined to retire, and declined it.'[1]

As the politics of Judge Cushing were not in harmony with the opinions professed by Otis and his school, he did not, in the latter part of his life, enjoy their full confidence. Questions, involving points of political controversy, arose in the courts; and the judges, from party bias, it was thought, failed to pronounce an impartial judgment. The following extract from Adams' diary may possibly owe its raciness, in part, to political antipathy. It is characteristic of Adams, however, if not of Cushing, and is quite curious. He had set out to attend the Court at Ipswich; 'overtook,' he says, 'Judge Cushing, in his old curricle, and two lean horses, and Dick, his negro, at his right hand, driving the curricle. This is the way of travelling in 1771; — a Judge of the Circuits, a Judge of the Superior Court, a Judge of the King's Bench, Common Pleas, and Exchequer, for the Province, travels with a pair of wretched old jades of horses, in a wretched old dung-cart of a curricle, and a negro, on the same seat with him, driving. But we shall have more glorious times anon, when the sterling salaries are ordered out of the revenue, to the judges, etc., as many most ardently wish, and the judges themselves, among the rest, I suppose. Stopped at Martin's, in Lynn, with Judge Cushing; oated, and drank a glass of wine, and heard him sigh and groan the sighs and groans of seventy-seven, though he kept active. He conversed in his usual, smiling, insinuating, doubt-

[1] Manuscript sketch of William Cushing, courteously submitted to my use, by Mr. Charles Cushing Paine, of Boston.

ing, scrupling strain.' [1] Adams, in other parts of his diary, does not hesitate to charge him with being jesuitical and false.

Judge Cushing lived a little more than six years after his resignation, in the enjoyment of a competent fortune, and surrounded by a numerous circle of relatives and friends.[2]

He was twice married. His second wife was Mary Cotton, a daughter of Josiah Cotton, of Plymouth, and the mother of the subject of our biography.

---

[1] Works of John Adams, Vol. II. p. 279. June 17th, 1771.

[2] He died at Scituate, March 14th, 1778.

CHAPTER II.

1732–1771.

HIS BIRTH, EDUCATION, AND PRACTICE AT THE BAR.

WILLIAM CUSHING, whose career we are now to trace, was the son of John and Mary Cushing, of whom we have made brief mention in the preceding chapter.

He was born at Scituate, in Massachusetts, March 1st, 1732. The particulars of his early years are meagre. He was prepared for College by Mr. Richard Fitzgerald, 'a veteran Latin schoolmaster,' and at the age of fifteen admitted a member of Harvard. He graduated in 1751. What was his progress through the college course of study, whether distinguished for talents or otherwise, is, at the present day, unknown. On leaving college, or shortly after, he became preceptor of the public grammar school in Roxbury. He held this situation about a year, and then entered upon the study of the law with the celebrated Jeremiah Gridley, 'the father of the Bar in Boston.'

How devoted to his profession was Gridley himself, and how high he placed the standard of professional acquirement in others, may be inferred from the advice he gave John Adams, when, as a young man, and an applicant for admission to the Bar, he sought Gridley's aid and countenance: 'I have a few pieces of advice to give you, Mr. Adams,' said he. 'One is, to pursue the study of the law, rather than the gain of it; pursue the gain of it enough to keep out of the briers, but give your main attention to the study of it. The next is, not to marry early; for an early marriage will obstruct your improvement; and, in the next place, it will involve you in expense. Another thing is, not to keep much company, for the application of a man who aims to be a lawyer must be incessant; his attention to his books must be constant, which is inconsistent with keeping much company. In the study of law, the common law, be sure, deserves your first and last attention; and he has conquered all the difficulties of this law, who is master of the Institutes. You must conquer the Institutes. The road of science is much easier now than it was when I set out; I began with Coke — Littleton, and broke through.' I asked his advice about studying Greek. He answered, 'It is a matter of mere curiosity.'[1]

Cushing remained in the office of Gridley until he was called to the Bar, in 1755. He began his practice in his native town of Scituate; but soon after removed to Pownalborough (now Dresden), in Maine. His father owned lands in that region, and this, it is supposed, was the cause of his going there.

Pownalborough was a frontier settlement; its population a collection of Protestants from Great Britain, Ireland, France, and Germany. The greater part of them were extremely poor, and very ignorant, without the means of either religious or secular instruction.[2] Among such a people there was doubtless a great deal of 'obscure contention;' and Cushing, from the outset, seems to have found no lack of professional employment.

---

[1] Works of John Adams, Vol. II. p. 46.

[2] Life of Rev. Jacob Bailey, pp. 79, 81. Bailey was a minister of the Church of England, and a missionary in this rude settlement.

When he fixed his residence in Maine, all the country east of Piscataqua River was included within the limits of one county. But, in 1760, two new counties were created out of this extensive territory; one of them, called Lincoln, had Pownalborough for its shire-town. Cushing was appointed Judge of Probate of this latter county, and held the post during a period of twelve years. But, of this period of his life neither tradition nor local history has taken note. We presume the even tenor of his way was uninterrupted by any remarkable incidents, and that the duties of his office were faithfully and satisfactorily performed.

CHAPTER III.

1771 – 1775.

A JUDGE OF THE MASSACHUSETTS SUPERIOR COURT.

In the latter part of the year 1771, Cushing's father resigned his seat on the Bench of the Superior Court of Massachusetts, and he was appointed to fill the vacancy. He now returned to his father's in Scituate, and 'on his death, inheriting the estate, which contained about four hundred acres, he continued to reside there for the rest of his life.' [1]

In 1774, Cushing, a bachelor of forty-two, married Miss Hannah Phillips, of Middletown, Connecticut, a blooming and highly accomplished young lady of twenty. She survived her husband, to whose comfort and happiness she was ever devoted, nearly a quarter of a century; dying in 1834, at the age of eighty years, and retaining to the last a vivid recollection of the scenes and events of former days.

When Cushing took his seat upon the Bench, the political affairs of the colonies were in a very inflamed condition. The popular dissatisfaction, in Massachusetts, was daily becoming more intense. Those who were in any way connected with the administration of the Royal authority were regarded with a jealous watchfulness. Judge Cushing's position was embarrassing; but his caution and reserve were equal to all its trials. From his appointment, until the out-

---

[1] MS. Sketch, by Mr. Chas. C. Paine.

break of the Revolution, in 1775, he took no part, either on the one side or the other, and carefully abstained from any expression of his opinions; so that it was equally unknown, whether he sympathised with the policy of the ministry, or the resistance of his countrymen. We cannot speak of this guarded neutrality with approbation. It lacks the saving grace of decision and courage. Cushing's position, however, was one of much delicacy. 'His associates on the bench, with the Governor and many of the principal persons of the Royal party, were the warm personal friends of his father, to whom of course he did not wish to give offence by any avowal of his political opinions; and on the other hand, his relative Thomas Cushing, Speaker of the House of Representatives, Robert Treat Paine, John Adams, and other influential members of the popular side, were his particular friends. So great were his moderation and prudence that he continued to enjoy the respect and good will of both parties without abatement.'[1]

Moderation was a distinguishing trait of Cushing's character. He seemed incapable of strong emotions. 'Grand, swelling strains of liberty,' he might not despise; but they were incapable to warm and animate him. On the other hand, sentiments of abhorrence and indignation were foreign to his nature. The excitement of the times, however, was too great, and the apprehensions of the popular leaders too lively, to enable him to enjoy his office with undisturbed tranquillity. Soon after his accession to the bench, a violent contest arose respecting the payment of the judges' salaries. Formerly they had been paid by the Province; but about this time the ministry

---

[1] MS. Sketch, by Chas. C. Paine.

determined that they should be paid by the Crown.[1] When this intelligence reached Boston, it occasioned a prodigious excitement. The change was denounced as 'big with fatal evils.'[2] The judges already held their commissions during the King's pleasure, and, hence, would be entirely dependent on the Crown, if they derived their salaries from the same source. When the Assembly met in January, 1773, they made the usual appropriations for the judges; but the Governor, anticipating the receipt of a royal warrant for their payment, witheld his assent to their grants.[3] The Assembly now resolved, that any one of the judges accepting his salary from the Crown, would discover to the world, that he had not a due sense of the importance of an impartial administration of justice; that he was an enemy to the Constitution, and had it in his heart to promote the establishment of an arbitrary government in the Province.

At the next session, in June, it was resolved, to be the duty of the judges to declare, without delay, whether they would receive their salaries from the Province or the Crown. If from the latter, then it would be the duty of the House to impeach them before the Governor and Council, as men disqualified to hold the important posts they sustained.

This notion of impeachment was original, it seems, with John Adams. 'At this period,' he says, 'the universal cry among the friends of their country was, 'What shall we do to be saved?' It was by all agreed, as the Governor was entirely dependent on the Crown, and the Council in danger of becoming so,

---

[1] This change was made Aug. 7th, 1772.

[2] Proceedings of the Boston Town Meeting, Oct. 28th, 1772; vide Gordon, vol. i., pp. 314–320; Bradford, vol. i., pp. 258–262.

[3] Mass. State Papers, pp. 365–367.

if the judges were made so too, the liberties of the country would be totally lost, and every man at the mercy of a few slaves of the Governor; but no man presumed to say what ought to be done, and what could be done. Intimations were frequently given, that this arrangement should not be submitted to. I understood very well what was meant, and I fully expected that if no expedient could be suggested, the judges would be obliged to go where Secretary Oliver had gone, to Liberty Tree, and compelled to take an oath to renounce the royal salaries. Some of these judges were men of resolution; and the Chief Justice, in particular, piqued himself so much upon it, and had so often gloried in it on the bench, that I shuddered at the expectation that the mob might put on him a coat of tar and feathers, if not put him to death. I had a real respect for the judges; three of them, Trowbridge, Cushing, and Brown, I could call my friends. Oliver and Ropes, abstracted from their politics, were amiable men, and all of them were very respectable and virtuous characters. I dreaded the effect upon the morals and tempers of the people, which must be produced by any violence offered to the persons of those who wore the robes and bore the sacred characters of judges; and moreover, I felt a strong aversion to such partial and irregular recurrences to original power. The poor people themselves, who by secret manœuvres are excited to insurrection, are seldom aware of the purposes for which they are set in motion, or of the consequences which may happen to themselves; and when once heated and in full career, they can neither manage themselves, nor be regulated by others.'[1]

[1] Works of John Adams, vol. ii., pp. 328–330.

Full af these reflections, he happened to dine, he says, with Mr. Samuel Winthrop, at New Boston, in company with several members of the general court and other gentlemen of the town. The conversation turned wholly on the topic of the day and the case of the judges. Adams expressed the opinion that they had a constitutional resource; which was nothing more nor less than an impeachment of the judges, by the House of Representatives, before the Council. The idea thus suggested was adopted, and shortly applied.

At the opening of the January session,[1] Judge Trowbridge informed the House that he had heretofore, and intended hereafter, to receive his salary from the Province, and not from the Crown. The other judges delayed their decision; but a method was adopted to obtain it. The House resolved, that, unless they should declare within three days, that they would receive their salaries from the General Assembly, and not from the Crown, decisive measures would be adopted. This action of the House brought the judges to a speedy conclusion, and within the specified time, Justices Ropes, Hutchinson, and Cushing declared their determination to receive their salaries from the Province.[2] But the Chief Justice said he could not decline the grants of the King, without his Majesty's leave, 'lest he should incur a censure from the best of sovereigns.'

Mrs. Warren, who was not altogether free from personal and party prejudices, thus speaks of this action of the judges: 'Two of the judges, Trowbridge and Ropes, readily complied with the demand, and relinquished the offensive stipend. A third was William Cushing, Esq.,

---

[1] 1774.

[2] Samuel Adams to Arthur Lee, April 4th, 1774; Force's Archives, vol. i., p. 238.

a gentleman rendered respectable in the eyes of all parties by his professional abilities and general integrity. He was a sensible, modest man, well acquainted with law, but remarkable for the secresy of his opinions: this kept up his reputation through all the ebullitions of discordant parties. He readily resigned the royal stipend, without any observations of his own; yet it was thought at the time that it was with a reluctance that his taciturnity could not conceal. By this silent address he retained the confidence of the Court faction, nor was he less a favorite among the Republicans.'[1]

The House of Representatives exhibited articles of impeachment against Chief Justice Oliver before the Council; but the Council would do nothing, and there they rested. However, they were printed in the newspapers, and indirectly effected all the good that was anticipated from them. For, when the Superior Court came to sit at Boston, in August,[2] both the grand and petit jurors refused to take their oaths, assigning among other reasons, that the Chief Justice had been charged with high crimes and misdemeanors by the late honorable House of Representatives, and that he had never been legally acquitted; but had been declared by that House to be unqualified to act

[1] Warren's American Revolution, vol. i., p. 117.

[2] 'Since the unwarrantable impeachment of the Chief Justice, I understand he has never taken his seat upon the bench, but he has promised me to attend the Superior Court, at Boston, towards the end of the month; and I hope he will preside also in said Court, to be held at Worcester, in September, notwithstanding the threats thrown out against him. I have engaged to meet him at Boston, to prevent violence, which, from the present system, I don't expect to meet with there; and I believe that I must attend him also at Worcester, where I am to expect it.' Governor Gage to the Earl of Dartmouth, August 27th, 1774; Force's Archives, vol. i., p. 741.

as Judge of that Court. In this dilemma, the Court adjourned until the next day, when the judges, with the exception of the Chief Justice, came into Court; 'and to the inexpressible grief of their fellow-citizens, went on to such business as is usually transacted without juries.'[1]

But the measures adopted by the popular leaders, to interrupt and thwart all judicial proceedings, together with the general determination of the people, that courts acting under the Royal Government, and in conflict, as was believed, with their charter, should not be permitted to sit, put an end, for the present, to the regular administration of justice in Massachusetts. The Boston Port Bill, and the subsequent acts for regulating the government of the Province, and for the more impartial administration of justice there, had produced a state of feeling that rendered the exercise of any branch of the Royal authority well-nigh impossible. 'Civil government,' thus wrote Gage to the Earl of Dartmouth, 'is near its end; the courts of justice expiring one after another; and where there is no other reason for not suffering them, it is, that the judges of the Inferior Courts, as well as the justices, are under the Governor's influence by the new acts, though the said acts don't take place, as to juries, till next month; but he may now

[1] Force's Archives, vol. i., p, 749. The propriety of General Gage's presence at Boston, at the opening of the Court, wonld seem to be vindicated by the following extract from a letter written by a gentleman in Boston, Aug. 29th: — 'To-morrow,' thus he wrote, 'will be the great, the important day here. Chief Justice Oliver, impeached by the Assembly last winter, for holding that office under his Majesty's appointment, will sit on the bench at the Superior Court; the Discontents vow he shall not; but the General has come hither from Salem to support him, — so we shall see which will prove the strongest.' Ibid., p. 744.

turn them, the judges and justices, out at pleasure, though he has as yet made no change in them. . . . . The judges of the Superior Court have been with me, in a body, to represent the impossibility of carrying on the business of their Court, in any part of the Province; that the force there was by far too small to protect them everywhere, and after all, no jurors would swear in; that it was needless laying fines, which they could not do on grand juries, there being no law for it in the Province; and withal, it would be in vain, the refusal being universal.'[1]

'As to the Courts,' thus wrote Joseph Hawley, a few months later, 'we must embarrass and retard them, by preventing suitors, jurors, witnesses, &c., going into them, by all ways and means, that I have not time now to explain. A sharp eye must be kept on them, that we may fully know the success of the attempts to establish the regulation so far as it respects the Courts. Sir, I think it of much importance to do this: as you regard your own life and your usefulness to your country, you should most attentively reflect on the steps and proceedings of the Court now sitting at Boston. If they get a grand jury, then they will probably obtain indictments of high treason, and indictments will not be procured without a view and respect to arrests and commitments, convictions, hangings, drawings, and quarterings. What your chance will be I need not tell you.'[2]

We have now arrived at the period, when all judicial authority, emanating from the Crown, was overthrown in Massachusetts. In the following chapter, however, we shall see that it was presently re-established by the Provincial Congress.

---

[1] Sept. 2d, 1774; Force's Archives, vol. i., p. 767.

[2] Hawley to Thos. Cushing, Feb. 22d, 1775. Journals of Mass. Provincial Congress, p. 751.

CHAPTER IV.

1775 – 1789.

CHIEF JUSTICE OF MASSACHUSETTS

CUSHING'S position as one of the royal judges, coupled with his impenetrable reserve on political subjects, exposed him to suspicion; but, doubtless, the respect entertained for him personally, prevented any unpleasant manifestation of it. Besides, the rapid progress of events soon compelled him to declare his sentiments and assume his ground. Alone, of all the royal judges, he took the side of his countrymen. That he acted decisively and satisfactorily, may be inferred from the fact that when the Provincial Congress re-organized the Judiciary, in the autumn of 1775, he was appointed one of the judges of the Superior Court.

In this position, he necessarily incurred great responsibility, and upon the supposition of defeat overtaking the efforts of his countrymen, great danger. For usurpation of the functions of justice — and usurpation it would be considered — would have exposed him, in case of disaster, to the severest punishment. He acted, nevertheless, with firmness; though, it would seem, somewhat doubtful of the grounds on which he proceeded. 'I can tell the grand jury the nullity of acts of Parliament,' — thus he wrote John Adams, who, under the new arrangement, had been appointed Chief Justice — 'but must leave you to prove it by the more powerful arguments of the *jus gladii divinum*, a power not peculiar to kings or ministers.'[1]

As the contest proceeded, Cushing perceived the irreconcilable views of the two countries, and that independence was essential to the security and welfare of his own. At a town meeting, in Scituate, on the 4th of June, 1776, he was appointed on a committee to draft instructions to the representatives of the town in the Provincial Congress, and thus expressed his sentiments upon the great question then agitating the public mind. 'The ministry of that kingdom,' (Great Britain,) — such is the language of the instructions, as written by Cushing — 'having formed the design of subjecting the Colonies to a distant, external and absolute power in all cases whatsoever, wherein the Colonies have not, and in the nature of things cannot have any share by representation, have, for a course of years past, exerted their utmost endeavors to put the same plan, so destructive to both countries, into execution; but finding it (through the noble and virtuous opposition of the sons of freedom) impracticable, they have had at length a fatal recourse to that which is still more repugnant to a free government, viz., a standing army — to fire and sword, to blood and devastation — calling in the aid of foreign troops, as well as endeavoring to stir up the savages of the wilderness, being determined to exercise their barbarities upon us, and, to all appearance, to extirpate, if practicable, the Americans from the face of the earth, unless they will tamely resign the rights of humanity, and to repeople this once happy country with the ready sons of vassalage.

'We therefore, apprehending that such subjection

[1] May 28th, 1776; Adams's Works, vol. ix., p. 390.

will be inconsistent with the just rights and blessings of society, unanimously instruct you to endeavor that our delegates in Congress be informed (in case that representative body shall think fit to declare the Colonies independent of Great Britain) of our readiness and determination to assist with our lives and fortunes, in support of that necessary measure.'

The town-meeting is the peculiar institution of New England; the original fountain, as it were, of the popular liberties; the practical school in which her citizens are taught the rights and duties of freemen. On this theatre, Cushing is said to have been invincible. He was an eloquent speaker; not eloquent in the highest sense; but easy in his elocution, and logical in his argument. 'His oratory,' says his Pastor, the Rev. Samuel Deane, 'was ready and flowing; but not of that overawing description with which some native orators, of more fiery mould, have transported audiences; but its excellence consisted in cool, deliberate judgment, and logical and lucid argumentation, which gave him eventually an advantage over those of more ardent temperaments.'[1]

On the resignation of John Adams, as Chief Justice of the Superior Court of Massachusetts[2] (Adams, by the bye, never served in that capacity, being occupied in the Continental Congress), Cushing succeeded to the vacant post. Of his labors, while presiding in this Court, but little has been transmitted that would interest the reader. He was, however, universally regarded by the Bar as an able Judge. His legal knowledge was accurate and extensive, and he always proved himself equal to the requirements of his position. He was eminent for the dignity and courtesy

[1] History of Scituate, p. 257.

[2] Adams resigned in Feb. 1777.

of his manner. There are yet living those who knew him as Chief Justice of Massachusetts; and they retain a strong impression of the respect which his *presence* inspired. 'I was personally acquainted with Judge Cushing during the last ten years of his life,' says the venerable and Rev. Dr. James Kendall, of Plymouth; 'was often at his house, and partook of the hospitality and kindness of his amiable and highly respected family. As a public man, and particularly as Chief Justice of the State, I knew him from my youth. My earliest impressions of Judge Cushing were received by hearing my father describe his bearing and manner, as presiding Judge, at the trial of the murderers of Dr. Spooner, of Petersham, in the county of Worcester, more than seventy years ago. My father lived in Sterling, twelve miles from Worcester, and was present at the trial of these criminals, four in number, including the wife of Dr. Spooner. I have a distinct recollection of the mild, and yet dignified manner, as described by my father, in which he presided at the trial, the impressiveness of his charge to the jury, and the solemnity and thrilling effect of the sentence pronounced by the Judge after conviction, not only upon the criminals, but also upon the Bar, and the whole audience assembled on this interesting and exciting occasion.'[1]

The air of superior dignity which peculiarly distinguished Chief Justice Cushing, was no doubt heightened by the large judicial wig, at that time worn by the Judges, and which he was among the last to give up. 'I remember the appearance of Judge Cushing myself,' says Mr. Hopkins, of Maine. 'I was very young at the few times when I saw him. It was some

---

[1] MS. Letter to the Author.

years before I entered upon the study of law. I very well remember, and perhaps I may never forget, the strong impression his appearance made upon my mind when I first saw him, as he was walking in a street in Portland. He was a man whose deportment surpassed all the ideas of personal dignity I had ever formed. His professional wig, I have no doubt, added much to the imposing effect of his external appearance.'[1]

The impression supposed to be made by dress, by externals, was carefully regarded by our ancestors. Besides, English custom dominated in this, as in weightier matters, and prescribed the mode. But, as mind becomes cultivated, and knowledge generally diffused, an appeal merely to the senses is no longer available — external appearance, solely, no longer inspires awe or begets respect. If peculiar, so as to designate a class or profession, it either ceases to make any impression at all, from being constantly observed, or excites ridicule instead of reverence. In either case, it is useless for its objects. 'The dress of the Judges before the Revolution,' it is stated in the Memoir of Governor Increase Sumner, 'and which was continued by them afterwards, was a black silk gown, worn over a full black suit, white bands, and a silk bag for the hair. This was worn by the Judges in civil causes, and criminal trials, excepting those for capital offences. In these, they wore scarlet robes, with black velvet collars, and cuffs to their large sleeves, and black velvet facings to their robes. The dignified appearance of the Judges, in either dress, made an impression upon the public mind of reverence for the authority of the law.'[2]

---

[1] Address before the Cumberland Bar of Maine, by J. D. Hopkins, 1833.

[2] Genealogical Register for April, 1854, p. 116.

Judge Cushing presided as Chief Justice in the Superior Court of Massachusetts for about twelve years. His whole period of service in that Court, as Associate and Chief Justice, before and subsequent to the Revolution, was about seventeen years. The labors of the Reporter, however, had not yet been invoked, and hence the record of this portion of his judicial career is meagre.

One of his decisions, as relating to an interesting event in the history of Massachusetts, will naturally arrest the reader's attention. The Constitution of that State, in the first article of the Bill of Rights, declared that all men were born free and equal, and had certain natural, essential, and unalienable rights, etc.[1] This general axiom, Cushing held, operated, *per se*, to abolish slavery in Massachusetts. The case is thus reported.

At the April term of the Superior Court, held at Worcester, in 1783, Nathaniel Jennison was tried for assault and battery on one Quacks. 'The justification is,' said the Chief Justice, in his charge to the jury, 'that Quacks is his slave; and to prove it, it is said that Quacks, when a child about nine months old, with his father and mother, was sold, by bill of sale, in 1754, about twenty-nine years ago, to Mr. Caldwell, now deceased; that when he died, Quacks was appraised as part of the personal estate, and set off to the widow in her share of the same; that Dr. Jennison, marrying her, was entitled to Quacks as his property; and, therefore, that he had a right to bring him home when he ran away, and that the defendant only took proper measures for that purpose. And the defendant's counsel also rely on some former laws of the

[1] This was the Constitution, adopted March 2, 1780.

Province, which give countenance to slavery. As to the doctrine of slavery, and the right of Christians to hold Africans in perpetual servitude, and sell and treat them as we do our horses and cattle, that (it is true) has been heretofore countenanced by the Province laws, but nowhere is it expressly enacted or established. It has been a usage; a usage which took its origin from the practice of some of the European nations, and the regulations of the British Government respecting the then Colonies for the benefit of trade and wealth. But whatever sentiments have formerly prevailed in this particular, or slid in upon us by the example of others, a different idea has taken place with the people of America, more favorable to the natural rights of mankind, and to that innate desire of liberty, with which Heaven, without regard to color, complexion, or shape of feature, has inspired all the human race. And upon this ground, our Constitution of Government, by which the people of this Commonwealth have solemnly bound themselves, sets out with declaring that all men are born free and equal, and that every subject is entitled to liberty, and to have it guarded by the laws, as well as life and property; and, in short, is totally repugnant to the idea of being born slaves.

'This being the case, I think the idea of slavery is inconsistent with our own conduct and Constitution, and there can be no such thing as perpetual servitude of a rational creature, unless his liberty is forfeited by some criminal conduct, or given up by personal consent or contract.'

Thus instructed, it is useless, perhaps, to add, that the verdict of the jury was *guilty*, and that with this trial slavery ceased to exist in Massachusetts. But, however the reader may commend the result of the doctrine laid down by the Chief Justice, it may well be questioned, whether the doctrine itself has any adequate foundation. When the Constitution of Massachusetts was adopted, slavery was an existing institution of the State; though, to be sure, its roots had not struck deep, nor spread far. It had been introduced in virtue of the commercial policy of the mother country, was accepted by the Colony, and regulated by its laws. Neither the Constitution nor any subsequent legislation had undertaken to abolish it. The general proposition asserted in the Bill of Rights, that all men are born free, etc., did not exist as a law for the Courts to expound and apply; but as a guide and land-mark for the Legislature. It might be a ground for the abolition of slavery by legislative authority; but could afford none, it would seem, for its overthrow by judicial authority. The decision of Judge Cushing, however, affected a system that was fast expiring, indeed, that could hardly be said to exist at all, and harmonized well with the general sentiment of the community.

From the close of the Revolution until the year 1787, the Courts of Massachusetts had to tread a rugged and difficult path. The war had entailed on the State an enormous debt. Inclusive of its proportion of the Federal debt, the amount exceeded fifteen millions of dollars. In addition to this, the several towns had contracted debts, to meet the requisitions upon them, and furnish supplies for the troops. Borne down by the pressure of taxation, and harrassed by distraints and executions, the people visited their exasperation on the Courts, through whose instrumentality the claims upon them were enforced. They had not expended their blood and substance, in the late war, to secure a liberty which, with a strange inconsistency, should transfer them to a jail, and their families to the alms-house. 'They could not realize that they had shed their blood in the field, to be worn out with burdensome taxes at home; or that they had contended, to secure to their creditors a right to drag them into courts and prisons.'[1] The Shays' insurrection was the natural result of these distresses and these feelings.

'The Courts and Judges were subjected during these times to great annoyances, and occasionally to much personal danger; frequently, the court-houses were surrounded and filled by people armed and highly excited, and the Judges were refused admittance at the inns, or food either for themselves or their horses. One occasion, in particular, has been often mentioned, when the Judges were exposed to imminent hazard of their lives. On arriving at the inn of a town where the court was to be held, they found the whole intervening space to the court-house filled by a mob of many hundred, armed, and resolved to prevent the opening of the court. The Chief Justice was applied to by a committee from the mob, and entreated to yield to their wishes; he replied, that the law appointed the court to be held at that time, and it was their duty to hold it accordingly; and, followed by his Associates, he proceeded into the street. His countenance was blanched to paleness, but his step was firm. As he advanced, the crowd opened before him, but slowly and sullenly; muskets rattled, and some bayonets rapped upon his breast; quietly and firmly, however, he moved on, reached the court-house, and the court was regularly opened. The respect and affection universally borne towards him

[1] Minot's History, p. 16.

contributed, without doubt, in no slight degree, to preserve the public support to the courts, and maintain their authority in this crisis.'[1]

During all these scenes of tumult and disorder, it is well attested that the Judiciary acted with becoming dignity and firmness. That Cushing enjoyed the confidence and respect of the people, is sufficiently evinced by the fact, that upon Governor Hancock declining a re-election in the canvass of 1785, committees from both parties invited the Chief Justice to be their united candidate for the post. This honor, however, he declined. Indeed, he steadily avoided, it would seem, all posts that would withdraw him from the Judiciary. In 1794, he was again solicited to be a candidate for Governor of Massachusetts. '*Entre nous*,' thus he wrote his friend, Increase Sumner, 'some gentlemen have proposed to me to stand for the first magistracy of our State; but many weighty reasons prompted me to decline the too high and arduous task. There is our good Lieut. Governor,[2] who stands in the direct line of promotion, and who has waded through a sea of political troubles, and grown old in labors for the good of his country; why not he?'[3]

Cushing continued in the Supreme Court of Massachusetts, as Chief Justice, until the organization of the Supreme Court of the United States, in 1789, when, as we shall see in the next chapter, he was appointed an Associate Justice of that tribunal.

---

[1] MS. Sketch, by Mr. Chas. C. Paine.

[2] Samuel Adams, who was chosen Governor.

[3] Memoir of Governor Increase Sumner, 'New England Genealogical Register,' p. 117.

CHAPTER V.

1789 - 1796.

ASSOCIATE JUDGE OF THE SUPREME COURT OF THE UNITED STATES.

THE Constitution adopted by the Federal Convention, and submitted to the States for their ratification, received Cushing's approval and support. He was elected a member of the Massachusetts Convention from his native town of Scituate, and took his seat in that body at its meeting in January, 1788. Hancock was chosen President, and Cushing Vice-President. In the absence of Hancock, from ill-health, Cushing presided over the deliberations of the Convention during a great part of the session.

The Convention numbered three hundred and sixty members; and when they first came together, a spirit strongly averse to the Constitution was manifested; and, on the final vote, only a majority of nineteen was obtained in its favor. Owing to his position, doubtless, as presiding officer, Cushing does not appear to have participated in the discussions which distinguished the sessions of the Convention.

The Constitution ratified by the requisite number of States, Washington was called by the universal voice of his countrymen to the highest post in the new government. At the election in Massachusetts, Cushing was chosen one of the Electors of President and Vice-President; and on the organization of the

Federal Government, he was appointed one of the Associate Justices of the Supreme Court.[1]

His commission was dated September 27, 1789.[2] He was present at the first term of the Supreme Court, held at New York, in February, 1790. It was probably his first appearance in that city; and he was accustomed to relate the following anecdote concerning it. We have elsewhere mentioned that he was among the last to give up the old-fashioned judicial wig. He wore it on this occasion, unconscious that its appearance was singular; but while walking in the street he noticed that about a hundred boys followed him, with marked attention and perfect silence. He thought it odd; but the incident excited little of his notice. At length, turning a corner, he was met by as many more, who turned around to another crowd behind them, and exclaimed, 'Hurrah! here he is!' This could not but excite more of his attention; but although it was apparent that he was the subject of the exclamation, he was utterly at a loss to divine the cause of it; but a sailor passing accidentally, and noticing the crowd, soon directed his eyes to the object f their attention. The sailor, too, was astonished, and involuntarily exclaimed, 'My eyes! what a wig!' Cushing was now let into the secret, and returning to his lodgings, sent for a peruke-maker, and obtained a more fashionable covering for his head. He never again wore the professional wig.[3]

We have elsewhere stated[4] that the first terms of

---

[1] See vol. i. of this work, pp. 383, 621

[2] The Associate Judges, and in the order of their appointment, were, Rutledge, Wilson, Cushing, Harrison, and Blair.

[3] Address of J. D. Hopkins, before the Cumberland Bar of Maine, 1833.

[4] Vol. i., p. 384.

the Supreme Court were attended with little or no business. Meanwhile, agreeably to the provisions of the Judiciary bill, Circuit Courts were held twice a year in each of the judicial districts. Much of the time of a judge in those days was spent in travelling; there were no railroads, and the best common roads were bad. While on the State bench, Cushing's rides extended into Maine, then a part of Massachusetts; and on the United States bench, as the circuits were then annually changed, he travelled over the whole Union, holding courts in Virginia, the Carolinas, and Georgia. His travelling equipage was a four-wheeled phæton, drawn by a pair of horses; which he drove. It was remarkable for its many ingenious arrangements (all of his contrivance) for carrying books, choice groceries, and other comforts. Mrs. Cushing always accompanied him, and generally read aloud while riding. His faithful servant, Prince, a jet-black Negro, whose parents had been slaves in the family, and who loved his master with unbounded affection, followed behind, in a one-horse vehicle, with the baggage.[1]

We shall now submit to the reader several of Cushing's judgments, while on the bench of the Supreme Court, which furnish, perhaps, the best criterion, that we possess, to form an opinion of his learning and ability.

In the case of Chisholm *v.* Georgia,[2] which involved the question, whether a State can be sued by a citizen of another State, he concurred in the affirmative opinion of the Court. He thought it resulted clearly from the letter of the Constitution, and was equally consistent with its spirit. To the suggestion, that

---

[1] C. C. Paine. [2] 2 Dallas, 419.

this would reduce the States to mere corporations, and take away all sovereignty, he thus replied: —

'As to corporations, all States whatever are corporations or bodies politic. The only question is, what are their powers? As to individual States and the United States, the Constitution marks the boundaries of powers. Whatever power is deposited with the Union by the people for their own necessary security, is so far a curtailing of the power and prerogatives of States. This is, as it were, a self-evident proposition; at least it cannot be contested. Thus the power of declaring war, making peace, raising and supporting armies for public defence, levying duties, excises and taxes, if necessary, with many other powers, are lodged in Congress; and are a most essential abridgment of State sovereignty. Again, the restrictions upon States: 'No State shall enter into any treaty, alliance, or confederation, coin money, emit bills of credit, make any thing but gold and silver a tender in payment of debts, or pass any law impairing the obligation of contracts;' these, with a number of others, are important restrictions of the power of States, and were thought necessary to maintain the Union; and to establish some fundamental, uniform principles of public justice, throughout the whole Union. So that, I think, no argument of force can be taken from the sovereignty of States. Where it has been abridged, it was thought necessary for the greater, indispensable good of the whole.'

We have elsewhere observed, that the decision in this case caused great alarm, and led to an amendment of the Constitution.[1]

In the case of Ware *v.* Hylton,[2] a case equally dis-

---

[1] See vol. i., p. 388. [2] 3 Dallas, 199.

tinguished for the important question involved, and the rare ability with which it was argued, Cushing discussed the point in issue with great force and clearness. That point was, whether the act of Virginia, passed during the war, sequestering British debts, was a bar to their recovery, notwithstanding the Treaty of 1783 provided that creditors on either side should meet with no lawful impediment to the recovery of the full value, in sterling money, of all *bona fide* debts theretofore contracted. Cushing held, with the majority of the Court, that the Treaty revived the debts in favor of the creditors, and removed the bar to a recovery which the law of Virginia had interposed.

'I shall not,' said he, 'question the right of a State to confiscate debts. Here is an act of the Assembly of Virginia, passed in 1777, respecting debts; which, contemplating to prevent the enemy deriving strength by the receipt of them during the war, provides that if any British debtor will pay his debt into the Loan Office, obtain a certificate and receipt as directed, he shall be discharged from so much of the debt. But an intent is expressed in the act not to confiscate, unless Great Britain should set the example. This act, it is said, works a discharge and a bar to the payer. If such payment is to be considered as a discharge, or a bar, so long as the act had force, the question occurs, — Was there a power, by the treaty, supposing it contained proper words, entirely to remove this law, and this bar, out of the creditor's way?'

The power he deemed undeniable, 'the treaty having been sanctioned, in all its parts, by the Constitution of the United States, as the supreme law of the land. Then arises the great question, upon the import of the fourth article of the treaty; and to me, the plain and obvious meaning of it goes to nullify, *ab initio*, all laws, or the impediments of any law, as far as they might have been designed to impair or impede the creditor's right or remedy against the original debtor. . . . The article, speaking of creditors, and *bona fide* debts heretofore contracted, plainly contemplates debts, as originally contracted, and creditors and original debtors; removing out of the way all legal impediments; so that a recovery might be had, as if no such laws had particularly interposed. The words, 'recovery of the full value in sterling money,' if they have force or meaning, must annihilate all tender-laws, making any thing a tender, but sterling money; and the other words, or at least the whole taken together, must, in like manner, remove all other impediments of law, aimed at the recovery of those debts. What has some force to confirm this construction, is the sense of all Europe, that such debts could not be touched by States, without a breach of public faith; and for that, and other reasons, no doubt, this provision was insisted upon, in full latitude, by the British negotiators. If the sense of the article be, as stated, it obviates, at once, all the ingenious, metaphysical, reasoning and refinement upon the words, *debt, discharge, extinguishment*, and affords an answer to the decision made in the time of the interregnum — that payment to the sequestors, was payment to the creditor. A State may make what rules it pleases; and those rules must necessarily have place within itself. But here is a treaty, the supreme law, which overrules all State laws upon the subject, to all intents and purposes; and that makes the difference. Diverse objections are made to this construction: that it is an odious one, and, as such, ought to be avoided; that treaties regard the existing state of things; that it would carry an imputation upon public faith; that it is founded upon the power of eminent domain, which ought not to be exercised, but upon the most urgent occasions; that the negotiators themselves did not think they had power to repeal laws of confiscation; because they, by the fifth article, only agreed, that Congress should recommend a repeal to the States.'

These objections Judge Cushing answers *seriatim*. 'As to the rule respecting odious constructions,' said he, 'that takes place where the meaning is doubtful, not where it is clear, as I think it is in this case. But it can hardly be considered as an odious thing, to inforce the payment of an honest debt, according to the true intent and meaning of the parties contracting; especially if, as in this case, the State having received the money, is bound in justice and honor, to indemnify the debtor, for what it in fact received. In whatever other lights this act of Assembly may be reviewed, I consider it in one, as containing a strong implied engagement, on the part of the State, to indemnify every one who should pay money under it, pursuant to the invitation it held out. . . .

'The provision, that 'creditors shall meet with no lawful impediment,' &c., is as absolute, unconditional, and peremptory, as words can well express, and made not to depend on the will and pleasure, or the optional conduct of any body of men whatever. To effect the object intended, there is no want of proper and strong language; there is no want of power, the treaty being sanctioned as the supreme law, by the Constitution of the United States, which nobody pretends to deny to be paramount and controlling to all State laws, and even State constitutions, whensoever they interfere or disagree.'

In the case of Penhallow *v.* Doane,[1] — a case of no special interest at this day, and only cited to give the reader an opportunity to see how Judge Cushing deals with legal subjects — this, among other points, was presented to the Court: whether the Court of Appeals, erected by the Continental Congress, had authority to reverse the sentences given in the Courts of Admiralty of the several States?

Cushing, Justice. — 'I concur with the rest of the Court, that the Court of Appeals, being a court under the Confederation of 1781, of all the States, and being a court for "determining finally, appeals in all cases of capture," and so being the highest court, the dernier resort in all such cases, their decision upon the jurisdiction and upon the merits of the cause, having heard the parties by their counsel, must be final and conclusive, to this, and all other courts. To this, as a Court of Admiralty, because it is a court of the same kind, as far as relates to prize, and without any controlling or revisionary powers over it. To this, as a Court of Common Law, because it is entirely a prize-matter, and not of common law cognizance. The cases, therefore, cited to show, that the common law is of general jurisdiction, and that the Court of King's Bench prohibits, controls, and keeps within their line, Admiralty courts, Spiritual courts, and other courts of a special, limited jurisdiction, do not, I conceive, touch this case. It is conceded by all, that the decision of a court competent is final and binding. Now, if the Court of Appeals was, under the Confederation of all the States, a court constituted "for determining finally appeals in all cases of capture," it was a court competent; and they have decided. Again;

---

[1] 3 Dallas, 54.

the Admiralty of England; why not equal reason here? . . .

'As to the original question of the powers of Congress, respecting captures, much has been well and eloquently said on both sides. I have no doubt of the sovereignty of the States, saving the powers delegated to Congress, being such as were "proper and necessary" to carry on, unitedly, the common defence in the open war that was carried on against this country, and in support of their liberties to the end of the contest. But, as has been said, I conceive we are concluded upon that point, by a decision heretofore made.

'The second exception in error is, that the sentence of the Court of Appeals was void by the death of Mr. Doane. That fact does not appear upon the record of the Court of Appeals, and I think we cannot reverse the decree in this incidental way, if it could be done by writ of error. If it was pleadable in abatement, it ought to have been pleaded as suggested there by the opposite party. On the contrary, it is implied by the record, that Doane was alive; otherwise he could not have been heard by his counsel, as the record sets forth; for a dead man could not have counsel or attorney. On the other hand, the letters of administration imply that he was dead at the time; but those letters were not before the Court, and therefore could not be a ground for their abating the suit, if it was abateable at all for such a cause. Here seems to be record against record, as far as implications go, and I take it to be an error in fact, for which, by the judicial act, there is to be no reversal. Upon this head, a case in *Sir Thos. Raymond* is cited by the counsel for the plaintiff in error, of trover by five plaintiffs — one dies — the rest proceed to verdict and judgment — and adjudged error, because every man is to recover according to the right he has at the time of bringing the action; and here each one was not, at the time of bringing the action, entitled to so much as at the death of one of the plaintiffs. But a case in *Chancery Cases*, p. 122, is more in point, — where money was made payable by the decree to a man that was dead, and yet adjudged, among other things, no error. But another matter, which seems well to rule this case, is, that, being a suit *in rem*, death does not abate it.'

These few specimens of Cushing's judicial judgments will enable the reader to form an estimate of his general ability. His mind was evidently well adapted to pursue legal investigations. 'As a judge,' says the Rev. Samuel Deane, 'he was eminently qualified by his learning, and not less by his unshaken integrity and deliberate temper. The writer of this notice first saw him on the bench in 1801, when his zenith brightness had probably abated, but he still remembers how forcibly his youthful mind was affected by the order and perspicuity with which he performed the duties of his high office, and the mild though commanding dignity with which he guided the bar.'[1]

With his acknowledged high qualities as a judge, and his eminent worth as a man, the reader will not be surprised, that he enjoyed the confidence and friendship of Washington; nor, as we shall see in the next chapter, that he was appointed by him to the highest post in the Judiciary.

[1] History of Scituate, p, 257.

CHAPTER VI.

1796–1810.

CHIEF JUSTICE OF THE UNITED STATES.

During Chief Justice Jay's absence in England, in the years 1794 and '95, negotiating the Treaty which has since borne his name, Cushing presided in his stead; and after the rejection of Rutledge, as we have related in a preceding volume, he was nominated to the Chief Justiceship, and unanimously confirmed. On the day this occurred, there was a large dinner-party at the President's. Cushing was one of the guests. On entering the dining-room, Washington, from the head of the table, directing his look to him, said in an emphatic tone, 'the Chief Justice of the United States will please take his seat on my right.' The Judge had heard nothing of the nomination, and was much affected at the announcement. His commission was made out, which he received the next day, and held for about a week, when, upon the ground of ill-health, he determined to resign it. Washington, for whom he entertained a profound veneration, endeavored to dissuade him from his purpose; but without avail.

As Cushing never actually presided as Chief Justice, the reader may doubt, whether, *stricti juris*, he ever held the office. If, however, he accepted the appointment, it is not material to the question, whether he discharged its duties. If, in taking his commission, he intimated his purpose to hold it; that is sufficient. Indeed, the mere act of receiving it, might, under the circumstances, manifest such purpose; and from that moment, he would be, *de jure*, Chief Justice. At any rate, all the obvious steps of the process were complete; he was nominated, confirmed, and commissioned.[1] Hence, in a work of this character, we should hardly feel justified in omitting a sketch of his life.

In politics, Cushing belonged to the Federal party, and shared its detestation of the excesses of the French Revolution, as well as its general opinion in favor of the alien and sedition laws. In a charge delivered to the Grand Jury of the District of Virginia, September 23d, 1798, he portrayed the horrors of the French Revolution, admonished them to be on their guard against French wiles, and the 'plot against the rights of nations and of mankind, and against all religion and virtue, order and decency.' He defended the sedition law, on the ground that it ameliorated the English law, by 'allowing the party accused to prove the truth of his assertions;' and upheld, with equal decision, the alien law.[2] The mildness of his character, however, the general moderation of his sentiments, together with his incapacity to entertain the acrimonious feelings that mingled with the political differences of the time, preserved him from the shafts of party warfare. 'He had,' says his friend, Mr. Deane, 'a felicity of manner, and an unblemished dignity of character, which enabled him to be open and decisive, without kindling the rage of opposition.

[1] Vide Marbury *v.* Madison, Cranch's Reports, vol. i., p. 158.

[2] Deane's Scituate, p. 405, note.

Cushing continued on the Bench till his death, which occurred September 13th, 1810, in the seventy-eighth year of his age. Ill-health interfered somewhat, in the latter years of his life, with the performance of his judicial duties, and, at his death, the business of his Court was a good deal in arrear. Indeed, he had prepared a letter of resignation of his office; 'but was called to resign life.'

CHAPTER VII.

CONCLUSION.

JUDGE CUSHING was of good stature, erect, graceful, and dignified. His complexion was fair, his eyes blue, and brilliant, his nose aquiline. In his dress, he adhered to the style of the Revolution; wearing a three-cornered hat, and small-clothes, with buckles in his shoes. 'In his bearing and manner,' says Dr. Kendall, 'he was a gentleman of the old chool, dignified, and yet affable and courteous in his conversation. . . . . . . As a politician, he was a Federalist, of the Washington school.'[1]

In private life he was universally beloved. The suavity of his manner, the moderation of his temper, his kindliness, purity, and simplicity, attracted and fixed the regards of all who knew him. He had a cheerful temperament, social disposition, and excelled in conversation. He looked on the bright side of human nature, was tender of private character, and equally unknown and incapable to say an unkind word of any one. When obliged to speak unfavorably of a person, it was often observed, that he invariably added something to his advantage. 'He was all that was amiable,' says Mr. Deane, 'always ready to instruct by useful discourse, and to make his friends happy by his cheerfulness.'[2] He was distinguished for his liberal hospitality. With the long journeys he

---

[1] MS. Letter to the Author.

[2] History of Scituate, p. 257.

was obliged to take, he had but little time, in each year, to be at home; but, while there, 'his mansion was a place of resort, not only by his fellow townsmen, but also by citizens of the neighboring towns and cities.'[1] His family attachments were strong, and having no children, 'his house was usually filled with his own and his wife's relations, who were numerous, and whom he always took great pleasure in seeing.'[2] His fortune was easy; consisting, in good part, of real estate.

Cushing's intellectual qualities were not of an extraordinary cast; but eminently respectable. He was of a singularly unaspiring nature; a man of peace, and averse to controversy. He neither opposed the mighty, nor went about to stop the current of a river. As we have already observed, his legal knowledge was extensive and accurate; and he enjoyed the confidence and respect of the Bar. His mind was strong, but sluggish. 'It was once said of him, that he had fine ideas in his head; but it required a beetle and wedge to get them out.'[3] He possessed literary tastes, 'and if we may judge by the numerous notes written with his own hand in margins, he read with the greatest care. He was a learned theologian; well acquainted with the controversies of the day, and though far from gathering heat in those controversies, he was conspicuously on the side of liberal Christianity. He used to speak of his acquaintance with Dr. Priestley, as a happy era of his life, and to read and talk of his works with approbation.'[4]

To this summary of Cushing's qualities, we are happy to add, from the pen of the venerable Josiah

---

[1] Rev. Dr. Kendall. [2] Mr. C. C. Paine. [3] Ibid.

[4] Deane's History of Scituate, pp. 257, 258.

Quincy, who has challenged, throughout a long and eminent career, the homage of all who reverence truth, courage, learning, and eloquence, the following portraiture of his moral and intellectual character:

'My acquaintance with Judge William Cushing,' says Mr. Quincy, 'was slight and occasional, and my impressions of his character were derived chiefly from observing him in Court, and from the information of others. His legal attainments were of high rank. His judgment sound, his habits laborious, and devoted to the duties of his occupation and station. His virtues of the pilgrim cast; pure in morals and inflexible in principle. But he was ambitious neither of literary nor political distinction. His nervous system was delicate, averse to all controversies, except those in which the pursuits of his profession involved him. In politics he took no active part; but they were conservative and decided. The friend of such men as John Adams, Francis Dana, and Oliver Ellsworth, all of whom entertained for him the highest respect, could not be otherwise than of an elevated cast of intellect and moral power. But the habits of his life were retired, and he sought his happiness in domestic life; desirous rather to be useful than to be known. Such are the general views I entertain of his character.'[1]

---

[1] MS. Letter to the Author.

THE LIFE

OF

OLIVER ELLSWORTH

THE

LIFE OF OLIVER ELLSWORTH.

CHAPTER I.

HIS ANCESTRY.

JOSIAH ELLSWORTH, the first of his name who came to this country, was a native, it is supposed, of Yorkshire, England. He settled at Windsor, in Connecticut, about the year 1650. He was but twenty-one at the time; and was known to his neighbors as Sergeant Ellsworth. The conjecture that he came from Yorkshire, is derived from Mr. John Ellsworth, who was a respectable merchant in London, at the beginning of the present century. He stated that it was a tradition in his family, which had long resided in Yorkshire, that a member of it had formerly removed to foreign parts; that he was a young man when he left, and had never returned. This tradition, it is supposed, indicates the first of the Connecticut Ellsworths.

The name itself is derived from that of a small village a few miles from Cambridge, in England. This village is situated on a rivulet, once remarkable for *Eels*. Hence, as the Saxon word, *worth*, signified *place*, the village was originally called *Eelsworth*; but afterwards, Ellsworth. And, as the custom formerly was for the first settler in a new place to take the name of the settlement, we have, in that circumstance, the origin of the family name.

Josiah Ellsworth, of whom we have but little information, continued to reside in Windsor until his death, which occurred in 1689. He left nine children. John, his fourth son, married and settled in Ellington, a township near Windsor. He had two sons, called John and David.

David was a respectable farmer, and lived in Windsor. He married Jemimah Leavitt, a lady of excellent character, good mind, and pious principles.

CHAPTER II.

1745 - 1771.

HIS BIRTH AND EDUCATION.

Oliver Ellsworth, an honored name in American history, was the son of David and Jemimah Ellsworth, and born at Windsor, Connecticut, on the 29th day of April, in the year 1745. His early years were passed on his father's farm, and, doubtless, gave no more indication of future distinction and usefulness than the childhood of his obscure playmates. Indeed, his mind developed slowly, and did not discover its distinguishing qualities until mature age. We have, therefore, no tales of precocity to relate, no marvellous feats, nothing to excite wonder or provoke incredulity. Like the sons of other farmers, he had the benefit of country life, air and exercise; advantages by no means to be despised. 'It may be thought whimsical, but it is truth,' says Goldsmith, 'I have found by experience, that they who have spent all their lives in cities, contract not only an effeminacy of habit, but even of thinking.'[1]

Young Ellsworth owed his opportunities of education to the strong desire that possessed his father that he should be a minister. While a lad he was placed under the instruction of Dr. Bellamy, a clergyman of considerable eminence, with whom he pursued the studies preparatory to his college course. At the age

[1] The Bee, No. VI.

of seventeen he entered Yale College, and remained a member of that institution for two years, when he removed to Nassau Hall, Princeton. This respectable college, at that time, was under the charge of President Finley, a gentleman of distinguished abilities as a preacher. He had greatly assisted Whitefield in his itinerant labors; and while thus employed was once seized by the civil authorities, at New Haven, Connecticut, and carried out of the Colony as a vagrant, under a law which prohibited itinerants from preaching in any parish without the consent of its settled minister.

Among the few incidents that have been preserved of this portion of Ellsworth's life, the following anecdote is, perhaps, most characteristic. It indicates a turn for special pleading, which might betoken the future lawyer. The students were prohibited to wear their hats within the college yard. Ellsworth, on one occasion, was arraigned for violating this law of the institution. He defended himself upon the ground that a hat was composed of two parts, the crown and the brim, and as his hat had no brim, which by the bye he had torn off, he could be guilty of no offence. This ingenious plea seems to have satisfied the scruples of his judges, and he escaped all punishment. We may add, that he was more remarked during his residence at college for his sportive disposition, and the interest he took in the college politics, than for any uncommon proficiency in the college course of study. His rank as a scholar, however, was respectable. He graduated in the year 1766, and received the degree of A. M.[1]

[1] From a statement in The National Portrait Gallery, it would seem that, after leaving college, he was employed as a teacher; but where, for what time, and with what success, does not appear.

In obedience to the earnest wish of his father, rather than from any predilection of his own, he commenced the study of theology with Doctor Smalley, a Connecticut clergyman of considerable local distinction. But points of faith had much less attraction for him than points of law; and the contests of the bar were more alluring than the prelections of the pulpit. It was not long before his father discovered that Oliver, in spite of entreaty, persuasion, or remonstrance, was determined to renounce the prospective dignity and glory of a village pastor, and seek his distinction in the paths of jurisprudence. He yielded, at length, to the wishes of his son, and after a year's study of theology, the embryo minister began the congenial study of the law.

His instructors in the lore of his future profession were the first Governor Griswold, with whom, and subsequently with Judge Root of Coventry, he pursued and completed his course of studies. The difficulties that beset the law at this time did not prove a source of discouragement to him.[1] He opposed to them perseverance and love of the pursuit. His text books, it is said, were Bacon's Abridgement and Jacobs' Law Dictionary, which he read attentively, and was then, viz., in 1771, called to the bar.

His education had not been obtained without incurring some pecuniary obligations, of which he determined, before beginning his career as a lawyer, to relieve himself. He possessed in his own right, whether by gift or otherwise I am uninformed, a tract of unimproved land on the Connecticut river, solely valuable for its timber. This, in vain, he attempted to sell. But, if land was not marketable,

---

[1] Vide vol i., pp. 34, 437.

wood was. Hence, instead of opening an office, and relying upon the uncertain gains of his profession to discharge his indebtedness, he proceeded to the forest with axe and woodman's rig, and in the course of a few months cut, and transported down the river to Hartford, wood enough to pay his debts. Resolution like this, in any walk of life, merits, if it does not always ensure, success.[1]

---

[1] Mr. Joseph Wood, from whose MS. I have obtained this anecdote, thus writes me respecting it:—'The fact concerning the woodland owned by him, I had from a gentleman who formerly resided in East Windsor, and was well acquainted with Judge E., and who lately died in this city,[1] over eighty years of age. He was not certain whether his father gave it to him, or he obtained it by his own exertions.' Oct. 5th, 1855.

[1] New Haven.

CHAPTER III.

1771-1784.

HIS PRACTICE AT THE BAR.

UNMINDFUL of the legal prescription that 'Mistress Common-Law should lye alone,' Ellsworth, soon after being called to the bar, married Miss Abigail Wolcott, a daughter of Mr. William Wolcott, of East Windsor. The Wolcotts were a very respectable family in Connecticut; the grandfather of Miss Abigail, though not deriving his birth 'from loins enthroned or princes of the earth,' had by his energy and abilities obtained wealth and honorable position in the Colony. But social differences, in a community where there was great equality of manners, were scarcely discernible, and constituted but a trifling obstacle to matrimonial unions;—good character, industrious habits, and mutual love, being the important and prevailing considerations.

At the time of his marriage it does not appear that the heart of Counsellor Ellsworth had yet been gladdened by a single fee. Though love is said to be blind, it has nevertheless very good powers of deglutition; and it was obvious to the pious and practical mind of David Ellsworth, that his son Oliver would require a more substantial diet than either Themis or Hymen promised to bestow. Accordingly, he offered him the lease of a small farm, in a wild, uncultivated state, that he owned in the north-west part of Windsor, in the parish of Wintonbury, which the sagacious attorney wisely accepted.

In this retired spot, he began his professional career. He had scarcely money enough, it is stated, when he went to live at the farm, to buy a load of rails. 'The materials with which the fences of his farm were to be constructed he wrought with his own hands from the trees that grew upon it, nor remitted this branch of labor until it was completely enclosed.'[1] He was compelled for several years, to rely almost wholly upon his agricultural labors for his support. His profession, which in the future was to be the source of fame and fortune, proved, during the first years of his practice, but a barren sceptre in his hands. He declared, that three pounds, Connecticut money, *per annum*, was the extent of his professional receipts for the first three years after being called to the bar. His circumstances were altogether unpromising and discouraging. He was too poor to keep either a horse or servant. His farm was situated about ten miles from Hartford, whither, when the Court was in session, he walked every morning, and returned in the same manner at night. One day, while going or returning from Court, he was met by a friend in his carriage, who asked him, 'why he went on foot so much?' 'Ah! friend W——,' said Ellsworth, 'we must all walk at some period of our lives, and I choose to do my walking in my younger days, while I am able.'[2] A significant reply, considering that the situation of the two friends was subsequently reversed.

Ellsworth's superior abilities seem to have been

---

[1] The National Portrait Gallery, vol. iv., art. Ellsworth.

[2] MS. by Mr. Wood.

unsuspected; but time sets all things even. The opportunity at length occurred, to discover to his neighbors what manner of stuff he was of. He was employed in a suit of some importance; and so ably and successfully did he conduct it, that he obtained a verdict for his client, and secured the favor of the community. 'He no longer went to Court with an empty docket.'[1] It was, I presume, during the trial of this cause, that he heard a stranger enquire, 'Who is that young man?—he speaks well;'—words of encouragement that were not unheeded or barren of fruit. They inspired confidence and hope. 'Of this incident he spoke, even in his latest years, to his children.'[2] His prospects brightened. Clients gradually increased; he was drawn from the obscurity in which he had hitherto been buried, and, in place of the scanty and meagre income, the joint product of manual toil and insignificant and occasional professional employment, it was not long before he had a large and lucrative practice.

Not very long after his first successful appearance at the bar, Ellsworth abandoned his little farm, with no violent regret we may well suppose, and took up his residence in Hartford.[3] He was soon appointed State's Attorney, an office of considerable emolument, which he held for several years. From this time, until public employments withdrew him from his profession, it is probable that Oliver Ellsworth had a larger practice than any lawyer of his day; at any rate than any of his cotemporaries of the Connecticut bar. The late Noah Webster, who was a student in Ellsworth's office, at the period of which we now speak, has stated that his docket frequently numbered

---

[1] MS. by Mr. Wood. [2] Nat. Portrait Gall., vol. iv., art. Ellsworth.

[3] This removal was probably in the autumn of 1775.

from a thousand to fifteen hundred cases; and that during the sessions of the courts his mind was subjected to a constant strain; there being scarcely a case tried in which he was not of counsel.[1]

In the preparation and trial of a cause, he discovered great tact, great powers of logic, great energy and earnestness of elocution. As an advocate, he stood at the head of the Connecticut bar. He was not, to be sure, deeply versed in the varied lore of his profession, nor had the circumstances of his life been propitious to any general acquisition of knowledge. But, 'the diligent study of the cases which arose in actual business, stored his mind with principles. Whatever was thus acquired, was firmly rooted in his memory; and thus, as he became eminent, he grew learned.' [2]

After he had obtained reputation both in professional and political life, a friend asked him what was the secret of his intellectual power. He said, in reply, that early in his career he discovered that he had no imagination; that the qualities of his mind promised so little that he became almost discouraged; that he then determined to study but one subject at a time, and not abandon it until he had fully mastered it. He said also, that in the practice of his profession he had, as a rule, given his attention to the main points

---

[1] The inhabitants of Connecticut, during the latter part of the last century, were somewhat noted for their litigious spirit; and this circumstance may serve to explain the unusual number of cases on Ellsworth's docket.

[2] Analectic Magazine, vol. iii., p. 385. This sketch of Ellsworth, though not full, and sometimes inaccurate in the detail of facts, is admirable in point of style, just in delineation of character, and instructive in reflection and remark. The writer steers clear of the beaten track of eulogy, and has the courage to distinguish and discriminate.

of a case, leaving the minor ones to shift for themselves.

This concentration of mind will carry far even an ordinary man; but Ellsworth's endowments, though wanting imagination, that central, combining and generalizing faculty, were not the endowments of an ordinary man. He had penetration, powers of discrimination and analysis, that enabled him to unfold with precision and perspicuity the difficulties of a question, to strip sophistry of its disguises, and maintain the view he wished to enforce. He did not, to be sure, either at the bar or in the senate, 'bring to the consideration of his subject that fertility of mind, and opulence of knowledge, which enable their possessor to examine his subject in every possible point of view, and to make every kind of information in some degree tributary to the investigation; but, like most men of powerful intellect, but little general cultivation, he seized at once upon the strongest point, and left it for no other. He did not enter the field of controversy in the glittering panoply of science, wielding at pleasure all her arms, but, like Hercules with his club, armed with a single weapon, but that one, powerful and massy.'[1]

All truly great men, all eminently successful men, are earnest men. They do with their might what their hands find to do. Thus it was with Ellsworth. He was not an orator, in the meaning of the schools. He had no glow of fancy, no grace, no splendor of diction, no passages of beauty or might; but he had an earnestness of tone, an energy of manner, directness, and simplicity of language, that went home to the hearts and understandings of his auditors. He

[1] Analectic Magazine, *supra*.

frequently, says Dr. Dwight, (whose redundancy of language and exaggeration of eulogy, however, renders it necessary to take his statements, *cum grano salis,*) 'poured out floods of eloquence which were irresistible and overwhelming.' His success with juries is said to have been unrivalled. He did not weary them with repetition and unnecessary detail. His concise, lucid and forcible arguments fixed and held their attention. Unlike his friend, Fisher Ames, he illustrated by a diagram, and not by a picture. 'He stated his matter skilfully and powerfully. He particularly excelled in a most luminous explanation and display of his subject.'[1]

'The remark has often been made by those who were eye and ear witnesses of its truth, that Mr. Ellsworth's clear and vivid apprehension, and lucid statement of the facts involved in a case, would frequently throw out a blaze of light that instantly dispelled all doubts and difficulties, to the surprise and admiration of every attendant.'[2] In addition to intellectual advantages, his bearing, though not after the model of Chesterfield, was dignified and impressive, and his character, from the outset, respected and esteemed.

Among the members of the Connecticut bar, with whom Ellsworth came most frequently in collision, was Doctor William Samuel Johnson, a son of Dr. Johnson, the first President of King's College. Johnson returned to Connecticut, from England, where he had resided several years as agent of the Colony, the very year Ellsworth was called to the bar. He was an accomplished scholar, and while in England, was

---

[1] Burke of Townshend; and, if contemporary accounts may be relied on, equally true of Ellsworth; though, to be sure, his style could hardly bear comparison with that of the former.

[2] MS. by Mr. Joseph Wood.

intimate with his namesake, Dr. Samuel Johnson, and his coterie of literary friends. He was also a learned lawyer, and graceful orator. 'When Dr. Johhson rose to address a jury,' said Trumbull, the author of McFingall, 'the polish and beauty of his style, his smooth and easy flow of words, and sweet, melodious voice, accompanied with grace and elegance of person and manner, delighted and charmed his hearers. But, when Ellsworth rose, the jury soon began to drop their heads, and, winking, looked up through their eyebrows, while his eloquence seemed to drive every idea into their very skulls in spite of them.'[1]

In concluding this chapter, we may add, that the profits of Ellsworth's practice were 'judiciously invested, and the fortune thus acquired was augmented, by the economy and simplicity of his mode of life, to a degree of wealth,' at that time, rare in Connecticut.[2] We may also further add, that after his withdrawal from the bar, and 'during the greater part of his public life, his family residence was at Windsor, where he lived plainly and unostentatiously.[3]

---

[1] MS. by Mr. Joseph Wood. [2] Analectic Magazine, p. 397.
[3] Ibid., p. 400

CHAPTER IV.

1775-1781.

HIS POLITICAL CAREER — SERVICE IN CONGRESS.

It was well-nigh impossible for a rising young lawyer, like Ellsworth, in the stirring times in which he lived, to keep aloof from politics. The causes of revolution, even before he had been called to the bar, were exciting the fears, and arousing the resentment of the Colonies. From the first he took the side of his countrymen, and throughout was a consistent and persistent Whig. He is said, on one or two occasions, when the enemy made incursions into Connecticut, to have served with the militia of his native county; but when this occurred, and whether he was ever in any action, does not appear. In truth, his tastes were not military, nor his talents fitted for that kind of life.

His first appearance on the stage of public affairs was as a member of the General Assembly of Connecticut, which assembled at Hartford in April, 1775, a few days after the action at Lexington. He had been chosen to represent his native town in that body. The impending struggle between the mother-country and her colonies, the spirit of resistance inflamed and diffused by the blood shed at Lexington, at once led the Connecticut Assembly to provide the means for actual warfare. With William Pitkin, Thos. Seymour, and Ezekiel Williams, Ellsworth was appointed a committee, called the *pay-table*, 'to examine, liquidate, adjust, settle, and give all needful orders' for the payment of accounts incurred for military purposes.

The duties of this committee were onerous, and, together with his professional engagements, would seem to have absorbed Ellsworth's time. His name does not again appear as a member of the Assembly. The details of this portion of his life, while presiding at the *pay-table*, are meagre, and could afford but little satisfaction to the reader, even if they were complete. Adjusting accounts cannot be supposed to afford very pleasurable occupation, even to the most practical mind; and doubtless, a journey to Albany, in the summer of 1776, to obtain from General Schuyler a warrant for the re-payment of the various sums expended for the Connecticut troops, who served in Canada the previous year, was to Ellsworth an agreeable relaxation.[1]

In October, 1777, he was elected by the Assembly of Connecticut a Delegate to the Continental Congress. He had six colleagues, 'one or more' of whom were empowered, when present, to represent the State. Subsequently, the Assembly required the presence of at least two of the delegates, in order to bind the State by their votes. By this arrangement the delegates could serve in Congress, or remain at home, as was mutually convenient. The arrangement, however, was a very bad one, and calculated to impair the usefulness of the representatives and impede the public business. 'It may easily be shown,' thus wrote Washington, on the 20th of August, 1780, 'that all the misfortunes we have met with in the military

---

[1] He went by order of the Assembly.

line, are to be attributed to short enlistments. *A great part of the embarrassments in the civil* flow from the same source. The derangement of the finances is essentially to be ascribed to it.'[1] The business of legislation and the science of politics require long experience and attentive study. How can a legislative body conceive and carry out a complete, connected system of policy, if its members are changed so often, that anything like harmony of opinion, or intelligent comprehension of the points on which they differ, is impossible? That people are best represented, who, viewing the acts of their representatives with watchful vigilance, continue them longest in service. Power to change, with wise forbearance to exercise it, preserves the rights and promotes the interests of the constituent.

Ellsworth did not take his seat in Congress until October, 1778. He was nominally a member for six years; but, being at intervals relieved by some one of his colleagues, his period of actual service did not extend over two or three years. But these were years of very peculiar interest and trial. Ruined finances, distress in the army, cabal in the diplomatic *corps*, dissensions in Congress, and inertness in the States, — these were among the distinguishing features of that gloomy period. The beginning of the Revolution was its golden age. Then the mere recommendations of Congress were scrupulously and vigilantly executed. But four years later, when Ellsworth became a member of that body, its *prestige* had departed. It was divided into cliques and factions. The public were of opinion that the States 'were badly represented, and the concerns of the nation horribly con-

---

[1] Gordon, vol. iii., p. 127.

ducted.'[1] The public too, while blaming others, were not exempt from blame themselves. They had become relaxed, and very feebly responded to the most judicious acts of Congress. That body could adopt measures, but had no power to enforce them — could

> —— 'utter oracles of dread,
> Like Friar Bacon's brazen head,
> But when a faction dared dispute 'em,
> Had ne'er an arm to execute 'em.'

When Ellsworth came to Congress he was but little, if at all, known beyond the limits of his native State, and there his reputation was chiefly for skill and ability as a lawyer. His political experience was the experience of a novice; and we may well suppose that his acquaintance with political science, as a theory, was but trifling. His practice, since he had practice, was absorbing; while his habit of confining his thoughts to the immediate subject requiring his attention, is inconsistent with the notion of any general or discursive study. His faculties were something hard and dry. They wanted flexibility, ease, and freedom of movement, and did not readily adapt themselves to new and various subjects. He did not, 'like Burke or Hamilton, possess that opulent and redundant mind, which, whatever may be the immediate subject of its contemplation, pours forth without effort the full flood of eloquence and reason, in large and various discourse, fraught with knowledge, and rich in moral and political wisdom.'[2] But he had business talents of a very high order, powers of investigation and reflection, uncommon powers of argument, sound judg-

---

[1] Washington's Writings, vol. vi., p. 142, and *ante*, vol. i., p. 242.

[2] Analectic Magazine, vol. iii., pp. 394, 395.

ment, steady application, ardor and devotion in pursuit of the public interests. While he continued in Congress 'he was particularly distinguished for his unyielding firmness and political courage, as well as for his powers in debate, and unwearied application in the discharge of public business.'[1] His service in the Continental Congress was an admirable preparation for service in the Federal Convention and the Senate of the United States, where he may be said to have stood,

—— 'if not first, in the very first line.'

Soon after Ellsworth's appearance in Congress he was appointed a member of two very important committees, viz., the Marine Committee, and the Committee of Appeals. The former, acting as a Board of Admiralty, had general charge of all naval affairs; and the latter heard and determined appeals from the several admiralty courts established in the different States, in cases of capture on the high seas. A case of the latter kind was brought before the committee, which, as it involved a conflict of decision and jurisdiction, attracted much attention at the time, and possesses features of interest even at the present day. The following are the material facts: —

Gideon Olmstead and others were captured by the enemy, and sent to Jamaica. Here they were put on board the Active, a British sloop, bound for New York with supplies for the British forces. They were employed in the navigation of the vessel; but in the course of the voyage they rose upon the master and crew, confined them to the cabin, and steered for New Jersey. They proceeded safely until within sight of

---

[1] Analectic Magazine, vol. iii., p. 387.

Egg Harbor, in that State, when they fell in with the Convention, an American brig, which took possession of the Active, and carried her to Philadelphia.

Obviously, Olmstead and his companions were entitled to the vessel, as their lawful prize; but, on trial of the question in the Admiralty of Pennsylvania, they were only adjudged a fourth part, whilst the residue was decreed to the officers and crew of the Convention. From this decision Olmstead appealed. The appeal was argued before the Committee of Appeals, and the judgment of the State court reversed: the decree being that the Active should be condemned as prize for the use of Olmstead and his companions. But the Pennsylvania judge, on the cause being remanded, contumaciously refused to execute this decree. The committee, without power to carry into effect their process, declined to proceed further in the matter; but, subsequently, their decision was sustained and enforced by the Supreme Court of the United States.[1]

In February, 1779, Ellsworth obtained leave of absence, and returned home. He did not again appear in Congress until the following December. His letters to Governor Trumbull and Oliver Wolcott, sr., which we shall now lay before the reader, will show the general character of the business that occupied the attention of that body while he was a member of it. His correspondence relates wholly to public affairs, and is not distinguished for those striking observations on men and things that impart to the letters of John Adams a living and peculiar interest. He had none of the passions that glowed in the breast of Adams, and gave animation and color to everything that fell from his lips or pen. Nor had he cultivated the art

---

[1] Vide U. S. vs Peters',5 Cranch Reports, 115.

of writing. His spoken style was superior to his written. His letters do not attract by any grace or vigor of expression. His meaning, however, is never dubious.

When Ellsworth returned to Congress, in December, 1779, the army were suffering the greatest privations. The Continental money had become so depreciated that it was wholly inadequate to the purchase of supplies. At one time, there was no bread in the camp for several days; and during the 'last week of December, and until the 8th of January, both officers and men were almost famishing through want.'[1] Without money and without credit, Congress now determined to make requisitions on the several States for specific supplies. A committee was appointed to report the quantities and kinds of supply each State ought to furnish as its quota. Of this committee Ellsworth was a member. Their report was substantially adopted by Congress. Meanwhile Washington had been compelled to adopt a very decisive measure. He informed the civil authorities of New Jersey, that, unless the army were relieved voluntarily, they must either disband or cater for themselves. He mentioned the kinds and quantities of provisions that he should expect from the several counties of the State, and the days on which they should be delivered. These demands were cheerfully and punctually complied with. Viewed in connection with these facts, the following letter from Ellsworth to Governor Trumbull will attract the reader's attention:[2] —

---

[1] Gordon, vol. iii., p. 42. 'The deficiency proceeded,' says the historian, 'from the absolute emptiness of the American magazines in every place, and the total want of money or credit to replenish them.'

[2] Dated at Philadelphia, January 14th, 1780.

Sir: — Congress have no late intelligence from Europe, nor do they yet learn the destination of the troops lately embarked from New York. Four American colonels, Morgan, Ely, &c., are out from New York, on short parole, with propositions drawn up by them and General Phillips, of the Convention troops, for a general exchange of prisoners, which bids fair to take place on the plan now proposed. It is referred by Congress to General Washington, with power to take measures thereon at his discretion.

'Much credit is due and given to Connecticut, for the supply of Beef said to be coming on from thence to the army, whose distress has been great, and yet remains critical, for want of provisions. Eight dollars have been given in its vicinity, by the soldiers, for a quart of meal, and a half a dollar for one ear of corn. Flour and grain are procured sufficient, it is said, for some months, and now forwarding as fast as may be; and every attention will in future be paid to furnish money for the Beef Department. The failure of that source, *the press*,[1] gives us, as was expectable, a violent shock, but, it is hoped, will be a salutary one. The system of taxation, urged by necessity, is now fast establishing itself. All the States in the Union, so far as I can be informed, are now buying and collecting, pursuant to the regulations of Congress; though in some of them, their Assemblies have not been together to consider of the quotas last required. Maryland Assembly has, indeed, been together, and adjourned without making any provision therefor, owing to their not being able to obtain a vote in the Senate for the sale of British and Tory property. But, as they have called on their

[1] Referring to the stop put to the issuing of bills of credit, in accordance to the Resolutions of Congress. See vol. i., p. 256.

people, at large, to show their sense on that question, and are soon to meet again, there is no doubt of that obstacle being removed, and that Maryland will fully and cheerfully furnish her quota. Greater unanimity has at no time, perhaps, prevailed in Congress than at present, or ever been more necessary.'

Pressed by the necessities of their situation, Congress, like an embarrassed debtor, resorted to expedients which proved wholly inadequate to the relief of the public distresses. That currency, which for five years had been the chief reliance for carrying on the war, was now nearly worthless, and, judged by its standard, supplies of every description were selling at the most exorbitant rates. Congress now conceived the project of a new limitation of prices; a project which, hitherto and now, proved ineffectual for its objects, was the source of general dissatisfaction, and calculated to weaken the patriotic zeal of the mass of the people. To adjust the details of the plan, a convention of commissioners from all the States was summoned to meet at Philadelphia.[1] Ellsworth was a member, and the following letter to Governor Trumbull relates, in part, to its proceedings: [2] —

'SIR: — Since the letter Mr. Sherman and myself did ourselves the honor of addressing your Excellency

---

[1] A convention of the five Eastern States had been held at Hartford, Ct., in the previous October, and proposed a regulation of prices on the basis of twenty for one. They also proposed a convention at Philadelphia, at the commencement of the year, in order that the plan might be adopted by all the States. Congress approved this proposal; but, meanwhile, urged the States to adopt the regulation at once, without waiting for a convention. Hildreth, vol. iii., p. 298.

[2] Dated Jan. 30, 1780.

by the last post, a commissioner has arrived from Massachusetts to the convention for a limitation of prices, which had adjourned *sine die.* Also a commission from Rhode Island, to their delegate in Congress, to the same purpose. Upon which, the Assembly of Pennsylvania, to whom their commissioner had made a report, have reappointed others to meet again, and a meeting thereupon has been made of commissioners from all the other States who attended before, except New Jersey, with the addition of Massachusetts and Rhode Island, at which also delegates from New York attended, though not specially authorized, and gave assurance that their State would abide the measures that might be adopted. The convention having again formed, now stands adjourned to Wednesday next, for New Jersey commissioners, who have been requested to come in. The result of which meeting will, perhaps, be a further adjournment to a distant day, to give Virginia, who has not yet done it, opportunity to appoint and send commissioners. It does not, indeed, appear what more can well be done at this time, as some of the commissioners present are not authorized to do anything, unless the convention shall be attended from all the States first proposed.

'In return for Lord Stirling's expedition to Staten Island, a part of the enemy, consisting of one hundred horse, and four hundred foot, last week surprised the outguards at Elizabethtown and Newark, and made four officers and about sixty men prisoners, and burned some public buildings at both places.

'The supplies and prospects of the army are now comfortable. The General was reduced to the necessity of demanding from the several counties in New Jersey specific supplies; with which they complied, even beyond the requisitions, with much spirit. Maryland is said to have fully complied with the requisition of Congress to that State, for fifteen hundred barrels of flour. Delaware has also exerted herself much in the same way. The Assembly of the State are now together, and seem disposed to furnish fifty thousand barrels of flour, requested of them, as also to go into such further specific supplies as may be necessary.

'South Carolina, justly apprehensive of her danger, is arming three regiments of Blacks. It is highly probable, unless the embarkation from New York should have blown to the West Indies, or suffered much in the storm, that we shall hear of an attack on Charleston. Though I trust there will be a defence sufficient, at least, to render it a serious one.[1] The town, situated on a neck less than one mile across, and not commanded by heights, is defensible, and well fortified on the land-side. The entrance of the harbor, being very narrow, is secured by a number of frigates, which are the largest that pass over the bar without taking out their guns.[2] Continental troops and militia are now marching Southward, but may not arrive in

---

[1] See vol. i., pp. 567–569.

[2] This was a great mistake. The American ships were incapable to defend the bar; and it was discovered that the enemy, with the tide and an easterly wind, could enter the harbor under full sail, and pass the Continental frigates at their station in Five-Fathom-Hole, or at any other station they might assume. The consequence was, that Commodore Whipple abandoned the defence of the bar, and retreated, first to Fort Moultrie, and then to Charleston. The impracticability of defending the bar ought to have been ascertained before the arrival of the British fleet, and in time to save the American ships. When it was ascertained, Charleston should have been abandoned, and the army preserved. The urgent wishes, however, of the inhabitants, and the civil authorities, together with the expectation of reinforcements, induced General Lincoln to hazard a defence.

season for the enemy's first attempts.[1] That policy which has long since directed the enemy to carry their operations and efforts Southward, seems now to be attended to, and there is much reason to expect that the active part of the next campaign will be in that quarter.

'I take the liberty to mention to your Excellency, that the situation of my affairs renders it necessary for me to return home by the beginning of March, and to express my wishes that some of the gentlemen, on the new election, may find it convenient to take their seats in Congress by that time.

'I am, sir,' &c.

The military operations at the South, whither active hostilities had been transferred, were now attracting all eyes, and were a subject of very general interest and speculation. On the 8th of February Ellsworth thus writes Governor Trumbull:[2] —

'No intelligence or communication has been had from Europe since I had the honor of addressing your Excellency last. The following is the substance of what, material, has since that time been received from the southward.

'Governor Watson of Georgia writes, the 15th of December, that their Assembly were then sitting at Augusta, — had appointed delegates to Congress, were arranging their force, securing their frontiers, and providing to co-operate in the expulsion of the enemy.

---

[1] The siege began on the first of April. On the 10th, Lincoln was reinforced by seven hundred Continental troops, under General Woodford; but this addition to his force was well-nigh neutralized by about the same number of North Carolina militia, whose term of enlistment had expired, quitting the lines and returning home.

[2] February 8th, 1780.

General Lincoln also writes from Charleston, the 19th and 22d of the same month, that the enemy remained quiet; that a ship with military stores from Philadelphia had very seasonably arrived; that the four Continental frigates ordered there from the eastward had also arrived, and brought in with them a British privateer of sixteen guns, and were in his possession, in addition to the French there before, — sufficient to secure their bar from insults, and keep open the communication for supplies; that the Spaniards had been up the Mississippi, and taken possession of the British settlements, and made nine hundred prisoners;[1] and that a considerable naval force, with four thousand troops on board, had sailed from the Havannah the beginning of December for Pensacola or Augustine, or both, which, however, the British army appeared to disbelieve, and had sent no reinforcement to either of these posts, and were in expectation of the arrival of troops from New York. There is every reason to believe, Sir, that Spain will make a serious diversion in the Floridas, to which, perhaps, we can have no objection, provided she does not extend her views on the Mississippi beyond the latitude of 31°, nor to an exclusive navigation of that river.

'The Convention of this place have concluded to adjourn to the first Tuesday of April, and to give notice thereof to Virginia, that she may then send commissioners, if she thinks proper, or otherwise let her determination be known.

'I have the honor,' &c.

---

[1] The English force on the Mississippi, consisting of British and German, under the command of Lieutenant-Colonel Dickson, did not amount to 500 men. They were captured after a siege of nine days.

The rapid depreciation of the paper-money, which soon reached forty for one, put an end to any hope of relief by regulation of prices. The emission of two hundred millions by Congress, the base emissions of the enemy, together with the emissions of the several States, had so multiplied the currency that it had become a drug in the market. Congress now began to perceive that, after the amount of their bills had gone beyond the purposes of a circulating medium, all additions to the quantity diminished the value, and this in a very rapid and irregular manner. Hence they determined to destroy all the paper-bills they had emitted, and substitute ten millions of new money, which was to be issued as the old bills were brought in. The latter were to be called in by taxes, in the course of a year, and for every twenty dollars of the old, one dollar of the new money was to be issued. This was to be redeemable, in specie, within six years, and in the meantime bear interest at the rate of five per cent, *per annum*. The new bills were to be issued on funds of the several States to be established for the purpose. This scheme was adopted on the 18th of March, 1780, and on the 20th Ellsworth and Sherman thus wrote Governor Trumbull in explanation of it:[1] —

'Sir: — The President will transmit to your Excellency the resolutions of Congress for sinking the Continental bills of credit, and issuing new bills on the credit of the several States, which we hope will be

---

[1] We may as well state in the outset that this new scheme proved ineffectual; that the new bills depreciated in the ratio of four to one, and Congress stopped their emission. Before the close of the following year they were compelled to rely on solid coin.

approved by your Excellency and the honorable General Assembly. It was judged impracticable to carry on the war with the present currency, and no other plan has been proposed that appeared so likely to relieve us from the embarrassments of a fluctuating currency, as that which has been adopted by Congress. The depreciation here has been at the rate of sixty for one, and in the Southern States from forty to fifty. Neither the scarcity, nor collection of taxes, has had any effect to appreciate or fix its value. 'Tis apprehended that the new bills will be effectually secured against depreciation from the smallness of the quantity to be in circulation, the funds provided for their redemption, the shortness of the period, and the payment of the annual interest. The preparing them under the direction of the Board of Treasury, and the insurance of payment by the United States in case any State shall by the events of the war be rendered incapable of redeeming them, will give them a currency throughout the United States, and be a security against counterfeits. The emission of bills will not only introduce a staple medium of trade, but will increase the revenue the amount of five millions of dollars equal to specie. The six-tenths of the bills to be emitted to enable the States to purchase the specific supplies called for by the resolution of the 25th of February last, and the remaining four-tenths will supply the Continental treasury for paying the army, &c., while the States are collecting the old bills for taxes. And although it is recommended to collect in the old Continental bills by monthly assessments, it may be expedient for the States to allow new bills to be exchanged for old, that the old may be drawn out of circulation as soon as possible, to prevent further counterfeits; and, if there should be scarcity of money, people might be allowed to pay their taxes in provisions, delivered at the magazines at the prices fixed by Congress. The new bills will be prepared and forwarded to the States as soon as possible.

'We hear that the Honorable Assembly have ordered a new emission of bills. We beg leave to submit to your Excellency, whether it will not be expedient to stop the issue of them, and adopt the plan recommended by Congress. We should be sorry to have that fail of the good effects expected from it by any act or omission on the part of the States. The same proportions are kept up in the present requisition as in the resolution of the 7th of October last, wherein Connecticut is rated much too high, but hope that wont prevent her compliance, at least to the amount of her quota. Perhaps her quota in the present circumstances would be more than one-eleventh part of the whole. Repeated assurances have been given by Congress that those States which do more than their proportion shall be equitably compensated.

'There is a Report before Congress for fixing the rate in specie at which the Loan-Office Certificates will be paid.

'It is reported that a new regulation of the Quarter-Master's and other staff departments will soon be established on the most economical plan, whereby much expense will be saved. They will be accommodated to the late regulation of making purchases by the States. The prices of the specific articles to be furnished by the States were estimated at about fifty per cent. above the prices of 1774. They include all expenses of purchasing and delivering them into the magazines. The motives for adopting that measure were, the rendering the supplies more certain and equable among the States, and to prevent fraud and abuses. And the aid of the States in procuring the supplies was to be absolutely necessary.

'By the letter from General Lincoln of the 22d ultimo, we are informed that part of the British forces that left New York landed at St. Johns and St. James islands, near Charleston — the numbers not ascertained, but he thinks there is a good prospect of making a successful opposition to them. Mr. Laurens expected to sail for Europe the 26th of February.

'We are, with the greatest respect,' &c.

Three days after the foregoing letter was written, namely, on the 23d of March, Ellsworth again wrote Trumbull, as follows; —

'Sir: — Permit me, as a private citizen, to express my wishes that the late resolutions of Congress on the subject of finance may meet your Excellency's approbation and support. Your Excellency must have long seen, with alarming apprehensions, the crisis to which a continued depreciation of the paper-currency would one day reduce our affairs. It is now, Sir, just at hand. Without more stability in the medium, and far more ample supplies in the Treasury than for months past, it will be impossible for our military operations to proceed, and the army must disband. The present moment is indeed critical, and if let slip the confusion and distress will be infinite. This, Sir, is precisely the point of time for the several legislatures to act decidedly, and in a manner that the world will forever call wise. It is now in their power, by a single operation, to give a sure establishment for public credit, to realise the public debt at its just value, and without adding to the burthens of the people to supply the Treasury. To furnish one common ground to unite their exertions upon for the accomplishment of these great purposes, your Excellency will perceive to be the spirit and design of the resolutions referred to. They speak a language too plain to need any comment. I will only add concerning them, that they have been the product of much labor and discussion, and though some States may have reason for thinking they are not the best possible, yet they are the best Congress could agree upon. And should they be rejected, I confess I do not well see on what ground the common exertions of the several States are to be united and continued hereafter. Your Excellency will forgive me the very great freedom of this letter, and permit me the honor of subscribing myself, with the greatest respect,' &c.

A joint letter from Sherman and Ellsworth to Trumbull, of the same date as the foregoing, but apparently written after the arrival of the mail which brought a communication from his Excellency, contained several particulars that may interest the reader: —

'Sir: — We are honored with your Excellency's dispatch, of the 10th instant, by Brown, and shall pay due attention to the matters and instructions therein communicated. In particular, with regard to debts due in Connecticut for beef purchased under the late Commissary-General Wadsworth, we shall again urge in Congress, as we repeatedly have done, the necessity of furnishing money to discharge them. But, Sir, there have been many and urgent calls for money, with which it has been impossible for Congress, with a nearly exhausted treasury, to comply. And the same difficulty will remain so long as the different

States are dilatory in collecting their quotas of money, or, when collected, apply it to other purposes than the payment of Connecticut warrants.

'The reduction of the battalions in the Continental army is a matter now before Congress, but is attended with difficulties. Though economy pleads strongly in favor of the measure, yet it is doubtful whether there will be sufficient time to adjust and settle the new arrangement of the army before they may be called to take the field; and, as every new arrangment is also found to be a new source of discontent, it is the opinion of some that the reduction should be postponed until there should be fewer causes of discontent in the army than exist at present. It has also been observed, that should the battalions not be reduced at this juncture, yet considerable saving may be made by the several States by forbearing to fill up vacancies in their respective lines, which are already numerous, should and may become more so. Our endeavors, however, shall not be wanting to carry our instructions on this head into effect.

'It is with pleasure we observe, from the acts transmitted to us, that, on the great and embarrassed subject of the public finances, the leading sentiments of the Assembly of Connecticut are much the same as in full discussion have been assented to in Congress, and we entertain the more confidence from the consideration that the measures which Congress, after so much deliberation, have recommended, will meet that concurrence and support from all the legislatures of these United States, as is essential to attaining the ends therein proposed. . . .

'By a delegate from South Carolina, just arrived, we learn that Charleston was safe on the first instant; that the enemy, who had occupied the adjacent islands, had appeared for some days motionless; that the garrison were in good spirits; that the North Carolina brigade of troops had arrived, and that the Virginia line were met on their march, though at the unexpected distance of four hundred miles.

'We have the honor,' &c.

On the 9th of May, Ellsworth wrote Governor Trumbull as follows. His description of the embarrassed condition of England will be likely to arrest the reader's attention: —

'Sir: — Your Excellency will probably before the receipt of this have been informed of the death of the Hon. Don Juan Demarlles,[1] the Spanish gentleman of distinction, who resided at this place. He died, after a short illness, the 28th of April, at Morristown, to which place he had accompanied the Minister of France, to pay their respects to the General and army. His remains were there interred, with the honors of war, and his funereal rites have been also here celebrated, this day, in the French chapel, with very great respect, and a lasting requiem sung to his soul. This gentleman, during his residence, appeared duly attentive to the political interests and views of this country, as well as his own, and waited with patience to see the ties between the two countries indissolubly formed by a ratification of the treaties of amity and commerce, which he expected would take place on the arrival of our Minister at the Court of Spain.

'Much anxiety prevails here to know the fate of Charleston, from which there are no accounts, to be

---

[1] *Quere* Mirales?

depended on, later than the 9th of April; nor does it appear from the papers published in New York on the 3d of this month, that any accounts have been received there later than ours. In addition to the other troops that had been detached from the main army and sent to General Lincoln, the Delaware regiment and the Maryland line went on a few days ago, and will arrive, it is hoped, in season to support the country, should the enemy be so fortunate as to gain a temporary advantage.

'There are very circumstantial accounts from New York, transmitted to General Washington, that Paul Jones is on the coast with a small squadron of five ships, and had lately chased some vessels into the Hook, and that a seventy-four-gun ship and some frigates were preparing in New York to go in quest of him. This may be true. It is unknown to Congress where he is.

'Several vessels have arrived, in this river, from St. Eustatia as late as the 23d of April, but bring no material intelligence in addition to what was here before, except that the formidable fleets in the West Indies were out of port, and that a very busy and important campaign was expected in that quarter.

'No official information has been received very lately from Europe; but from the current of publications on that side of the water, and especially the English papers, it does not appear that any power has yet been found sufficiently uninformed to join Great Britain in the wicked and romantic attempts of reducing to obedience what she yet styles her rebellious colonies. And, as she cannot obtain assistance, she seems willing to have it believed that she stands in need of none, and accordingly goes on with a show and pretensions of being sufficient for all things of herself — much, perhaps, as a merchant sometimes on the eve of bankruptcy makes an uncommon parade of wealth and business, in order to keep up the delusion until chance may have had time to achieve something in his favor. The comparison, however, fails in this respect, that it is no secret to the world that the circumstances of Great Britain are bad, and that her wisest men are filled with consternation. She is ready to be crushed with the weight of her own debt, which is accumulating upon her by the whole expense of the war, and for which she is already mortgaged to pay forever an annual interest of seven millions sterling. Her revenues being fully charged with the interest, it is impossible for her ever to reduce the principal but by a sponge or revolution, and as impossible for her to go on much further in borrowing. She is also embarrassed with the claims of oppressed Ireland, which may perhaps advance upon her, and she is less able to contest them. . . . Add to which, county conventions, in spite of the ministry, are now forming in various parts of England, under the first characters of the nation, for reducing within due bounds the influence of the crown and the public expenditures; or, which is the same thing, oversetting the present venal and Utopian system of administration. From these marks of the weakness and dissolution she bears within herself, it is reasonable to expect that Great Britain will ere long cease from troubling us; and, unless she can speedily regain the sovereignty of the seas, she may be reduced, from her insular situation, to hold her own existence at the mercy of her enemies. The use good men in America will derive from these considerations will be of encouragement to persevere in the present contest, and continue working with the Lord until, by his good pleasure, the great business of our political salvation shall be fully accomplished.

'It must, I know, be supporting to your Excellency to observe that the State over which you have the honor to preside are sufficiently impressed with these sentiments already, and do not need additional arguments laid before them to comply with their duty and their interest. Their sense and determination expressed by the General Assembly in their late sessions at Hartford, are a proof, and at the same time exhibit to the world a conviction, of the never-failing resources a wise and virtuous republic has within itself. I thought it my duty to read in Congress the accounts I had received from Connecticut, and was kept in countenance by their just approbation. And it is devoutly to be wished that the well-timed and animating example of so respectable a State may have its due influence with the rest. A number of their assemblies, as New York, New Jersey, Pennsylvania, Maryland, and Virginia, are, it is said, now convened, or convening, and will be informed, through the channel of the Philadelphia papers, if not otherwise, what Connecticut has done.

'I have the honor,' &c.

There is something in the pecuniary vitality of England that baffles the speculations of the economist, and renders all conjectures as to the extent of her resources apparently futile. If Ellsworth at this time had been told that, after the exertions and expenditures of the American war, England, instead of sinking into weakness and infirmity, would set out afresh in the career of prosperity, would enlarge and consolidate her empire in the East, open new sources of commerce, increase her military strength, and for nearly a quarter of a century wage war with the most formidable power of modern times, — that, in addition to the support of her own fleets and armies, she would subsidize her allies — that she would do all this with apparent ease, — her credit never doubted, her resources never failing — and come out of the contest, at last, victorious over all her foes, and then surpass all other nations in the career of commerce and industrial enterprise, — his imagination would have rejected, as wild and chimerical, what living men have beheld.

'By the inclosed paper, of this day,' thus Ellsworth wrote Trumbull on the 6th of June, 'your Excellency will see the Spaniards are in possession of Mobile. There are no late official accounts from South Carolina. But, from a variety of circumstances, there is much reason to apprehend that Charleston is in the hands of the enemy, and that the garrison capitulated about the 12th of May. The war will probably be very serious with us this campaign, and it is to be wished all may expect and be prepared for it.

'Some of the new bills for Connecticut will, we hope, be forwarded the beginning of next week. What the Eastern States have done on the resolutions of the 18th of March, your Excellency is fully informed. New York has adopted the measure with unanimity and spirit, and pledged their forfeited estates as a fund for their bills. The doings of this State your Excellency will see in the inclosed paper. The Assembly of Delaware are convening again, and it is hoped will have wisdom and firmness to do right. Maryland meets again the 7th of this month. Mr. Jenefer, a delegate from that State, says they will undoubtedly adopt the measure and execute it, as not only the people, but a decided majority both in the

Senate and Assembly, approve it. A question arose, when their Assembly were last together, between them and the Senate, whether the new bills should be a tendry. On this they grew warm, and adjourned. They have probably by this time cooled, and discovered that they were disputing about a circumstance not very essential. Virginia Assembly are together, and there is every reason to believe that they will adopt the measure pretty unanimously.

'There is nothing very late from Europe, nor any other particulars yet received of the engagement in the West Indies than what is taken from the English accounts.

'We hear nothing yet of the arrival of the French fleet, but shall begin to look out for them in a week or ten days.

'I have the honor,' &c.

As late as the 8th of June definite intelligence of the fall of Charleston had not reached Congress. On that day Ellsworth wrote Trumbull, that 'the various accounts we have from the southward still leave it a matter of doubt whether Charleston is taken or not. Though it is now generally believed to have been safe on the 12th of May, and by many as late as the 18th. A body of the enemy marched into New Jersey the 7th, as far as Springfield. Some skirmishing has ensued. Whether the object is foraging, or attempting the camp at Morristown, or to make a show of their force, is uncertain.

'Letters from Martinique, as late as the 13th of May, mention no further particulars of the engagement of the 17th of April, than that the English fleet, in a shattered condition, put into the St. Lawrence; and that the French fleet, with the troops on board, continued out, and, it was hoped, would be able to effect a descent upon some of the English islands.

'A very large quantity of military stores and provisions are said to have arrived in the West Indies from France. We do not yet hear of the arrival of the fleet expected on the coast. More than forty sail of merchantmen have arrived in the Chesapeake and Delaware in the course of ten days. Prices and exchange are falling. There has been no depreciation of the currency here for about three months.

'Your Excellency will doubtless receive from the President a resolution for advancing a sum of the moneys of the United States, when such there shall be not otherwise appropriated, to the French Commissary, Mons. De Corny, to be replaced in specie on the arrival of their fleet. It is, indeed, to be wished that the United States had money, at this time in Connecticut and other States, that could be advanced for such exchange, as evident and essential benefits might be derived therefrom. But, at present, it cannot be supposed that they have much money anywhere. Of this the Minister (of France) was frankly told before the resolution passed, that he might not be thereby disappointed; and it was doubtful whether there would soon be any considerable sums in the Treasury, or Loan Office of Connecticut, for which Congress would have right to draw. It is earnestly his wish to do all in his power for establishing the credit of the paper-currency; and I will take the liberty to suggest to your Excellency, as I did to the Minister, that should the United States have money on hand, which they could so exchange, it might be of public utility could such exchanges be made with individual States or persons. He has received of this State £17,000 of their new bills, similar to those lately struck off for

Connecticut, to replace the same in specie when the fleet arrives. It would be well if the specie which the French may bring into this country could, with their approbation and convenience, be placed in the public treasury, and their purchases made with the same currency as ours.

'Two or three hundred thousand dollars of the new bills for Connecticut will be sent forward on Monday next. If the holders of the old bills should be desirous or willing to exchange them for the new at their relative value, this might perhaps be effected, under proper restrictions, through the hands of a public agent, or agents, who should receive and carry the old bills into the Loan Office, to be destroyed, and obtain credit therefor to the State, as part of its quota to be brought in, and who could receive the six-tenths in behalf of the State, or, at the rate of one for forty, to the proprietors of the bills received, in retaining one-tenth for the State. This thought I have taken the liberty to suggest to the consideration of your Excellency, conceiving it to be immaterial to the United States what method, consistent with good faith, any State shall take to expedite the gathering and bringing its quota to be destroyed. To what lengths it may be expedient for the State to lay open its funds, so that persons possessed of money in other States should be disposed to give the preference to Connecticut funds, might come in and take the benefit of them to the eventual exclusion of some of its own citizens, as the case may be, your Excellency will be most competent to determine.

'I have the honor,' &c.

Charleston had now been in the hands of the enemy a full month, yet, on the 13th of June, no official information of its fall had reached Philadelphia — so difficult was the transmission of intelligence. On that day, Ellsworth thus wrote Trumbull: —

'Sir: — Though we are yet without official information respecting Charleston, there scarce remains a doubt of its being taken, and that the garrison surrendered, on terms, on the 12th of May. The capitulation, published in New York, is in this city, but I have not seen it, to note the particulars it contains. General Gates is ordered to the southward, to take command. The enemy remains in force at Elizabethtown Point. The object is yet unascertained.

'I have forwarded, by the bearer, 120,000 dollars of the new bills for Connecticut, and have more on hand, to be forwarded in a few days.

'The State of New Jersey has also adopted the measure recommended on the 18th of March.

'I beg leave to express my sincere condolence with your Excellency for the loss of Mrs. Trumbull.'

Ten days later, viz., on the 23d of June, Ellsworth again wrote the Governor: —

'I enclose, for your Excellency's perusal, the papers last published here. The enemy have gained some advantages, at the southward, since the surrender of Charleston; but it is to be hoped, from the exertions now making in North Carolina and Virginia, that they will not be able to proceed much farther. The enemy in New Jersey remained, on the 20th of this month, inactive at Elizabethtown Point. It is certain a fleet has returned to New York from Charleston, and, according to the best information yet obtained, has brought General Clinton and a considerable part of his troops. It is said that Admiral Arbuthnot has also returned. General Lincoln arrived this day at Congress, and has requested an enquiry into his conduct in his loss of Charleston. Mr. Laurens having been prevented from going to Holland, Mr. John Adams, or, if inconvenient for him, Mr. Dana, is authorized to transact [business] until Mr. Laurens, or some other appointed in his room, shall arrive.

'Your Excellency, I presume, has too perfect a knowledge of the state of the army, and too frequent representations of public exigencies from Congress, their Committee at camp, and the General, to leave it in my power to add anything on those subjects. Mr. Huntington is nearly through the smallpox, and I hope will soon leave me at liberty to return home.

'I have the honor,' &c.

On the first of August he thus wrote Governor Trumbull: —

'Sir: — My health being reduced so low as not to admit of my constant attendance in Congress, and the situation of my family and affairs making it necessary for me soon to return home, I propose, Sir, to return the beginning of autumn, of which I hope your Excellency will not disapprove. I have written to Mr. Law, who I supposed would come to the next Congress, acquainting him with my circumstances, and requesting him to come by the first of September, or sooner, if he could. And I take the liberty to request your Excellency, in case Mr. Law should by any means fail of coming, that some other gentleman in the delegation, as shall be most convenient for them, may be called on.

'Nothing very important, of late, has passed in Congress. There is, at present, a representation from all the States, except North Carolina. The Court of France has undertaken to guarantee a loan, for these States, of ten millions of livres.[1] Present assurances have been received of the friendly dispositions of the King of Prussia. There is no account yet of the proposed mediation having made any further progress than to be offered. Probably Great Britain will not be hasty in accepting it, if she believes as delusively as her minister writes, that America is on the point of submission. There is, perhaps, too great an opposition of interests in this mediation, for either of the parties at war to be willing to risk their claims with it further than circumstances may require.

'We have nothing later from the southward than is contained in the enclosed papers.

'I have the honor,' &c.

Soon after the date of the foregoing letter, Ellsworth returned to Connecticut, and did not resume his seat in Congress until June, 1781.

---

[1] $1,851,851.

CHAPTER V.

1781–1783.

SERVICE IN CONGRESS CONTINUED.

It would be of little satisfaction to the reader to enumerate the various committees upon which Ellsworth served during the time he remained in Congress, in the summer of 1781; neither would the detail illustrate his character, nor the history of that period. The war was approaching its close, but the decisive blow had not yet been struck. The army was unpaid; the paper-money had fallen nearly out of circulation, and supplies could only be obtained for specie. The finances, however, were now under very efficient control. Congress had abandoned the old system of boards and committees; and the Departments of Foreign Affairs, War, Marine, and Finance, were each placed under a single head.[1] Robert Morris had charge of the Finance Department, and how important were his services, how ardent and successful his efforts in the most critical moments, history has delighted to record.

---

[1] Robert R. Livingston was placed at the head of the Department for Foreign Affairs, and Lincoln at the head of the War Department. Instead of the Committee for hearing Appeals in cases of prize, a Court of Appeals, consisting of three judges, was instituted. The business of the Marine Committee was placed in the hands of the Superintendent of Finance.

When Ellsworth returned to Congress in December, 1782, great changas had taken place. Cornwallis had surrendered, possession of the Southern States had been recovered, and the resolution of the House of Commons against any further prosecution of the war on the American continent, evinced very clearly that the country was soon to enjoy the blessings of peace.

This prospect, after the distresses of a long and exhausting war, was hailed with unfeigned satisfaction. But the difficulties which surrounded Congress were still great and pressing. The States, relieved of impending danger, — their soil no longer occupied by hostile forces — sunk into utter inertness. Instead of the fervid patriotism that animated the people at the beginning of the war, party-spirit or selfish views now seemed to be the prevailing motives of their conduct. The languor of the several States, — their inability or unwillingness to carry out the recommendations, or comply with the measures, of Congress — occasioned the greatest solicitude, and were a source of well-founded alarm. The public creditors had become impatient, and the discontent of the army threatened the most serious consequences. It was absolutely necessary that measures should be adopted to restore the public credit; but how this should be done, how a permanent revenue should be provided, how raised and collected, were questions of great difficulty, and occasioned long and able debates. On one hand, those who favored a strong central government were anxious that the revenue should be collected under the authority of Congress; and, on the other, the advocates of State authority would leave the public engagements to be provided for by the several States.

Among those who would still trust to the vigor and public spirit of the States, — unreliable as that vigor and public spirit had hitherto proved — was Ellsworth: and he would do this from expediency and virtual necessity. His argument, certainly, is forcible. On one side he felt the necessity of Continental funds for making good the Continental engagements, but, on the other, desponded of a unanimous concurrence of the States in such an establishment. He observed, that it was a question of great importance how far the Federal Government could or ought to exert coercion against delinquent members of the Confederacy, and that without such coercion no certainty could attend the Constitutional mode, which referred everything to the unanimous punctuality of thirteen different councils. Considering, therefore, a Continental revenue as unattainable, and periodical requisitions from Congress as inadequate, he was inclined to make trial of the middle mode of permanent State-funds, to be provided at the recommendation of Congress, and appropriated to the discharge of the common debt.[1]

He substantially concurred in Rutledge's scheme of an impost, as described in the life of that gentleman.[2] He suggested, however, several modifications. He concurred in the expediency of new-modelling the plan of the impost by defining the period of its continuance; by leaving to the States the nomination, and to Congress the appointment, of collectors, or *vice versa*, and by a more determinate appropriation of the revenue — the first object to which it ought to be applied was, he thought, the foreign debt. This object claimed a preference, as well from the hope of facilitating further aids from that quarter, as from the

[1] Madison Papers, vol. i., p. 291.

[2] Vol. i., p. 593.

disputes into which a failure might embroil the United States. The prejudices against making a provision for foreign debts, which should not include domestic ones, was unjust, and might be satisfied by immediately requiring a tax, in discharge of which Loan-Office certificates should be receivable. State-funds, for the domestic debts, would be proper for subsequent consideration.[1]

The scheme of revenue finally adopted by Congress, viz., a tax on land and duties on imports,[2] received his support. With Hamilton and Madison, he was appointed a committee to prepare an address to the States in explanation and recommendation of it. It was written by Mr. Madison, and sets forth, with eloquence and ability, the necessity of providing for the Federal debt.[3]

Having thus briefly explained Ellsworth's views upon the interesting question of revenue, we shall now recur to his correspondence, and relate the history of contemporary affairs in his own language. On the 23d of April, 1783, he thus writes Oliver Wolcott, sr.:[4] —

'Dear Sir: — I hope you reached home safe, and found your family well, and yourself also in better health than is possible to be enjoyed in the fog of this city. Your recess from business, after long confinement, must, I think, afford you some pleasure, and to see the fruits of your labor — peace and independence — much more.

---

[1] Madison Papers, vol. i., pp. 309, 310.

[2] Vide vol. i., pp. 594, 595.

[3] This address is printed in the Appendix to the first volume of the Madison Papers.

[4] Ellsworth returned to Connecticut in February, but again took his seat in Congress in April.

'Congress, since you left it, have ratified the provisional treaty, and ordered the prisoners to be released, and also that the public horses and other now useless property be sold; and has passed the report on revenue with alteration of the duty on salt to five *per cent.*, and the duty on all wines, except Madeira, which stands at twelve-ninetieths to six-ninetieths of a dollar. We have nothing more yet of the treaty. Late private letters from Europe mention that preliminaries were not signed by the Dutch, but that at last they had received such offers from the British as the French Court advised them to accept, and that there was no doubt but they would; also, that they had appointed a Mr. Van Birkel their Ambassador to these States. A letter has been received from Mr. Dana, at Petersburgh, of the 15th of January. He had not then assumed a public character, nor made any advances towards a treaty of commerce, nor indeed could make any to purpose till he should first pave the way, according to the niggardly custom of that Court, with about £10,000 sterling in presents to her ministers. He also thought it very probable that a war would take place between Russia and the Porte, on account of the Khan of Crimea, who had been deposed by the Tartars of that Independency.

'Sir Guy Carleton has written to Congress to appoint a person to attend at New York, to see the seventh article of the treaty, relating to American property, duly observed, as he expects soon to begin an embarkation. Most of the Tories are gone from there to Nova Scotia, cursing their King all the way. . . .

'Colonel Dyer, I suppose, is well. With Mrs. Trumbull and his new span, and Doctor Holton as an aid, he set off last Saturday for an airing to Wilmington, and is not yet returned.'

On the 6th of May he again wrote Wolcott: —

'Dear Sir: — I am happy to find, by your letter of the 25th of April, that you were safe at home and in perfect good humor, and that you propose, by and bye, writing a treatise to keep everybody else so. I hope, Sir, you will send me one of the first impressions, which I shall certainly stand in need of, if I do not get away from here sooner than present prospects indicate. But it seems, Sir, that you are not quite out of the noise of politics, though you are happily removed from this seat of them. That horrid clamor, of which you speak, about commutation, — a mere change of a name, indeed — though it excites neither the idea of guilt nor fear in your mind, does very illy become a people of sense, especially in the very moment of their salvation, when every heart and voice ought to be joined in praise.[1] But so it is, Sir. The Princes of the Power of the Air can raise storms any time when they have occasion for them, having elements to work upon, and which, like the roaring sea, casteth up mire and dirt, and are easily set in motion.

'We are not yet favored with the definitive treaty. The completion of it is said to have been delayed for the approbation of the Emperor of Germany and the Empress of Russia; as a compliment to them, I sup-

[1] Ellsworth here refers to the act of Congress commuting the half-pay for life (of officers) into five years' full-pay, in a gross amount, certificates to be issued for it, bearing interest at six per cent. This measure was very generally condemned in New England, where the feeling was strong against any extra pay whatever.

pose, for having so far interested themselves as to offer their mediation to bring it about.

'General Washington and Sir Guy Carleton have an appointment to meet this day at Tappan, to confer about the evacuation of posts and other matters in the seventh article of the treaty. Nothing yet appears to induce a suspicion that the treaty will fail of being carried into effect, on both sides, as fast as the nature of the case will admit. Certainly, we cannot wish to see it violated and annulled; nor has Great Britain so much reason to be dissatisfied, under all circumstances, as North, Fox, and their partisans pretend, — for their object probably is, to hunt down the present minister, and to transfer the popular odium from the criminal to the executioner. If Great Britain, induced thereto by the folly of a former administration, must make us independent of herself, it is wise in her to do it with a grace, and in a manner that shall also keep us independent of France. This principle was, no doubt, well explained and enforced by Messrs. Adams and Jay. But it would have been weakness in a British minister not to have adopted it, and in as large an extent as in the present treaty seems to have been done, even as to the Loyalists, who are said to have been sacrificed for nothing.[1] I believe the true interest of the British

[1] If sacrificed in the treaty, the Loyalists, in large numbers, were provided for by Parliamentary allowance. Their application for indemnity was favorably received: out of five thousand and seventy claims that were presented, only nine hundred and fifty-four were abandoned or rejected; among the remaining number about fifteen millions of dollars were distributed. In addition to this sum, provision was made for those who had lost lucrative offices. Besides, the confiscating laws were generally repealed, and many of them returned to this country and got possession of their property.

nation is better secured by peopling a colony with them, than it could have been by re-instating them with us. Their number is said to be near thirty thousand.

'A number of officers from Sir Guy Carleton are now going on to take charge of the British prisoners at Lancaster and elsewhere, and conduct them by land to New York. Sir Guy expects soon to be superseded or relieved by General Gray. Three months' pay is like to be made to the army when they shall be disbanded: one-third in cash, and the rest in Mr. Morris's notes. He will continue in office until the engagements he shall enter into for this purpose, and those that he has already entered into, which are not yet performed, shall be fulfilled.

'Congress are busy in the peace arrangements, and I now think will not have a recess the ensuing summer.

'Should this find you at Hartford, as I hope it will, I must beg your influence with Mr. Huntington to come forward to Congress as soon as he can, as Colonel Dyer does not propose to stay much longer, and there is danger of Congress being without a representation of nine States, which would greatly embarrass the business they have now generally to transact. I hope Mr. Strong, or some other gentleman, will also soon be ready to relieve me. I do not, and dare not, think of staying through the summer.

'I was favored with your letter from Danbury, which, as Brown was here, I omitted to answer till he should return, which did not happen till I received your other letter of the 25th. I shall be very happy, Sir, to receive your letters as long as I stay here, and to merit the continuance of your confidence as long as

I live. With compliments to Mrs. Wolcott and your daughters, I am,' &c.

Most of the distinguished men of the Revolution, after the contest was ended, retained but little of hostile feeling towards Great Britain. With the mass of the people, however, resentment was too deeply rooted to be easily eradicated. At the South, too, where the war had entailed more personal suffering and loss than elsewhere, a spirit of animosity had been aroused, which was shared by all classes. Rutledge, we have seen, manifested to the last an intense and unconquerable aversion to Great Britain.[1] But at the North the leading men had far more sympathy with England than with France. Suspicion of the designs of the French Court, which Jay and Adams early imbibed and communicated to Congress — the course pursued by Vergennes with respect to the fisheries and the public lands — had induced a distrust of France, which subsequent events were not calculated to efface. Besides, they regarded the prostration of Great Britain as likely to be injurious to their own country and subversive of the best interests of Europe. Among those who shared this opinion were Jay and Ellsworth. We have seen that the former, early in the war, while he would risk all for independence, nevertheless, wished well to Old England.[2] The following letter from Ellsworth to Governor Trumbull, dated May 13th, 1783, among other particulars, will give a hint as to the sentiments he entertained towards the mother-country: —

'Sir: — Little has occurred here worth your Excellency's notice, since Colonel Dyer addressed you by

---

[1] Vol. i., pp. 629, 630. [2] Ibid., p. 193.

messenger Brown. An interview has been had between General Washington and Sir Guy Carleton, at Orangetown, for sundry purposes relating to the execution of the seventh article of the provisional treaty. Every assurance is given by the latter that New York, with Penobscot, shall be evacuated as soon as shipping necessary for that purpose can be procured, which he has sent for. Commissioners on the part of the United States are appointed to superintend, with others on the part of the British, the embarkation, to prevent any property being carried away, which by the treaty was stipulated to be left. It is not probable our army will disband till the embarkation takes place. The army are like to be furnished with three months' pay at the time of disbanding. Part of it must be paper anticipation. Mr. Morris will continue in office until the engagements necessary to be entered into for that purpose shall be discharged. The troops of the Southern army, composing the Pennsylvania, Maryland, and Virginia lines, are sent for, to be brought into their respective States, in order to their being discharged.

'Congress are now busied in reducing, as fast as may be, the public expenditures, and settling the necessary peace arrangements. A plan of revenue for funding the public debt, which has taken up much time in Congress, will be immediately forwarded for the consideration of the State, accompanied with the documents necessary to give information relating to that important subject. As might naturally be expected at the close of so long a war, we find a considerable debt on our hands, which, all will agree, it much concerns the national character and prosperity to provide for, however various may be the opinions as to the mode of doing it.

'It is, I think, Sir, also of much importance at this time, that the accounts of the several States with the United States should be liquidated and brought to an equitable adjustment. Unless this is done, it will be impossible [to have] mutual confidence and a good understanding among them, or to obviate the objections which almost every one in its turn makes against complying with the requisitions necessary for the common interest and safety. Commissioners for liquidating these accounts are now gone, and going, into the States. The necessary instructions for the one nominated for Connecticut, I understand by Mr. Morris, are sent forward, and I hope, if approved by the State, he will be able immediately to proceed to business.

'We are not yet, Sir, favored with the Definitive Treaty of Peace, which is now daily expected. The completion of it is supposed to be somewhat delayed to consult the approbation of the Emperor of Germany and the Empress of Russia, who particularly interested themselves in the restoration of a general peace.

'By the enclosed paper your Excellency will perceive that another change has taken place in the British ministry. Not seeming in a humor to be satisfied, that fickle nation one day sacrifices a Premier for continuing the war, and the next day another for putting an end to it. The truth, perhaps, is, that Great Britain, not having been able to accomplish her purposes either by fighting or treating, finds it more convenient to charge the failure to a deficiency in her servants, than to acknowledge what the world perceives to be the case, a deficiency in her resources and power. It is no secret that her debt is so increased as to require, together with her peace establishment, a million and a half sterling annually more than her revenue amounts to. This circumstance alone made it necessary for her, at all events, to purchase peace, and will probably be sufficient security for her good behavior for a long time yet to come. Neither the safety of this country, or [nor] the balance of power of Europe, requires that Great Britain should be at all more reduced than she in fact is; and it is by avoiding that distraction of councils and corruption of manners that have brought her down, that America can hope to rise or long enjoy the blessings of a revolution, which, under the auspices of Heaven, she has gloriously accomplished.'

The following letter to Governor Trumbull, dated June 4th, 1783, so far as it relates to the coalition between Lord North and Fox, and to the question then pending in Congress as to the propriety of having resident ministers at the various foreign courts, is quite curious: —

'Sir: — Colonel Dyer has lately left Congress, and will fully inform you of the state of affairs to that time, and leave very little for me to communicate to your Excellency. A packet just arrived at New York from Falmouth, it is represented, brings information that the Definitive Treaty was signed, and that the British were to leave this coast, at farthest, by the first of August. The packet also brings a list of the new British ministry, established the 2d of April, which I take the liberty to enclose. From the strange coalition of which it is formed, there is little reason to doubt but that another change of a partial nature will follow, as soon as the present convulsive state of that nation shall have subsided. Lord North, who is the fixed favorite of his sovereign, and a man of the most system, business, and address, will easily find means to lay aside Mr. Fox and his coadjutors when he can well do without them, as he has already done with regard to one set of opponents, whom he let come forward to perish in the odium of exciting measures which he had rendered necessary.

'A letter from Mr. Dumas to the Secretary of Foreign Affairs advises, that Mr. Van Birkle, Ambassador from their High Mightinesses the States General to these United States, was to sail for America the first of this month.

'A question, which has been more than once agitated in Congress, on the expediency of an interchange of ministers with foreign courts, except on special occasions, is yet undecided, and probably will receive no direct decision. While, on the one hand, respectability abroad, facility of acquiring and extending useful information, and the long-established custom of European nations, except the uncivilized Turk and mountain-barricaded Swiss, plead strongly in the affirmative; considerations of economy and simplicity of manners, so necessary to be observed in republics, and factious intrigues, so necessary for them to avoid, have much weight in the opposite scale.

'Congress have appointed Oliver Pollock, late Agent of the United States at New Orleans, their Agent to reside at the Havannah. It is to be hoped, we shall not ultimately fail of the valuable trade of that island, though its ports are at present shut against us, owing, it is said, in some measure to abuses committed there under the American flag by foreigners who wished to render it obnoxious.

'We hear from the Assembly of Virginia, that the House of Delegates, notwithstanding they so unanimously and recently voted a repeal of their act granting to the United States the impost first recommended by Congress, had given liberty for a bill to be brought in for complying with the requisition of the impost, as it now stands, and that there was a great probability the act would pass. This is the only Assembly from which we have yet heard upon that subject, and from which, next to that of Rhode Island, the greatest opposition was apprehended.

'A very liberal offer is made by Maryland, to induce Congress to fix its residence at Annapolis. One less so had before been made by the State of New York, of the town of Kingston. Which, or whether either of them, will be accepted is uncertain; though it is generally agreed that Congress should remove to a place of less expense, less avocation, and less influence, than are to be expected in a commercial and opulent city. . . .

'I have the honor to be,' &c.

The following letter, written a few days after the foregoing, namely, on the 18th of June, 1783, relates chiefly to the progress of negotiations abroad: —

'Sir: — . . . Nothing official has been received here from Europe since I had the honor of addressing your Excellency by messenger Brown, except a letter from Mr. Laurens, of the 5th of April, at London, mentioning the appointment of David Hartley, Esq., in the room of Mr. Oswald, to finish the American negotiations, and that, from conversing with several of the new ministry, particularly the Duke of Portland and Mr. Fox, he was satisfied of their disposition, that they should proceed with liberality and dispatch. Another letter, of the 23d of April, from Doctor Franklin's secretary, mentioning the arrival of Mr. Hartley in France, and that the Doctor was then gone, in company with him, from Passy to Versailles; and a letter from Mr. Dana, at Petersburgh, of the last of February, mentioning that he expected it would be two months, according to the dilatory course of such business at that court, before the commercial treaty with them, which he was upon, would be finished.

'The furloughed part of the army are on their way home. Some have arrived here from the southward. They receive three months' pay, but all in Mr. Morris's notes, which run six months.

'I do not learn, Sir, that any of the legislatures this way, or to the southward, have yet passed upon the plan of revenue proposed by Congress, except those of New Jersey and Maryland, neither of which has as yet adopted it fully: the first having granted the impost as requested, but the other funds only for one year; the latter having granted the impost, and postponed the rest to another session.

'Mr. Huntington is not yet arrived. I hope he is near at hand, and that he has at least one colleague with him.

'I have the honor,' &c.

It is mentioned in the preceding letter, that some of the furloughed troops from the southward had arrived at Philadelphia, and that provision had been made to give them three months' pay. Some delay in preparing Mr. Morris's notes, in which the payment was to be made, led to a mutiny among these and other Pennsylvania troops, which interrupted the proceedings of Congress, and induced an adjournment to Princeton, whence Ellsworth, on the 10th of July, thus wrote Governor Trumbull: —

'Sir: — I should have acknowledged the tenor of your Excellency's letter, of the 23d of June, by Jesse Brown, of whom I received it on his return, but he made no stay here. He will have informed your Excellency of the adjournment of Congress to this place. They were prevented going on with business at Philadelphia by a mutiny, in the Pennsylvania line, of about five hundred men, who had formed there, under a board of sergeants, for a redress of grievances, and taken the command of the city and magazine, and had proceeded so far as, with fixed bayonets, to surround the State House in which Congress and the Council of the State were sitting, — threatening destruction, if their demands were not complied with in twenty minutes. Some officers of a higher rank, as was then supposed, and since appears, were the instigators of the plot — two of whom have fled. Congress, by a committee,[1] whose report is herewith inclosed, called on President Dickinson and his Council to turn out their militia, and suppress the mutiny; but they had not spirit or power enough to do so, or did not think it necessary. After waiting in this situation for some days, and appearances of menace and further violence still continuing, Congress judged it expedient to adjourn to this place, which they did on the 27th of June — expecting, at the same time, that their removal out of the reach of the mutineers, with its being known that a detachment of Eastern troops was ordered from the main army, might, by convincing them they were to expect coercion, instead of compliance, disconnect and disperse them. The expectation was in some measure answered. The detachment from the army is, notwithstanding, gone forward to

[1] This committee consisted of Hamilton, Ellsworth, and Peters.

disarm such of the mutineers as may not have dispersed, and bring to trial such of the principal actors as can be apprehended, and also to prevent further disorder upon the arrival of the Pennsylvania line from the South.

'How long Congress will remain here is uncertain. They will hardly return to Philadelphia, without some assurance of protection, or even then with the intention to stay longer than till accommodations shall be elsewhere prepared for a fixed residence. But, Sir, it will soon be of very little consequence where Congress go, if they are not made respectable, as well as responsible, which can never be done without giving them a power to perform engagements, as well as to make them. It was, indeed, intended to have given them this power, in the Confederation, by declaring their contracts and requisitions for the common defence sacredly binding on the States; but in practice it amounts to nothing. Most of the States recognise these contracts and comply with the requisitions so far only as suits their particular opinion and convenience. And they are the more disposed, at present, to go on in this way, from the irregularities it has already introduced, and a mistaken idea that the danger is over — not duly reflecting on the calamities of a disunion and anarchy, or their rapid approach to such a state. There *must*, Sir, be a revenue somehow established, that can be relied on, and applied for national purposes, as the exigencies arise, independent of the will or views of a single State, or it will be impossible to support national faith or national existence. The powers of Congress must be adequate to the purposes of their constitution. It is possible, there may be abuses and misapplication, still it is better to hazard *something*, than to hazard *all*.

'I am glad to be informed, Sir, that the two Messrs. Huntington will be here soon. Business has been much delayed for the want of a sufficient representation.

'We have nothing official concerning the Definitive Treaty later than by a letter from Doctor Franklin, about the 20th of April. It had been delayed by the tardiness of the Dutch, but more for the want of a British ministry; but was then progressing. Mr. Hartley, who has succeeded Mr. Oswald, was very acceptable, and, as the Doctor adds, an old acquaintance of his, and a lover of peace.

'Accounts from New York say that an embarkation of the German troops is taking place, and that a treaty is to be expected very soon. The commercial treaty with Sweden is arrived. Denmark also desires one. The Journals requested by your Excellency shall be sent.

'I have the honor,' &c.

In August, or the latter part of July, Ellsworth returned home, and did not again take his seat in the Continental Congress. Although re-elected by the Legislature of Connecticut, he declined the service. He also declined the appointment, tendered him by Congress in the following year, of Commissioner of the Treasury.

He had now served his native State with ability in the councils of the Confederacy, and we shall see, in the following chapter, that that ability was equally employed, though in a different capacity, at home.

CHAPTER VI.

1780 – 1784.

A MEMBER OF THE GOVERNOR'S COUNCIL.

WHILE a Delegate to Congress, Ellsworth, in the year 1780, was elected a Member of the Governor's Council, or the Upper House, as it was styled. This post he held, by successive re-elections, until 1784. The Council, in the Connecticut system, was a coordinate branch of the Legislature, and also constituted the Supreme Court of Errors, with legal and equitable jurisdiction.[1] Ellsworth, when present, took an active part, it is said, in its deliberations, and had unrivalled influence over his colleagues. He was conscientious and faithful in the discharge of his duties. His habits of thought were slow and laborious, and his mind did not reach its conclusions without long and anxious reflection; but whatever labor was necessary, to fix and confirm his opinion, he did not fail to bestow.

'Whenever any important case was under consideration in the Council or Court of Errors,' says Mr. Wood, 'Mr. Ellsworth, in the recess, if one occurred, retired to his lodgings, and continued travelling the floor, unconscious of any thing except the operations of his

[1] It consisted of the Lieutenant-Governor and twelve Assistants.

mind, until he went through his course of thought and research. During this time his lips were in motion, and an indistinct utterance kept up, intermingled with pinches of snuff as often as once a minute, till he arrived at his conclusions. His mind, then, seemed to find instant relief, and he gave himself up to amusement and cheerful conversation. In these moments of relaxation he frequently delighted himself with the sports and prattle of children. When the Board were at Hartford, a little lad, by the name of John Bull, who lived in the neighborhood of Mr. Ellsworth's lodgings, found out that he was a very amusing playmate at a certain hour of the day, and therefore regularly made his appearance at the door, to have a romping with his jocose companion.'[1]

This simplicity of tastes, this love of children — in themselves a more valuable testimony to the goodness and kindliness of his nature than all labored eulogies — characterized Ellsworth through life. Neither the weight of public cares, nor the strife of politics, corrupted or hardened the native purity of his heart. 'The love of children,' says one of his biographers, 'had always been one of his prominent traits of character. From the chicanery and selfishness of mankind he turned, with renewed pleasure, to their simplicity. It was remarked of him, in early life, that, when deeply engaged in those absorbing studies which afterwards won for him fortune and renown, he daily spent some time in caressing his neighbor's children. He even seemed disappointed when any circumstance prevented this accustomed intercourse. Though there were long periods in which he was compelled to seclude himself from the pleasures of the

---

[1] MS. Memoir by Mr. Joseph Wood.

domestic circle, yet he would sometimes permit his own little ones to enter his study when occupied in the severest toils of thought, and draw pictures for their amusement. "I like to indulge them in this way," he observed, "and when it is necessary to deny them, I send them to their mother." As they advanced in age, their improvement and the formation of their habits were felt by him in their full importance. The incalculable worth of time, the duty of industry, the folly of extravagance, the necessity of rectitude and piety, were impressed both by precept and example.'[1]

So great was the deference paid to Ellsworth by the members of the Connecticut Council, that it frequently happened, after the majority had expressed their opinion, a question, a suggestion from him, induced a reconsideration and reversal of decision. And, in general, his direct, simple, and lucid statement of the points in issue determined the judgment of the Court. We have, however, no specimens of this portion of his judicial career, and must rely on contemporary testimony as to the merit and importance of his services. He continued a Member of the Council, as we have already mentioned, until 1784, when he was appointed a Judge of the Superior Court of Connecticut. In this latter position we shall view him in the following chapter.

---

[1] National Portrait Gallery, vol. iv. Art. 'Ellsworth.'

CHAPTER VII.

1784-1789.

A JUDGE OF THE SUPERIOR COURT OF CONNECTICUT.

THE career of Ellsworth as a Judge of the Superior Court of Connecticut does not present many points of especial interest. The decisions of the Court, while he was a member of it, are chiefly collected in Kirby's Reports. Few of his opinions, however, are reported *in extenso*, and the cases themselves do not possess much of novelty or interest. When he came to the Bench, the law in Connecticut was in an uncertain and unsettled state. A good deal of embarrassment had arisen from the attempt to reject such part of the common law as was supposed to be inapplicable to the situation of a community distinguished for 'the equal distribution of property, simplicity of manners, and agricultural habits and employments.' But in determining what was applicable and what inapplicable, great uncertainty and contradiction naturally arose in the decisions of the Courts. 'For the principles of their decisions were soon forgot, or misunderstood, or erroneously reported from memory. Hence arose a confusion in the determinations of our Courts, the rules of property became uncertain, and litigation proportionably increased.'[1]

[1] Kirby's Reports, Preface.

The publication of Kirby's Reports was a very important step towards establishing a uniform and permanent system of law in Connecticut. Though the cases at the present day may not be regarded as throwing any very important light on the principles of jurisprudence, they must, historically, be viewed with interest. With these few preliminary observations, we shall now lay before the reader several of Ellsworth's opinions, which will give a favorable impression of his general ability, even if they do not particularly display his character as a jurist.

In Hobby *v.* Finch, &c.,[1] Ellsworth dissented from the judgment of the Court, and held that an advertisement that lands are to be sold at public auction, with the terms of sale, &c., is not a sufficient memorandum in writing within the statute for the prevention of frauds and perjuries, and, consequently, that the vendor could not be held to a performance of his agreement. He thus stated the grounds of his opinion. 'First. Because the declaration is ill. It doth not appear that the plaintiff paid or offered to pay, or secure the sum he bid for the land, nor that he bid any sum that would have justified the administrators in passing a deed. Nor is there any averment of the value of the land, or any rule of damages given. Secondly. The advertisement is no evidence or memorandum of agreement on which the action is grounded. The agreement was made at the time the land was bid off, and was made and expressed on the one part by the bid made for the land, and on the other part by striking it off. Here the minds of the parties met, and the substance of the agreement, as thus expressed, was, that the plaintiff should have the land for the

---

[1] Kirby's Reports, pp. 14, 16.

sum he had then bid for it, and that a deed should be executed accordingly. The advertisement doth not express this agreement, nor either part of it; nor was any reference had to the advertisement in forming this agreement, farther than as to the mode of payment. That this sale was at public auction makes no difference. It is as requisite, by the statute, that public sales of land should be guarded as private ones, and it is as easy to be done. A memorandum of the sale might be taken in writing from the vendor, and would hardly be refused, if required at the time of the sale or agreement. I think the statute extends to this case, and that it has not been complied with.'

In Hart *v.* Smith,[1] Ellsworth again dissented from the judgment of the Court, which was, that assumpsit would not lie for money paid by mistake in the settlement of an account; though, if the mistake was apparent on the face of the account, a special action on the case, pointing out such mistake, might be sustained.

'It is an established principle of law,' said Ellsworth in his dissenting opinion, 'founded in the most apparent justice, that an action will lie for money paid by mistake; and it makes no difference whether the mistake happens in the settlement of an account, or of any other matter. It is sufficient, to maintain the action, that there has been a settlement, and a mistake therein, whereby the defendant has obtained money of the plaintiff, which in conscience he ought not to retain. The difficulty lies in showing with clearness and certainty that the mistake has happened, which in *all cases* cannot be done; as where a settlement is made in gross, without computation or regard had to particulars; so where a settlement is made on compu-

[1] Kirby's Reports, p. 127.

tation, but the evidence of the computation is not preserved, and only a receipt is given, to show that a settlement has been made. But other cases there are, in which the mistakes are clear and certain; as where they have happened by a miscast, a mistaken or double entry, and the account or statement is preserved for inspection, as in the present case; so where the mistake has happened by the misconception of a fact, which afterwards comes to light; as when a loss has been allowed on a policy of insurance, and the vessel afterwards safely arrives. Whenever the mistake is apparent, or, from the nature and circumstances of it, clearly demonstrable, a remedy may and ought to be admitted; nor will the admission of it invalidate the settlement of the parties, which may still be left to operate, so far forth as the same was understandingly made. Ratifying the errors or mistakes of a settlement does not destroy it, but only makes it what the parties designed it should be; and the Court, in the trial of every such case, will confine the plaintiff to lay his finger at once upon the mistake, and not suffer him unnecessarily to ramble over the settlement.' Having thus established a right of recovery, he proceeds to inquire whether such recovery may be had in an action of *indebitatus assumpsit*. 'This is a kind of action,' said he, 'well known in our practice, as well as in the common law of England; and from the equity of the principles on which it proceeds, and the extensiveness of the remedy it gives, is highly favored. It lies generally when one has secured money belonging to another, without any valuable consideration on the receiver's part; for the law construes this to be money had and received to the use of the owner only; it is in the nature of a bill in equity, and is applicable to almost every case where the defendant has received money which, *ex equo et bono*, he ought not to retain; and particularly where he has obtained it by imposition or mistake, as in the present case. . . . As the trial is on equitable principles, the defendant may, under the general issue of *non assumpsit*, disprove the facts set up by the plaintiff, or set up other and independent facts, to rebut the equity of the plaintiff's demand. The generality both of the charge and defence are supposed to be adapted to the nature and design of the action.'

In Adams *v.* Kellogg,[1] the Court held that a *feme-covert* cannot devise real estate to her husband. The opinion of Ellsworth upon this question is very full and instructive. Starting with the proposition that the right to direct the succession of estates by will is not a natural, but a municipal right, a mere creature of law, he thus proceeds: 'Admitting, however, that a right of devising estate was a natural right, it would not follow that a *feme-covert* has it, though there be no statute to take it away. Many natural rights are controlled by long use and custom, which may be evincive of common consent, and acquire, to every purpose, the force of law. Others are controlled by the reason of the case, arising out of some special relation or condition. We have no statute to divest a *feme-covert* of her personal estate; and yet nobody doubts but, by the act or condition of coverture, it becomes the husband's; nor have we any that she shall not contract and bind her person and estate, as a *feme-sole* may; yet she cannot do it. It cannot, then, be inferred that a *feme-covert* has power to devise an estate, from the score of natural right. As to her supposed common law right to devise her estate, there has not been

[1] Kirby's Reports, pp. 195, 438.

a custom or any adjudications to found it upon, either in this country or that from which we emigrated.

'The right of *devising* is of a much later date than that of *heiring* estates, both being political inventions, but not equally the offspring of necessity. The latter we trace to Abraham's time; the former only to Solon's, who introduced it into the Athenian code, to supply the want of heirs where there was no issue. From thence, with some enlargement, it was copied into the Roman twelve tables; and has at length, by very slow degrees, and with some alterations, been adopted by the greatest part of Europe. Denmark, Sweden, and Poland, however, had not the use of wills, either of real or personal estate, at the beginning of the present century, and I am not certain that they have yet.

'With regard to the latitude in which the Romans admitted the use of wills, who extended it to *feme-coverts*, a diversity of circumstances ought to be noted. Marriage, by their law, formed a much slighter union of persons and property than is the case with us. A wife might contract and bind her person and estate, and maintain actions in her own name; nor was the husband holden for her debts, contracted before or after marriage, nor civiliter for her trespasses. She might retain and manage her personal as well as other estate, except what she saw fit to advance to her husband, to entitle her to a jointure; and this, if his circumstances declined, she might recover back again, and have an action against him for it; and nothing more than consent of parties was necessary to dissolve the marriage. Consonant enough to this state of things was the wife's power to make a will. A son could not do it, while his father lived, because he was under the power of the father, and considered as one with him.

From this heathenish source sprung the idea of a *feme-covert's* power to make a will, and has been absurdly adopted by some Christian nations, whom clerical influence has been sufficient to shackle with the *civil law.*'

Having shown that, neither by natural or common or statute law, has a *feme-covert* the right to devise her estate, he thus concludes:

'With regard to the policy of extending such a power to *feme-coverts*, it may be remarked, that there is not the same reason for it as there was for the statute empowering a husband to sell his wife's lands, with her consent. From a sale of them she might have comfort and necessary support, but not from a devise. Besides, the freedom of her consent in that case is to be evinced, as fully as it may, by examination before a magistrate; which circumstance also, as well as that of recording, gives immediate notoriety to the transaction, that all concerned may scrutinize it while it can be done to advantage. Nor do the general reasons urged for the institution of wills seem to extend to the case of a *feme-covert.* That of their use in aiding family government does not, because the government is not placed in her hands. Nor does that of their utility in stimulating to industry and economy; for her exertion adds nothing to the stock she is to dispose of. The crumbling down of overgrown estates need not be mentioned here. The possession of this power must be as inconvenient for *feme-coverts* as it is unnecessary. It must subject them to endless teasing and family discord, as well as frequently their heirs, and sometimes their children, to the loss of property, which the law has been studious to preserve for them. Add to which, exposed as they are to coercions imperceptible to others, and dangerous for them to disclose;

placed in the power of a husband, whose solicitations they cannot resist, and whose commands, in all things lawful, it is their duty to obey. Their wills, taken in a corner, and concealed from the world till they have left it, can afford but very uncertain evidence of the real wishes of their hearts. Political considerations, therefore, so far as they can be of weight, serve to confirm the opinion, that a *feme-covert* has not power to dispose of her estate by will.'

Having thus given the general reader an opportunity to observe in what manner Ellsworth acquits himself in the discussion of legal questions, we do not propose to trace further his services while on the Bench of the Superior Court of Connecticut. Indeed, as, in most of the cases, the individual opinions of the Judges are not reported, such a labor would fail to throw any additional light upon this portion of his career. Upon one interesting subject of inquiry we have been unable to obtain any precise information, and that is, respecting the opinions he entertained of the barbarous criminal code at this time in force in Connecticut. The punishments inflicted on offenders — whipping, cropping, branding with a hot iron, exposure with a halter round the neck, &c. — were directly calculated to destroy all pride of character, all desire, or even chance of reformation. Whether Ellsworth was in advance of his contemporaries, and in favor of ameliorating a code thus brutal in its character, is unknown to us. Taking leave of him, for the present, in his judicial character, we shall now view him on the broader theatre of public affairs.

CHAPTER VIII.

1787.

THE FEDERAL CONVENTION.

THE absence of any general authority to provide means for the payment of the public debt, and regulate commerce, together with the distracted counsels of the several States, threatened to involve the affairs of the United States in anarchy and confusion. 'Our situation,' thus wrote Madison, 'is becoming every day more and more critical. No money comes into the Federal Treasury, no respect is paid to the Federal authority, and people of reflection unanimously agree that the existing Confederacy is tottering to its foundation.'[1] In this crisis of the body-politic, the Federal Convention assembled at Philadelphia, in May, 1787.[2] It was composed of the most distinguished abilities and character that the country could boast. Over its deliberations presided Washington; the genial wisdom of Franklin illustrated its debates; the trained mind, extensive information, and reflective habits of Madison; the fertile resources, the ready and trenchant talents of Gouverneur Morris; the liberal views and sound sense of Charles Cotesworth Pinckney; the in-

---

[1] Madison to Randolph, February 25th, 1787. Madison Papers, p. 619.

[2] Vol. I., pp. 373–376, 601, 602.

flexible integrity and unbending republicanism of Colonel Mason; the rare genius of Hamilton; the penetrating mind and persuasive eloquence of Rufus King—were all displayed on this conspicuous theatre, and more or less determined the course and result of the Convention. But, whatever is due to the merits of others, 'it is owing,' says Mr. Calhoun, 'it is owing — I speak it here, in honor of New England and the Northern States — it is owing mainly to the States of Connecticut and New Jersey that we have a Federal, instead of a National Government; that we have the best Government, instead of the most despotic and intolerable, on the earth. Who were the men of these States to whom we are indebted for this admirable Government? I will name them. Their names ought to be engraven on brass, and live forever. They were Chief Justice Ellsworth, Roger Sherman, and Judge Patterson of New Jersey. The other States further south were blind; they did not see the future. But to the sagacity and coolness of these three men, aided by a few others, but not so prominent, we owe the present Constitution.'[1]

Ellsworth had long perceived the necessity of reorganizing the Federal authority so as to give it a revenue independent of the States; but that object attained, he would preserve the latter in their integrity, and give the General Government no more control over them than was requisite to enforce the powers with which it might be entrusted. In other words, he would enlarge the authority of the Confederation, rather than substitute an entirely different system. As the favorite scheme of government proposed

---

[1] Calhoun's Works, vol. iv., p. 354. Remarks on Simmons's Resolutions.

to the Convention departed widely from his views, it was his endeavor, in the discussions that ensued, to make that scheme as nearly conformable to his sentiments as possible. He was among the most earnest, as he certainly was among the ablest, advocates of what was termed the States-Rights party.

His colleagues in the convention, from Connecticut, were Roger Sherman and William Samuel Johnson. Sherman was practical, laborious, and well-informed; but his mind was neither richly, nor variously, endowed. His distinguishing qualities were good sense, adroitness in the management of affairs, sound judgment, and unwearied application. His grave demeanor, austere virtue, and practical wisdom, were all calculated to impress the minds, and insure the confidence of his constituents. Ellsworth entertained for him the profoundest respect, and endeavored, it is said, to form his own character on Sherman's model. 'This,' remarked John Adams, 'was praise enough for both.'[1]

Johnson was wholly unlike Sherman. He was naturally attracted to the *literæ humaniores*, and was distinguished for liberal culture and graceful eloquence. In masculinity, in talents for affairs, in logic and labor, he was inferior to his colleagues; but, in extent and variety of information, in scholarship, in oratory, in all that attracts the eye and captivates the heart, he was their superior.

Ellsworth objected to the term *National* Government, and proposed, instead, the Government of *the United States*. This, he said, was the proper title. He wished the plan of the Convention to go forth as an amendment of the Articles of the Confederation, since,

---

[1] Portrait Gallery, vol. iv. Art. 'Ellsworth.'

under this idea, the authority of the Legislatures could ratify it. If they are unwilling, the people will be so too. If the plan goes forth to the people for ratification, several succeeding conventions within the States would be unavoidable. He did not like these conventions. They were better fitted to pull down than to build up Constitutions.[1]

The existence and agency of the States he deemed indispensable. Without their co-operation it would be impossible, he said, to support a republican government over so great an extent of country. An army could scarcely render it practicable. The largest States were the worst governed. Virginia is obliged to acknowledge her incapacity to extend her government to Kentucky; Massachusetts cannot keep the peace one hundred miles from her capital, and is now forming an army for its support. How long Pennsylvania might be free from a like situation could not be foreseen. If the principles and materials of our government are not adequate to the extent of these single States, how can it be imagined that they can support a single government throughout the United States? The only chance of supporting a general government lies in grafting it on those of the individual States.[2]

Under a National Government, he said, he should participate in the national security; but that was all. What he wanted was domestic happiness. The National Government could not descend to the local

---

[1] Madison Papers, vol. ii., p. 908. The scheme introduced into the Convention by Mr. Patterson of New Jersey, which was purely Federal, and excluded the idea of any departure from the principle of the Confederation, was concerted among the members from Connecticut, New York, New Jersey, and Delaware, with, as is supposed, Mr. Martin of Maryland. Ibid., p. 812, note.

[2] Madison Papers, vol. ii., p. 957.

objects on which this depended. It could only embrace objects of a general nature. He turned his eyes, therefore, for the preservation of his rights, to the State Governments. From these alone he would derive the greatest happiness he expected in this life. His happiness depended on their existence, as much as a newborn infant on its mother for nourishment. If this reasoning was not satisfactory, he had nothing to add that could be so.[1]

He would not only preserve the identity of the States, but their equality also; and as a means to secure this, he insisted that, in the Senate, each State should have an equality of suffrage. When it was decided that, in the first branch of the Legislature, the representation of the several States should be according to population, Ellsworth remarked, that he was not sorry at the result. He hoped it would become a ground of compromise with regard to the second branch. They were partly national, and partly Federal, he said. The proportional representation in the first branch was conformable to the national principle, and would secure the large States against the small. An equality of voices was conformable to the Federal principle, and was necessary to secure the small States against the large. He trusted that, on this middle ground, a compromise would take place. He did not see that it could on any other; and if no compromise should take place, their meeting would not only be in vain, but worse than in vain. To the eastward, he was sure Massachusetts was the only State that would listen to a proposition for excluding the States, as equal political societies, from an equal voice

[1] Madison Papers, vol. ii., p. 1014. With these views it is, perhaps, unnecessary to say that he opposed the idea of Congress having a negative on the State laws.

in both branches. The others would risk every consequence rather than part with so clear a right. An attempt to deprive them of it was at once cutting the body of America in two. The large States, he conceived, would, notwithstanding the equality of votes, have an influence that would maintain their superiority. Holland, as had been admitted, had, notwithstanding a like equality in the Dutch Confederacy, a prevailing influence in the public measures. The power of self-defence was essential to the small States. Nature had given it to the smallest insect of the creation. He could never admit that there was no danger of combinations among the large States. They would, like individuals, find out and avail themselves of the advantage to be gained by it. It was true the danger would be greater if they were contiguous, and had a more immediate and common interest. A defensive combination of the small States was rendered more difficult by their greater number. He would mention another consideration of great weight. The existing Confederation was founded on the equality of the States in the article of suffrage; was it meant to pay no regard to this antecedent plighted faith? Let a strong Executive, a Judiciary, a Legislative power, be created; but let not too much be attempted, by which all may be lost. He was not in general, he said, a half-way man; yet he preferred doing half the good we could, rather than do nothing at all. The other half may be added when the necessity should be more fully experienced.[1]

An equal vote to each State in the Senate, he maintained, was essential to save the few from being destroyed by the many. If security was all that the

---

[1] Madison Papers, vol. ii., p. 998.

great States wished for, the first branch secured them. His position was not the result of partial or local views. The State he represented belonged neither to the class of large or small States, but held a middle rank.[1]

Against this notion of an equal representation in the Senate was arrayed a very strong opposition — an opposition which numbered in its ranks Franklin, Madison, King, Pinckney, Wilson, and, indeed, a majority of the Delegates.

Madison said, if it was conceded, the minority could negative the will of the majority of the people; could extort measures, by making them a condition of their assent to other necessary measures; could obtrude measures on the majority, by virtue of the peculiar powers which would be vested in the Senate; and that the evil would increase with every new State that might be admitted. Besides, it would give a perpetual preponderance to the Northern against the Southern scale. Wilson objected to equality of votes in the Senate, because the small States might control the Government, as they had done in the Continental Congress.

Ellsworth, in reply, asked two questions — one of Mr. Wilson, whether he had ever seen a good measure fail in Congress for want of a majority of States in its favor?—the other of Mr. Madison, whether a negative lodged with a majority of States, even the smallest, could be more dangerous than the qualified negative proposed to be lodged in a single Executive Magistrate, who must be taken from some one State?

At first, Ellsworth was in favor of paying the members of Congress out of the treasuries of their respective States. In opposition to this proposition, Hamil-

---

[1] Madison Papers, vol. ii., p. 1003.

ton pressed the distinction between the State Governments and the people. The former, he said, would be the rivals of the General Government. The State Legislatures ought not, therefore, to be the paymasters of the latter. In reply to this, Ellsworth said, if they were jealous of the State Governments, the latter would be equally jealous of them. 'If, on going home,' said he, 'I tell them we gave the General Government such powers because we could not trust you, will they adopt it? And without their approbation it is a nullity?'[1] Again, 'if the Senate was meant to strengthen the Government, it ought to have the confidence of the States. The States will have an interest in keeping up a representation, and will make such provision for supporting the members as will ensure their attendance.'[2]

But his views upon this subject were successfully answered by Madison. They would subvert, he maintained, the end intended by allowing the Senate a duration of six years; they would hold their places during the pleasure of the State Legislatures. 'The motion,' said he, 'would make the Senate, like Congress,[3] the mere agents and advocates of State interests and views, instead of being the impartial umpires and guardians of justice and the general good.'[4]

It has been said of Ellsworth, that, after he had formed his opinion, he was very pertinacious in adhering to it; but, on this occasion, he was convinced of the impolicy of payment by the States, and gracefully acknowledged his error. He said that, on reflection, he had become satisfied that too much dependence on

[1] Madison Papers, p. 935. 'Those who pay,' said Hamilton, 'are the masters of those who are paid.' Ibid., p. 934.

[2] Ibid., p. 970.

[3] The Continental Congress.

[4] Madison Papers, p. 971.

the States would be produced by this mode of payment. He moved, therefore, that the members of Congress should be paid out of the treasury of the United States.

He was of opinion that the number of Representatives should not be large, not only on the ground of expense, but for the reason that the public business would be more promptly and better conducted with a small representation. He was in favor, too, of an annual election of Representatives. 'The people were fond of frequent elections,' he said, 'and might be safely indulged in one branch of the Legislature.' He opposed the proposition to make the privilege of an elector dependent on a property qualification. 'Ought not every man who pays a tax,' he inquired, 'to vote for the Representative who is to levy and dispose of his money?' At any rate, if a pecuniary qualification was to be insisted on, leave the several States to fix the amount, and not attempt a provision for it in the Constitution. He would also make members of Congress ineligible to public offices. 'If rewards are to circulate only within the Legislature, merit out of it,' he said, 'will be discouraged.'

Gouverneur Morris urged the danger of admitting strangers into our public councils, and hence proposed fourteen years' citizenship, as a qualification for Senators. But Ellsworth was opposed to the motion, as discouraging meritorious aliens from emigrating to this country. Rutledge, too, proposed that a residence of seven years in a State should be required, to entitle one to be elected a Representative to Congress. Ellsworth, on the contrary, thought seven years too long a term. He thought one year sufficient, but seemed to have no objection to three years.

He was opposed to conferring on Congress the

power to issue paper-money. The mischiefs of that description of money were fresh in the public mind, and had excited the disgust of all the respectable part of America. 'Paper-money can in no case be necessary,' he said. 'Give the Government credit, and other resources will offer. The power may do harm, never good.'

Rutledge was in favor of the Union assuming the debts of the States, inasmuch as they were incurred in the common defence, and especially as taxes on imports, the only sure source of revenue, were to be given to the common Government. Ellsworth thought the assumption would naturally follow, so far as the State debts ought in equity to be assumed.

Over the militia of the States, he would give the General Government all necessary authority; but was opposed to the idea of the latter making laws for their regulation and discipline, except when they were in the actual service of the United States. 'The whole authority over the militia,' he said, 'ought by no means to be taken away from the States, whose consequence would pine away to nothing after such a sacrifice of power. He thought the general authority could not sufficiently pervade the Union for such a purpose, nor could it accommodate itself to the local genius of the people. It must be vain to ask the States to give the militia out of their hands.' Besides, he deemed a uniform militia law impracticable. 'Three or four shillings,' he said, 'as a penalty will enforce obedience better, in New England, than forty lashes in some other places.'

On the question proportioning representation to direct taxation, and both to the white and three-fifths of the black inhabitants, Ellsworth voted in the affirmative. His colleague, Doctor Johnson, was of opinion that wealth and population were the true, equitable rules of representation, but these two principles resolved themselves into one; population being the best measure of wealth. He concluded, therefore, that the number of people ought to be established as the rule, and that all descriptions, including blacks *equally* with the whites, ought to fall within the computation.

Notwithstanding the provision of the Constitution which gives the slaveholding States a representation based, in part, on three-fifths of their black population, excited a good deal of discussion and opposition in the Convention, and has since been the subject of much jealousy and unfriendly criticism, it is difficult to conceive any valid objection to it. Indeed, it would be difficult to answer satisfactorily Doctor Johnson's view of the matter, viz., that the blacks should stand on an equality with the whites. The negroes constituted a large portion of the population of the Southern States. They were the laboring, producing population. Why should other States scrutinize the character of that population, and discriminate against it? If the rule of representation between confederating States is population, why should not that population be enumerated irrespective of its condition? Any representation of the slave population, however, was warmly opposed by many of the leading members of the Convention, and by none more warmly than Gouverneur Morris. 'Upon what principle,' he demanded, 'is it that the slaves shall be computed in the representation? Are they men? Then make them citizens, and let them vote. Are they property? Why, then, is no other property included? The houses in this city [Philadelphia] are worth more than all the wretched slaves who cover the rice swamps of South Carolina. . . . Let it not be said that direct taxation is to be proportioned to representation. It is idle to suppose that the General Government can stretch its hand directly into the pockets of the people, scattered over so vast a country. They can only do it through the medium of exports, imports, and excises. For what, then, are all the sacrifices to be made? He would sooner submit himself to a tax for paying for all the negroes in the United States, than saddle posterity with such a Constitution.'

It was also urged against slave representation, that it would encourage the slave trade, inasmuch as every accession of that class of population would proportionably increase the votes of the slaveholding States in the National Government. And to the slave trade there was a very strong opposition. Maryland and Virginia had already prohibited it; but if allowed by the General Government, their action would be in vain. Fresh supplies of wretched Africans, said Gouverneur Morris, would increase the danger of attack, and the difficulty of defence. The right of importing, said Luther Martin, was unreasonable, because slaves weakened one part of the Union which the other parts were bound to protect.

Ellsworth, on the other hand, would not intermeddle with the subject. 'Let every State import what it pleases,' he said. 'The morality or wisdom of slavery are considerations belonging to the States themselves. What enriches a part enriches the whole, and the States are the best judges of their particular interest. The old Confederation had not meddled with this point. He did not see any greater necessity for bringing it within the policy of the new one.'

In reply to Colonel Mason, who said that slaves produced the most pernicious effect on manners, that every master of slaves is born a petty tyrant, Ellsworth remarked, that, as he had never owned a slave, he could not judge of the effects of slavery on character. He said, however, 'that, if it was to be considered in a moral light, we ought to go further, and free those already in the country. As slaves also multiply so fast in Virginia and Maryland, that it is cheaper to raise than import them, whilst in the sickly rice swamps foreign supplies are necessary, if we go no further than is urged, we shall be unjust towards South Carolina and Georgia. Let us not intermeddle. As population increases, poor laborers will be so plenty as to render slaves useless. Slavery, in time, will not be a speck in our country. Provision is already made in Connecticut for abolishing it; and the abolition has already taken place in Massachusetts. As to the danger of insurrections from foreign influence, that will become a motive to kind treatment of the slaves.'

General Pinckney, in order to get rid of one difficulty that had been started, moved to refer the subject to the Committee, in order that slaves might be made liable to an equal tax with other imports, which he thought right. Gouverneur Morris wished the whole subject to be committed, including the clauses relating to taxes on exports, and a navigation act. These things, he said, might form a bargain among the Northern and Southern States. We have elsewhere stated that a proposition had already been reported, that no navigation act should be passed without the assent of two-thirds of the members present in each House — a proposition exceedingly distasteful to most of the Northern States, and which they were desirous to get rid of.[1]

Ellsworth, however, was for taking the plan as it

---

[1] Vol. i., p. 610.

was. He would concede the right of importing slaves, without compromise or equivalent. 'This widening of opinions,' he said, 'had a threatening aspect. If we do not agree on this middle and moderate ground, he was afraid we should lose two States, with such others as may be disposed to stand aloof—should fly into a variety of shapes and directions, and most probably into several Confederations, and not without bloodshed.' Accordingly, he voted against a reference of the clause as to a navigation act.

On the question as to the mode of appointing the Executive, three plans were proposed. First, appointment by Congress, with ineligibility for a second term. Secondly, an election by the people at large. Thirdly, appointment by Electors chosen for that purpose by the States.

To the first mode, it was objected, that it would be attended with intrigues and contentions: to the second, that while, perhaps, fittest in itself, yet the people might be misled by designing men; and, besides, the right of suffrage was more diffusive in the Northern than in the Southern States, and the latter would have no influence in the election, on the score of the negroes: to the third, Ellsworth gave his support. His plan proposed the appointment by Electors, chosen by the Legislatures of the States, according to a prescribed ratio. To the mode of election, that is, by Electors, a majority of States assented; but it was left to the Legislatures of the several States to determine how the Electors should be chosen.

Ellsworth favored six years as the term of the Executive office. 'If the elections be too frequent,' he said, 'the Executive will not be firm enough. There must be duties which will make him unpopular for the moment. There will be *outs* as well as *ins*. His administration, therefore, will be attacked and misrepresented.' He would not make him ineligible. He should be re-elected, if his conduct proved him worthy of it. 'And he will be more likely," said he, 'to render himself worthy of it, if he be rewardable with it. The most eminent characters, also, will be more willing to accept the trust under this condition, than if they foresee a necessary degradation at a fixed period.' He approved heartily of the proposition to associate the National Judiciary with the Executive in the revisionary power. 'The aid of the Judges,' he said, 'will give more wisdom and firmness to the Executive. They will possess a systematic and accurate knowledge of the laws, which the Executive cannot be expected always to possess. The law of nations will also frequently come into question. Of this the Judges alone will have competent information.' But this expedient was shown, as we think, to be unwise, and was judiciously rejected.

To the idea, however, of an Executive Council, Ellsworth was very much wedded, and on a subsequent day he renewed the subject. He conceived there ought to be a Council; and his proposition was, that it should be composed of the President of the Senate, the Chief Justice, and the Ministers as they might be established for the Departments of Foreign and Domestic Affairs — War, Finance, and Marine — who should advise but not conclude the President. This proposition, however, shared the fate of the first, and was rejected.

Ellsworth urged the appointment of the Federal Judiciary by the Senate, rather than the President; but, in the absence of that mode, he would give to the Senate the nomination, subject to the President's approval. He thought the Senators, coming from all parts of the country, would have a better knowledge of characters than the Executive; and, besides, the latter would be more open to caresses and intrigues than the former. This view of the subject was favorably received, but was not finally adopted.

We have now laid before the reader the opinions which Ellsworth espoused in the Federal Convention. We have seen that, in the outset, he declared himself in favor of a ratification of their proceedings by the Legislatures of the States, rather than by conventions. On that point he was very strenuous, and made an elaborate speech in its support. He thought more was to be expected from the Legislatures, than from the people. To the objections of Colonel Mason, that the Legislatures had no authority to ratify, and if they had, their successors, having equal authority, could rescind their acts, he replied, that a new set of ideas seemed to have crept in since the Articles of Confederation were established. 'Conventions of the people were not then thought of. The Legislatures were considered as competent. Their ratification had been acquiesced in without complaint. To whom have Congress applied, on subsequent occasions, for further powers? To the Legislatures, not to the people.' Besides, they existed as a Federal society, united by a charter which admitted of alterations by the Legislative authority of the States. As to the second point, he could not admit that it was well-founded. 'An act to which the States, by their Legislatures, make themselves parties, becomes a compact from which no one of the parties can recede of itself.'

The plan of the Convention, however, was referred to conventions; and in the next chapter we shall see the part he took in the Convention assembled to pronounce upon it, in Connecticut. We should here observe, however, that, during the final proceedings of the Federal Convention, Ellsworth was absent; and, from that circumstance, his name was not attached to the Constitution. But, although objecting to some of the details of that instrument, he was, nevertheless, prepared, as we shall presently see, to give it his earnest and unqualified support.

CHAPTER IX.

1788.

THE CONNECTICUT CONVENTION.

Ellsworth was a member of the Connecticut Convention, which assembled at Hartford, in January, 1788, and opened the debates on the proposed Constitution. He made two speeches — one in explanation of the scheme of government recommended by the Federal Convention; the other on the power of Congress to lay taxes. These speeches — as giving the reader an idea of his style and ability in treating political subjects — will naturally find a place here. It should be observed, however, that they are not altogether an accurate representation of his views, as was publicly stated by him soon after their appearance. On opening the discussion, he thus addressed the Convention: —

'Mr. President: — It is observable that there is no preface to the proposed Constitution; but it evidently presupposes two things — one is, the necessity of a Federal Government; the other is, the inefficacy of the old articles of Confederation. A Union is necessary for the purposes of a national defence. United, we are strong; divided, we are weak. It is easy for hostile nations to sweep off a number of separate States, one after another. Witness the States in the neighborhood of ancient Rome. They were successively subdued by that ambitious city, which they might have conquered with the utmost ease, if they had been united. Witness the Canaanitish nations, whose divided situation rendered them an easy prey. Witness England, which, when divided into separate States, was twice conquered by an inferior force. Thus it always happened to small States, and to great ones, if divided. Or if, to avoid this, they connect themselves with some powerful State, their situation is not much better. This shows us the necessity of combining our whole force, and, as to national purposes, becoming one State.

'A Union, Sir, is likewise necessary, considered with relation to economy. Small States have enemies, as well as great ones. They must provide for their defence. The expense of it, which would be moderate for a large Kingdom, would be intolerable to a petty State. The Dutch are wealthy, but they are one of the smallest of the European nations, and their taxes are higher than in any other country of Europe. Their taxes amount to forty shillings per head, when those of England do not exceed half that sum. We must unite, in order to preserve peace among ourselves. If we be divided, what is to prevent wars from breaking out among the States? States, as well as individuals, are subject to ambition, to avarice, to those jarring passions which disturb the peace of society. What is to check these? If there be a parental hand over the whole, this, and nothing else, can restrain the unruly conduct of the members. Union is necessary to preserve commutative justice between the States. If divided, what is to prevent the large States from oppressing the small? What is to defend us from the ambition and rapacity of New York, when she has spread over that vast territory which she claims and holds? Do we not already see in her the seeds of an overbearing ambition? On our other side there is a large and powerful State. Have we not already begun to be tributaries? If we do not improve the present critical time — if we do not unite — shall we not be like Issachar of old, a strong ass crouching down between two burdens? New Jersey and Delaware have done this, and have adopted the Constitution unanimously.

'A more energetic system is necessary. The present is merely advisory. It has no coercive power. Without this, government is ineffectual, or rather is no government at all. But, it is said, "such a power is not necessary. States will not do wrong. They need only to be told their duty, and they will do it." I ask, Sir, what warrant is there for this assertion? Do not States do wrong? Whence come wars? One of two hostile nations must be in the wrong. But, it is said, "Among sister States, this can never be presumed." But we do not know that. When friends become enemies, their enmity is the most virulent. The seventeen provinces of the Netherlands were once confederated; they fought under the same banner. Antwerp, hard pressed by Philip, applied to the other States for relief. Holland, a rival in trade, opposed and prevented the needed succors. Antwerp was made a sacrifice. I wish I could say there were no deeds of similar injustice springing up among us. Is there not, in one of our States, injustice too barefaced for Eastern despotism? That State is small; it does little hurt to any but itself. But it has a spirit that would make a Tophet of the Universe.[1] But some will say, "We formerly did well without any Union."

[1] Rhode Island is here alluded to.

I answer, our situation is materially changed. While Great Britain held her authority, she awed us. She appointed Governors and Councils for the American Provinces. She had a negative upon our laws. But, now, our circumstances are so altered, that there is no arguing what we shall be from what we have been. It is said, that other Confederacies have not had the principle of coercion. Is this so? Let us attend to those Confederacies which have resembled our own. Some time before Alexander, the Grecian States confederated together. The Amphictyonic Council, consisting of deputies from those States, met at Delphos, and had authority to regulate the general interests of Greece. This Council did enforce its decrees by coercion. . . . After the death of Alexander, the Achæan league was formed. The decrees of this Confederacy were enforced by dint of arms.'

He points out other instances of Confederacies having a coercive power, and thus proceeds: 'But, to come nearer home, Mr. President, have we not seen and felt the necessity of such a coercive power? What was the consequence of the want of it during the late war, particularly towards the close? A few States bore the burden of the war. While we, and one or two more of the States, were paying eighty or a hundred dollars per man to recruit the Continental army, the regiments of some States had scarcely men enough to wait on their officers. Since the close of the war, some of the States have done nothing towards complying with the requisitions of Congress. Others, who did something at first, seeing that they were left to bear the whole burden, have become equally remiss. What is the consequence? To what shifts have we been driven? To the wretched expedient of negotiating new loans in Europe, to pay the interest of the foreign debt. And, what is still worse, we have been obliged to apply the new loans to the support of our own civil government at home. Another ill-consequence of this want of energy, is, that treaties are not performed. The treaty of peace with Great Britain was a very favorable one for us. But it did not happen perfectly to please some of the States, and they would not comply with it. The consequence is, Britain charges us with the breach, and refuses to deliver up the forts on our Northern frontier.

'Our being tributaries to our sister States is in consequence of the want of a Federal system. The State of New York raises sixty or eighty thousand pounds a year by impost. Connecticut consumes about one-third of the goods upon which this impost is laid, and, consequently, pays one-third of this sum to New York. If we import by the medium of Massachusetts, she has an impost, and to her we pay tribute. If this is done when we have the shadow of a National Government, what shall we not suffer when even that shadow is gone! If we go on as we have done, what is to become of the foreign debt? Will sovereign nations forgive us this debt, because we neglect to pay? or will they levy by reprisals, as the law of nations authorizes them? Will our weakness induce Spain to relinquish the exclusive navigation of the Mississippi, or the territory which she claims on the east side of that river? Will our weakness induce the British to give up the Northern posts? If a war breaks out, and our situation invites our enemies to make war, how are we to defend ourselves? Has Government the means to enlist a man, or buy an ox? Or shall we rally the remainder of our old army? The European nations I believe to be not friendly to us. They were pleased to see us disconnected from Great Britain; they are pleased to see us disunited among ourselves. If we continue so, how easy it is for them to portion us out among them, as they did the Kingdom of Poland! But, supposing this is not done, if we suffer the Union to expire, the least that may be expected is, that the European Powers will form alliances, some with one State, and some with another, and play the States off one against another, and that we shall be involved in all the labyrinths of European politics. But I do not wish to continue the painful recital; enough has been said to show that a power in the General Government to enforce the decrees of the Union is absolutely necessary.

'The Constitution before us is a complete system of Legislative, Judicial, and Executive power. It was designed to supply the defects of the former system; and, I believe, upon a full discussion, it will be found calculated to answer the purposes for which it was designed.'

His next speech, on the power of Congress to lay taxes, will be likely to impress the reader very favorably. Mr. Webster, on reading an extract from it in the Senate, referred to Ellsworth as 'a gentleman who has left behind him, on the records of the Government of his country, proofs of the clearest intelligence, and of the utmost purity and integrity of character.'[1]

'Mr. President: — This is a most important clause in the Constitution; and the gentlemen do well to offer all the objections which they have against it. Through the whole of this debate, I have attended to the objections which have been made against this clause; and I think them all to be unfounded. The

---

[1] Webster's Works, vol. iii., p. 485.

clause is general; it gives the General Legislature "power to lay and collect taxes, duties, imposts, and excises; to pay the debts, and provide for the common defence and general welfare of the United States." There are three objections against this clause: first, that it is too extensive, as it extends to all the objects of taxation; secondly, that it is partial; thirdly, that Congress ought not to have power to lay taxes at all. The first objection is, that this clause extends to all the objects of taxation. But, though it does extend to all, it does not extend to them exclusively. It does not say that Congress shall have all these sources of revenue, and the States none. All, excepting the imposts, still lie open to the States. This State owes a debt; it must provide for the payment of it. So do all the other States. This will not escape the attention of Congress. When making calculations to raise a revenue, they will bear this in mind. They will not take away that which is necessary for the States. They are the head, and will take care that the members do not perish. The State debt, which now lies heavy upon us, arose from the want of powers in the Federal system. Give the necessary powers to the National Government, and the State will not be again necessitated to involve itself in debt for its defence in war. It will lie upon the National Government to defend all the States, to defend all its members from hostile attacks. The United States will bear the whole burden of war. It is necessary that the power of the General Legislature should extend to all the objects of taxation, that Government should be able to command all the resources of the country; because no man can tell what our exigences may be. Wars have now become rather wars of the purse than of the sword. Government must, therefore, be able to command the whole power of the purse; otherwise, a hostile nation may look into our Constitution, see what resources are in the power of Government, and calculate to go a little beyond us; thus they may obtain a decided superiority over us, and reduce us to the utmost distress. A Government which can command but half its resources, is like a man with but one arm to defend himself.

'The second objection is, that the impost is not a proper mode of taxation; that it is partial to the Southern States. I confess I am mortified when I find gentlemen supposing that their Delegates in Convention were inattentive to their duty, and made a sacrifice of the interests of their constituents. If, however, the impost be a partial mode, this circumstance, high as my opinion of it is, would weaken my attachment to it; for I abhor partiality. But I think there are three special reasons why an impost is the best way of raising a national revenue. The first is, that it is the most fruitful and easy way. All nations have found it to be so. Direct taxation can go but little way towards raising a revenue. To raise money in this way, people must be provident; they must constantly be laying up money to answer the demands of the collector. But you cannot make the people thus provident. If you would do anything to the purpose, you must come in when they are spending, and take a part with them. This does not take away the tools of a man's business, or the necessary utensils of his family. It only comes in when he is taking his pleasure, and feels generous; when he is laying out a shilling for superfluities, it takes twopence of it for public use, and the remainder will do him as much good as the whole. I will instance two facts, which show how easily and insensibly a revenue is raised by indirect taxation. I suppose people in general are not sensible that we pay a tax to the State of New York. Yet it is an incontrovertible fact, that we, the people of Connecticut, pay annually into the treasury of New York more than fifty thousand dollars. . . . All nations have seen the necessity and propriety of raising a revenue by indirect taxation, by duties upon articles of consumption. . . . The experiments which have been made in our own country show the productive nature of indirect taxes. The imports into the United States amount to a very large sum. They never will be less, but will continue to increase for centuries to come. As the population of our country increases, the imports will necessarily increase. They will increase, because our citizens will choose to be farmers, living independently on their freeholds, rather than to be manufacturers, and work for a groat a day. . . . It is a strong argument in favor of an impost, that the collectors of it will interfere less with the internal police of the States than any other species of taxation. It does not fill the country with revenue officers; but is confined to the sea-coast, and is chiefly a water operation. Another weighty reason in favor of this branch of the revenue is, if we do not give it to Congress, the individual States will have it. It will give some States an opportunity of oppressing others, and destroy all harmony between them. If we would have the States friendly to each other, let us take away this bone of contention, and place it, as it ought in justice to be placed, in the hands of the General Government.

'"But," says an honorable gentleman near me, "the impost will be a partial tax; the Southern States will pay but little, in comparison with the Northern." I ask, what is the reason for this assertion? Why, says he, we live in a cold climate, and want warming. Do not they live in a hot climate, and want quenching? Until you get as far south as the Carolinas, there is no material difference in the quantity of clothing which is worn. In Virginia, they have the same course of clothing that we have; in Carolina, they have a great deal of cold, raw, chilly weather; even in Georgia, the river Savannah has been crossed upon the ice. And if they do not wear quite so great a quantity of clothing in those States as with us, yet people of rank wear that which is of a much more expensive kind. In these States, we manufacture one-half of our clothing, and all our tools of husbandry; in those, they manufacture none, nor ever will. They will not manufacture, because they find it much more profitable to cultivate their lands, which are exceedingly fertile. Hence they import almost everything, not excepting the carriages in which they ride, the hoes with which they till the ground, and the boots which they wear. If we doubt of the extent of their importations, let us look at their exports. So exceedingly fertile and profitable are their lands, that a hundred large ships are every year loaded with rice and indigo from the single port of Charleston. The rich return of these cargoes of immense value will all be subject to the impost. Nothing is omitted; a duty is to be paid upon the blacks which they import. From Virginia, their exports are valued at a million sterling per annum. The single article of tobacco amounts to seven or eight hundred thousand. How does this come back? Not in money; for the Virginians are poor, to a proverb, in money. They anticipate their crops; they spend faster than they earn. They are ever in debt. Their rich exports return in eatables, in drinkables, and in wearables. All these are subject to the impost. In Maryland, their exports are as great in proportion as those in Virginia. The imports and exports of the Southern States are quite as great, in proportion, as those of the Northern. Where, then, exists this partiality which has been objected? It exists nowhere but in the uninformed mind.

'But there is one objection, Mr. President, which is broad enough to cover the whole subject. Says the objector, Congress ought not to have power to raise any money at all. Why? Because they have the power of the sword; and, if we give them the power of the purse, they are despotic. But, I ask, Sir, if ever there were a government without the power of the sword and the purse? This is not a new-coined phrase; but it is misapplied. It belongs to quite another subject. It was brought into use in Great Britain, where they have a King vested with hereditary power. Here, say they, it is dangerous to place the power of the sword and the purse in the hands of one man, who claims an authority independent of the people; therefore, we will have a Parliament. But, the King and Parliament together, the supreme power of the nation, they have the sword and the purse. And they must have both; else, how could the country be defended? For the sword without the purse is of no effect; it is a sword in the scabbard. But does it follow, because it is dangerous to give the power of the sword and purse to an hereditary Prince, who is independent of the people, that, therefore, it is dangerous to give it to the Parliament — to Congress, which is your Parliament — to men appointed by yourselves, and dependent upon yourselves? This argument amounts to this; you must cut a man in two in the middle, to prevent his hurting himself. . . . This

Constitution defines the extent of the powers of the General Government. If the General Legislature should, at any time, overleap their limits, the Judicial Department is a constitutional check. If the United States go beyond their powers, if they make a law which the Constitution does not authorize, it is void; the judicial power, the national judges, who, to secure their impartiality, are to be made independent, will declare it to be void. On the other hand, if the States go beyond their limits, if they make a law which is a usurpation upon the General Government, the law is void; and upright, independent judges will declare it to be so. Still, however, if the United States and the individual States will quarrel, if they want to fight, they may do it, and no frame of government can possibly prevent it. It is sufficient for this Constitution, that, so far from laying them under a necessity of contending, it provides every reasonable check against it. But, perhaps, at some time or other, there will be a contest; the States may rise against the General Government. If this do take place, if all the States combine, if all oppose, the whole will not eat up the members, but the measure which is opposed to the sense of the people will prove abortive. In republics, it is a fundamental principle that the majority govern, and that the minority comply with the general voice. How contrary, then, to republican principles, how humiliating, is our present position! A single State can rise up, and put a veto upon the most important public measures. We have seen this actually take place. A single State has controlled the general voice of the Union; a minority, a very small minority, has governed us. So far is this from being consistent with republican principles, that it is, in effect, the worst species of monarchy. Hence, we see how necessary for the Union is a coercive principle. No man pretends the contrary; we all see and feel this necessity. The only question is, shall it be a coercion of law, or a coercion of arms? There is no other possible alternative. Where will those who oppose a coercion of law come out? Where will they end? A necessary consequence of their principles is a war of the States one against the other. I am for coercion by law — that coercion which acts only upon delinquent individuals. This Constitution does not attempt to coerce sovereign States, in their political capacity. No coercion is applicable to such bodies, but that of an armed force. If we should attempt to execute the laws of the Union by sending an armed force against a delinquent State, it would involve the good and bad, the innocent and guilty, in the same calamity. But this legal coercion singles out the guilty individual, and punishes him for breaking the laws of the Union. All men will see the reasonableness of this; they will acquiesce, and say, Let the guilty suffer.' . . .

The reporter of the Debates in the Connecticut Convention says, 'that the Constitution was canvassed fully and critically. Every objection was raised against it, which the ingenuity and invention of its opposers could devise. The writer of this account could wish to exhibit to public view (though he is sensible he could do it but imperfectly) the whole debates upon this interesting subject; but is unable to do it. Suffice it to say, that all the objections to the Constitution vanished before the learning and eloquence of a Johnson, the genuine good sense and discernment of a Sherman, and the Demosthenian energy of an Ellsworth.'

The men who had risen to eminence in Connecticut since the beginning of the Revolutionary troubles, and who now exercised a controlling influence upon public opinion, were found, with scarcely an exception, the advocates of the proposed Constitution. With such support, it is not surprising that the Connecticut Convention should ratify it by an overwhelming majority. The vote stood, one hundred and twenty-eight in favor, and forty against ratification.

CHAPTER X.

1789 – 1796.

MEMBER OF THE UNITED STATES SENATE.

THE first Congress under the new Constitution met at New York, March 4th, 1789. Ellsworth and Johnson appeared and took their seats as Senators from Connecticut. A quorum of members, however, did not assemble until the 6th of April. The business of the Senate, with a single exception, both Legislative and Executive, was transacted with closed doors, until the second session of the third Congress. We have, therefore, but a meagre official report of the part Ellsworth enacted in that body. From collateral sources, however, we know that his services were very important, and elicited the highest encomiums of those who witnessed them. We have already observed that he had business talents of a very high order; and they found an appropriate field for their display, in organizing and putting in operation the new Government. Without precisely such talents, the affairs of mankind would sink into confusion and disorder. Without them the operations of government could not go on. Yet eloquence attracts more immediate attention, and wins more general applause. This could hardly be otherwise. The latter appeals directly to our senses and feelings, while the former affect us only in their noiseless results. Eloquence, as a means to raise the spirits and rally the energies of mankind, in some great crisis, cannot be too highly estimated. In some instances it has averted the downfall of States, and in others restored their liberties. The career of the renowned orators of the world shows how vast and abiding has been its influence. But, when the critical moment is overpast, when the resolutions which it has inspired are to be carried into effect, then another order of ability is required. Then, the actor assumes the superior place; then, a Patrick Henry yields to a Washington, and a Lee to a Jay. It is true, powers of eloquence and powers of action may be combined in the same person, as has been seen in very conspicuous instances; but, for the most part, they appear separately, or in very disproportionate union.

The day after the Senate was in a capacity to act, Ellsworth was appointed Chairman of a Committee to bring in a bill for organizing the Judiciary of the United States. This labor chiefly devolved on him, though, doubtless, he was materially assisted by the aid and suggestions of his colleague, Dr. Johnson, and Judge Patterson of New Jersey, who were members of the Committee. The original bill, in his handwriting, is still preserved in the archives of the Government. It passed with but little alteration from the original draft. It is unknown what arguments were employed against it in the Senate; but, in the House, it was decried as wholly unnecessary; as establishing a government within a government, which would jostle and finally destroy each other. A Supreme Court, with appellate jurisdiction, together with State Courts of Admiralty, was the only system, it was said, that the necessities or wishes of the people required. Livermore, of New Hampshire, declared that he could not conceive the occasion of the new system, 'unless it be to plague mankind.'

The reasons that determined Ellsworth in dividing the States into districts, and instituting inferior Federal Courts, are stated in a letter to his friend, Judge Law, of Connecticut: —

'To annex to State Courts jurisdiction, which they had not before, as of admiralty cases, and, perhaps, of offences against the United States, would be constituting the Judges of them, *pro tanto*, Federal Judges, and, of course, they would continue such during good behavior, and on fixed salaries, which, in many cases, would illy comport with their present tenures of office. Besides, if the State Courts, as such, could take cognizance of those offences, it might not be safe for the General Government to put the trial and punishment of them entirely out of its own hands. One Federal Judge, at least, resident in each State, appears unavoidable; and without creating any more, or much enhancing the expense, there may be Circuit Courts, which would give system to the Department, settle many cases in the States that would otherwise go to the Supreme Court, and provide for the higher grades of offences. . . . I consider a proper arrangement of the Judiciary, however difficult to establish, among the best securities the Government will have; and question much if any will be found at once more economical, systematic, and efficient, than the one under consideration.'[1]

---

[1] Oliver Ellsworth to Hon. Richard Law, New York, August 4th, 1789. The letter from which this extract was taken was courteously placed at my disposal by Mr. Edward Law, of the Philadelphia Bar, and a grandson of Judge Law. The letter itself, however, had previously been printed in 'Wharton's State Trials.'

The first session of Congress was chiefly occupied in creating the different Departments of the Government, and putting the new system into operation. The second session, which commenced at New York, on the 8th of January, 1790, found an ample field for discussion in Hamilton's report for the maintenance of the public credit. The plan recommended by the Secretary was admirably calculated to strengthen the Federal Government, and attach to it the most powerful classes in the community. By assuming the State debts, the whole body of creditors had a direct interest in giving the Government a cordial support. A project so extensive, in its consequences, as the American Funding System, very naturally provoked the warm opposition of the advocates of State sovereignty, as contra-distinguished from the advocates of Federal principles.

Ellsworth, known in the Federal Convention for his zealous advocacy of the independence and co-ordination of the several States, was wise enough to perceive that, after their acceptance of the proposed scheme of government, it was folly to cripple its power, and impede its benefits, by endeavoring to narrow and circumscribe the authority with which it was actually invested. The powers of the Constitution, he justly argued, were all vested, parted from the people, from the States, and vested in the Government which the Constitution contemplated;[1] that Government he would strengthen and confirm. He would give it all needed constitutional facilities to discharge its various functions, and perform its various obligations. Hence, to the general features of Hamilton's financial scheme,

[1] Argument on President's power of removal. Adams's Works, vol. iii., p. 409.

he gave his energetic support; but to several of the details he objected.

'Our friend, Mr. Ellsworth,' wrote Wolcott, at that time Auditor in the Treasury, . . . 'has been of opinion that it was not expedient to attempt to fund the public debt at a higher rate of interest than four per cent. That this sum, punctually paid, would answer the expectations of the creditors, the requirements of justice, and would better secure the public honor than a promise of a higher division, which would, under the circumstances of this country, be attended with greater risque of failure. He has also been dissatisfied with the Secretary's proposal of leaving one-third of the debt unfunded for ten years, as this measure would tend to encourage speculations, and would leave, after ten years, a great burden upon the the country, with little advantage to the creditors, who would alienate their demands to foreigners, who would purchase that part of the debt at a low rate. These opinions have been supported by him with all that boldness and reason which give him a predominant influence in the Senate.'[1]

Thus early had Ellsworth achieved that position in the Senate which he maintained, with increasing reputation, so long as he continued a member of that body. He was, says John Adams, the firmest pillar of Washington's whole Administration, in the Senate.[2]

Soon after the opening of the second session of Congress, the President communicated to them the interesting fact that North Carolina had ratified the Con-

---

[1] Gibbs's Federal Administrations, vol. i., p. 49, July 20th, 1790.

[2] Adams's Works, vol. x, pp. 108, 112. Vide post, p. 182.

stitution; and, on the 1st of June, that Rhode Island had done the same. This latter State had shown a very persistent determination to remain independent; but a bill which passed the Senate, and was pending in the House, to prevent 'goods, wares, and merchandizes' from being brought thence into the United States, doubtless convinced her that she could not profitably hold herself aloof from the Union. Besides, the same bill authorized the demand of a sum of money from her; being, probably, her proportion of the public debt. It was to this measure, doubtless, that Ellsworth refers in the following letter to a friend: —

'Rhode Island,' he says, 'is, at length, brought into the Union, and by a pretty bold measure in Congress, which would have exposed me to some censure had it not produced the effect which I expected it would, and which, in fact, it has done. But "all's well that ends well." The Constitution is now adopted by all the States, and I have much satisfaction, and perhaps some vanity, in seeing, at length, a great work finished, for which I have long labored incessantly.'[1]

In August, Congress adjourned to meet at Philadelphia, on the first Monday of December, that city having been fixed upon as the temporary, and the Potomac as the permanent seat of Government.[2] The seeds of a powerful opposition to the Administration had already begun to germinate. 'The Northern

---

[1] New York, June 7th, 1790.

[2] The Potomac, it is probable, would not have been fixed on as the seat of Government, had it not been conceded as a 'countervailing advantage' to the funding of the State debts — the Northern States desiring the latter, and the Southern the former. The two measures were passed as a compromise.

States,' thus wrote Wolcott, 'are somewhat unhappy with respect to high salaries and pensions, the Middle States are vexed at the assumption of the State debts, and the Southern planters are execrating the politics of the Quakers.'[1] Virginia voted that the assumption of the State debts was unconstitutional; the Legislature of North Carolina was not less hostile to the scheme; but the measure which more strongly tended than any other, at this particular time, to divide the community into distinct parties, was the charter of a National Bank.

When Congress assembled in December, the Secretary of the Treasury recommended the creation of a Bank as a necessary instrument for the custody and transmission of the public monies. He also recommended a duty on ardent spirits, whether imported or distilled in this country. Both these important measures received the support of Ellsworth. When the latter resulted in the outbreak known as the Whiskey Insurrection, he thus wrote his friend Wolcott:—

'The use of military force against the insurgents I

---

[1] Federal Administrations, by Gibbs, vol. i., p. 58; September 21st, 1790. The petition of the Quakers, signed on behalf of the Yearly Meeting, for Pennsylvania, New Jersey, Delaware, and the western parts of Maryland and Virginia, asking Congress whether 'it be not, in reality, within your power to exercise justice and mercy, which, if adhered to, we cannot doubt, must produce the abolition of the slave trade,' had occasioned much angry debate in Congress, and much feeling in the slaveholding States. The petition of the Quakers was followed by one from the Pennsylvania Abolition Society, of which Franklin was President, urging upon Congress 'to countenance the restoration of liberty to the unhappy men, who, alone, in this land of freedom, are degraded into perpetual bondage.' These petitions, and the subsequent debates, had excited a good deal of alarm.

believe to be indispensable, and a measure in which the Executive may rely on the approbation and steady support of Connecticut, and New England generally. . . . As to a call on the militia of this State, it certainly should not take place, unless it appears that a force deemed adequate cannot be obtained nearer home. . . . Should the Executive, however, who seldom mistakes, and, as we believe, never, judge it expedient to call for a detachment of the Connecticut militia, a call a few weeks hence would be less inconvenient for them than at present; but little time would be necessary to prepare. As to compensation — the soul of patriotism — they have been accustomed, as you know, to as much pay, or the assurance of it, as their time was supposed to be worth, the privates about forty dollars a month, which they would the more expect in a tour that they should conceive not to be properly their own, but to result from the delinquency of others.'[1]

The first Congress expired on the third of March, and with it terminated Ellsworth's term in the Senate, he having been drawn in the class whose seats were to be vacated at the end of the second year. He was re-elected, however, by the Connecticut Legislature, and took his seat at the opening of the second Congress in October. His labors henceforward were of the most interesting character. The domestic policy of the Government had, south of New England, stimulated into activity a powerful opposition. Its foreign policy, as the French revolution began to develop its tremendous energies, inflamed the elements of discontent into the highest exasperation. The Jay treaty, as we

[1] August 24th, 1794. Federal Administration, vol. i., p. 158.

shall presently see, furnished an object upon which the whole virulence of the opposition was concentrated.

The grave questions that constantly arose in the Senate — questions of constitutional law, questions of policy, requiring study and research — taxed a conscientious mind like Ellsworth's to its utmost capacity. The field of investigation was new and unexplored; but not until every part of it was carefully examined, did he form his conclusions. His career in the Senate 'contributed much to evolve the latent powers of his vigorous mind, which was roused and elevated by the collision of powerful talents, and the ardent investigation of great questions. Every important point which came under discussion in the Senate was examined by him with the most laborious application, and revolved again and again with the most unremitted and ardent meditation. During the course of such an investigation, his mind seemed to be tasked to its utmost strength; and he would pass whole days, and sometimes nights, in walking up and down his chamber, absorbed in mental labor. It was almost impossible to divert his attention towards any other object, before he had thoroughly formed his conclusions on the subject which engaged him. When, at last, the question which had thus excited him was finally determined, he appeared at once relieved from a weight of thought, and was left languid and exhausted, as if he had been wearied out by severe bodily labor. When he had once definitely made up his opinion, after this mature and impartial examination, he was immovably firm in his purpose, and was often thought somewhat too strenuous and uncompromising in the support of his own particular views.'[1]

[1] Analectic Magazine, vol. iii., p. 391.

The opening of the French Revolution was hailed, in the United States, by men of all parties, as an auspicious event. The Constitution of 1791 was very generally approved; but when the National Convention inaugurated another revolution, abolished the newly-established Constitution, and brought the King to the scaffold, a great change ensued in the sentiments of the Federalists. They perceived that all this violence, these torrents of blood, instead of promoting the cause of liberty and free government, must end in the iron rule of despotism. The Republicans, on the contrary, regarded the overthrow of monarchy, and the establishment of a Republic in France, as the precursor of the final triumph of free principles. When, therefore, the friendly aid of the United States was invoked by France, in the war then raging, a large portion of the people were cordially in favor of granting it. Beyond the sympathy which was really felt for the French, thousands believed that the treaty of alliance bound the United States to join in the war, and that gratitude and good faith required this sacrifice at their hands. Besides, the course of Great Britain towards the United States, since their independence had been achieved, in part the result of our own conduct in obstructing the payment of British debts, and in part the result of 'a national insolence against us'[1] — heightened and increased the resentment which a long and distressing war had engendered.

News of the war between France on one hand, and Great Britain and Holland on the other, arrived in this country in the spring of 1793. Genet, the new French Minister, came at the same time. Inspired

[1] John Adams.

with all the zeal and enthusiasm that inflamed the partisans of Robespierre and Danton, and endowed with a good share of the audacity which characterized the latter, he was determined to force the United States to take a part in the war. He proceeded in the most extraordinary manner, issued naval and military commissions, and gave orders for fitting out and arming privateers.

The Administration, after careful deliberation, determined to observe a strict neutrality, 'and pursue a conduct friendly and impartial towards the belligerent Powers.' Washington's proclamation to that effect was issued on the 22d of April, 1793, and occasioned the greatest dissatisfaction on the part of the Opposition. It increased the bitterness of party animosity, and brought upon the Administration the concentrated force of party virulence.

Ellsworth, believing that neutrality was important to the best interests of his country, zealously defended the measure, and gave to Washington his cordial and unwavering support. The hectoring and insolent conduct of Genet, supported and applauded as it was by the Jacobin societies, was too intolerable to be borne, and the Administration soon decided to put an end to his mission. A letter, requesting his recall, was despatched on the 16th of August, and with what effect the following extract of a letter from Ellsworth to Judge Law will show: — 'As to the war between this country and England,' thus he writes, 'so much dreaded by some and wished for by others, I think it will not take place. Complaint of M. Genet has been made to his Court, with a request of his recall. The answer is, that they disapprove of his conduct, and will immediately recall him. The fact, however, is, that he has not done but part of the mischief he was sent to do.'[1]

The course of the Administration in preserving the peace of the country, in maintaining the principles set forth in the President's proclamation of neutrality, had the effect, united with other causes of dissatisfaction, such as the assumption of the State debts, and the creation of a National Bank, to give the Opposition a majority in the House. To that majority, the conduct of Great Britain towards this country—a conduct chiefly owing, as we have had occasion to remark, to insolence, and a determination to make our neutrality inconvenient and unprofitable—was a subject of great indignation. As a means of retaliation, Mr. Madison introduced his commercial resolutions, based on a previous report of Jefferson's, proposing restrictions and additional duties on the manufactures and navigation of nations not having commercial treaties with the United States, and a reduction of duties on the tonnage of vessels belonging to nations having such treaties.

These resolutions of Madison were aimed at Great Britain, with whom we had no treaty of commerce, and designed to favor France, with whom we had. Among the Federalists, they were regarded with alarm and great disapprobation. Undoubtedly, they were calculated to complicate affairs with England, and, if adopted, might have resulted in war. Nevertheless, we cannot help thinking that they proposed a proper means of retaliation. The effect of their introduction

---

[1] Ellsworth to Law, January 20th, 1794. 'One more Genet in this country,' wrote Chauncey Goodrich to Oliver Wolcott, 'will make us sick of diplomatiques. If we want to do any business abroad, give some good fellow a letter of attorney, and let him do it.' Federal Administrations, vol. i., p. 130.

into the House was the conception of a special mission to England. While the Administration neglected no means to put the country in a state of defence, they would, nevertheless, preserve peace, if it could be done consistently with honor and safety. To Ellsworth, it is believed, belongs the credit of suggesting the means of attaining this object.

While the discussion on Madison's resolutions was proceeding, in the latter part of February, or the 1st of March, Ellsworth, Strong, Rufus King, and Cabot, held a consultation on the condition of affairs. The result of their deliberations was the proposition of an immediate special mission to England. This, it was thought, would have the effect to stay further proceedings in Congress, and avert an impending war. Ellsworth was deputed to confer with the President, and recommend to him the project of a mission, and Jay or Hamilton as the proper person to fill it. Accordingly, he had an interview with Washington, and a long and familiar conversation upon the threatening aspect of public affairs. The President evinced great concern, and said, 'Well, Mr. Ellsworth, what can be done?' The latter replied by stating that the result of the deliberations of himself and friends was, that an immediate special mission to England ought to be instituted. 'After a few further observations and inquiries, General Washington asked Mr. Ellsworth who, in case that course should be adopted, would, in his opinion, be a proper person for that appointment. Mr. Ellsworth replied, naming the persons they had agreed to recommend to the President. From the conversation with General Washington at this interview, as well as from the tenor of all his previous private correspondence and public communications to Congress, it was apparently to him a new project. At the close of the conversation, as

Mr. Ellsworth rose to depart, "Well, Sir," said the President, "I will take this subject into consideration."'[1]

On the 5th of April, 1794, Ellsworth thus wrote Oliver Wolcott, senior: — 'I thank you for your letter, received some time since, and for your opinion of Mr. Madison's propositions. Probably you do not mistake, in supposing them to be insidious, and incapable of producing any other effect than mischief. They have not, however, yet passed, and I trust will not. The debts of the South, which were, doubtless, among the causes of the late revolution, have ever since operated to obstruct its benefits, by opposing compulsive energy of government, generating mist and irritation between this country and Great Britain, and, of course, giving a baleful ascendency to French influence. Under these auspices, an extensive combination of the wicked and the weak has been arranged for some time past, and will probably continue its efforts to disturb the peace of this country, so long as the European contest continues in its present state of dubiety. Some precipitate measures are now contemplated in Congress; but I hope in a few days we shall see the business turned into a channel of negotiation, and a respectable special Envoy sent to London, on the subject of commercial spoliations. A negotiation of this kind, with proper interior arrangements to give it weight, would, I presume, save us from war.'[2]

It was believed by the Federalists, that the virulence manifested in Virginia and the South against

---

[1] MS. by Mr. Joseph Wood. Pitkin, in his History, says, that such a proposition was made to General Washington on the 10th of March, this probably being the date of Ellsworth's interview with him.

[2] Federal Administrations, vol. i., p. 134.

England, and the opposition to measures which gave additional strength and vigor to the General Government, was in consequence of the extensive debts owing in those States. The planters supposed that the Revolution had thrown them off: but the treaty revived them, and the Federal Courts furnished the means of prosecuting them. 'The prospect of poverty, and dependence on the Scotch merchants, is what they cannot view with patience.'[1] It was supposed that another war with England was desired by them as a means of finally extinguishing these perplexing claims, or that they wished so far to weaken the Federal authority as would render their recovery impossible. But motives of this character, while they might have had influence in individual cases, or in this or that locality, are inadequate to explain the general opposition to the Administration which now began to organize itself, and especially at the South. There were cogent causes of war against England; there was a natural and strong sympathy for France; and, on the part of those who had objected to the Constitution on the ground that, in its practical operation, it would be likely to overshadow and destroy the independence of the States, there was a lively apprehension that the domestic policy of the Government would lead directly to consolidation. Here, then, we have sufficient grounds, without imputing dishonorable motives, on which a party might desire war with England, and at the same time wish to circumscribe the Federal authority.

On the 16th of April, Jay was nominated as special Envoy to England, and after a discussion of three days, he was confirmed by a vote of eighteen against

[1] Wolcott to Wolcott, senior, February 8th, 1793. Ibid. vol. i., pp. 85, 86.

eight.[1] On the very day the nomination was made to the Senate, Ellsworth thus wrote Wolcott: — 'In a late letter,' he says, 'I suggested to you the idea of turning our grievances into a channel of negotiation. I now venture to assure you that Mr. Jay will be sent as special Envoy to the Court of London, with such powers and instructions as probably will produce the desired effect. His nomination will come forward this day or to-morrow. He is now here, and has this moment informed me of his determination to accept the appointment, if it shall be made. This, Sir, will be a mortifying movement to those who have endeavored, by every possible means, to prevent a reconciliation between this country and Great Britain. . . . The embargo, I trust, will not be continued beyond the thirty days for which it was laid. It ought not to have been laid at all.'[2]

The embargo referred to by Ellsworth, and which it seems he opposed, was among the number of defensive measures that Congress thought the situation of the country demanded; such as the fortification of the principal posts, the raising a corps of engineers, and obtaining a supply of arms. Madison's propositions were defeated,[3] and in June Congress adjourned.

The outbreak of the Western insurrection, to which we have already alluded, and the success of Jay's mission, were now objects of great solicitude. We have seen, in a previous volume, the progress and result of that mission.[4] On the 8th of June, 1795, the Jay

---

[1] Vol. i., p. 403.

[2] April 16th, 1794. Federal Administrations, vol. i., p. 135. The embargo was laid March 26th, and continued until May 25th.

[3] They were defeated in the Senate by the casting-vote of the Vice-President.

[4] Vol. i., pp. 401–414.

treaty was laid before the Senate, specially convened to consider it. Its provisions were discussed with much acrimony; but in the end it was finally ratified.

When the public were put in possession of the treaty, their indignation kept no bounds. Washington's hesitation, real or apparent, to give it his sanction, increased the noise and tumult of popular opposition. Ellsworth, who had taken a prominent part in the inception of the mission, and earnestly defended its results, was not a little restive under what seemed wavering or indecision on the part of the President. His solicitude as to the decision of the Executive was intense. He could not sleep, and 'continued day and night, for about a fortnight, walking his hall in the most intense anxiety as to the result, and scarcely closed his eyes in sound sleep for several successive nights.'[1]

On the 15th of August, he wrote Wolcott as follows:—'If the President decides wrong, or does not decide soon, his good fortune will forsake him. N. E.[2] is tolerably quiet, and will be more so as the subject becomes more understood; but I am to be responsible only for Connecticut.'[3] Five days later, having, meanwhile, been informed that Washington had signed the treaty, he wrote Wolcott again. 'I am glad the President,' he says, 'has done, at last, what I am unwilling to believe he ever hesitated about, and the delay of which has not been without hazard and some mischief. The crisis admits not of the appearance of indecision, and, much less, of steering any course but one. There is less reason to be anxious for the Eastern

[1] MS. Memoir by Mr. J. Wood. [2] New England.
[3] Federal Administrations, vol. i., p. 225.

quarter than there was some weeks since. . . . Governor Huntington was here yesterday, on his way to Dartmouth, and loves peace so well, that, to make sure of it, he wishes we had taken the twelfth article too.'[1]

When Congress assembled in the following December, it soon became manifest that the House would not, without serious opposition, appropriate the money necessary to carry the treaty into effect. 'They are just now entering upon the anxious discussion,' wrote Ellsworth, 'and will, I trust, after spending a great deal of time in doubtful debate and menacing movements, finally conclude that there would be too much responsibility in deciding wrong.'[2] A call was made upon the President, to lay before the House the papers relating to the negotiation; but, after mature reflection, he decided that compliance with the call was improper. Ellsworth, who had, in the meanwhile, become Chief Justice, drew up an argument against the right of the House to demand the papers; and the grounds upon which the Executive proceeded, although severely criticised at the time, were obviously just and constitutional.

We have seen that Rutledge's opposition to the treaty was warmly resented by the leading Federalists, and, among others, by Ellsworth. When the Chief Justiceship was tendered Rutledge, his sentiments respecting the treaty were unknown; indeed, at that time, he was not aware of its contents, and, of course, had formed no opinion. Whether Washington shared in the general surprise, when it became known that Rutledge had ranked himself among the opponents of the treaty, does not appear; but whether he

---

[1] Federal Administrations, vol. i., p. 226.

[2] Ellsworth to Wolcott, senior, March 8th, 1796. Ibid., p. 306.

did or not, his obvious course was to submit the nomination to the Senate. 'With regard to Mr. Rutledge,' wrote Ellsworth, 'it certainly was difficult, after he had come, not to commission him. If the evil is without remedy, we must, as in other cases, make the best of it. Believe not, my dear Sir, that I have feelings on this occasion which are not common to all well-disposed friends of the Government.'[1] It was unknown to the Federalists that Rutledge had been actually commissioned since the 1st of July, and that the instrument itself remained in the State Department, as a mere matter of convenience, until he should arrive in Philadelphia to hold the August term of the Supreme Court.[2] But, however indignant and surprised they were at the announcement of his promotion to the highest post in the Judiciary, following close, as it did, upon the publication of his speech on the treaty, they did not, we are persuaded, finally reject his nomination on merely political grounds. The unhappy condition of his intellect had become known, and his rejection, as we have elsewhere observed, was doubtless the dictate of prudence.[3] We shall presently see that this rejection resulted in Ellsworth's promotion to the vacant post. Meanwhile, we may glance at the condition of parties in the country.

The opposition to the Administration was steadily increasing, and gaining consistency and confidence. They had already obtained a majority in the House of Representatives, and the Federalists looked forward to the election of Jefferson, as the successor of Washington, as by no means an improbable event. This prospect was a source of lively apprehension and

[1] Ellsworth to Wolcott, August 20th, 1795. Federal Administrations, vol. i., p. 226.

[2] See vol. i., p. 632, 638. [3] Ibid., p. 641.

alarm. Ellsworth was among those who believed that the highest and best interests of the country would be unsafe in Jefferson's hands; that his animosity towards England, and his partiality for France, would hurry him into a line of conduct injurious, if not destructive, to its peace, welfare, and harmony. His opinion of Jefferson is disclosed in the following extract of a letter written after his death: —

'The late Judge Ellsworth, of Connecticut,' says the writer, 'was universally considered one of the most profound men in our country. He was one of the real nobles of nature. When I was at Congress, in the winter of 1797, Mr. Ellsworth was a member of the Senate, and we boarded at the same house.[1] At the election the fall before, Mr. Jefferson was the competitor of Mr. Adams for the Presidency, and came near to gaining the office. The circumstance excited much anxiety and alarm amongst the Federal members in Congress. I was one evening sitting alone with Mr. Ellsworth, when I asked him the question, Why the apprehensions of Mr. Jefferson's being President should occasion so much alarm? at the same time observing that it could not be supposed he was an enemy to his country, or would designedly do anything to injure the Government as constitutionally established. Mr. Ellsworth, after a short pause, replied, "No," it is not apprehended that Jefferson is an enemy to his country, or that he would designedly do anything wrong. But it is known he is a visionary man, an enthusiastic disciple of the French Revolution, and an enemy to

---

[1] The writer has mistaken the year: in 1797, Ellsworth was Chief Justice, and not a Senator.

whatever would encourage commercial enterprise, or give energy to the Government. It is apprehended that, if he were President, he would take little or no responsibility on himself. The nation would be, as it were, without a head. Everything would be referred to Congress. A lax, intriguing kind of policy, would be adopted; and while arts were practised to give direction to popular sentiment, Mr. Jefferson would affect to be directed by the will of the nation. There would be no national energy. Our character would sink, and our weakness invite contempt and insult. Though Mr. Jefferson would have no thoughts of war, his zeal in the French cause, and enmity to Great Britain, would render him liable to secret influence, that would tend to the adoption of measures calculated to produce war with England, though it was not intended, and the nation might be plunged into a war wholly unprepared."'

We shall see, hereafter, that, when Jefferson was actually elected President, Ellsworth was disposed to yield to the unwelcome choice, without murmur or complaint.[1]

Ellsworth's service in the Senate was very laborious. The subjects that engaged his attention were of great magnitude and variety. Questions of constitutional law, finance, commerce, and political economy, were to be investigated and opinions formed. The faithful manner with which he performed his duties did much to open and expand his mind. 'A distinguished gentleman, whose early and constant habits of intimacy with Mr. Ellsworth afforded him the most ample opportunities of observing the progress and character of

---

[1] See post p. 259.

his mind, has expressed his opinion, that in no part of his life did he display a more evident and remarkable development and progressive improvement of talent than during the term of his service in the Senate of the United States. This period extended nearly to the fifty-second year of his age, long before which time of life the intellectual powers of most men have arrived at their full maturity, and, if not perfectly stationary, are at least become awkward and unpliable to any new trains of thought, or unaccustomed mode of mental exertion.'[1]

The measures of Washington's administration he supported with a zeal and ability surpassed by no member of the Senate. Though ardent and energetic in advocating his line of policy, he was too earnest, sincere, and true, to employ any other weapons than those drawn from reason and legitimate argument. As a 'parliamentary orator, his characteristic features were strength and originality of thought. In argument and debate he was always powerful and impressive, frequently ardent and animated; yet this ardor was rather the earnest vehemence of strong reason, than the glow of imagination, or the warm burst of feeling. With few of the external graces of the orator; with little ornament or polish of language; not very copious; not very flowing; he had, in an uncommon degree, the power of commanding attention and enforcing conviction. He satisfied or subdued the reason, with little endeavor either to excite the feelings, or to gratify the fancy.'[2] Without indulging in personalities, there was yet a severity in his argumentation, a vigor and vehemence of manner, that was sometimes as annoying to the discomfited advocate of opposing

[1] Analectic Magazine, vol. iii., p. 392.

[2] Ibid., p. 402.

views as sarcasm and invective. On one occasion, Gunn, of Georgia, smarting under a speech of Ellsworth's, expressed a determination to send him a challenge. This would have been a very safe proceeding, as it was well known that Ellsworth was a member of the church, and would not fight. However, several Georgia gentlemen, who concurred in the propriety of his remarks, called upon him, and urged him to accept the challenge, if sent, and permit one of them to act as his proxy in the business. But Ellsworth, doubtless, was too good a Christian to assent to such an arrangement. However, the fact that it had been proposed came to the knowledge of Gunn, and from that or some other cause he forbore to send the challenge.[1]

Ellsworth's colloquial talents were of a distinguished order, and the delight of every social circle in which he appeared. During the greater part of his service in the Senate, society in Philadelphia was very much divided, according to the party and political affinities of its members. Hence, his associations were very much, if not exclusively, confined to families whose politics were the same as his own. The house of his friend Wolcott was a pleasant resort to him. 'In his parlor, of an evening,' says the late Hon. Joseph Hopkinson, referring to Wolcott and the Federal society of Philadelphia, 'you would meet more or less company of that description. Leading members of the Senate and House of Representatives, especially from New England, were habitually there, and sometimes at my house. When I mention such names as Ellsworth, Ames, Griswold, Goodrich, Tracy, &c., you may imagine what a rich and intellectual society it

[1] On the authority of Mr. Jos. Wood's MS. Memoir.

was. I will not say that we have no such men now, but I don't know where they are.'[1]

Ellsworth, when voting for the rejection of Rutledge, as he, doubtless, did, little anticipated that the ermine would finally fall upon him. But, when Cushing, to whom the vacant post was assigned, declined the too arduous honor, as he conceived it to be, it was conferred upon Ellsworth. After much deliberation and doubt he accepted the appointment, and resigned his seat in the Senate. 'It is, Sir, my duty to acquaint you,' thus he wrote the Governor of Connecticut, 'that I have, with some hesitation, accepted an appointment in the Judiciary of the United States, which of course vacates my seat in the Senate. This step, I hope, will not be regarded as disrespectful to a State which I have so long had the honor to serve, and whose interests must forever remain precious to my heart.'[2]

The Governor, in his reply, as well as in letters to other friends, doubtless spoke the gratification and approval of Connecticut at the promotion of her distinguished son. 'Mr. Ellsworth's appointment,' he says, in a letter to Jonathan Trumbull, 'will be very satisfactory to all who are willing to be pleased. If our country shall be preserved from anarchy and confusion, it must be from men of his character.'[3] 'The established principles and abilities of Mr. Ellsworth,' he writes his son, 'render his appointment proper.'[4] 'I doubt not but that the State,' thus he writes Ells-

---

[1] Federal Administrations, vol. i., pp. 162, 163.

[2] Ellsworth to Oliver Wolcott, senior, March 8th, 1796. Federal Administrations, vol. i., p. 306.

[3] March 14th, 1796. Ibid., p. 322.

[4] Oliver Wolcott, senior, to Oliver Wolcott, junior, March 21st, 1796. Ibid.

worth himself, 'would very reluctantly part with your services under their immediate appointment, but upon the conviction that they will be rendered more extensively useful by your discharging the duties of the very important office to which you are appointed. . . . Accept, Sir, my sincere wishes that your present appointment may be as agreeable to yourself as, I doubt not, it will be useful to your country.'[1]

However valuable an acquisition to the Judiciary were the abilities and character of Ellsworth, Adams seems to think that his services, in the actual state of parties, were more needed in the Senate than on the Bench. He says the Democratic societies had long been laying their trains, 'to explode Washington, to sacrifice Adams, and bring in Jefferson. . . . Washington was aware of this, and prudently retreated. But what had he done before he left the chair? Ellsworth, firmest pillar of his whole Administration in the Senate, he had promoted to the high office of Chief Justice of the United States; King he had sent Ambassador to London; Strong was pleased to resign, as well as Cabot; Hamilton had fled from his unpopularity to the Bar in New York; Ames to that in Boston; and Murray was ordered by Washington to Holland. The utmost efforts of Ellsworth, King, and Strong, in the Senate, had scarcely been sufficient to hold the head of Washington's administration above water during the whole of his eight years.' Adams adds, that if, during his own Administration, Ellsworth, King, and Strong had been in the Senate, 'the world would never have heard of the disgraceful cabals and unconstitutional proceedings of that body.'[2]

---

[1] March 29th, 1796. Federal Administrations, vol. i., p. 324.

[2] Letter to James Lloyd, January, 1815. Adams's Works, vol. x.,

Adams, as Vice-President, was a witness of Ellsworth's labors in the Senate during the whole period of his service in that body. That he occupied the high position he assigns him is confirmed by the testimony of a political opponent, whose active spirit and subtle intellect gave him, at one time, a commanding influence in the politics of the country. We refer to Aaron Burr, who was a member of the Senate during the latter part of Ellsworth's connection with that body. Mr. Goodrich, speaking of a private claim which was disallowed by the Senate says, 'Oliver Ellsworth, a man of great pertinacity of character, as well as wisdom in the conduct of affairs, had acquired immense influence in that body; it being said by Aaron Burr, that if he should chance to spell the name of the Deity with two *ds*, it would take the Senate three weeks to expunge the superfluous letter! He was generally opposed to money grants, from a just anxiety as to the means of the Government, and hence was called the "Cerberus of the treasury." This formidable Senator opposed the bill in Colonel Ely's favor, and it was, consequently, defeated.'[1]

---

pp. 108–112. By 'the disgraceful cabals and unconstitutional proceedings' of the Senate, Mr. Adams, doubtless, refers to the character of the opposition that manifested itself, on the part of leading Federal Senators, to some of his official acts, and especially to his re-election.

[1] Goodrich's Recollections, vol. i., p. 536.

CHAPTER XI.

1796 – 1800.

CHIEF JUSTICE OF THE UNITED STATES.

Ellsworth, on the 4th of March, 1796, received the appointment of Chief Justice of the United States. He hesitated to accept this honorable position. He doubted his fitness for the office. 'In the course of his practice and judicial duties in Connecticut, at that time wholly an agricultural State, he had little inducement or opportunity to make himself familiar with the principles of commercial law, and his acquaintance with foreign and national jurisprudence was almost wholly confined to those subjects which had fallen under his investigation in the discharge of his Senatorial and other public duties. Besides, he had now, for several years, been drawn aside, by political pursuits, from the practice of his profession; and no man who does not, in some degree, judge from his own experience, can completely realize how evanescent and fleeting are the impressions left upon the memory by all those branches of professional knowledge which do not depend upon general principles of reason, but, as must of necessity be the case with regard to a considerable part of every system of positive law, are either altogether arbitrary, or founded upon technical reasoning, and analogy to a series of precedents.

'Immediately upon his appointment, he commenced a very extensive course of legal studies upon those points in which he felt himself especially deficient, and pursued it with unremitted application in every interval of public employment. It is probable, too, that he had underrated his previous acquirements, for neither the public, nor the Bar in any part of the Union, remarked any deficiency in legal learning; nor did he ever display, in any of his judicial opinions, that unwieldly show of citations and crude mass of reading in which those to whom learning is not yet familiar are so fond of indulging. Independently of that general ability and business cast of character which fitted him for almost every situation in which he might be placed, he was remarkably well adapted for this office. If there was any station for which he was peculiarly formed by nature, it was that of a Judge. His habits of patient and impartial investigation, his sound and accurate judgment, and his quick perception, all conspired to render him every way worthy of the station which he filled; and had his appointment been made somewhat earlier in life, his mind more liberalized and adorned in youth by general learning and elegant literature, and in mature age more concentrated towards the single object of legal science, he would, doubtless, have ranked among the most accomplished and able magistrates of any age or nation. Amid all the comparative disadvantages under which he labored, although a less splendid, he was probably not a less useful officer; and if he threw little new light upon the great principles of natural justice or commercial law, he most certainly performed all the ordinary duties of his important and laborious office, not merely with ability, but with patience, diligence, and strict integrity. He rose rapidly in public opinion, and the estimation of the Bar; and in a period of violent party rancor, the purity and impartiality of his judicial character was untarnished even by suspicion.'[1]

When Ellsworth received his appointment as Chief Justice, the Supreme Court was sitting at Philadelphia, and he presided during the remainder of the term. There was much in his personal appearance and bearing to grace the distinguished position he occupied. He was tall, erect, and dignified; his large blue eyes, well set under heavy and highly intellectual brows, were firm and penetrating. His silk robe and powdered hair, it is said, heightened his natural advantages, and gave him, in the seat of justice, a dignity of demeanor which was felt by all who appeared before him. And yet, withal, there was a characteristic plainness about him, a homeliness, that was unmistakeable. His manners were simple and unaffected. He was patient, attentive, impartial, and laborious. In learning, he was not inferior to his successor, Chief Justice Marshall; in labor, he was, at least, his equal. 'His patience and diligent attention, united to his quickness of apprehension, and the clearness of his perceptions, contributed to great despatch of business and soundness of decisions. His opinions at bar, as they are preserved in the reports, are concise and perspicuous. Seizing the leading points in the case, and throwing aside all adventitious circumstances, he established the principle clearly and definitely, without any ostentatious parade of legal research, or far-sought ingenuity of argument.'[2]

The dignity, courtesy, and ability of Chief Justice Ellsworth secured to him, everywhere, the confidence and esteem of the Bar. His simplicity, purity, and

---

[1] Analectic Magazine, vol. iii., pp. 393, 394. [2] Ibid., p. 402.

modesty compelled affection and respect. Yet his nature was resolute, and he knew what was due to himself, as well as what belonged to others. No one felt inclined to brow-beat him, and if the attempt had been made, no man would have vindicated his personal dignity, and the dignity of the Bench, with more spirit and decision. The following anecdote may illustrate this feature of his character. While holding a Circuit Court at Philadelphia, with Judge Chase, who was somewhat disappointed, it is said, at not obtaining the place occupied by Judge Ellsworth,[1] a cause came on for trial, in which Mr. Ingersoll was of counsel. He began his argument, but had not proceeded far before Judge Chase exclaimed, 'There is no dispute about that, Mr. Ingersoll, the point is well settled, and there is no need of arguing it.' Mr. Ingersoll then stated his second point, but had scarcely begun to enforce it, before he was again interrupted by Judge Chase with, 'that is well settled, Mr. Ingersoll, you need not spend time to argue it.' Mr. Ingersoll, evidently vexed and disconcerted at these annoying interruptions, nevertheless, proceeded to lay down his third point, when he was, in like manner, again interrupted. Indignant at this treatment, he abandoned his argument and took his seat. 'The Chief Justice had now borne with his Associate as long as respect for himself and the Court would allow; and taking out his snuff-box, and as his custom was, tapping it on the side preparatory to abstracting a pinch, said to Mr. Ingersoll, with an emphatic manner and meaning not misunderstood by his Associate, 'The Court has ex-

---

[1] Judge Chase had been appointed an Associate Judge of the Supreme Court on the 27th of January, 1796, a few weeks previous to Ellsworth's appointment.

pressed no opinion, Sir, upon these points, and when it does, you will hear it from the proper organ of the Court. You will proceed, Sir, and I pledge you my word you shall not be interrupted again;' then turned his face towards Judge Chase with a withering look of rebuke, under which the judge, with all his nerve and daring, fairly quailed.'[1]

In March, the first term of the Supreme Court, at which Ellsworth presided, adjourned; and immediately after, he sailed for Savannah, to hold there a term of the Circuit Court. The Duke de Liancourt was a passenger on board the same ship. 'One of my fellow-passengers,' says the Duke, 'was Mr. Ellsworth, of Connecticut, recently appointed Chief Justice of the United States. All the Americans who were with us, and they were almost all young people, showed him no more regard than if he had been one of the negroes; though he be, next after the President, the first person in the United States, or perhaps, indeed, the very first. Disrespect to their seniors, and to persons in public office, seems to be strongly affected among the Americans; such, at least, is the humor of the rude and ill-bred among them.'[2]

Accustomed to the ceremonial of courts, and the supreme deference with which official persons were treated under the old regime in France, the Duke de Liancourt was, naturally enough, perhaps, shocked that the Chief Justice of the United States should meet with no more consideration than any private gentleman. But we may be sure that, to the Chief Justice himself, any other style of treatment would

---

[1] On the authority of Mr. Uriah Tracy, Senator, at that time, from Connecticut. MS. by Mr. Jos. Wood.

[2] The Duke de Liancourt's Travels, vol. i., p. 553.

have been as distasteful as it might have been agreeable and pleasing to the French Peer.

Ellsworth's charges to grand juries were, in many respects, admirable for matter and manner. They were brief, pointed, and perspicuous. The following is his address to the Grand Jury at Savannah, delivered on the 25th of April, 1796:—

'Gentlemen of the Grand Jury. This Court has cognizance of all offences against the United States committed within the District of Georgia, or elsewhere, without the jurisdiction of any particular State, by persons afterwards found within this District. After all such offences you will, therefore, enquire and due presentment make. Your duty may, perhaps, be unpleasant; but it is too important not to be faithfully performed. To provide in the organization that reason shall prescribe laws, is of little avail, if passions are left to control them. Institutions without respect, laws violated with impunity, are, to a Republic, the symptoms and seeds of death. No transgression is too small, nor any transgression too great, for animadversion. Happily for our laws, they are not written in blood, that we should blush to read them, or hesitate to execute them. They breathe the spirit of a parent, and expect the benefits of correction, not from severity, but from certainty. Reformation is never lost sight of, till depravity becomes, or is presumed to be, incorrigible. Imposed, as restraints here are, not by the jealousy of usurpation, nor the capriciousness of insensibility; but as aids to virtue, and guards to right, they have a high claim to be rendered efficient.

'Nor is this claim more heightened by the purity of their source, and the mildness of their genius, than by the magnitude of the interests they embrace. The national laws are the national ligatures and vehicles of life. Though they pervade a country as diversified in habits, as it is vast in extent, yet they give to the whole harmony of interest and unity of design. They are the means by which it pleases Heaven to make, of weak and discordant parts, one great people, and to bestow upon them unexampled prosperity. And, so long as America shall continue to have one will organically expressed and enforced, must she continue to rise in opulence and respect.

'Let the man, or combination of men, who, from whatever motive, oppose partial to general will, and would disjoint their country to the sport of fortune, feel their impotence and error. Admonished by the fate of Republics which have gone before us, we should profit by their mistakes. Impetuosity in legislation, and instability in execution, are the rocks on which they perished. Against the former, indeed, we hold a security which they were ignorant of, by a representation instead of the aggregate, and by a distribution of the legislative power to maturing and balancing bodies, instead of the subjection of it to momentary impulse, and the predominance of faction. Yet, from the danger of inexecution we are not exempt. Strength of virtue is not, alone, sufficient; there must be strength of arm, or the experiment is hopeless. Numerous are the vices, and as obstinate the prejudices, and as daring as restless is the ambition, which perpetually hazard the national peace. And they certainly require that, to the authority vested in the Executive Department, there be added liberal confidence, and the unceasing co-operation of all good citizens for its support. Let, then, there be vigilance — constant vigilance and fidelity for the execution of laws — of laws made by all, and having for their object the good of all. So let us rear an empire sacred to the rights of man; and commend a government of reason to the nations of the earth.'[1]

The alien and sedition acts, which caused such an outcry at the time, and still furnish the substratum or adornment of many an excited political harangue, were deemed by Ellsworth, in the actual circumstances of the country, apparently on the eve of a war with France, as eminently proper measures.[2] Besides, he was of opinion that the sedition act was an amelioration of the common law, and did not create a new offence. The following charge was delivered to a grand jury, at a time when the spirit of resentment and opposition to these two celebrated enactments was at its height:—

'Gentlemen of the Grand Jury. Placed as the guardians of the laws, you have in trust the Government itself—a government, let me remark, entitled to affection, as well as support—a government legitimate in its origin, free in its principles, and tested by effects, eminently beneficent. If we look upon it as it is, the palladium of American liberty, and ground of national hope, our solicitude for its preservation will increase with the dangers to which it is exposed. The fondness for novelty, and extravagant anticipation of good, which aided the Government at its outset, must, from an eight years' experiment of what any government on earth would realize, have given way to disgust, and the project of some new theory.

---

[1] MSS.

[2] There were, at the time of the passage of these acts, about 30,000 Frenchmen in the United States, as well as other foreigners, who ardently sympathized with them.

'Less to have been expected is the baneful influence of those elements of disorganization, and tenets of impiety, which have been propagated with a zeal that would have done honor to a better cause. . . . It is manifest that, unhinged and imperious, the mind revolts at every institution which can preserve order, or protect right, while the heart, demoralized, becomes insensible to social and civil obligations. So radically hostile to free government are the impassioned and impious. It is further observable that evils which annoy us, by a disingenuous ascription to causes that have no agency in producing them, are made extensively the means of seduction. With concern I add, that, whatever disaffection has sprung from these sources, or the common incidents of government, or from untowardness of temper, or spirit of party, has not failed to cherish, to ripen, and to marshal, a spirit, alas! which our circumspection has been incompetent to prevent, and which mischief seems incompetent to satisfy. While it estranges honest men, poisons the sources of public confidence, and palsies the hand of administration, it opens a door to foreign influence, that destroying angel of republics.

'If, from the indications within, we derive an argument for vigilance and firmness in the execution of laws, how much is it strengthened by the convulsive aspect of exterior affairs? Whether allured by caresses, or impelled by violence, the object is still to separate the people from the Government. Yes, the avowed object is to separate the people from the Government, and, of course, to prepare them, by sedition and rebellion, for a new order of things. We trust in God that foreign government is not to prevail here! but without prompt support and energy given to our own, our trust is mere presumption.'[1] . . .

In a letter to Timothy Pickering, then Secretary of State, the Chief Justice thus explains his opinions respecting the sedition act; the most unpopular act, perhaps, with which the history of the Federal party is associated: —

'I thank you,' he says, 'for sending me the charge of that pains-taking Judge Addison,[2] who seems to be a light shining in darkness, though the darkness comprehends him not. He is doubtless, correct in supposing that the sedition act does not create an offence, but rather, by permitting the truth of a libel to be given in justification, causes that, in some cases, not to be an offence which was one before. Nor does it devise a new mode of punishment, but restricts the power which previously existed to fine and imprison. But, as to the constitutional difficulty, who will say, negating the right to publish slander and sedition is "abridging the freedom of speech or of the press," of a right which ever belonged to it? or will show us how Congress, if prohibited to authorize punishment for speaking in any case, could authorize it for perjury? of which nobody has yet doubted. If a repeal of the act is to take place this season, I think the preamble, in order to prevent misapprehension, and withal to make a little saving for our friend Marshall's address, should read thus: — "Whereas, the increasing danger and depravity of the present time require that the law against seditous practices *should be restored to its former rigor*, therefore, &c." I congratulate you on

[1] MSS. [2] Of Pennsylvania.

the late success of the British; not that they had not power enough before, but because the French had too much; and, besides, if the latter had obtained the victory, they would not have thanked God for it.'[1]

We have given the reader an opportunity to judge of the style and character of Chief Justice Ellsworth's charges to grand juries. We may now add, that, as presiding judge on the Circuit, he gained great applause. He had a ready facility in the despatch of business, and in all parts of the country was respected for his able and impartial discharge of his duties. Williams's case is the only one where the judgment of the Chief Justice was subjected to the crucible of violent criticism, and angry denunciation. And, even in this instance, the purity and integrity of the judge escaped all imputation; it was only the political consequences of the doctrine that he enunciated which excited animadversion. But the doctrine itself, so far as judicial opinion and exposition are concerned, is today the law of the United States. Considered, however, on the broad ground of natural right, and political expediency, it may well be doubted whether, in its full extent, it can be sustained. Certainly, our Government, thus far, has shown no disposition to be governed by it. The doctrine laid down by Ellsworth in the Williams' case was, that there is no right of expatriation; and, consequently, that allegiance is not dissoluble by the act of the citizen alone.

Williams, an American by birth, was indicted for accepting a commission from France, and committing hostilities against the British, contrary to the treaty between Great Britain and the United States. He did

[1] MS. Letter, December 12th, 1798.

not deny the acts charged against him, but put his defence on the ground that he was no longer a citizen of the United States, that he was a naturalized citizen of France, where he had resided since 1792, with the exception of a five months' absence, and hence had a right to engage in the service of his adopted country. Evidence to this effect, Ellsworth regarded as wholly irrelevant and inoperative. He thus stated his opinion: —

'The common law of this country,' said he, 'remains the same as it was before the Revolution. The present question is to be decided by two great principles; one is, that all the members of a civil community are bound to each other by compact; the other is, that one of the parties to this compact cannot dissolve it by his own act. The compact between our community and its members is, that the community will protect its members; and on the part of the members, that they will at all times be obedient to the laws of the community, and faithful in its defence. This compact distinguishes our Government from those which are founded in violence or fraud. It necessarily results, that the members cannot dissolve this compact, without the consent or default of the community. There has been here no consent; no default. Default is not pretended. Express consent is not claimed; but it has been argued, that the consent of the community is implied by its policy, its condition, and its acts.

'In countries so crowded with inhabitants that the means of subsistence are difficult to be obtained, it is reason and policy to permit emigration. But our policy is different; for our country is but sparsely settled, and we have no inhabitants to spare. Consent has been argued from the condition of the country;

because we were in a state of peace. But, though we were in peace, the war had commenced in Europe. We wished to have nothing to do with the war; but the war would have something to do with us. It has been extremely difficult for us to keep out of this war; the progress of it has threatened to involve us. It has been necessary for our Government to be vigilant in restraining our own citizens from those acts which would involve us in hostilities. The most visionary writers on this subject do not contend for the principle in the unlimited extent, that a citizen may, at any and at all times, renounce his own, and join himself to a foreign country.

'Consent has been argued from the acts of our Government, permitting the naturalization of foreigners. When a foreigner presents himself here, and proves himself to be of a good moral character, well affected to the Constitution and Government of the United States, and a friend to the good order and happiness of civil society; if he has resided here the time prescribed by law, we grant him the privilege of a citizen. We do not inquire what his relation is to his own country; we have not the means of knowing, and the inquiry would be indelicate; we leave him to judge of that. If he embarrasses himself by contracting contradictory obligations, the fault and the folly are his own. But this implies no consent of the Government, that our own citizens should expatriate themselves. Therefore, it is my opinion that these facts, which the prisoner offers to prove in his defence, are totally irrelevant,' &c.

With this opinion of the Chief Justice to guide them, the jury found no difficulty in bringing in a verdict of guilty. Williams was then sentenced to four months' imprisonment, and to pay a fine of a thousand dollars. He was, however, subsequently pardoned, and his fine remitted.

The opinions of Chief Justice Ellsworth, while on the Bench of the Supreme Court, and reported by Dallas, are not of a character to interest the general reader; but, as showing his manner of discussing legal questions, we shall cite one or two of them at length. Meanwhile, we may observe that the following opinion, delivered at a Circuit Court in North Carolina, is, probably, the most elaborate decision of the Chief Justice that has been preserved. We are not aware that it has ever been printed. The question involved was of the same character as in the case of Ware *v.* Hylton,[1] which we have noticed in the lives of Cushing and Marshall; but with this difference, that in the former the debt was absolutely confiscated, while in the latter it was only sequestered, The whole subject, as will be seen, is discussed with great vigor and clearness: —

'It is admitted,' said the Chief Justice, 'that the bond on which this action is brought was executed by the defendant to the plaintiffs, and that the plaintiffs have not been paid. But the defendant pleads that, since the execution of the bond, a war has existed in which the plaintiffs were enemies; and that, during that war, this debt was confiscated, and the money paid into the Treasury of the State. And the plaintiffs reply that, by the treaty which terminated the war, it was stipulated "that creditors on either side should meet with no lawful impediments in the way

[1] Dallas' Reports, vol. iii., p. 199.

of the recovery of *bona fide* debts heretofore contracted."

'Debts contracted to an alien are not extinguished by the intervention of a war with his nation. His remedy is suspended while the war lasts; because it would be dangerous to admit him into the country, or to correspond with agents in it, and also because a transfer of treasure from the country to his nation would diminish the ability of the former, and increase that of the latter, to prosecute the war. But with the termination of hostilities, these reasons and the suspension of the remedy cease.

'As to the confiscation here alleged, it is, doubtless, [true] that enemy debts, so far as consists in barring the creditors, and compelling payment from the debtors for the use of the public, can be confiscated; and that, on principles of equity, though, perhaps, not of policy, they may be; for their confiscation, as well as that of property of any kind, may serve as an indemnity for the expenses of war, and as a security against future aggressions. That such confiscations have fallen into disuse, not from the duty which one nation, independent of treaties, owes to another, but from a commercial policy which European nations have found a common, and, indeed, strong interest in supporting. Civil war which terminates in a severance of empire does, perhaps less than any other, justify the confiscation of debts, because of the special relation and confidence subsisting at the time they were contracted. And it may have been owing to this consideration, as well as others, that the American States, in the late Revolution, so generally forbore to confiscate the debts of British subjects. In Virginia, they were only sequestered. In South Carolina, all debts, to whomsoever due, were excepted from confiscation; as well, in Georgia, of British merchants and others residing in Great Britain.[1] And in the other States, except this, I do not recollect that British debts were touched. Certain, it is, that the recommendation of Congress on the subject of confiscation did not extend to them. North Carolina, however, judging for herself in a moment of severe pressure, exercised the sovereign power of passing a confiscation act, which extends, among others, to the debts of the plaintiffs: providing, however, at the same time, as to all debts which should be paid into the treasury under that act, that the State would indemnify the debtors, should they be obliged to pay again.

'Allowing, then, that the debt in question was, in fact, and of right confiscated, can the plaintiffs recover by the treaty of 1783?

'The fourth article of that treaty is in the following words: — "It is agreed that creditors on either side shall meet with no lawful impediment to a recovery of the full value, in sterling money, of all *bona fide* debts heretofore contracted." There is no doubt but the debt in question was a *bona fide* debt, and, therefore, contracted; *i. e.*, prior to the treaty. To bring it within the article, it is also requisite that the debtor and creditor should have been on different *sides* with reference to the parties to the treaty. And as the defendant was confessedly a citizen of the United States, it must appear that the plaintiffs were subjects of the King of Great Britain. And it is pretty clear, from the pleadings and the laws of the State, that they were so. It is true that, on the 4th of July, 1776, when North Carolina became an independent

[1] Georgia suspended, but did not confiscate; and in the case of Georgia *v.* Brailsford, it was held that the creditors could recover. Vide vol. i., p. 392, *et seq.*

State, they were inhabitants thereof, though natives of Great Britain, and might have been claimed and holden as citizens, whatever were their sentiments or inclinations. But the State afterwards, in 1777, liberally gave to them, and others similarly circumstanced, the option of taking an oath of allegiance, or of departing the State under a prohibition ever to return; with the indulgence of a time to settle their estates, and remove their effects. They chose the latter, and ever after adhered to the King of Great Britain, and must, therefore, be regarded as on the British side.

'It is also pertinent to the inquiry, whether the debt in question be within the before recited article, to notice the objection stated by the defendant's counsel, viz., that, at the date of the treaty, what is now sued for as a debt was not a debt, but a nonentity; payment having been made, and a discharge effected, under the act of confiscation, and, therefore, that the stipulation concerning debts did not reach it.

'In the first place, it is not strictly true that in this case there was no debt at the date of the treaty. A debt is created by contract, and exists till the contract is performed. Legislative interference to exonerate a debtor from the performance of his contract, whether upon or without conditions, or to take from the creditor the protection of law, does not in strictness destroy the debt, thought it may the local remedy for it. The debt remains, and, in a foreign country, payment is frequently enforced.

'Secondly. It was manifestly the design of the stipulation that where debts had been, heretofore, contracted, there should be no bar to their recovery from the operation of laws passed subsequent to the contracts. To adopt a narrower construction of the article would be to leave creditors to a harder fate than they have been left to by any modern treaty.

'Upon a view, then, of all the circumstances of the case, it must be considered as one within the stipulation, that there should be "no legal impediment to a recovery;" and it is not to be doubted that impediments created by the act of confiscation are "legal" impediments. They must, therefore, be disregarded if the treaty is a rule of decision. Whether it is so, or not, remains to be considered.

'Here, it is contended by the counsel for the defendant, that the confiscation act has not been repealed by the State; that the treaty could not repeal or annul it; and, therefore, that it remains in force, and secures the defendant; and further, that a repeal of it could not take from him a right vested, to stand discharged.

'As to the opinion that a treaty does not annul a statute, so far as there is an interference, it is unsound. A statute is a declaration of the public will, and of high authority; but it is controllable by the public will subsequently declared; hence the maxim, that, when two statutes are opposed to each other, the latter abrogates the former. Nor is it material, as to the effect of the public will, what organ it is declared by, provided it be an organ constitutionally authorized to make the declaration. A treaty, when it is in fact made, is, with regard to each nation that is a party to it, a national act; an expression of the national will, as much so as a statute can be: and does, therefore, of necessity annul any prior statute, so far as there is an interference. The supposition that the public can have two wills, at the same time, repugnant to each other — one expressed by a statute and another by a treaty — is absurd.

'The treaty now under consideration was made, on the part of the United States, by a Congress composed of Deputies from each State, to whom was delegated, by the Articles of Confederation expressly, "the sole and exclusive right and power of entering into treaties and alliances;" and laws ratified or made by them became a complete national act, and the act and law of every State. If, however, a subsequent sanction of this State were necessary to make it a law here, it has been had and repeated.'

He refers to the act of 1787, declaring the treaty a law in the State, and to the adoption of the Constitution of the United States in 1789, which declares, that all treaties which had been or might be made under the authority of the United States, should be the supreme law of the land; and thus proceeds: 'Surely, then, the treaty is now law in this State; and the confiscation act, so far as the treaty interferes with it, is annulled.

'With regard to the remaining suggestion, that annulling the confiscation act will not annul the defendant's right of discharge acquired while the act was in force, it is true, the repeal of the law does not destroy what has been well done under it. But, admitting the right claimed by the defendant to be as substantial as a right of property can be, yet he may be deprived of it if the treaty so requires. It is justifiable, and frequent in the adjustment of national differences, to concede, for the safety of the State, rights of individuals; and they are afterwards indemnified, or not, according to circumstances. What is more material to be here noted is, that the right or obstacle in question, whatever it may amount to, has been created by law, and not by the creditor, and comes, therefore, within the description of legal impediments; all of which, in this case, the treaty, I apprehend, removes. Let judgment be for the plaintiffs.'[1]

In the case of Wiscart *v.* Dauchy,[2] the question arose, how the appellate jurisdiction of the Supreme Court was to be exercised, whether by appeal or writ of error. The Court held that the Constitution and act of Congress contemplated the latter mode alone.

Ellsworth, *Chief Justice.* . . . 'The Constitution, distributing the judicial power of the United States, vests in the Supreme Court an original, as well as an appellate jurisdiction. The original jurisdiction, however, is confined to cases affecting Ambassadors, other public Ministers, and Consuls, and those in which a State shall be a party. In all other cases, only an appellate jurisdiction is given to the Court; and even the appellate jurisdiction is likewise qualified, inasmuch as it is given, "with such exceptions, and under such regulations, as the Congress shall make." Here, then, is the ground, and the only ground, on which we can sustain an appeal. If Congress has provided no rule to regulate our proceedings, we cannot exercise an appellate jurisdiction; and if the rule is provided, we cannot depart from it. The question, therefore, on the constitutional point of an appellate jurisdiction is, simply, whether Congress has established any rule for regulating its exercise?

'It is to be considered, then, that the judicial statute of the United States speaks of an appeal and of a writ of error; but it does not confound the terms, nor use

[1] MSS. The names of the parties in this case are not known to me.

[2] Dallas' Reports, vol. iii., p. 321.

them promiscuously. They are to be understood, when used, according to their ordinary acceptation, unless something appears in the act itself to control, modify, or change the fixed and technical sense which they have previously borne. An appeal is a process of civil law origin, and removes a cause entirely, subjecting the fact, as well as the law, to a review and re-trial; but a writ of error is a process of common law origin, and it removes nothing for a re-examination but the law. Does the statute observe this obvious distinction? I think it does. In the twenty-first section there is a provision for allowing an appeal in Admiralty and maritime causes from the District to the Circuit Court; but it is declared that the matter in dispute must exceed the value of three hundred dollars, or no appeal can be sustained; and yet, in the preceding section, we find that decrees and judgments in civil actions may be removed, by writ of error, from the District to the Circuit Court, though the value of the matter in dispute barely exceeds fifty dollars. It is unnecessary, however, to make any remark on this apparent diversity. The only question is, whether the civil actions here spoken of include causes of Admiralty and maritime jurisdiction? Now, the term civil actions would, from its natural import, embrace every species of suit which is not of a *criminal* kind; and, when it is considered that the District Court has a a criminal as well as a civil jurisdiction, it is clear, that the term was used by the Legislature, not to distinguish between Admiralty causes, and other civil actions, but to exclude the idea of removing judgments in criminal prosecutions from an inferior to a superior tribunal. Besides, the language of the first member of the twenty-second section seems calculated to obviate every doubt. It is there said, that final decrees and judgments in civil actions in a District Court may be removed into the Circuit Court upon a writ of error; and since there cannot be a decree in the District Court in any case, except cases of Admiralty and maritime jurisdiction, it follows, of course, that such cases must be intended, and that, if they are removed at all, it can only be done by writ of error.

'In this way, therefore, the appellate jurisdiction of the Circuit Court is to be exercised; but it remains to inquire, whether any provision is made for the exercise of the appellate jurisdiction of the Supreme Court; and I think there is, by unequivocal words of reference. Thus, the twenty-second section of the act declares, that "*upon a like process*," that is, upon a writ of error, final judgments and decrees in *civil actions* (a description still employed in contradistinction to criminal prosecutions) and suits in equity in the Circuit Court, may here be re-examined, and reversed or affirmed. Among the causes liable to be thus brought hither upon a writ of error, are such as had been previously removed into the Circuit Court, "by appeal from a District Court," which can only be causes of Admiralty and maritime jurisdiction. . . .

'The law may, indeed, be improper and inconvenient; but it is of more importance, for a judicial determination, to ascertain what the law is, than to speculate upon what it ought to be. If, however, the construction, that a statement of facts by the Circuit Court is conclusive, would amount to a denial of justice, would be oppressively injurious to individuals, or would be productive of any general mischief, I should, then, be disposed to resort to any other rational exposition of the law which would not be attended with these deprecated consequences. But, surely, it cannot be deemed a denial of justice, that a man shall not be permitted to try his cause two or three times over. If he has one opportunity for the trial of all the parts of his case, justice is satisfied; and even if the decision of the Circuit Court had been made final, no denial of justice could be imputed to our Government; much less can the imputation be fairly made, because the law directs that, in cases of appeal, part shall be decided by one tribunal, and part by another; the facts by the Court below, and the law by this Court. Such distribution of jurisdiction has long been established in England.'[1]

In the case of Wilson *v.* Daniel,[2] which was error from the Circuit Court of Virginia, two questions were presented for the consideration of the Court. They are thus stated and answered: —

Ellsworth, *Chief Justice.* 'There have been two exceptions taken to the record in the present case. First. That the judgment of the inferior Court is so defective, that a writ of error will not lie upon it. It is evident, however, that the judgment is not merely interlocutory; but is in its nature final, and goes to the whole merits of the case. Though imperfect and informal, it is a judgment on which an execution could issue; and as the defendant below might be thus injured by it, we are unanimously of opinion, that he is entitled to a writ of error. The second exception is, that the judgment is not for a sum of sufficient magnitude to give jurisdiction to this Court. On this exception there exists a diversity of sentiment; but it is

[1] The act of Congress of March 3d, 1803, provided for an *appeal* instead of a *writ of error*.

[2] Dallas' Reports, vol. iii., p. 401.

the prevailing opinion, that we are not to regard the verdict, or judgment, as the rule for ascertaining the value of the matter in dispute between the parties. By the judicial statute, it is provided that certain decisions of the Circuit Court, in certain cases, may be reversed on a writ of error in the Supreme Court; but it is declared that the matter in dispute must exceed the sum or value of two thousand dollars. To ascertain, then, the matter in dispute, we must recur to the foundation of the original controversy — to the matter in dispute when the action was instituted. The descriptive words of the law point emphatically to this criterion; and in common understanding the thing demanded (as in the present instance the penalty of a bond), and not the thing found, constitutes the matter in dispute between the parties.

'The construction which is thus given not only comports with every word in the law, but enables us to avoid an inconvenience, which would otherwise affect the impartial administration of justice. For, if the sum or value, found by a verdict, was considered as the rule to ascertain the magnitude of the matter in dispute, then, whenever less than two thousand dollars was found, a defendant could have no relief against the most erroneous and injurious judgment, though the plaintiff would have a right to a removal and revision of the cause, his demand, which is alone to govern him, being more than two thousand dollars. It is not to be presumed that the Legislature intended to give any party such an advantage over his antagonist; and it ought to be avoided, as it may be avoided, by the fair and reasonable interpretation which has been pronounced.'

If the reader is anxious to trace the Chief Justice

through the reports, he can examine the case of La Vengeance; The ship Phœbe Ann; Brown *v.* Barry; Wilson *v.* Daniel; Clark *v.* Russell; Sims *v.* Irvine; and Turner *v.* The Bank of North America.[1] He will, however, find but little in the character of the questions discussed in these cases to interest him, and will be likely to carry away from the examination but a small addition to his stock of legal knowledge. We have, however, in the course of the present chapter, endeavored to give him an opportunity to form an opinion as to Ellsworth's judicial abilities. It only remains to add, that he continued on the Bench as Chief Justice until the latter part of the year 1800, when he resigned his commission. He had, however, as we shall see in the next chapter, been absent in Europe during the previous year, engaged in the negotiation of a treaty with France. Part of the occurrences that finally resulted in his appointment as Envoy to Paris, took place while he was Chief Justice, and excited in him, as in the friends of the Government and the Administration generally, both anxiety and indignation. We have thought, however, that it would be more convenient to the reader to relate, with all practicable brevity, the history of our troubles with France, and Ellsworth's connection with it, in a separate chapter.

Meanwhile, we may observe, that Ellsworth, active, ardent, and vehement as he had been in the politics of his time, was singularly exempted from that rancor, that bitterness of attack which pursued, with more or less persistency, all the leading public characters of that period, and especially the leading charac-

[1] Dallas' Reports, vol. iii., pp. 297, 319, 365, 401, 415, 425; Ibid., vol. iv., p. 8.

ters of his own party. The integrity of his motives, his candor and sincerity, seem never to have been questioned. If thus spared by political opponents, we may well suppose that to his friends he was an object of unqualified respect and affection. Thus was he regarded by Washington, of whose Administration he was such an efficient supporter. Whether they enjoyed the confidence and esteem of that distinguished person has become, in our day, a sort of test by which the public characters of the Revolution are more or less tried. This, we venture to say, is not altogether a just mode of decision. Washington was not infallible. His justice, his integrity, his calm, cautious judgment, his moderation in every variety of situation, and his undoubted patriotism, are qualities universally and justly accorded him. But he was not exempt from failings; in other words, he was human. He was liable to be deceived, and was deceived, by artful men whose professions of attachment were calculated to lull distrust, and open the way to his confidence. Hence, it has occurred, that men whose patriotism was questionable, whose services were of no very great importance, and whose talents — talents chiefly for dexterity and intrigue, were employed for their own personal aggrandizement, have, by the parade of their intercourse with Washington, been held up to the view of posterity as patriots, and heroes of unimpeachable worth.

That Ellsworth was one of the men upon whom Washington relied; that he was among the most vigorous and influential supporters of his Administration; that he could not fail to be respected for the tone and firmness of his principles, is all very true. But Ellsworth was a man whose virtue carried with it its own attestation, and required no endorsement, no letter of commendation, to insure its acknowledgment. It is not, therefore, as a sort of witness to character that we lay before the reader the following letter; but as showing the intimate friendship that existed between these distinguished persons: —

'Dear Sir: — Before I leave this city, which will be within less than twenty-four hours,' thus did Washington write Ellsworth when he had ceased to be President, 'permit me, in acknowledging the receipt of your kind and affectionate note of the 6th, to offer you the thanks of a grateful heart for the sentiments you have expressed in my favor, and for those attentions with which you have always honored me. In return, I pray you to accept all my good wishes for the perfect restoration of your health, and for all the happiness this life can afford. As your official duty will necessarily call you to the southward, I will take the liberty of adding, that it will always give me pleasure to see you at Mount Vernon as you pass and repass.

'With unfeigned esteem and regard, in which Mrs. Washington joins me, I am always and affectionately yours,

'GEORGE WASHINGTON.'[1]

---

[1] MS. Letter, dated March 8th, 1797, four days after the expiration of his term of office.

CHAPTER XII.

1799–1800.

ENVOY EXTRAORDINARY TO FRANCE.

THE outbreak of the French Revolution, as we have before remarked, was hailed in this country with unaffected joy and enthusiasm. To this country the French patriots, as they were styled, naturally turned for sympathy and gratulation, and at a later moment for active assistance and material aid. But, when the Administration of Washington, on a comprehensive survey of the condition of the United States, and the complicated affairs of Europe, determined on neutrality, as the policy dictated by wisdom, by an enlightened view of our interests, it produced an exasperation of feeling at Paris, that might have resulted in an immediate declaration of war, had it not been known that the line of conduct adopted by the Administration was disapproved and denounced by the Opposition, which was numerous and increasing. Indeed, the opinion was firmly held that, on this question of neutrality, the Administration were unsupported by the American people. Genet's extraordinary conduct, in issuing commissions, and giving orders for fitting out and arming privateers, was owing, in great measure, to this undoubted persuasion.

But, if war was not actually declared, in every

respect, short of that, our country was treated with the greatest insolence by our former ally. Our commerce was harassed in every quarter, and in every article; our seamen often abused, generally imprisoned, and treated in other respects like enemies.[1] But these outrages affected very differently the supporters of the Administration and their opponents. The latter charged, that little else could be expected from the line of conduct pursued by the Administration; by its alleged sympathy with Great Britain, and disregard of the obligations this country owed to France. If war was to be declared at all, it was said, it should be against Great Britain, which had been the greatest offender.

When, therefore, peace, 'amity, commerce, and navigation,' were secured with that Government, in consequence of the Jay treaty, the utmost exasperation was manifested on the part of France, and found a ready sympathy in this country. It was not so much that the treaty had objectionable features, as that any treaty should be made at all. In October, 1796, the French Government issued an *arrêt*, directing the seizure of British property on board of American vessels, and provisions bound for England. This was in violation of the treaty of 1778; but that they affected to regard as having ceased the moment the Jay treaty was ratified. By successive orders, the commerce of the United States was made the lawful prey of French cruisers; the necessities of the French treasury, and the unfriendly disposition of the American authorities, being the motives, and, indeed, the pretexts for this wholesale robbery and plunder.

---

[1] Mr. Monroe's description of the state of things, in July, 1794, at the time of his arrival in France, and just after the execution of Robespierre.

The recall of Monroe was construed as another evidence of the unfriendly sentiments of our Government, and another ground of justification of the robber policy of France. This gentleman was recalled upon what subsequently seemed, from his explanations, a misapprehension of his real conduct. It was thought, and for strong apparent reasons, that he had omitted to explain the views and course of the United States, although furnished with all requisite documents for that purpose; but, according to his statements, when specific objections to the conduct of his Government were urged, he did employ the arguments for its vindication with which he had been charged. These objections, however, it so happened, were not stated until a very late moment; thus giving the Administration at home ground of suspicion that neglect, or some more reprehensible cause, had kept their Ambassador in a state of passivity. But this exculpation of Mr. Monroe, in the light of more recent revelations, is hardly satisfactory. M. Thiers, in his history of the French Revolution, declares that Monroe urged the Directory to submit to the wrongs inflicted by President Washington, in order to leave him without excuse, to enlighten the Americans, and effect a different choice at the next election. If this be so, if the sources of M. Thiers' information are authentic, in what a melancholy light is the conduct of Monroe exhibited. Instead of being the independent representative of his country, he was merely the representative of party views, and partisan sentiments.

General Charles Cotesworth Pinckney, a gentleman of ability, frankness, candor, and integrity, was sent over as Monroe's successor. He was not received. 'Cards of hospitality were refused him, and he was threatened with being subjected to the jurisdiction of the Minister of Police; but, with becoming firmness, he insisted on the protection of the law of nations due to him as the known Minister of a foreign Power.'[1] Towards the latter end of January, 1797, he received written notice to quit the territories of France, and accordingly proceeded to Amsterdam, where he waited for instructions from home. The French Government protested that it would not receive another Minister Plenipotentiary from the United States until the grievances of France were redressed; the chief grievance being the Jay treaty. To its own list of outrages, it now added an act annulling the principle of *free ships, free goods,* incorporated into the treaty of 1778, and declaring all Americans serving in British vessels pirates, to be treated with the utmost rigor.

The news from France induced President Adams to convene Congress at an extra session, on the 15th day of May.[2] What measures should be adopted in the present conjuncture was a subject of general interest and inquiry. Hamilton was of opinion that a commission extraordinary, with Mr. Madison a member of it, should be sent to France *to explain, demand, negotiate,* &c.[3] Ellsworth's ideas may be gathered from the following letter, written at Springfield, Massachusetts, the day before Congress assembled:—

'Since leaving Philadelphia,' he says, 'I have attended courts in New York, Connecticut, and Vermont, and been in the western parts of Massachusetts and New Hampshire, and found everywhere an increased and increasing attachment to the Government;

---

[1] President's Message to Congress, of May 16th, 1797.

[2] 1797.

[3] Hamilton to Wolcott, March 30th, 1797. Federal Administrations, vol. i., p. 484.

and I have no doubt that any measure which, in the present crisis, it may judge expedient to adopt, will have general acquiescence and support from this quarter of the Union. All expect that Congress will do something, though there seems to be no settled opinion what that will or ought to be. Probably an embargo till the next meeting of Congress, removable by the President, and accompanied with the trial of a special Envoy, would be the most satisfactory. And it may be the best measure that will be found practicable; but of this, your information from the South, and from Europe, must better enable you to judge. Should the idea of an Envoy be admitted, may not some able character from the Eastward, and Mr. Pinckney, be joined in the commission, with plenary power, however, to either, in the absence of the other.'[1]

The President's speech at the opening of Congress, firm, patriotic, resolute, and dignified, was cordially received. He expressed, what was the general wish and opinion of the friends of his Administration, a desire for peace, and an intention to renew negotiations to secure it. At the same time, he recommended measures for defence, and preparation for resistance, if that should finally be rendered necessary. 'Since writing you from Springfield,' says Ellsworth, in a letter to Wolcott from Boston, 'I have attended court at Portsmouth, and have now been some days at this place. The President's speech is well received, and if well answered by both Houses, as we expect, will do much good at home and abroad. I repeat that neither Congress nor the Executive need hesitate about any proper measures, from an apprehension that public

[1] Ellsworth to Wolcott, May 14th, 1797. Federal Administrations, vol. i., p. 523.

opinion and spirit will not support them. There is still, however, such diversity of opinion among the best of men, as to the means expedient to be taken, that I can give no useful information on that point, and perhaps went too far in the conjecture I hazarded in my former letter.'[1]

The President, according to his intention to renew negotiations, as declared to Congress, sent out an extraordinary commission to treat with the French Government, which was composed of General Pinckney, John Marshall, and Elbridge Gerry. The progress and result of their mission is stated in the subsequent life of Marshall. We shall not, therefore, dwell upon the details here. Generally, we may observe, that they were treated with the greatest rudeness and indignity, and could accomplish no good end without first assenting to terms that would have compromised the honor and essential interests of their country. When the treatment to which they had been subjected, and the terms of negotiation which had been proposed to them became known to their countrymen, on the publication of their despatches, a general outburst of patriotic feeling was everywhere witnessed. This confirmed and supported the just sentiments of Congress, and immediate measures were adopted to put the country in a state of preparation for war. Additions were made to the Navy, and the Navy Department created. The President was empowered to raise a Provisional Army, in case of war being declared against the United States, or actual invasion, or imminent danger of invasion before the next meeting of Congress. This army was to consist of ten thousand

[1] Ellsworth to Wolcott, May 29th, 1797. MS. See also Federal Administrations, vol. i., p. 540.

men, enlisted for a term not exceeding three years, together with such volunteers as the President might accept. Finally, the armed vessels of the United States were authorized to capture and bring into port any French armed vessel depredating on American commerce; all commercial intercourse between the two countries and their dependencies was suspended, and merchant vessels, in addition to resisting capture, were now authorized to make recaptures.

'I will never send another Minister to France,' said the President to Congress, after it appeared that the negotiation had ceased, 'without assurances that he will be received, respected, and honored as the representative of a great, free, powerful, and independent nation.'[1]

With an army[2] raised and to be raised, with Washington at its head as Lieutenant-General, with all our accumulated grievances unredressed, and no opening for the resumption of negotiation, the prospect certainly was, that war must ensue. Such was the expectation through the summer of 1798. No change visible to the public eye was discernible in the French counsels. Preparation for hostilities went on. Further retaliatory measures were adopted by Congress.[3] The public pulse beat high and strong. The position of

---

[1] President's Speech to Congress, June 21st, 1798.

[2] Twelve additional regiments were added to the regular army, together with some light dragoons, to continue during the pending difficulties with France.

[3] Such as the suspension of the treaties between the two countries, and instructions to our public ships to capture any French armed vessel whatever, with a view to condemnation, and permission to issue commissions to private armed vessels.

the Government, and the sentiments of the people, were in harmony. The cup of reconciliation, to use the language of Washington, in accepting the command of the army, had been exhausted to the last drop, and they could with pure hearts appeal to Heaven for the justice of their cause, and trust the result to Providence.[1] And yet, it has been absurdly pretended that the Federal leaders, especially Hamilton, had ulterior views, and while preparing for the conflict with France, were, by means of these very war measures, by aid of the military forces, either directly or indirectly, bent on effecting such changes in the Constitution as would perpetuate their power, or even substituting a monarchy in place of the Federal Republic. It is to be regretted, that this charge of a past age, made in a time of party animosity, the suggestion of excited fears, or disappointed hopes, should be reproduced in this, and arguments adduced to give it currency and support. Upon what insubstantial grounds all such suspicions or conjectures were built then, or are constructed now, any one may perceive who will take the trouble to read the tissue of evidence with which they are attempted to be supported.[2] Nothing, it seems to us, can be more destitute of any real foundation.

In the temper, and with the preparations we have described, Congress adjourned on the 19th of July. The President retired to his farm at Quincy. While there, he was called upon to determine the relative rank of the three Major-Generals whose offices had been created by the act of Congress augmenting the

---

[1] Washington to Adams. Writings of Washington, vol. ii., p. 261.

[2] See Writings of Jefferson, and Life and Works of John Adams, vol. i., chap. x., *passim*.

regular army. His own conduct in regard to this question of rank had not been altogether consistent; but, in the end, he was compelled, much to his disgust and annoyance, to appoint Hamilton as second in command. Washington's letter to him, respecting the appointment of officers — a letter whose blunt and imperative tone no man would have resented more highly than Washington himself, had it been addressed to him under similar circumstances — effected a compliance with his wishes.[1] No doubt the abilities of Hamilton, and perhaps the expectation of the public, made his appointment, in the rank second only to the Commander-in-chief, expedient and proper. But both Knox and Pinckney were superior to him in former rank, and the President assumed the ground that the rules of military service, as well as delicacy and propriety, required that, in the present arrangement, their precedence should be preserved. There certainly was great force in this view of the subject, although, as the organization was a new one, appointments might be made, according to strict military ideas, without reference to antecedent rank; yet, considering Knox's services in the Revolution, and his service in the War Department, the President might well feel great reluctance, even if that reluctance had not been stimulated by hatred to Hamilton, to put him last on the list. But his wishes were disregarded, and he was compelled, under circumstances really amounting to *duresse*, to give Hamilton the superior place. In consequence, Knox, who really had much ground for chagrin, declined his appointment; but Pinckney, waiving all considerations of rank, accepted his.

We have no doubt that Adams, seeing how powerful

---

[1] September 25, 1798. Writings of Washington, vol. xi.

was the weight of General Hamilton, the hold he had on the mind of Washington, on the Federal party, on the wealthiest and most powerful classes of his countrymen, felt, and naturally enough too, that with his position in the army, in case of war, he could bring a combination of influence to bear on the Executive, in any contested point, to which he must yield, or be crushed. In a word, that General Hamilton would virtually dictate his line of conduct, and probably, at the next election, obtain his place.[1] This situation, and this prospect, would have aroused a spirit less proud, less resolute, than the spirit of John Adams; but when viewed through the medium of his impatient and jealous temper, it became intolerable. Here, then, we venture to think, is to be found the impelling bias that determined his opinion in favor of another mission to France, on receiving certain assurances that a Minister would be received.

Whether the measure itself was, under the circumstances, a wise one, whether consistent with the position our Government had assumed, must be determined, not altogether, nor chiefly by the result, for subsequent and accidental causes may give a prosperous issue to the most ill-judged scheme, but on a view of the situation of affairs as they existed at the time it was conceived.

In considering this question, every dispassionate mind, we think, will agree, that the wrongs and insults of France to this country justified war; that war being waived, it was not demanding too much, considering that two of our attempts at reconciliation had

[1] In one of his letters to Cunningham, Adams says:—'The British faction was determined to have a war with France, and Alexander Hamilton at the head of the army, and then President of the United States.'

been rejected with indignity and outrage, to require of France, if she desired peace, to take the initiative, and send hither a Minister to negotiate. This step would evince her sincerity, and give unmistakeable evidence of pacific sentiments. Either a declaration of war, or leaving France to take the requisite steps to insure peace by sending a Minister to this Government, was obviously the course prescribed to the Administration by considerations of dignity, by the regard due to the national honor, and a just sense of the national character. The latter alternative was what the friends of the Administration required. But, suddenly, without consultation with them, without even intimating his purpose to his Cabinet, the President, on the 18th of February, 1799, nominated a Minister to France. It struck everybody with astonishment — friends and foes alike. Form whatever opinion we may as to the propriety of the measure itself, the mode adopted by the President in accomplishing it must be deemed erratic and unwise. It was very much like stealing a march upon his friends. Surely, this was not the course to inspire or retain confidence! In truth, highly as we must respect and applaud the abilities and revolutionary services of President Adams, much as we must venerate many points of his character, it is, nevertheless, obvious that he was not fitted for a leader, or to be at the head of the Government. He had not sufficient repose of character, steadiness, discretion, and temper for such a post.

But, on what grounds did he proceed in making the nomination? Had he received assurances that his Envoy would be 'received, respected, and honored as the Representative of a great, free, powerful, and independent nation.' Assurances, indeed, of this character, had been received from M. Talleyrand, and through as regular a channel, perhaps, as could be expected; but the previous conduct of M. Talleyrand had been marked by such circumstances of intrigue and indirection, as to afford no ground of reliance on his sincerity. Indeed, the leading supporters of the Administration believed his professions to be illusory; that they were intended to distract our counsels, impede our measures for defence, and foster internal divisions in the country.

Mr. Adams, however, proceeded on a different hypothesis, and we have mentioned the probable bias that led to his decision. At the same time, it is obvious, that he regarded the assurances of M. Talleyrand with misgiving. The very message nominating Murray as Minister, contained this language: —

'If the Senate shall advise and consent to his appointment, effectual care shall be taken that he shall not go to France without direct and unequivocal assurances from the French Government, signified by their Minister of Foreign Relations, that he shall be received in character; shall enjoy the privileges attached to his character by the law of nations; and that a Minister of equal rank, title, and powers, shall be appointed to treat with him — to discuss and conclude all controversies between the two Republics by a new treaty.'

If the assurances already received from Talleyrand were deemed reliable, and as made in good faith, why did not the President send his Minister to France, without waiting for other assurances? If they were not sufficiently reliable and satisfactory for that purpose, why did he nominate a Minister at all?

In truth, the President could not well help feeling, that risking another Minister at Paris, on the mere faith of M. Talleyrand's professions, would, presumptively, expose our Government to a repetition of previous insults and indignities, and consequent humiliation. But such was his restiveness, under the overshadowing influence of the military chiefs, that he could not forego the opportunity of an opening, however small; of a chance, however doubtful, to be relieved of it. No doubt he was attached to the good of his country; but, to say that personal considerations did not mingle with his patriotism in this important act of his life — that he did not dread Hamilton, and wish to conciliate the opposition — is what a careful study of the transaction will scarcely warrant.

When the message of the President, nominating Murray as Minister Plenipotentiary to the French Republic, was received in the Senate, it was referred to a committee for consideration. This committee had an interview with the President, the result of which was, that he consented to nominate a commission, in room of Murray as sole Minister. Accordingly, on the 25th of February, 1799, he nominated 'Oliver Ellsworth, Esq., Chief Justice of the United States, Patrick Henry, Esq., late Governor of Virginia, and William Vans Murray, Esq., our Minister resident at the Hague, to be Envoys Extraordinary and Ministers Plenipotentiary to the French Republic; with full powers to discuss and settle, by a treaty, all controversies between the United States and France. It is not intended that the former of these gentlemen shall embark for Europe, until they shall have received from the Executive Directory assurances, signified by their Secretary of Foreign Relations, that they shall be received in character; that they shall enjoy all the prerogatives attached to the character by the law of nations; and that a Minister, or Ministers, of equal powers, shall be appointed and commissioned to treat with them.'

Mr. Henry declined his appointment, on account of his age, and Governor William R. Davie, of North Carolina, was appointed in his place. Ellsworth, it is said, disapproved the mission, and accepted his commission with reluctance. This is doubtless true; but none of his correspondence bearing directly on either point has, to my knowledge, been preserved. There is evidence, however, that he did not view the mission with the same heightened sentiments that animated his friends; nor with such feelings as he discovered in the crisis of the Jay treaty. He occupied, in truth, a position of *quasi* neutrality between Adams, Hamilton, and their respective friends, although his sympathies leaned strongly to the side of the latter.

On the 30th of July, a letter was received from M. Talleyrand, containing the assurances required by the President as conditional to the embarkation of our Envoys.

'It was certainly unnecessary,' said he in the communication that contained these assurances, 'to suffer so many months to elapse for the mere confirmation of what I have already declared to Mr. Gerry, and which, after his departure, I caused to be declared to you [Mr. Murray] at the Hague.'

This quiet censure of the President for requiring a repetition of assurances which he had already made the ground of important public action was the natural result of the imputation cast on M. Talleyrand's sincerity by the mere fact of demanding it. The President, however, deemed it far below the dignity of his position, 'to take any notice of Talleyrand's impertinent regrets, and insinuations of superfluities.'[1]

He instructed the Secretary of State to request our Envoys, that, 'laying aside all other employments, they make immediate preparations for embarking. Whether together or asunder, from a northern, a southern, or a middle port, I leave to them. I am willing to send Truxton, or Barry, or Talbot, with them; consult the Secretary of the Navy and Heads of Department on this point. Although I have little confidence in the issue of this business, I wish to delay nothing, to omit nothing.'[2] Why, then, fly in the face of the best opinion of his day, and begin a business, in the issue of which he had so little confidence?

Instructions for our Envoys were prepared, and no obstacle seemed to interpose to their departure. But, about the 1st of September, news arrived of another revolution at Paris. The Directory, with the exception of Barras, was changed, the clubs were revived, and appearances were portentous of 'another reign of democratic fury, and sanguinary anarchy.' As the men who had given the assurances relative to the mission were no longer in power, and as their successors might possibly disavow them, it was thought by the Cabinet that a temporary suspension of the embassy was expedient. A letter to that effect was written to the President by the Secretary of State, which expressed the sentiments of all the members of the Cabinet, with the exception of the Attorney-General. Ellsworth concurred with them in opinion, and at the

[1] Adams' Works, vol. ix., p. 10. Letter to Pickering, August 6th, 1799.

[2] Ibid. 'Our operations and preparations,' said he in the same letter, 'by sea and land, are not to be relaxed in the smallest degree. On the contrary, I wish them to be animated with fresh energy.'

suggestion of Mr. Pickering, as it would seem, and perhaps of Wolcott also, he wrote a guarded letter to the President, from Hartford, as follows: —

'Sir: — If the present convulsion in France, and symptoms of a greater change at hand, should induce you, as many seem to expect, to postpone for a short time the mission to that country, I wish for the earliest notice of it. The Circuit Court in this State and Vermont fell through last spring from the indisposition of Judge Chase, and must now fall through again from the indisposition of Judge Cushing, unless I attend them. I am beginning the Court here, and should proceed on to Vermont, if I was sure of not being called on, in the meantime, to embark. It is, Sir, my duty to obey, not advise, and I have only to hope that you will not disapprove of the method I take to learn the speediest intimation of yours.

'I have the honor,' &c.[1]

On the same day, he thus wrote to Mr. Pickering:

'Dear Sir: — I have lately received your favors of the 11th, 13th, and 16th, containing a great deal of important matter, and shall have the honor to write you an answer the moment I can get free from the Circuit here, which I am obliged to attend, owing to the indisposition of Judge Cushing, and to the business, to which I am obliged to pay double attention to repair the loss of the last term through the indisposition of Judge Chase. I have this day wrote a letter to the President, from which he will easily collect my

[1] Adams' Works, vol. ix., p. 31. September 18th [19th; *query*], 1799.

opinion concerning a temporary suspension of the mission to France, though I have endeavored to write in a manner that could not give offence.

'I am, dear Sir,' &c.[1]

Ellsworth was not very sanguine as to the effect of his letter upon the President. 'Possibly,' thus he wrote Wolcott, 'my letter to him a few days since may have for answer that the Envoys are not to embark till it can be better seen to whom they should be addressed; but this is more indulgence than I anticipate.'[2] The reply he received, however, was more favorable to his views than he expected. 'The convulsions in France,' wrote the President, 'the change of the Directory, and the prognostics of greater change, will certainly induce me to postpone, for a longer or shorter time, the mission to Paris. I wish you to pursue your office of Chief Justice of the United States without interruption, till you are requested to embark. You will receive from the Secretary of State letters which will occupy your leisure hours. I should be happy to have your own opinion upon all points. We may have further information from Europe. If your departure for Europe should be postponed to the 20th of October, or even to the 1st of November, as safe and as short a passage may be expected as at any other season of the year. This is all I can say at present.'[3]

---

[1] MS. Letter. It is dated September 19th; but this may be an error of the transcriber; possibly it should be the 18th.

[2] Federal Administrations, vol. ii., p. 265. Sept. 20th, 1799.

[3] Adams' Works, vol. ix., p. 34. September 22d, 1799. On the 9th of September, the President had written a private letter to Stoddart, the Secretary of the Navy, in which he used this language: — 'I have no reason nor motive to precipitate the departure of the

The substantial part of the President's letter Ellsworth communicated to Pickering on the 26th of September, but unaccompanied by any remark.[1] On the 1st of October, however, he thus wrote Wolcott: —

'Judge Cushing has finally relieved me from Vermont, and the President, in his very great wisdom, has suspended my destiny to France, so that I have time to sit down to think; and I think that the prospects of that distracted country and of Europe, and of course our own, begin to brighten. Pray indulge the same thought, if you can, for you certainly stand in need of it.

'Very sincerely yours,' &c.[2]

The Cabinet thought if the President should meet them at Trenton, whither the public offices had been removed on account of the yellow fever at Philadelphia, before any final decision was made respecting the mission to France, it would be 'an eligible step.' They wrote him to that effect, through the Secretary of State, on the 24th of September. 'Governor Davie,' thus he wrote, in communicating the opinion of

---

Envoys. If any information of recent events in Europe should arrive, which, in the opinion of the Heads of Department, or of the Envoys themselves, would render any alteration in their instructions necessary or expedient, I am perfectly willing that their departure should be suspended until I can be informed of it, or until I can join you. I am well aware of the possibility of events which may render a suspension of the mission, for a time, very proper. France has always been a pendulum. The extremest vibration to the left has always been suddenly followed by the extremest vibration to the right. I fear, however, that the extremest vibration has not yet been swung.' Ibid., p. 19.

[1] MS. Letter, September 26th, 1799.

[2] Federal Administrations, vol. ii., p. 266.

himself and colleagues, 'will probably be here the first week in October, and Judge Ellsworth will doubtless be ready to meet him; or if you should conclude to come on, the Judge would certainly be gratified in waiting to accompany you.'[1] A letter from Stoddart, the Secretary of the Navy, written the 13th of September, and entering at large upon the reasons, public and personal, in favor of the President's going to Trenton at so important a moment, had already induced him to undertake the journey.[2]

On his way to Trenton, he called and saw Ellsworth at Windsor. 'I was, the evening before last,' thus wrote the latter to Pickering, on the 5th of October, 'honored with a call from the President of half an hour; but nothing passed respecting my going to Trenton. I have, notwithstanding, presumed to write him by this day's mail, as follows: — "Since you passed on, I have concluded to meet Governor Davie at Trenton, which he probably will expect, and which, besides putting it in our power to pay you our joint respects, and to receive as fully any communication of your views as you may wish to make, may enable me to accompany him eastward, *should you continue inclined* to such suspension of our mission as, under present aspect, universal opinion, I believe, and certainly my own, would justify. It is a matter of some regret, Sir, that I did not consult you on the proposition of this visit; but if I err, experience has taught me that you can excuse."[3] Governor Davie will doubtless arrive before me, and I hope will be made comfortable

---

[1] Adams' Works, vol. ix., p. 36. Pickering to Adams, September 24th.

[2] See Stoddart's Letter, and Adams' Reply of September 21st, in Adams' Works, vol. ix., pp. 25, 33.

[3] This letter is printed in Adams' Works, vol. ix., p. 37.

and easy. It will be Thursday evening or Friday morning next before I shall have the pleasure of seeing you and him.

'In the meantime, I am,' &c.[1]

As the President had an intimation that Ellsworth might go to Trenton, in Pickering's letter of the 24th of September, it is a little singular that, while at Windsor, he should make no allusion to it. Ellsworth himself had not yet, it would appear, determined to go. Doubtless, Pickering had suggested the propriety of his presence at Trenton; but, apparently, not until after the President's departure did he conclude to make the journey. As it was a subject of deliberation, however, a question yet to be decided, he afterwards regrets that he did not consult with the President respecting it. Was there any indirection in this, as has been insinuated?[2]

Mr. Adams, in his labored defence of his conduct respecting the French mission, published originally in the columns of the Boston Patriot,[3] thus describes his visit to Ellsworth: — 'On my way,' he says, 'I called upon Chief Justice Ellsworth, at his seat in Windsor, and had a conversation of perhaps two hours[4] with him. He was perfectly candid. Whatever should be the determination, he was ready at an hour's warning to comply. If it was thought best to embark immediately, he was ready. If it was judged more expedient to postpone it for a little time, though that might subject him to a winter voyage, that danger had no weight with him. If it was concluded to defer it till the spring, he was willing to wait. In this dis-

[1] MS. Letter.

[2] Adams' Works, vol. ix., p. 38, note.

[3] In the year 1809.

[4] Ellsworth says *half an hour*.

position I took leave of him. He gave me no intimation that he had any thought of a journey to Trenton.'[1]

Although Adams had received intimation, as we have already seen, that Ellsworth might go to Trenton, he was very mistrustful as to the object of the journey. 'I transiently asked one of the Heads of Departments,' he says, 'whether Ellsworth and Hamilton had come all the way from Windsor and New York to persuade me to countermand the mission. . . .. I know of no motive of Mr. Ellsworth's journey. However, I have already acknowledged that Mr. Ellsworth's conduct was perfectly proper. He urged no influence or argument for counteracting or postponing the mission.'[2]

Ellsworth's opinion, however, in favor of suspending the mission was well understood by the President. It was so declared in the letter announcing his intention to go to Trenton. And, evidently, from the language of that letter, Mr. Adams, while at Windsor, had concurred in its propriety. At any rate, he had indicated that he was not committed to an adverse opinion.

Adams arrived at Trenton on the 10th of October. The convulsion in France, the revolution in the Directory which had resulted in the retirement of all the members but Barras, including Talleyrand himself, and which had induced the President to write Ellsworth that he should postpone, for a longer or shorter time, the mission to Paris, still presented the same pressing arguments for delay. But they were reinforced, and rendered more impressive by news from Europe which arrived at Trenton on the 13th of Octo-

---

[1] Adams' Works, vol. ix., p. 252. [2] Ibid., p. 299.

ber. The British, under the Duke of York, had landed in Holland, the Dutch fleet had been captured, and Suwarrow was victorious in Switzerland. It might be premature to argue, from these successes, that the Bourbons were likely to be presently restored; but in the unsettled state of the French Government, united with the gloomy state of their military affairs, there was every inducement for a *masterly inactivity* on our part; a wise observation of the progress of events before committing the Government by positive acts. At all events, delay could work no possible harm. In the meantime, the new Government would have an opportunity to renew the assurances insisted upon from the discarded Directors. But the President, stimulated, no doubt, in part, by the suspicion that there was a combination, with Hamilton at its head, to defeat the mission altogether, determined that the Envoys should immediately proceed, although, as we shall presently see, without any confidence in the success of their mission.

In two or three days after Adams arrived at Trenton, Ellsworth came. Governor Davie had already been there several days. They were invited to dine with the President alone, in order that they might converse with entire freedom. 'At table,' says the host, 'Mr. Ellsworth expressed an opinion somewhat similar to that of the Heads of Departments, and the public opinion at Trenton. "Is it possible, Chief Justice," said I, "that you can seriously believe that the Bourbons are, or will be soon, restored to the throne of France?" "Why," said Mr. Ellsworth, smiling, "*it looks a good deal so.*" "I should not be afraid to stake my life upon it, that they will not be restored in seven years, if they ever are," was my reply. And then I entered into a long detail of my reasons for this opinion. They would be too tedious to enumerate here, and time has superseded the necessity of them. The result of the conversation was, that Mr. Davie was decidedly for embarking immediately, as he always had been from his first arrival, and Mr. Ellsworth declared himself satisfied, and willing to embark as soon as I pleased.'[1]

The inference from the foregoing language clearly is, that the conversation thus described took place before the order to embark was given; and that Ellsworth was convinced of the propriety of the Envoys proceeding on the mission. But it is stated, on the contrary, that it occurred after the order to embark had been given,[2] when, of course, any refutation or contestation of the President's reasoning would be useless and uncalled for. It is also stated, that Ellsworth, instead of being 'satisfied and willing to embark,' disapproved of the mission to the last; that, on personal grounds, he was anxious to remain, and would have refused to go at all, but for the apprehension that Burr or Madison would be sent in his place.[3]

The President's reasoning on the consequences of the mission was recited by Ellsworth to Pickering and Wolcott. 'The President thinks the French Government,' thus wrote Pickering to Washington, 'will not accept the terms which the Envoys are instructed to propose; that they will speedily return; and that he shall have to recommend to Congress a declaration of war. . . . But as to the French negotiations producing a war with England; if it did, England could not hurt us! This last idea was part of Mr. Ellsworth's recital

[1] Adams' Works, vol. ix., p. 254.

[2] Federal Administrations, vol. ii., p. 273. Mr. Gibbs, however, it will be observed, gives no authority for his statement.

[3] Ibid.

to Mr. Wolcott and me. I had not patience to hear more, but have desired Mr. Wolcott to commit the whole recital to writing, which he promised to do. And yet the President has, several times, in his letters to me from Quincy, mentioned the vast importance of keeping on good terms with England.'[1]

On the evening of the 15th of October, the President summoned the Cabinet to a meeting. The instructions to the Envoys were discussed, amended, and unanimously approved. They separated about 11 o'clock. Nothing had been said as to the delay of the mission; but early the next morning the President, without consultation, or intimation of his purpose, gave his final orders for the departure of the Envoys by the 1st of November.

---

[1] Federal Administrations, vol. ii., p. 280. Writings of Washington, vol. xi., p. 572. October 24th, 1799.

CHAPTER XIII.

1799–1800.

CONTINUATION OF THE MISSION TO FRANCE.

IN the preparation of the instructions to the Envoys, Ellsworth was freely consulted. 'I propose to send a copy of the draught of instructions to Mr. Ellsworth,' wrote the Secretary of State to the President, 'and to invite his observations upon them, as it is important that he should be satisfied. And if want of time should prevent a second transmission of the instructions to you (which, however, I think will not be the case), may I take the liberty of proposing, if your judgment should not be definitively made up on particular points, that we may, if Mr. Ellsworth should desire it, and we all concur in opinion with him, make alterations in the draught? Provided that none of the ultimata be varied, except that which prescribes the mode of organizing the Board of Commissioners.'[1]

In his reply, the President said:—'I am glad you have sent a copy to the Chief Justice. I had several long conversations with him last winter, on the whole subject. He appears to me to agree most perfectly in sentiment with me upon every point of our policy towards France and England; and this policy was

[1] Adams' Works, vol. ix., pp. 23, 24. September 11th, 1799.

founded only in perfect purity of moral sentiment, natural equity, and Christian faith towards both nations. I am, therefore, under no hesitation in the propriety of sending the draught to him, nor in consenting that, if want of time should prevent a second transmission of the instructions to me, the Heads of Department, in concert with him, may make alterations in the draught, within the limitations you propose. Indeed, Mr. Ellsworth is so great a master of business, and his colleagues are so intelligent, that I should not be afraid to allow them a greater latitude of discretion, if it were not unfair to lay upon them alone the burden of the dangerous responsibility that may accompany this business.'[1]

The following are Ellsworth's observations on the draught of instructions, contained in a letter to the Secretary of State: —

'Dear Sir: — Having given your draught of instructions such perusal as the hurry and pressure of a court, crowding two terms into one, admits of, I remark, with all the freedom you invite, that to insist that the French Government acknowledge its orders to be piratical, or, which is the same, *absolutely* engage to pay for the depredations committed under them, is, I believe, unusually degrading, and which would probably defeat the negotiation, and place us in the wrong. The alternative of insisting that the fifth Commissioner shall be a foreigner is more than was insisted with Great Britain, and a ground, as I apprehend, hardly sufficient to risk a failure upon, though an eligible arrangement to attempt. The style of the instructions

---

Adams' Works, vol. ix., p. 31. September 19th, 1799.

is certainly nowhere heightened beyond the provocation received; yet in some few instances, which will readily occur to you on revision, is more spirited, as it seems to me, than can be necessary to impress the Envoys, or than, in the event of publication, would be evidential of that sincerity and conciliatory temper with which the business should appear to be conducted. I still think well of Governor Davie, and believe Mr. Murray to be honest. Younger, somewhat, than myself, it is not strange if they discover more promptitude to obey an honorary call.

'I am,' &c.[1]

Two weeks later, on the 5th of October, he thus wrote: —

'Dear Sir: — I have been favored with your letter of the 28th ultimo. Mr. M.'s [Murray] reasons for thinking that the French, in the state of things contemplated by our mission, would not abandon their construction of the treaty with respect to the *role d'equipage*, are among those which led me to doubt the expediency of *insisting* that they should do it, or even of *insisting* that the fifth Commissioner should be a foreigner, which they would consider as abandoning the chance for their construction, unless they could so arrange the choice as to obtain a foreigner who was or might be corrupted. But I confess, Sir, that I have not skill enough to calculate a week beforehand for the meridian of France, nor hardly for our own. I am as satisfied as Mr. M. can be of the rectitude of our construction, and as sensible that Commissioners,

---

[1] MSS. September 20th, 1799.

as under the British treaty, would give us but an equal chance to establish or lose it.'[1]

As an indispensable condition of a treaty, our Envoys were instructed that it must contain a stipulation, making compensation for all losses and damages sustained by citizens of the United States in consequence of irregular or illegal capture or condemnation of their vessels and other property under color of authority or commissions from the French Republic, or its agents. And all captures or condemnations were deemed irregular or illegal, when contrary to the law of nations, or the stipulations of the treaty of 1778 while that treaty remained in force. This idea of compensation, we shall presently see, prevented the negotiation of a treaty, and resulted in a temporary settlement, which left the points that could not then be adjusted, for future arrangement.

The Envoys sailed for France, on the 3d of November, in the frigate United States, Captain Barry, who had instructions to land them in any French port they might prefer, or touch at any other ports which they might desire. They arrived at Lisbon on the 27th, where they had previously agreed to touch. Ellsworth suffered much during the passage from seasickness. Indeed, his vigorous frame had already lost somewhat of its elasticity and tone from 'some of the infirmities of approaching age,' and was not very well fortified to resist the unfavorable influences of a stormy winter's voyage.

At Lisbon, they were informed of the revolution of the 18th Brumaire, which had resulted in the overthrow of the Directory, and the virtual concentration

[1] MSS. The remainder of this letter we have quoted, ante, p. 229.

of authority in the hands of Napoleon, as first Consul. They were a good deal embarrassed what course to pursue. Their letters of credence might not avail them with the new rulers; and thus their mission, if not frustrated, at all events, delayed. However, they finally determined to sail for L'Orient, and thence proceed to Paris, if their information should justify that step. Accordingly, on the 21st of December they set sail; but they encountered a severe gale, which continued nearly a fortnight, drove them out of their course, and finally induced them to steer for Corunna, in Spain, where they disembarked. Ellsworth's sufferings were extreme, and from their effects he never recovered. The consequences were aggravated by the journey he was now compelled to undertake through Spain and France to Paris.

On the 17th of January, the Envoys despatched a courier to that city with a letter to the Minister of Foreign Relations, announcing their arrival at Corunna, and requesting that passports might be sent them for the journey to Paris. Ten days later they left Corunna, and on the 9th of February arrived at Burgos, where they met their courier, on his return. He brought a letter from Talleyrand, saying, that they 'were expected with impatience, and would be received with warmth;' and that the form of their letters of credence was immaterial, and would be no obstacle to entering upon the negotiation. Thus assured, they left Burgos on the 11th of February; and after a long and most disagreeable journey, in the course of which they endured great fatigue, privation, and hardship, they arrived at Paris on the 2d of March. Mr. Murray, from the Hague, had arrived the evening before. Talleyrand was at once informed of their presence in Paris. His reception and treatment of them was all that could be desired. On the 8th, they were presented to the First Consul in form. Joseph Bonaparte, M. Fleurieu, formerly Minister of Marine, and M. Roederer, then Counsellor of State, were appointed to conduct the negotiation on the part of France. But the indisposition of Joseph Bonaparte prevented immediate attention to the business, and it was not until the 2d of April that the negotiators had their first conference. It was then discovered that the powers of the French Ministers were not sufficiently full and explicit; and a further delay of several days took place, in order that they might obtain an enlargement of their authority. When that was accomplished, the negotiation commenced.

On the part of the United States, it was chiefly, nay, almost exclusively, conducted by Ellsworth. It was a new, and unaccustomed scene to him; and it has been said, that 'although his usual vigor of mind did not desert him, he appeared in it to less advantage than in any other situation in which he was placed in the course of his long and active life. But slightly acquainted with the arts, the forms, and the ambiguous and guarded language of diplomacy, he frequently laid himself open to his adroit adversaries, and it required all his firmness to recover the ground thus incautiously lost. He was thought by the wily diplomatists of the French Court, to have wasted much time and talent in endeavoring to prove to them the right or wrong of every position which was advanced in the course of the negotiation, while *they* regarded the whole business as a mere matter of bargain and compromise; this, however, is an error of judgment, if it be one, which I trust our country will never wish to see corrected in any of her public agents. When it is considered that in addition to the difficulty of the business in which he was engaged, and the novelty of his situation, Judge Ellsworth was, during this period, suffering under the attacks of severe disease, it will not be wondered at, that, in some minor points, the treaty which he formed did not fully answer the just claims and expectations of the American people. It was, however, in all probability, the best that could be procured, and, as such, was ratified by the President and Senate.'[1]

Whatever want of facility or tact Ellsworth may have discovered in the conduct of this negotiation, it is certain that the honor and essential interests of his country could not have been entrusted to more capable hands. He may, possibly, from inexperience, have been discomfitted in the skirmishing business of the negotiation; but, it is clear, that in the adjustment finally made, he obtained all for his country, that, under the actual circumstances, could be obtained. Nobody could have done better. It became, at last, a simple question, whether all our differences should be left unaccommodated, or a temporary arrangement be made, which would secure peace, without at all sacrificing our rights or interests. To be sure, less was obtained in some respects, than could be wished; but, the same argument that was employed to sustain the Jay Treaty, was equally applicable to this negotiation.

To the claim of indemnity for depredations on our commerce, the French Ministers answered, that if allowed, the Treaties, for whose infractions the claim had chiefly arisen, must be restored. The reply was, that those treaties, having been violated by one party, and renounced by the other, a priority had since attached in favor of the treaty with Great Britain, which

[1] Analectic Magazine, vol. iii., p. 396.

conceded certain exculsive rights to that country, and which, seemingly, could not consistently be restored to France. But this view of the subject, the French Ministers would not entertain, and 'there appeared no alternative, but to abandon indemnities, or, as a means of saving them, to renew, at least partially, the treaty of commerce. Whether in fact it could, or could not be renewed, consistently with good faith, then became a question for thorough investigation.' The considerations that presented themselves to the minds of the American Ministers, and which they communicated to the American government, in the journal of their proceedings,[1] induced the opinion, that every part of the former treaties might be renewed without any breach of good faith whatever. They, accordingly, offered a renewal, with limitations of the 17th article, of the commercial treaty, 'which, without compromising the interests of the United States, would have given to France what her Ministers had particularly insisted on, as essential to her honor, and what they had given reason to expect would be deemed satisfactory.'

But this overture only served to enlarge the demands of the French Ministers, who now insisted upon a total renewal of the treaties, without exception or limitation, which brought the negotiation to a stand. 'The American Ministers, however, after a deliberation of some days, the progress of events in Europe continuing, in the meantime, to grow more unfavorable to their success, made an ulterior advance, going the whole length of what had been last insisted on. They offered an unlimited recognition of the former treaties,

[1] MSS. dated Oct. 4, 1800. The essential portions of it have been printed by Mr. Gibbs, in the Federal Administrations, vol. ii, p. 436–438.

though accompanied with a provision to extinguish such privileges claimed under them, as were detrimental to the United States, by a pecuniary equivalent to be made out of the indemnities which should be awarded to American citizens. A compensation, which, though it might have cancelled but a small portion of the indemnities, was, nevertheless, a liberal one, for privileges which the French Ministers had often admitted to be of little use to France, under the construction which the American government had given to the treaties.'

This offer, though it covered the avowed objects of the French government, secured an engagement to pay indemnities, as well as the power to extinguish the obnoxious parts of the treaties. But the French Ministers, wishing to avoid any engagement of this kind, now abandoned the principles upon which the negotiation had, for some time, proceeded, and insisted that 'it was indispensable to the granting of indemnities, not only that the treaties should have an unqualified recognition, but that their future operations should not be varied in any particulars for any consideration or compensation whatever. In short, they thought proper to add what was unnecessary, that their real object was to avoid any indemnities, and that it was not in their power to pay them. No time was requisite for the American Ministers to intimate that it had become useless to pursue the negotiation any further.

'It accorded as little with their views, as with their instructions, to subject their country perpetually to the mischievous effects of those treaties, in order to obtain a promise of indemnity at a remote period, a promise which might as easily prove delusive, as it would reluctantly be made; especially, as under the guaranty of the treaty of alliance, the United States might be immediately called upon for succors, which if not furnished, would of itself be a sufficient pretext to render abortive the hope of indemnity. It only remained for the [Envoys] to quit France, leaving the United States involved in a contest; and, according to appearances, soon alone in a contest, which it might be as difficult for them to relinquish with honor, as to pursue with a prospect of advantage; or else to propose a temporary settlement, reserving for a definite adjustment, points which could not then be satisfactorily settled, and providing, in the meantime, against a state of things of which neither party could profit. They elected the latter, and the result has been the signature of a Convention.'

The reasons thus assigned for abandoning the idea of a treaty, and concluding a Convention, it seems to us, are unanswerable. Indeed, a treaty of the character contemplated by their instructions was utterly out of the question. If, therefore, the Convention preserved peace, without yielding any essential interest, or sacrificing, in any point, the national honor, the Envoys deserved the praise and gratitude of their country. What, then, were the terms of this celebrated Convention? They are thus summarily described in a letter from Gouverneur Morris to Hamilton: —

'It' [the Convention,] 'contains, among other things, a stipulation that, as the parties cannot agree about the old treaties, nor the indemnities mutually due, or claimed, they will negotiate further about them at a convenient period, and until they shall have agreed on those points, the treaty shall have no operation; but the relations of the two countries shall be regulated by that Convention; that public ships, which have been, or may be taken, shall be mutually restored; that property captured or not yet definitely condemned, shall be restored on proof of ownership; that debts shall be paid; that the vessels of the two nations, and their privateers, as well as their prizes, shall be treated in the respective ports of each other, as those of the nation the most favored; that free ships shall make free goods, and the converse; that when neutral ships are convoyed, the word of the officer commanding the convoy shall be taken, and no visit allowed; that when armed ships shall be permitted to enter with their prizes, they shall not be obliged to pay any duty, nor shall the prizes be seized, nor shall the officers of the place make examination concerning the lawfulness of such prizes; but this stipulation is not to extend beyond the most favored nation; that privateers belonging to an enemy shall not fit their ships, sell or exchange their prizes, or purchase provisions, except what may be needful to go to the next ports of their own country. Finally, this Convention is unlimited in its duration; such, my dear sir, is the result of our French negotiation, which evidently places us in a critical situation.'[1]

But not so thought Hamilton. To be sure, he did not altogether approve the result attained by our Envoys; indeed, at first, he very much disapproved it. But reflection led him to defend many of the provisions contained in the Convention, and maintain the propriety of its entire ratification. 'In my opinion,' thus he wrote Morris, 'there is nothing in it contrary to our treaty with Great Britain. The annulling of our former treaties was an act of reprisal in consequence of hostile differences, of which no other power had a right to benefit; and which, upon an accommo-

[1] Works of Hamilton, vol. vi., p. 492. Dec. 19th, 1800.

dation, might have been rescinded, even to the restoration of the *statu quo*. Great Britain is now, in this respect, in a better situation than she was when she made the treaty. She has so far no good cause to complain. There are, indeed, features which will not be pleasant to the British Cabinet, particularly the principle that free ships shall make free goods, and that the flag of ships of war shall protect. As these are points upon which France was endeavoring to form hostile combinations against Great Britain, the giving place to them in the Convention will have an unfriendly countenance towards her; and as it regards good understanding between her and us, is to be regretted in the present moment. Yet, we had a right to make these stipulations, and as they may be fairly *supposed* to be advantageous to us, they are not, in fact, indications of enmity. They give no real cause of umbrage, and, considering the general interests of Great Britain, and her particular situation, it does not seem probable that they will produce on her part a hostile conduct.

'As to the indemnification for spoliations, that was rather to be wished than expected, while France is laying the whole world under contribution. The people of this country will not endure that a definitive rupture with France shall be hazarded on this ground. If this Convention is not closed, the leaving of the whole subject open will render it easier for the Jacobin Administration to make a worse thing. On the whole, the least evil is to ratify. The contrary would finish the ruin of the Federal party, and endanger our internal tranquillity. It is better to risk the dangers on the other hand, than on this side.''

[1] Hamilton's Works, vol. vi., p. 496, Dec. 24, 1800.

When it is remembered how high a spirit of resentment had been engendered against France in consequence of her aggressions, insults, and indignities, it cannot excite surprise, that the results of the negotiation, especially in impassioned minds, should have awakened a feeling of keen disappointment. They demanded compensation; indemnity for the past and security for the future. That the latter was obtained; that the former was not abandoned, but left for future adjustment; that this was the best result, then attainable; that in its train it brought all the blessings of peace, did not satisfy men whose minds had been inflamed by wrong and outrage, and did not sufficiently advert to the circumstances that surrounded the objects at which they aimed. Nevertheless, the Convention with France must, in the light of history, be pronounced wise and beneficial; and, as such, redound to the honor of our Envoys.

Among those who most warmly condemned its provisions, and disapproved the course of Ellsworth in assenting to them, were his intimate friends, Wolcott and Pickering. To the former he thus wrote, from Havre:—

'You will see our proceedings and their result. Be assured more could not be done without too great a sacrifice, and as the reign of Jacobinism is over in France, and appearances are strong in favor of a general peace, I hope you will think it was better to sign a Convention, than to do nothing. Sufferings at sea, and by a winter's journey through Spain, gave me an obstinate gravel, which, by wounding the kidneys has drawn and fixed my wandering gout to those parts. My pains are constant, and, at times excruciating; they do not permit me to discharge my official duties.

I have, therefore, sent my resignation of the office of Chief Justice, and shall, after spending a few weeks in England, retire for winter quarters to the south of France.'[1]

Referring to Wolcott's intention to resign his post as Secretary of the Treasury, and which he subsequently carried into effect, Ellsworth, in a postscript to his letter, thus advises him:—

'You certainly did right not to resign, and you must not think of resigning, let what changes may take place, at least till I see you. Though our country pays badly, it is the only one in the world worth working for. The happiness it enjoys, and which it may increase, is so much superior to what the nations of Europe do, or ever can enjoy, that no one who is able to preserve and increase that happiness ought to quit her service, while he can remain in it with bread and honor. Of the first, a little suffices you; and of the latter, it is not in the power of rapine or malevolence to deprive you. They cannot do without you, and dare not put you out. Remember, my dear friend, my charge; keep in till I see you.'

To Pickering, who had been removed from the State Department, he thus wrote:—

'My best efforts, and those of my colleagues, have not obtained all that justice required, or which the policy of France should have given. Enough is, however done, if ratified, to extricate the United States from a contest, which it might be as difficult to relin-

[1] Federal Administrations, vol. ii., p 434, Oct. 16th, 1800.

quish with honor, as to pursue with a prospect of advantage. A partial saving is also made for captured property; guards are provided against future abuses, as well, perhaps, as they can be by stipulations, and our country is disentangled from its former connections. As the reign of Jacobinism in France is over, and appearances are strong in favor of a general peace, I hope you will think it was better to do this, than to have done nothing.' [1]

But, to both Wolcott and Pickering, who were men of strong political antipathies, and had been connected with the administration of the government while the difficulties with France were pending, the result of the negotiation was very distasteful. 'You will read the treaty, which was signed with France,' thus wrote the former to the latter, 'with astonishment. I can account for it only on the supposition that the vigor of Mr. Ellsworth's mind has been enfeebled by sickness. The Senate are, I understand, much embarrassed, though they will probably advise a conditional ratification. It is now certain that the mission has proved as unfortunate as we considered it at the time it was instituted. The country must be dishonored by an unequal treaty, or must incur the risk of having its dispute with France unsettled, after a general peace with Europe. The probability of this event during the present winter is understood to be increasing.' [2]

Pickering thus replies: 'The treaty with France, as you suppose, has excited my astonishment. Davie and Murray always appeared to me fond of the mis-

[1] Federal Administrations, vol. ii., p. 463, Oct. 16th, 1800.
[2] Ibid., p. 461, Dec. 28th, 1800.

sion, and I supposed that they had made the treaty; but, when informed that our friend, our highly respected and respectable friend, Mr. E———, was most urgent for its adoption, my regret equalled my astonishment. The fact can be solved only on the ground which you have suggested.'[1] But all this is the language of feeling. Reason decides differently. A calm, dispassionate, and comprehensive survey of all the circumstances attending the negotiation, as well as the result finally attained by it, will show that the mind of Ellsworth, unaffected by the distressing malady that afflicted him, exhibited all its usual vigor, and accomplished undeniable good for his country.

The Convention with France was submitted to the Senate on the 15th of December, and finally ratified by them, with the exception of the second article, which postponed the former treaties, and the mutual claims for indemnity, for future negotiation. This article the Senate desired to have expunged, and another article substituted, limiting the duration of the Convention to eight years. The President accepted the ratification in this form, though at the same time, declaring that, had it been unconditional, it would have been more conformable to his opinion. It was not, however, until Jefferson's accession to the Presidency, that the ratifications were exchanged. Bonaparte assented to the modifications made by the Senate, with this proviso, 'that by this retrenchment, the two States renounce their respective pretensions, which were the object of the 2d article.' Our government accepted the Convention as thus altered, and on the 21st of December, 1801, it was finally promulgated. The effect of the condition attached by Napoleon, was

---

[1] Federal Administrations, vol. ii., p. 462, Jan. 3d. 1801.

to relieve France of all liability for the depredations on our commerce, amounting in the aggregate to over twenty millions of dollars. Whether our government, by thus exonerating France from the claims of our citizens, and for a partial equivalent too, became bound to pay them, has been a subject of much discussion, and contrariety of opinion. But it is foreign to our task to present the arguments employed on either side.

CHAPTER XIV.

1800–1801.

INCIDENTS OF HIS RESIDENCE IN EUROPE.

DURING his residence in Paris, Ellsworth became acquainted with many of the celebrated characters, who, in one department or other of public life, had risen to distinction. Under the vigorous sway of the First Consul, confidence was fast being restored, the pursuits of business received a fresh impulse, and general satisfaction pervaded the country. The universal speculation and inquiry awakened by the Revolution, however, were still active, and discussions on religion, and politics continued to agitate the *salons* of Paris.

In a conversation with Volney, on the subject of government, the latter read, or described to Ellsworth, a plan which he had formed for France. He dwelt upon it with much enthusiasm, as a system calculated to advance his countrymen to a state of perfection. Ellsworth listened patiently to all the details of the philosopher's project, and then remarked, 'There is one thing, Mr. Volney, for which you have made no provision.' 'And, pray sir, what is that?' 'The selfishness of man,' replied Ellsworth. 'Ah! said Volney, 'that's the d—l on't.'[1]

On another occasion, the conversation turned on religion, when Volney declared, 'in the most direct manner, his entire disbelief of the existence of God, a Providence, and a future state.' Not long after, M. Volney passed Mr. Ellsworth, at an early hour, in the Champs Elysees, on horseback. 'I see, friend Volney,' said Mr. Ellsworth, 'that although you disbelieve the existence of a God, you are willing to take some pains to preserve your life and health.' 'Yes,' answered Volney, 'this horse is my Providence.'[2]

Ellsworth became quite intimate with Talleyrand, and in a familiar conversation with him, on one occasion, respecting American institutions, the celebrated *diplomat* said, 'Mr. Ellsworth, how can we establish among our people republican principles, and free institutions.' 'In the first place, sir,' replied Ellsworth, 'you must establish a judicial tribunal. Let your judges be some of the first men in the nation; give them ample salaries, a hundred thousand francs a year, if necessary, sufficient to place them above the danger of bribery; and set them above the reach of the Government. The nation will soon find that in that court all have equal rights and privileges. Lower courts will easily be established on similar principles, and other institutions will follow of course.' 'I know it, I know it,' replied Talleyrand, 'but Frenchmen, Mr. Ellsworth, are always in a hurry. They cannot wait such a slow process.'[3] And if they could, they might find in the end, that an impartial administration of law may well consist with the most perfect despo-

[1] Mr. Wood's MSS. [2] Dwight's Travels, vol. iv., p. 225.
[3] Mr. Wood's MSS.

tism. Bad laws, impartially administered, is no phenomenon, either in free or despotic States. And such a system existing in a despotism, we mean the impartial administration of bad laws, is more likely to destroy the very vitals of a people than to reform the principles of their government. An independent judiciary, enlisting under the banner of reform, making common cause against the government from which they derive their support, is a spectacle which mankind are not very likely to witness. On the contrary, they will, until human nature is radically changed, resist innovation, and endeavor to preserve the whole condition of things on its original foundation.

On the conclusion of the negotiation, Joseph Bonaparte celebrated the auspicious event by a splendid fête, at his chateau at Marfontane, about eighteen miles north of Paris. Oliver Ellsworth, Jr., who had accompanied his father in the capacity of private Secretary, thus describes the incidents of this interesting occasion :—

'We arrived' he says, 'at the village of Marfontane, about 2 o'clock, P. M.,[1] where we found a large number of the French magistrates assembled at the chateau of Joseph Bonaparte. The First Consul arrived about 4 o'clock. His entrance into the chateau was announced by the firing of cannon, and bands of music playing. During the afternoon, the company amused themselves by walking in the park, or gardens attached to the chateau, which are laid out in English style, affording picturesque views. Behind the chateau is a canal; and in front, at a small distance, is a park with rocky, barren hills, topped by an ancient tower on one

[1] October 3d, 1800.

side, and a large natural pond, with islands interspersed, and fine cultivated hills, here and there, on the other.

'In the evening, after the final signature of the treaty by the French and American ministers, it was presented for ratification to the First Consul, upon which occasion, about 8 in the evening, cannon were fired to announce the ratification. About 9 o'clock, the guests, consisting of about 110 persons, were conducted to the supper tables, spread in three large halls. The principal, called *Union Hall*, was superbly decorated and illuminated, hung with verdant wreaths and numerous inscriptions commemorating the 4th of July, 1776, and other periods and places celebrated by important actions in America during the struggle for independence. Among the inscriptions were frequently seen the letters F. A., France and America, with views of the Federal city, of Philadelphia, and Havre de Grace, the port from which the American ministers were to embark. An angel was represented flying with the olive branch from Havre de Grace to Philadelphia.

'The second hall, called *Salle de Washington*, was adorned with the bust of Washington, the French and American flags side by side.

'The third hall, called *Salle de Franklin*, contained a bust of Doctor Franklin. The design of these decorations seemed to be principally the commemoration of the American Independence and French Liberty, and that was the spirit of the toasts given at table. The toast of the French Consul was "The memory of those who have fallen in the defence of French and American Liberty." The toast of the second Consul, Cambaceres, was, "The successor of Washington."

'After supper, about 10 o'clock, there was a splendid and ingenious display of fire works exhibited in the gardens, the chateau and other buildings being illuminated during the evening. Next followed a fine concert of music. About 12 o'clock, two short, but interesting comedies were performed in the private theatre within the chateau. The actors and actresses were the best that Paris could afford. At the conclusion of one of the plays, a song, complimentary to the United States, was sung. At the close of the performances, about 2 o'clock, A. M., some of the company took their beds, some took a second supper, and some their exit for Paris at 3 o'clock.

'While walking in the gardens with Mr. Roderer, son of the French Commissioner, he informed me that Joseph Bonaparte proposed raising a marble monument, in the garden, in commemoration of the signing of the treaty between France and the United States.

'From Marfontane, the Envoys and suite took their departure, on the 4th of October, for Havre de Grace, and reached St. Denis in the afternoon, whence they were obliged to send back to Paris for stronger carriages.' [1]

They arrived at Havre de Grace on the evening of the 6th, too late to take passage in the Portsmouth, which might have sailed that morning, but as the tide would not allow her to go to sea only once in eight or ten days, she could not again sail till after the middle of the month. Mr. Ellsworth's health was so much impaired, that his physician told him it would be dangerous for him to attempt a passage across the ocean after the middle of October. As no other opportunity offered until the 19th, though he had gone to Havre with the intention of embarking, he came to the reso-

---

[1] MSS.

lution to spend the winter in the south of France. In the meantime, he determined to visit England, chiefly with the view of testing the efficacy of the mineral waters at Bath. He was carried to that country in the Portsmouth. His son returned home with Governor Davie, bringing with him his father's resignation of the office of Chief Justice.

In England, Ellsworth doubtless found himself in a more congenial atmosphere than in France. He was familiar with the laws, government, and social institutions of the country. Besides, the tie of language will always, more or less, bind the American to his ancestral home. The tone of society, too, and habits of life, no doubt, were more in unison with his feelings, than in Paris. But that he was out of his proper element in this latter city, as has been suggested, seems to be a mere supposition, without any adequate foundation. True, he was 'now advanced in years, infirm in health, almost unacquainted with the French language, with little taste for the fine arts;' but we doubt if it can be justly said that he was 'severe and rigid in his morals and habits of life.'[1] Purity of morals by no means implies austerity; on the contrary, it may well consist with pleasantry, with social gaiety and ease. Ellsworth's spirits were naturally buoyant, and his humor playful and sportive. That he found sources of amusement and instruction 'in gay and luxurious Paris,' notwithstanding the disadvantages under which he labored from ill-health, and want of familiarity with the language, may well be imagined. He had acted a distinguished part on the great theatre of affairs; he was there brought into contact with men who had acted a similar part. Surely, in the

[1] Analectic Magazine, vol. iii., p. 396.

interchange of opinion, in witnessing the scenes of the Revolution, and an unaccustomed condition of society, he could not fail to find much to give a pleasing stimulus to his mind, and gratify a liberal curiosity.

On his arrival in England, Ellsworth appears to have proceeded at once to Bath. He soon abandoned the idea of returning again to France, and remained in England until his departure for the United States, in the following spring. In January, he thus wrote his friend Rufus King, then resident minister of the United States at the Court of St. James: —

'I propose going to London about the middle of next month, and shall probably embark there. And I hope to be able to carry home your good bargain, for America will want a new wonder by the time I shall arrive.'[1]

In the following letter, he thus playfully refers to his health, and the defeat of the Federalists: —

'Dear Sir: — As you have lived long and well enough to begin to die, you should welcome the gout in your joints, as the best means to protract the process, and give lucid intervals. The Bath waters, I believe, seldom cure this disease, though they mitigate and shorten its paroxysms; and are, also, of great use when needed to fix it to the extremities. This effect, however, is more than they are likely to produce for me, while my kidneys are weakened by the constant laceration of sand. They have somewhat increased my appetite and spirits, and promoted the discharge of calcareous matter, though I do not perceive that

[1] MSS. Bath, January 20th, 1801.

they check its formation. I hope we shall next have better bodies.

So, the anti-Feds. are now to support their own administration, and take a turn at rolling stones up hill. Good men will get a breathing spell, and the credulous will learn to understand the game of *out and in*.'[1] . . . . .

Three days later he again wrote King, and as follows: —

'Dear Sir: — . . . . . You do not, surely, mistake the fear of Jefferson for the gout; because you think, as I do, that he dare not run the ship aground, nor essentially deviate from that course which has, hitherto, rendered her voyage so prosperous.[2] His party, *also*, must support the government while he administers it; and if others are consistent, and do the same, the government may even be consolidated, and acquire new confidence. It may be well, however, for your letters to guard against that despondency of some, who, always believing that the government must soon die, will be apt to say it can never die in better hands.

'Probably, England will block up the Sound; but she must let the American trade pass, which will facilitate to her essential supplies, and avoid grounds of complaint to the United States, at a time, on every account, the most improper to furnish them. Perhaps, you may think it expedient to drop a hint or two to Lord Grenville on this subject, though the right train of reflections upon it seem pretty obvious.'[3] . . . . .

On his arrival in London, Ellsworth was an object

---

[1] MS. letter to Rufus King, Jan. 21st, 1801.

[2] See ante, chap. x., p. 177. [3] MS., January 24th, 1801.

of marked attention on the part of the Court, the leading public men, as well as the Bench and the bar. Says Mr. King, in a letter to the Secretary of State:—

'Whatever may have been the temper or inclination of this Government in a different posture of its affairs, and before the Convention with France was published, its sentiments in respect to that instrument, and the distinguished manner in which Mr. Ellsworth has been received by the Court, have a tendency to show that, at present, it has no animosity or unusual prejudice against us; on the contrary, those who disseminate its opinions, encourage the people to bear their distresses arising from the dearness of bread, by holding forth to them the abundant harvest of America, and a prospect of a great supply from that source.'[1]

Ellsworth visited Westminster Hall, and 'was taken to a seat on the King's Bench, where Lord Kenyon — then rapidly approaching the close of his long tenure, and in the last year of that old-fashioned green coat, which Mr. Erskine declared had been bought nearly a quarter of a century before — was sitting with Judge Le Blanc and Judge Grose. It was, as is said, during the train of arguments which are reported in the beginning of the first volume of Mr. East, that the American Chief Justice visited Westminster Hall. The famous case of Rex *v.* Waddington was then before the Court, in which all the leaders of the bar were retained; and at the inception of which, a scuffle is said to have taken place near Mr. Garrow's chambers, between the emissaries of the two contending interests, each seeking to be the first at the door of that eminent

[1] MS.

advocate. Mr. Law led off for the defendants in the proceeding in arrest of judgment, and was followed by Mr. Erskine, Mr. Garrow, and Mr. Scott. Notwithstanding Mr. Jay's previous appearance at the Court of St. James, and the cotemporaneous presence there of Mr. King, the fame of their accomplishments had not reached the King's Bench, whose precincts they had probably never invaded; and it was, consequently, with great curiosity that the elder lawyers, whose notions of America had been derived from the kidnapping cases, which were the only precipitate cast on the reports of the privy council by the current of colonial litigation, spied out the American Chief Justice. Mr. Ellsworth's simple, but dignified carriage, so much like, as is said, that of his successor on the bench, was in happy contrast to the awkwardness of the English Chief Justice; and as soon as it was discovered that, though his worn and marked features bore a stamp which had not then become familiar to the English eye, he was neither an Indian nor a Jacobin, two things regarded as equally beyond the limit of civilized sympathy, he was surrounded by a knot of lawyers, curious to know how the common law stood transplanting. Still, the obscurity which hung about the history of the American Republic, could not but produce some confusion; and it was with this view of the supposed creolishness of the American people — a hybrid between the Englishman and the Indian, mingling the distinctive powers of each without that power of perpetuating them, which the old philosophers thought only belonged to unmixed races — that Judge Grose, with an air, it is said, of grave delicacy, inquired whether the obstruction of the course of descent had not turned fee simples into life estates. Perhaps, to the same uncertainty may be traced the question which Mr. Garrow is said to have addressed to the American judge, 'Pray, Chief Justice, in what cases do the half-blood in America take by descent?'[1]

With a natural curiosity, Ellsworth endeavored to obtain some knowledge of the origin and history of his family; and with what result, we have already seen.[2] Occasional travel, current politics, and news from America, served to relieve the tedium of disease, and preserve the elasticity of his spirits. The censure, however, bestowed on his negotiation by his friends at home, seems to have wounded him; and, especially, the imputation, that it was the consequence of an impaired intellect. Thus he wrote Mr. King, from Bath, on the 26th of February:—

'My Dear Sir:—I am very sorry to hear that his Majesty has been deranged, and still more so to learn that I am supposed to be in the same predicament. I devoutly hope that a similar imputation will not extend to our government; but that it will continue to have respect, though mine is lost in its service. What more is, at present, to be done in France, will, at least, fall to the lot of some one not prejudged distracted for undertaking it.

'It is strange, that after your letter to the Secretary of State, (of which, if you see no impropriety, I hope you will favor me with a copy, or an extract,) it could have been supposed that G. B. [Great Britain], had a right to complain; and even without that letter it ought to have been sufficient, that by an uncontested rule of construction, there is implied and understood a saving for the operation of prior treaties.[3]

---

[1] American State Trials, Preliminary Notes. [2] Ante. chap. i.

[3] The extract thus asked for, is the one, doubtless, that we have printed, Ante. p. 260. Mr. Jefferson was among those who, errone-

'The 3d article, including a restoration of the frigate, had, as you know, its real reciprocity in that part of the 4th which secured the restoration of about forty valuable merchantmen, chiefly letters of marque, on such proofs of ownership as they were known to be furnished with. If the rights of war had attached, restoring the latter was a much greater sacrifice than that of the former; and if there had not been war there was nothing humiliating nor unusual in the restorations on either side.

'The 2d article was harmless; and by admitting the inoperation of the former treaties, silenced a claim which would have been continued, and might have become embarrassing.

'As to the provisions respecting future captures and commerce, we might be satisfied with them quite as long as France, by observing, would avoid an occasion to revise them. To have expressed a limitation of years to the Convention was truly compatible with the idea of a further and definitive treaty, embracing the claims of indemnity which we were not at liberty to abandon. But I will not trouble you with remarks as obvious as they are now become useless.

Very truly yours.' [1]

Though the Convention with France was submitted to the Senate on the 15th of December, that body did not finally act upon it until the third of the following February. Ellsworth, naturally, was anxious to learn the result, which, from various intimations, seemed to be involved in a good deal of doubt.

---

ously, thought the Convention with France would 'endanger the compromitting us with Great Britain.'

[1] MS.

'I am truly thankful, my dear sir,' thus he wrote King on the 3d of March, 'for your package of this day, as I shall be for every scrap of American intelligence, till we know the fate of two questions, both too important for passion to decide. There is now more hope of the Convention than from the Boston account. It was not a copy of that instrument that I enclosed to General Hamilton; but a few observations respecting it, intended to guard against surprise. It is, indeed, strange that the Secretary of State should omit to acknowledge your interesting letter, and that there should be so much evidence of the Senate's being unacquainted with its import. I lament, sir, as much as you can the embarrassments of this country as well as that they are not better understood in our own.' [1]

In the course of a few days intelligence arrived that the Convention with France had been ratified, with the exception of the 2d article. This modification, Ellsworth regarded as impairing the value of the negotiation. 'The exception of the 2d article,' he wrote King on the 17th of March, 'makes the instrument rather worse for us, as it leaves more room for France to claim anteriority, in the point of interference. And, I think it most likely that she will accede to the alteration.' [2]

Five days later, and after hearing the result of the protracted contest between Jefferson and Burr, in the House of Representatives, he thus wrote Mr. King:—

'So, then, my dear sir, after thirty trials, fortune has given us the best of a bad bargain. I think the Feds. have acquired less reputation by the con-

---

[1] MS. [2] MS.

test than the public would have lost had they suc ceeded. . . . . .

'I have just engaged a passage from Bristol, not as I for some time expected to New York, but in the Nancy, Capt. Orn, for Boston, who has been detained a week by the weather, and must now wait till the 27th or 28th, for a spring tide. I cannot, therefore, you see, go to London, though I have certainly more desire to go than while it was generally supposed that the Convention with France was rejected; and while, of course, it must have been supposed that the American Negotiators had disregarded their instructions. Your negotiation about the debts probably does not progress much at present, though I hope there yet continues a prospect of its having a favorable issue. Pray, inform me how far, according to your and Mr. Williams' account, the French have executed the 4th article of the Convention.'[1]

On the 29th he again wrote King, and from Bristol where he was now waiting to embark.

'Your seasonable and well-directed discourses with Mr. Otto, could scarcely, my dear sir, fail of being useful. It was certainly time for G. B. to disembarrass our Spanish commerce, and if she only pursues her own interest, she will be more cautious, especially at present, how she checks our intercourse with any nation, either under pretext of blockades, or by abusing the right of search. It is, doubtless, time, also, that her Vice Admiralty Courts should be so reformed as to be more competent, and more disposed to do their duty.

---

[1] MSS., March 22d, 1801.

'I know not when, or by whom you will be succeeded; but am confident that it will be by no one till you request it, which must not be till our differences with this country are settled, and should not be till our treaty with her has been received. I pray Mrs. King to accept my best wishes, and am, my dear sir, with much obligation, and sensibility,

Your affectionate friend.'[1]

Ellsworth had now been in the service of his country, in high and responsible posts, more than a quarter of a century. With health fatally impaired, he now returned home, with the intention to retire altogether from public life.

---

[1] MSS.

CHAPTER XV.

1801 – 1807.

MEMBER OF THE GOVERNOR'S COUNCIL.

FROM the Bath waters Ellsworth had derived no permanent benefit, although the more distressing symptoms of his disease were alleviated. The voyage home was a severe trial to his impaired constitution. The change in his appearance was obvious and painful. To his family it was truly affecting. They were looking out for his return home with eager expectation. His carriage had been sent forward to meet him. 'At his beautiful mansion in Windsor all was joyful expectancy. His children listened to the echo of every approaching wheel, and saddened at perceiving that it had not brought their father. At length his own carriage was, indeed, descried. The whole family group hastened forth to welcome him. Wife, and son, and daughter, and servant born in his house, were there. It was a thrilling moment. The profound Statesman, whose wealth and fame had been purchased by no sacrifice of virtue, wearied with those services which had rendered his name illustrious, was coming to share the repose of his native shades, and to be parted from them no more. He alighted from his carriage. But he spoke not to his wife. He returned not the embrace of his children. He glanced not even at his twin boys, the youngest of that beloved circle. Leaning over his gate, and covering his face, he first silently breathed a prayer of gratitude to that Being who gave him once more to see his habitation in safety and in peace. He took not the full cup of joy that was pressed to his lips until it had been hallowed by devotion.'[1]

'The lingering disease and ultimate death of a favorite son, a youth of much promise, which took place about this time, contributed, together with the infirm and precarious state of his own health, to depress his spirits as much as a mind naturally so firm and vigorous could be affected by external circumstances.'[2]

The son here referred to was Oliver Ellsworth, Jr., who had accompanied his father to Europe in the capacity of Private Secretary. His health was naturally frail, and had been further impaired by severe application to his studies. His voyage, and residence in Europe, had failed to benefit him, and soon after his return to this country, he went to the West Indies to try the efficacy of a more genial climate. But his disease had progressed too far for effectual relief, and his death soon followed.

Although Ellsworth had determined to pass his remaining life in retirement, yet, when in the year following his return from Europe, he was elected a member of the Governor's Council; 'he did not refuse the call of public duty, and continued in this station the remainder of his life, faithfully attending to the public

---

[1] National Portrait Gallery, vol. iv., Art. 'Ellsworth.'

[2] Analectic Magazine, vol. iii., p. 397.

business in spite of the attacks of disease, and the pressure of domestic affliction. . . . . . His seat in the Council made him, *ex officio*, a member of the Board of Fellows of Yale College; and he entered very zealously into all the concerns and interests of that highly respectable and important institution. His official duties were the more laborious, because, during the time in which he held a seat in the Council, that body exercised the double powers of a constituent branch of the Legislature, and of the final Court of Appeals from all inferior State jurisdictions. He was particularly attentive to this latter department of his duty.'[1]

The decisions of the Council, acting as a Supreme Court of Errors, are collected in Day's Connecticut Reports. The individual opinions of the members, however, are not reported; and, consequently, we are unable to determine the precise share Ellsworth had in the judgments of the court. That his influence on the minds of his brethren was as controlling as eighteen years before, when he was a member of the same court, may naturally be presumed. For, in addition to the weight of acknowledged talents, he now united the authority of age, and long and distinguished public service.

In May, 1807, the Legislature of Connecticut remodeled their judiciary. In place of the existing system, they organized three Circuit Courts, and formed a new Court of Appeals. In order, it is said, to give greater dignity to the system thus established, Ellsworth was appointed Chief Justice of the State. He accepted the appointment; but before the adjourn-

---

[1] Analectic Magazine, vol. iii., p. 397.

ment of the Legislature, who, in thus honoring him did honor to themselves, and the State they represented, a severe attack of his painful disease warned him that his life was approaching its close and parting. Hence, this last honorable testimonial to his virtues and abilities, from the representatives of a State he loved and had served, he felt compelled to decline.

CHAPTER XVI.

1807.

CONCLUSION.

ELLSWORTH'S home, on the banks of the Connecticut, at Windsor, afforded him a delightful retreat from the cares of public life. He was fond of the country; was well acquainted with agriculture, practically and scientifically, and derived great satisfaction in attending to the cultivation of his farm. 'His leisure was chiefly passed in agricultural occupations. During this period he published, in one of the Connecticut journals, a series of brief essays on rural affairs, some of which contained a very whimsical mixture of agriculture and politics.'[1] Before the value of gypsum was generally known in this country, he called the attention of the agricultural community, through the medium of these essays, to its importance. But his Connecticut neighbors, it is said, held 'book knowledge,' and the speculations of a jurist and statesman upon such topics, at rather a cheap rate. This fact, however, does not detract from the value of his contributions to the current literature of agriculture.

His style of living was simple and unostentatious;

[1] Analectic Magazine, vol. iii., p. 398.

his intercourse with his neighbors frank and easy. They found in him, at all times, a safe counsellor and friend. In the affairs of individuals, the church, the parish, the town, and State, his advice was freely given. In politics, he manifested great interest to the last, and frequently entered into their details 'with more warmth, perhaps, than became his age and character.'[1] He was an earnest believer in christianity, and a constant attendant on public worship. 'His example before his household was calculated to impress the importance of that religion which he revered and loved. Guests occasionally present at their morning and evening devotions were solemnized by the fervor and sublimity of his prayers. He inculcated on all under his roof a reverence for the Sabbath; and was in the habit of gathering them around him, and reading them a sermon, in addition to the public worship of the day. During the changes of an eventful life, the fluctuations of revolution, the interruptions incidental to high office, the gaiety of the Court of France, and the desultory habits imposed by foreign travel, he never overlooked the sacred obligations of the Sabbath, or shunned to give infidelity a reason for the hope that was in him. As he approached the close of life, the inspired volume, which had from youth been his guide and counsellor, became more and more dear. Like a new book, it revealed to him unknown treasures. . . . . . Day and night, while he stood on the verge of a higher existence, did his soul, disengaging itself from earthly things, search the Scriptures of truth with solemnity and delight.'[2] It may be added that books of theology, especially Dr. Lardner's, en-

---

[1] Analectic Magazine, vol. iii., p. 398.

[2] National Portrait Gallery, vol. iv., Art. 'Ellsworth.'

gaged his attention in this period of comparative leisure; and that on points of faith, his belief, for the most part, conformed to the prevailing New England standard.

In all his habits and tastes, there was an unaffected simplicity. He often visited a mineral spring in Suffield, Connecticut, for the benefit of his health. On one occasion, the wife of the proprietor of the Springs declined his application for board, saying, that she 'could not entertain a great man like him in a suitable manner.' 'But, madam,' said he, 'do you not have bread.' 'Oh, yes sir, and milk, too.' 'Very well,' was the reply, 'that is all the food I need.' The fears of the good woman were dissipated, and she received him willingly.

In his rambles, while at Suffield, 'he often seated himself by the stone wall on the common, where the children of the neighborhood soon gathered around him, first from curiosity, and afterwards manifested their interest in him by the regularity of their attendance. The occasion was improved by imparting instruction, and he smilingly remarked to my father, in reply to a suggestion of his, 'Mr. Leavitt, time is not lost while I can teach these children something which will always be remembered by them.'[1]

Upon every recurrence of the paroxysms that characterized his distressing malady, the health of Ellsworth grew more and more feeble. Though he experienced flattering intervals of relief, he could have but little hope of ultimate recovery. His sufferings in the latter stages of his disease were very great, and 'during his last sickness he was at times deprived of his reason. In his lucid intervals, the observations which

[1] MS. letter.

he made, and the sentiments which he expressed, concerning the nature, excellence, and rewards of Christianity, were declared by those who were present, not only to have been pious, ardent, and sublime, but wonderful.'[1]

He died on the 26th of November, 1807, in the sixty-third year of his age. His funeral took place on the 28th, and his remains were followed to the grave by a numerous concourse of his fellow-citizens, who had come from all the surrounding country to pay the last tribute of respect to their deceased countryman. He was buried in the cemetery near his accustomed place of worship, on the north bank of the Farmington river, where a neat monument, with an appropriate inscription, has been erected to his memory.

'Oliver Ellsworth,' says Dr. Dwight, 'was formed to be a great man.' His person was tall, dignified, and commanding. Without haughtiness, there was yet in his manners and aspect, something that everywhere, and at all times, compelled respect. The prevailing expression of his countenance was grave and serious. His forehead was high and broad; his eyes blue and penetrating. His features were regular, and well-proportioned, but plain withal. The portrait by Trumbull, it is said, gives a pretty accurate idea of his personal appearance. His social, moral, and intellectual qualities were of a character to challenge respect and esteem. No man was more modest and unassuming; more 'just, frank, kind, and obliging in his deportment.' He was eminently social in his disposition, and mingled freely with all classes on an easy and friendly footing. The turn of his mind was practical, and this, together with the circumstances of his early years, had

[1] Dr. Dwight.

rendered him familiar with the details and ordinary business of life. At the south, in the court-yard of a public house, when the stage-coach had sustained some injury, the inquiry was once made, 'who is that gentlemen who understands everything, and is eloquent about a coach-wheel?' 'The Chief Justice of the United States,' was the reply.[1] In the administration of his private affairs, he was methodical, careful, and economical; but, though his prudence in pecuniary matters was somewhat severe, he, nevertheless, gave liberally to any useful or benevolent object.

He was an uncommonly agreeable man,[2] and the delight of the social circle. His conversational talents, as we have elsewhere remarked, were of a high order; he was sprightly, engaging, and instructive. If particularly interested in the conversation, he became animated, his countenance beamed with intelligence, and his manner and language were eloquent and impressive. If, at the tea table, at such a time, he would take cup after cup of his favorite beverage, wholly unconscious of the number, until his attention was called to it.

His high moral qualities were universally acknowledged; the shafts of calumny were never aimed at him. 'In the elevated course assigned him by his country, he moved not only secure from the lip of slander, and without a blot upon his fair fame, but with that true dignity which always accompanies real greatness.'[3] The sincerity of his principles no man doubted. 'The purity and excellence of his character,' says Dr. Dwight, 'are rare in any station; and in

---

[1] National Portrait Gallery, vol. iv., Art. 'Ellsworth.'

[2] Dr. Dwight. See Dwight's Travels, vol. i, p. 301–304.

[3] American Register for 1807, p. 96.

the higher walks of life are almost unknown.'[1] Truth and justice were essential attributes of his character.

The endowments of his mind were of a sound and valuable sort. Others have had more brilliant qualities; few more practically useful ones. He had not the glance of genius; he did not descend to his subject from above, but rose to it by regular gradations of logic. His habits of thought were slow and laborious. Inference, not intuition, distinguished the operations of his mind. His subject absorbed and pre-occupied him. He was not addicted to books; had little sense of the beautiful, and not much creative power. 'He was formed by nature more for the discharge of active duties, than for contemplative study or abstract science.' But, for strength of reason, for sagacity, wisdom, and sound, good sense in the conduct of affairs; for moderation of temper, and general ability, it may be doubted, if New England has yet produced his superior.

---

[1] Dwight's Travels, *supra.*

THE LIFE

OF

JOHN MARSHALL.

THE

LIFE OF JOHN MARSHALL.

CHAPTER I.

HIS ANCESTRY.

JOHN MARSHALL, the grandfather of Chief Justice Marshall, was a native of Wales, and emigrated to America about the year 1730. He settled in Westmoreland County, which, not inaptly, has been termed 'the Athens of Virginia' — Washington, Monroe, and the Lees having been born there. Here he married Elizabeth Markham, a native of England, who bore him four sons and five daughters.

John Marshall was a planter, but does not appear to have been a very prosperous one. His estate, called 'Forest,' though consisting of several hundred acres, was comparatively unproductive. It was inherited by his eldest son, Thomas, who subsequently removed to Fauquier County. He settled at a place called Germantown, and resided there for several years.

Thomas Marshall and Washington were born in the same neighborhood, were companions in boyhood, and friends ever after. Both became practical surveyors, and in the pursuits of a common profession, and afterwards, in the service of a common country, their friendship and association were preserved. On the outbreak of the Revolution, Thomas Marshall was placed in command of the third Virginia regiment, serving as Continental troops, and in that capacity performed arduous and meritorious service. He was at Trenton and Brandywine, and in the latter battle bore a conspicuous part.

The natural abilities of Thomas Marshall were uncommonly vigorous, and were improved, not only by observation and reflection, but by extensive acquaintance with books. Though his means were limited, and his early advantages of education slight, he had purchased and made himself familiar with most of the standard works of English literature. By his neighbors and acquaintance he was held in the highest estimation for sound sense, and general ability. By his children he was equally beloved and admired. 'I have myself,' says Judge Story, 'often heard the Chief Justice speak of him in terms of the deepest affection and reverence. I do not here refer to his public remarks; but to his private and familiar conversations with me, when there was no other listener. Indeed, he never named his father, on these occasions, without dwelling on his character with a fond and winning enthusiasm. It was a theme on which he broke out with a spontaneous eloquence; and, in the spirit of the most persuasive confidence, he would delight to expatiate upon his virtues and talents. "My father," (would he say, with kindled feelings and emphasis,) "my father was a far abler man than any of his sons. To him I owe the solid foundation of all my own success in life."'[1]

---

[1] Discourse upon the Life, &c., of John Marshall.

About the time of his removal from Westmoreland to Fauquier County, Thomas Marshall married Miss Mary Keith, respecting whom we have been able to obtain only one or two trifling particulars. If, however, the character and talents of her children may be taken as the reflection of her own, she must have possessed great merit and understanding.

CHAPTER II.

1755—1775.

HIS BIRTH AND EDUCATION.

JOHN MARSHALL, the eldest of fifteen children, was the son of Thomas and Mary Marshall, and born at a locality called Germantown, in Fauquier County, Virginia, on the 24th day of September, 1755. When he was quite young, the family moved to Goose's Creek, under Manassa's Gap, near the Blue Ridge, and still later to Oak Hill, where they were living at the commencement of the Revolution.[1] His father, a planter and surveyor like his friend Colonel Washington, led a very retired life, owing no doubt to the narrowness of his fortune, and the studiousness of his disposition. The region of country, too, in which he lived, was very sparsely settled; there were no schools in the neighborhood, and the duty of instructing his children chiefly devolved on him. How cheerfully and faithfully he performed it, the remark of the Chief Justice, which we have already quoted, that to his father he owed the solid foundation of all his success in life, is an ample testimony.

To him he was indebted for that love of literature, which continued fresh and warm down to the very closing scenes of his life. 'At the age of twelve [he]

[1] Howe's Virginia Historical Collections, page 262.

had transcribed the whole of Pope's Essay on Man, and some of his moral essays, and had committed to memory many of the most interesting passages of that distinguished poet. The love of poetry, thus awakened in his warm and vigorous mind, soon exerted a commanding influence over it. He became enamored of the classical writers of the old English school, of Milton, and Shakspeare, and Dryden, and Pope; and was instructed by their solid sense, and beautiful imagery. In the enthusiasm of youth, he often indulged himself in poetical compositions, and freely gave up his leisure hours to those dreamings with the muses, which (say what we may) constitute with many the purest source of pleasure in the gayer scenes of life, and the sweetest consolation in the hours of adversity.'[1]

In study, in healthful sports, and amidst the genial and virtuous influence of his home, the early boyhood of John Marshall passed happily away. He was particularly fortunate in being reared among numerous brothers and sisters. It has been often remarked that children growing up, under such circumstances, are the more apt, on that account, to make good men and women. They constitute a little community among themselves, and learn betimes that respect for social rights and duties, that mutual accommodation and forbearance, which fit them for useful and pleasant association in those corporate communities in which their lives are to be passed.

At fourteen, he was sent to Westmoreland, a hundred miles away, where he commenced the study of Latin. His teacher was the Rev. Mr. Campbell, a very respectable clergyman, with whom he remained a year. One of his fellow-students, a lad of far infe-

---

[1] Discourse on the Life, &c., of John Marshall, by Joseph Story.

rior capacity, but who afterwards became President of the United States, was James Monroe. On his return home, which was about the time of his father's removal to Oak Hill, young Marshall continued the study of Latin another year, under the Rev. Mr. Thompson, a Scotch clergyman, who had just settled in the parish, and resided in his father's family. This was all the aid he ever received from teachers in his study of the classics. With Mr. Thompson he had begun the reading of Horace and Livy; but how far his own unassisted efforts subsequently carried him, I am unable to say. As his stock of classical lore, however, was never very extensive, we may, perhaps, presume that, in the absence of classical tuition, he turned with more ardor to the study of English literature. Here he had the assistance and sympathy of his father, who was not only the kind and considerate parent, but the friend and companion of his son. 'My father,' thus he wrote long after, 'superintended the English part of my education, and to his care I am indebted for any thing valuable which I may have acquired in my youth. He was my only intelligent companion, and was both a watchful parent, and an affectionate, instructive friend. The young men within my reach were entirely uncultivated; and the time passed with them was devoted to hardy, athletic exercises.'

But not to study alone, nor to the companionship of such a father, is the eminence of John Marshall to be solely attributed. In addition to the native vigor of his faculties, much was owing to the circumstances amid which he grew up. In a thinly populated region of country, he had, necessarily, but little society, his mind was thrown upon itself, and his lonely meditations created and confirmed habits of thought and reflection. The wild and mountainous scenery, too, that surrounded him, could not fail to affect a mind like his; reverent, and impressible to the varied charms of nature. The simple style of living, too, then common in that part of Virginia, the easy and friendly footing on which all social intercourse was conducted, were not lost on Marshall. Both were afterwards perceptible in his characteristic simplicity, and ready sympathy with humanity, in all its relations, without regard to rank or fortune, which, with his other qualities, so endeared him to his countrymen. 'He ever recurred with fondness to that primitive mode of life, when he partook, with a keen relish, balm tea and mush, and when the females used thorns for pins.'[1] He was fond of athletic exercises, and, naturally enough in a region abounding in game, of field sports also. These tastes and habits gave him a firm, robust constitution, and, even in his years, he exhibited the vigor and freshness of youth.

Having selected the law as his future profession, he began the study of it about the time he was entering on the eighteenth year of his age. He had not, however, made much progress in the perusal of Blackstone's Commentaries, before the threatening aspect of public affairs withdrew and concentrated his energies upon very different pursuits. In the next chapter, we shall view the future Chief Justice as a soldier.

---

[1] Howe's Virginia Historical Collections, page 263.

CHAPTER III.

1775–1780.

HIS MILITARY SERVICES.

Times of Revolution are necessarily times of great intellectual activity. All minds are alert, anxious, and inquiring. Whether the cause of Revolution be political or religious, discussion and investigation are presupposed. Mankind are not apt to change existing establishments without very thorough conviction of the necessity of such change. And that conviction is not wrought in a day. Fixed habits, inherited attachments, interest in the past, and hopes in the future, all plead against innovation. When, therefore, all the various considerations that urge men to submit to the present order of things are overpowered by the weight of opposing considerations, it may readily be supposed that, in the conflict that has taken place, the minds of men have been thoroughly aroused, abstracted from ordinary pursuits, and fixed on objects of a larger and more comprehensive character.

It was in the midst of the fermentation and excitement immediately preceding actual hostilities between Great Britain and her American colonies, that John Marshall received his first lessons in practical politics. His father was a staunch Whig, who believed that the pretensions of Great Britain, if submitted to, would result in the political enslavement of himself and posterity. The son could hardly fail to catch the tone and partake the sentiments of his father. But, whatever his natural bias, yet not blindly, nor with unreasoning facility, did he espouse the prevailing opinions. He investigated the grounds of the controversy. The various political essays of the day he read attentively. Full of youthful ardor, and looking forward to the time when discussion would give way to arms, he enrolled himself in a company of volunteers, in order to learn something of the rudiments of military science. In the spring of 1775 he was appointed Lieutenant in a militia company of the neighborhood, and, soon after, first Lieutenant in a company of minute-men. In this latter capacity, as we shall presently see, he was called into active service.

On the 20th of April, Lord Dunmore, in consequence of the hostile attitude of the Virginians, had the powder in the magazine at Williamsburg removed on board a man-of-war. This proceeding produced a feeling of great exasperation throughout Virginia, and was increased by the threat of Dunmore that he would fire Williamsburg, and proclaim freedom to the slaves, if injury should befall himself, or the officers who had acted in the execution of his orders. It was in the midst of the prevailing excitement, when the whole body of the people were fully aroused, that news arrived of the action at Lexington. This startling intelligence increased the ferment. An appeal to arms and the God of Hosts seemed now to be inevitable. It is at this critical moment that we have our first view of John Marshall. It is now that we get our first distinct impression of his youthful appearance. His company had assembled, according to previous notice, about ten miles from his father's residence. A kinsman and cotemporary, who was present at their place of meeting, has thus described him as he then and there appeared: —

'It was in May, 1775. He was then a youth of nineteen. The muster-field was some twenty miles distant from the Court-house, and in a section of country peopled by tillers of the earth. Rumors of the occurrences near Boston had circulated with the effect of alarm and agitation, but without the means of ascertaining the truth, for not a newspaper was printed nearer than Williamsburg, nor was one taken within the bounds of the militia company, though large. The Captain had called the company together, and was expected to attend, but did not. John Marshall had been appointed Lieutenant to it. His father had formerly commanded it. Soon after Lieutenant Marshall's appearance on the ground, those who knew him clustered about him to greet him, others from curiosity and to hear the news.

'He proceeded to inform the company that the Captain would not be there, and that he had been appointed Lieutenant instead of a better; that he had come to meet them as fellow-soldiers, who were likely to be called on to defend their country, and their own rights and liberties, invaded by the British; that there had been a battle at Lexington, in Massachusetts, between the British and Americans, in which the Americans were victorious, but that more fighting was expected; that soldiers were called for, and that it was time to brighten their fire-arms, and learn to use them in the field; and that, if they would fall into a single line, he would show them the new manual exercise, for which purpose he had brought his gun,—bringing it up to his shoulder. The sergeants put the men in line, and their fugleman presented himself in front to the right.

'His figure,' says his venerable kinsman, 'I have now before me. He was about six feet high, straight and rather slender, of dark complexion, showing little if any rosy red, yet good health, the outline of the face nearly a circle, and within that, eyes dark to blackness, strong and penetrating, beaming with intelligence and good nature; an upright forehead, rather low, was terminated in a horizontal line by a mass of raven-black hair of unusual thickness and strength; the features of the face were in harmony with this outline, and the temples fully developed. The result of this combination was interesting and very agreeable. The body and limbs indicated agility, rather than strength, in which, however, he was by no means deficient. He wore a purple or pale blue hunting shirt, and trowsers of the same material, fringed with white. A round black hat, mounted with the buck's-tail for a cockade, crowned the figure and the man. He went through the manual exercise by word and motion, deliberately pronounced and performed, in the presence of the company, before he required the men to imitate him; and then proceeded to exercise them, with the most perfect temper. Never did man possess a temper more happy, or, if otherwise, more subdued or better disciplined.

'After a few lessons, the company were dismissed, and informed that, if they wished to hear more about the war, and would form a circle around him, he would tell them what he understood about it. The circle was formed, and he addressed the company for something like an hour. I remember, for I was near him, that he spoke, at the close of his speech, of the minute battalion, about to be raised, and said he was going into it, and expected to be joined by many of his hearers. He then challenged an acquaintance to a game of quoits, and they closed the day with foot-races and other athletic exercises, at which there was no betting. He had walked ten miles to the muster-field, and returned the same distance on foot to his father's house at Oak Hill, where he arrived a little after sunset.'[1]

Thus and so was John Marshall, in the freshness of youth, and thus, in the main, did he continue through life. The same simplicity, naturalness, good nature, happy temperament, open, manly, and sincere disposition, were at all times remarked, and secured to him the unaffected love of his countrymen. They could admire the exhibition of his pre-eminent talents, but qualities like these were needed to attract and fix the affection of their hearts.

The occurrences to the northward, and the hostile attitude of parties at home, the liability and expectation of being called into immediate service, induced the volunteers of Culpepper, Orange, and Fauquier Counties, to constitute themselves a regiment of minute men. This was, doubtless, the organization to which young Marshall referred, in his address to the militia, as about to be formed. They were the first minute men raised in Virginia, and numbered about three hundred and fifty men. Lawrence Taliaferro was chosen their Colonel, Edward Stevens, Lieutenant-Colonel, and Thomas Marshall, the father of the Chief Justice, Major. The future Chief Justice himself received the appointment of first Lieutenant in one of the companies of this regiment.

---

[1] Eulogy on John Marshall by Horace Binney, pp. 22–24.

These were the citizen soldiery, who, John Randolph said in the Senate of the United States, in one of his discursive speeches, 'were raised in a minute, armed in a minute, marched in a minute, fought in a minute, and vanquished in a minute.' Their appearance was calculated to strike terror into the hearts of an enemy. They were dressed in green hunting-shirts, 'home-spun, home-woven, and home-made,' with the words, '*Liberty or Death*,' in large white letters, on their bosoms. 'They wore in their hats buck-tails, and in their belts, tomahawks and scalping-knives. Their savage, warlike appearance, excited the terror of the inhabitants as they marched through the country to Williamsburg.'[1] Lord Dunmore told his troops before the action at the Great Bridge, which we shall presently describe, that if they fell into the hands of the *shirt-men*, they would be scalped; an apprehension, it is said, which induced several of them to prefer death to captivity. To the honor of the *shirt-men*, however, it should be observed, that they treated the British prisoners with great kindness — a kindness which was felt and gratefully acknowledged.

Early in June, Lord Dunmore, apprehensive of his personal safety, fled on board a man-of-war. With the British shipping, off the coast of Virginia, at his command, he possessed the means of annoying the Virginians, without being able to strike any very effective blow. Through the summer and autumn of 1775, both parties were kept upon the alert, but nothing of a very serious character occurred. At length, on the 7th of November, Dunmore proclaimed martial law, denounced as traitors all who were capable of bearing arms and did not resort to His Majesty's standard,

[1] Howe's Virginia Historical Collections, p. 238.

and offered freedom to all slaves 'appertaining to rebels' who would join His Majesty's troops. He set up his standard in Norfolk and Princess Anne, prescribed an oath of allegiance, and, from among the Loyalists, received a considerable accession to his force.

At Suffolk, eighteen miles south-west of Norfolk, the Virginians had collected provisions for their troops. To capture these provisions was an object of importance to Lord Dunmore. To prevent it, was an object of equal importance to the Virginians. The Provisional Government had kept a steady eye on his lordship's movements, and clearly perceived the danger of permitting him to retain a foothold at Norfolk. They despatched Colonel Woodford, with a detachment of minute men, including Marshall's company, to protect the provisions at Suffolk, and relieve Norfolk from the presence of the enemy. The engagement which we are now to relate, was the result.

About twelve miles from Norfolk, on the only practicable road to Suffolk, was the Great Bridge, as it was termed, and built over the southern branch of Elizabeth River. Here Dunmore, apprised of Woodford's movements, erected a stockade fort, and supplied it with a numerous artillery. The position was a strong one, surrounded on all sides by water and marshes, and only accessible by a long dike. This was commanded by his cannon, as well as the bridge and the causeway on the other side, over which the Americans must pass. The Governor's troops, however, were not equal to his intrenchments. They consisted of two hundred regulars, a corps of Norfolk Loyalists, and 'a shapeless mass of varlets of every color.' [1]

---

[1] Botta.

When Woodford arrived at the bridge, he threw up a breastwork at the extremity of the causeway on his side. Neither party seemed disposed to begin the attack. Several days passed, without any serious movement on either side. In numbers and character, the Virginians were much superior to the enemy. True, for the most part, they were unused to warfare, but being chiefly young men, they were full of enthusiasm, and ready for action. It was here and now, that Lieutenant Marshall had his first experience of war. In the action which ensued, he is said to have borne an honorable part.

The enemy were induced to begin the attack by stratagem. A servant of Major Marshall's, after being instructed in the part he was to play, deserted to the enemy, and reported that there were not at the bridge more than three hundred *shirt-men*. This tale Lord Dunmore believed, and accordingly despatched his regular troops, together with about three hundred blacks and Loyalists, to drive the Virginians from their position. The attack was made on the 9th of December. Captain Fordyce, a brave and accomplished officer, led the attacking party. As they advanced along the causeway to storm the breastwork, they were exposed to the deadly fire of the American riflemen. The effect was overwhelming. The action did not last more than twenty or thirty minutes; but the enemy were totally routed. Lord Dunmore abandoned his intrenchments, spiked his cannon, and again fled to his ships.

On the fourteenth, the Americans entered Norfolk. Here Marshall remained with his corps, until the town was bombarded and burned by the British shipping, on the 1st of January following.

In July, 1776, he was appointed first Lieutenant in

the eleventh Virginia regiment, and, in the following winter, joined the army in camp at Morristown. That army, notwithstanding the successes at Trenton and Princeton, was in the most wretched condition, both as to numbers and *materiel.* Washington's letter to the Governor and Council of Connecticut, describing the actual state of affairs, is said to have drawn tears from those who heard it read.[1] 'Nothing but a good face and false appearances,' he subsequently wrote, 'have enabled us hitherto to deceive the enemy respecting our strength.'[2]

It was the fortune of young Marshall to follow the standard of his country in the gloomiest period of the war; a period, when patient endurance of suffering was the highest quality the soldier could display. In May, when the campaign of 1777 was about opening, he received the appointment of Captain. In this subordinate post he was not in a position to attract the eye of the historian, and, consequently, we are without any detailed account of his actual conduct in the field. Suffice it to say, therefore, that he was engaged in the action at Iron Hill, which preluded the Battle of Brandywine, when the corps to which he was attached did memorable service. Indeed, the Virginia troops behaved, in this battle, with the greatest gallantry, and merited universal praise. But the victory, or the results of victory, remained with the British. In the course of a few days, General Howe made his triumphal entry into Philadelphia.[3]

Then followed the Battle of Germantown,[4] a battle which would have resulted in favor of the Americans, had not victory been snatched from their grasp, in

---

[1] Gordon, vol. ii., p. 170.

[2] Ibid., p. 198.

[3] September 26th, 1777.

[4] October 3d, 1777.

the manner thus described by one of the American Generals. 'At Germantown,' he says, 'fortune smiled on our arms for hours. The enemy were broke, dispersed, and flying on all quarters; we were in possession of their whole encampment, together with their artillery park, &c. A *wind-mill* attack was made on a house into which six light companies had thrown themselves to avoid our bayonets; this gave time to the enemy to rally; our troops were deceived by this attack; taking it for something formidable, they fell back to assist in what they deemed a serious matter. The enemy finding themselves no further pursued, and believing it to be a retreat, followed. Confusion ensued, and we ran away from the arms of victory ready to receive us.' [1]

Marshall was with the column that halted to attack Chew's House — an attack to which the ill success of the day is undoubtedly attributable. No further serious engagement took place between the two armies during this campaign; and on the 19th of December, Washington, with his exhausted troops, went into winter quarters at Valley Forge. The cold was extreme; yet his men were without clothes to cover their nakedness, without blankets to lie on, and without shoes, so that their marches could be traced by the blood from their feet. They were as often without provisions as with. But these men, taking up their winter quarters within a day's march of the enemy, without a house or hut to cover them, till they could be built, pinched by hunger, and stiffened by cold, submitted to hardships and privations like these without a murmur. Well might Washington declare without arrogance, or the smallest deviation from truth, 'that no history, now extant,

[1] Gordon, vol. ii., p. 235.

can furnish an instance of an army's suffering such uncommon hardships as ours has done, and bearing them with the same patience and fortitude.'[1]

Marshall's mess-mates, during this memorable winter, were Lieutenant Robert Porterfield, Captain Charles Porterfield, Captain Johnson, and Lieutenant Philip Slaughter. The latter has described the sufferings they endured from want of food and clothing. 'Most of the officers gave to their almost naked soldiers nearly the whole of their clothing, reserving only that they themselves had on. Slaughter was reduced to a single shirt. While this was being washed, he wrapped himself in a blanket. From the breast of his only shirt he had wrist-bands and a collar made, to complete his uniform for parade. Many of his brother officers were still worse off, having no under garment at all; and not one soldier in five had a blanket. They all lived in rude huts, and the snow was knee-deep the whole winter. Washington daily invited the officers, in rotation, to dine with him at his private table; but, for want of decent clothing, few were enabled to attend. Slaughter being so much better provided, frequently went in place of others, that, as he said, "his regiment might be represented." While in this starving condition, the country people brought food to the camp. Often the Dutch women were seen riding in, sitting on bags on their horses' backs, holding two or three bushels each of apple pies, baked sufficiently hard to be thrown across the room without breaking. These were purchased eagerly, eaten with avidity, and considered a great luxury.'

Slaughter says, 'Marshall was the best-tempered man he ever knew. During their sufferings at Valley

[1] Washington's Writings, vol. v., pp. 321, 329.

Forge, nothing discouraged, nothing disturbed him; if he had only bread to eat, it was just as well; if only meat, it made no difference. If any of the officers murmured at their deprivations, he would shame them by good-natured raillery, or encourage them by his own exuberance of spirits. He was an excellent companion; and idolized by the soldiers, and his brother officers, whose gloomy hours were enlivened by his inexhaustible fund of anecdote.'[1]

A further testimony, as to the estimation in which he was held by his brother officers, is found in the following extract. 'When the writer of this article first saw him,' says a cotemporary, 'he held the commission of Captain in that regiment.[2] It was in the trying, severe winter of 1777–8, a few months after the disastrous battles of Brandywine and Germantown had tested his firmness, hardihood, and heroism. The spot where we acquired our earliest information of him, was the famous hutted encampment at Valley Forge, about thirty miles from Philadelphia. By his appearance then, we supposed him about twenty-two or twenty-three years of age. Even so early in life, we recollect that he appeared to us *primus inter pares*, for, amidst the many commissioned officers, he was discriminated for superior intelligence. Our informant, Colonel Ball, of another regiment in the same line, represented him as a young man, not only brave, but signally intelligent. Indeed, all those who intimately knew him, affirmed that his capacity was held in such estimation by many of his brother officers, that, in many disputes of a certain description, he was constantly chosen arbiter; and that officers, irritated by

---

[1] Howe's Virginia Historical Collections, pp. 239, 266.

[2] Eleventh Virginia Regiment.

differences, or animated by debate, often submitted the contested points to his judgment, which, being in writing, and accompanied, as it commonly was, by sound reasons in support of his decision, obtained general acquiescence.'[1]

He was often employed, during this period of his military life, as Deputy Judge Advocate. The performance of the duties of this post extended his acquaintance among the officers of the army. It was now that he became acquainted with Colonel Hamilton, who was acting as aid-de-camp of the Commander-in-chief. 'Of Hamilton,' says Judge Story, 'he always spoke in the most unreserved manner, as a soldier and statesman of consummate ability; and, in point of comprehensiveness of mind, purity of patriotism, and soundness of principles, as among the first that had ever graced the councils of any nation. His services to the American Republic he deemed to have been of inestimable value, and such as had eminently conduced to its stability, its prosperity, and its true glory.'[2] But, notwithstanding the deep respect he always entertained for Hamilton, 'whose unreserved friendship, at a subsequent period of his life, he familiarly enjoyed,' we shall hereafter see that, when the man by whose hand he had fallen, was brought before him on a charge of treason, he held the scales of justice with so nice a poise, he held up before the prisoner the shield of the law with so firm a hand, that if it did not excite the surprise, at least, provoked the indignation of the Chief Executive Magistrate, who pressed the conviction of Burr with a zeal that seemingly had its root in vindictiveness.

---

[1] North American Review for January, 1828, p. 8.

[2] Story's Discourse on the Life, &c., of John Marshall, p. 16

The possession of Philadelphia promised so little advantage to the Royal forces, and, indeed, exposed them to such danger, that the British Ministry sent out orders, in the spring of 1778, for its speedy evacuation. These orders reached Sir Henry Clinton, who had superseded Sir William Howe, early in June. He immediately addressed himself to the task of executing them. In the night of the 18th, the city was evacuated. The American army was immediately put in motion, with the view to harass and impede the progress of the enemy.

Marshall was in the Battle of Monmouth, which succeeded. He remained with the army through the campaign, as well as during the following winter. In the campaign of 1779, it was his fortune to be connected with or engaged in two of the most brilliant actions that distinguished it. He was with Wayne at the assault of Stony Point, on the night of the 16th of June, and with the detachment to cover the retreat of Major Lee, after his surprise of the enemy's post at Powle's Hook, on the 19th of July; an enterprise which threw a lustre upon the American arms. He continued with the army until the close of the year, when a part of the Virginia line was sent to South Carolina, to co-operate in the defence of that State. It so happened, that he was attached to the other part, whose term of enlistment now expired. Being thus without command, he, with other supernumeraries, was directed to return home, in order to take charge of such men as the State might raise for them.

No further opportunity for active military service occurred, until the arrival in Virginia of the British army under General Leslie, in October, 1780. Captain Marshall now joined the small force under Baron Steuben, who had been left by General Greene, (while on his way to assume the command of the Southern army,) to direct the defence of the State. General Leslie, however, finding that Lord Cornwallis could not effect a junction with him, an object which was essential to the success of the plan for the reduction of Virginia, finally sailed for Charleston.

Late in December, the State was again invaded by Arnold. Marshall joined the forces collected to oppose him, and continued in service until Arnold retired to Portsmouth, in the latter part of the following January. As there was still a redundancy of officers in the Virginia line, he now resigned his commission; and for the future we shall view him in a different walk of life.

CHAPTER IV.

HIS PRACTICE AT THE BAR.

1781 — 1799.

During the season of inaction following his return to Virginia, in the winter of 1779–80, Marshall resumed the study of the law. He attended, at William and Mary's College, a course of law lectures by Mr. Wythe, better known afterwards as Chancellor Wythe, and lectures upon natural philosophy by Mr. Madison, then President of the College, and subsequently Bishop of Virginia. He was connected with the institution until the summer vacation of 1780, and soon after was admitted to the Bar. But, in the tumult of war, the courts of law were suspended in Virginia, and not reopened until after the capture of Cornwallis, in October, 1781. From the termination of Arnold's invasion, when he resigned his commission, until he began his practice upon the re-opening of the Courts, Marshall devoted himself, with unremitting attention, to the study of his future profession.

It was at this period of his life, either in the summer of 1780 or 1781, that he undertook a journey to Philadelphia on foot, in order to be inoculated for the small-pox. He walked at the rate of thirty-five miles a day. On his arrival, such was his shabby appearance, that he was refused admission into one of the hotels; his long beard, and worn-out garments, probably suggesting the idea that his purse was not adequate to his entertainment.[1] But to the man who had undergone the hardships of Morristown and Valley Forge, who had been reduced almost to nakedness, any garb that served the purpose of a covering, must have seemed sufficient for any occasion. In truth, he was at all times careless of his dress, particularly in early life; and once, as we shall presently relate, lost a generous fee in consequence.

He began his professional career in Fauquier, his native county; but, in the course of two years, removed to Richmond, where he continued to reside until his death. His stock of legal knowledge, as we may infer from the short time he had devoted to its acquisition, was not very extensive; but it was said of the Virginians, more than a hundred and fifty years ago, that, being naturally of good parts, they neither require nor admire as much learning as they do in Britain.[2] At any rate, such was the felicity of Marshall's understanding, that on a slender foundation of legal science he soon raised himself to the highest reputation in his profession. He attributed his early success at the Bar to the friendship of his old com-

---

[1] Southern Literary Messenger, vol. ii., p. 183.

[2] 'The Present State of Virginia; by Hugh Jones, A.M., Chaplain to the Honorable Assembly, and lately Minister of Jamestown, in Virginia.' The Reverend author seems to have been charmed with his residence among the Virginians, and thus asserts their superiority over all the other colonists: — 'If New England,' he says, 'be called a receptacle of Dissenters, and an Amsterdam of religion, Pennsylvania a nursery of Quakers, Maryland the retirement of Roman Catholics, North Carolina the refuge of runaways, and South Carolina the delight of Buccaneers and Pyrates, Virginia may be justly esteemed the happy retreat of true Britons, and true churchmen for the most part; neither soaring too high, nor dropping too low, consequently should merit the greater esteem and encouragement.'

panions in arms. 'They knew,' he would say, 'that I felt their wrongs, and sympathized in their sufferings, and had partaken of their labors, and that I vindicated their claims upon their country with a warm and constant earnestness.'[1] We have seen how strong was their attachment to him. 'I myself,' says Judge Story, 'have often heard him spoken of by some of these veterans in terms of the warmest praise. In an especial manner the Revolutionary officers of the Virginia line (now "few and faint, but fearless still") appeared almost to idolize him, as an old friend and companion in arms, enjoying their unqualified confidence.'[2]

They knew his abilities, his integrity, and loved him for the goodness of his heart. Strangers, on the contrary, judging from external appearances, might not so readily have given him credit for qualities that would insure success at the Bar. For, though easy, frank, friendly, and cordial in his manners, and social in his habits, he was yet negligent in his dress, not very studious, and with nothing in his exterior to attract clients. The following anecdote is characteristic of his rustic appearance, at a time when his comprehension and grasp of mind had already attracted the attention of the Bench and Bar, and he was advancing with sure steps to the head of his profession. He 'was one morning strolling through the streets of Richmond, attired in a plain linen roundabout and shorts, with his hat under his arm, from which he was eating cherries, when he stopped in the porch of the Eagle hotel, indulged in some little pleasantry with the landlord, and then passed on. Mr. P., an elderly

---

[1] New York Review, vol. iii., p. 333.

[2] Discourse upon the Life, &c., of John Marshall, p. 16.

gentleman from the country, then present, who had a case coming on before the Court of Appeals, was referred by the landlord to Marshall, as the best advocate for him to employ; but the careless, languid air of the young lawyer had so prejudiced Mr. P., that he refused to engage him. On entering Court, Mr. P. was a second time referred by the Clerk of the Court, and a second time he declined. At this moment entered Mr. V., a venerable-looking legal gentleman, in a powdered wig and black coat, whose dignified appearance produced such an impression on Mr. P. that he at once engaged him. In the first case which came on, Marshall and Mr. V. each addressed the Court. The vast inferiority of his advocate was so apparent, that, at the close of the case, Mr. P. introduced himself to young Marshall, frankly stated the prejudice which had caused him, in opposition to advice, to employ Mr. V.; that he extremely regretted his error, but knew not how to remedy it. He had come into the city with one hundred dollars, as his lawyer's fee, which he had paid, and had but five left, which, if Marshall chose, he would cheerfully give him, for assisting in the case. Marshall, pleased with the incident, accepted the offer, not, however, without passing a sly joke at the *omnipotence* of a powdered wig and black coat.'[1]

Marshall's rise at the Bar was rapid. Once placed in the line of employment, his extraordinary talents could hardly fail to make the same impression on whoever witnessed their display, as on Mr. P.. For, without possessing scarcely a single attribute that we naturally ascribe to the orator, without beauty of style, melody of voice, grace of person, or charm of manner, he, nevertheless, was as distinguished as an advocate,

---

[1] Howe's Virginia Historical Collections, p. 266.

as he afterwards became as a judge. The qualities that gave him such pre-eminence at the Bar are thus delineated by the graceful pen of Mr. Wirt: —

'This extraordinary man,' says Mr. Wirt, 'without the aid of fancy, without the advantages of person, voice, attitude, gesture, or any of the ornaments of an orator, deserves to be considered as one of the most eloquent men in the world; if eloquence may be said to consist in the power of seizing the attention with irresistible force, and never permitting it to elude the grasp, until the hearer has received the conviction which the speaker intends. His voice is dry and hard; his attitude, in his most effective orations, was often extremely awkward; while all his gesture proceeded from his right arm, and consisted merely in a perpendicular swing of it, from about the elevation of his head to the bar, behind which he was accustomed to stand. As to fancy, if she hold a seat in his mind at all, his gigantic genius tramples with disdain on all her flower-decked plats and blooming parterres. How then, you will ask, how is it possible, that such a man can hold the attention of an audience enchained through a speech of even ordinary length? I will tell you. He possesses one original, and almost supernatural faculty; the faculty of developing a subject by a single glance of his mind, and detecting at once the very point on which every controversy depends. No matter what the question; though ten times more knotty than "the gnarled oak," the lightning of heaven is not more rapid, or more resistless, than his astonishing penetration. Nor does the exercise of it seem to cost him an effort. On the contrary, it is as easy as vision. I am persuaded, that his eyes do not fly over a landscape, and take in its various objects with more promptitude and facility, than his mind embraces and analyzes the most complex subject.

'Possessing, while at the Bar, this intellectual elevation, which enabled him to look down and comprehend the whole ground at once, he determined immediately, and without difficulty, on which side the question might be most advantageously approached and assailed. In a bad cause, his art consisted in laying his premises so remotely from the point directly in debate, or else in terms so general and so specious, that the hearer, seeing no consequence which could be drawn from them, was just as willing to admit them as not; but, his premises once admitted, the demonstration, however distant, followed as certainly, as cogently, as inevitably, as any demonstration in Euclid. All his eloquence consists in the apparently deep self-conviction, and emphatic earnestness of his manner; the correspondent simplicity and energy of his style; the close and logical connection of his thoughts; and the easy gradations by which he opens his lights on the attentive minds of his hearers. The audience are never permitted to pause for a moment. There is no stopping to weave garlands of flowers, to hang in festoons around a favorite argument. On the contrary, every sentence is progressive; every idea sheds new light on the subject; the listener is kept perpetually in that sweetly pleasurable vibration, with which the mind of man always receives new truths; the dawn advances with easy but unremitting pace; the subject opens gradually on the view; until, rising, in high relief, in all its native colors and proportions, the argument is consummated, by the conviction of the delighted hearer.'[1]

---

[1] The British Spy, pp. 178–181.

If Marshall, as he first appeared at the Bar, did not bear a finished resemblance to the picture thus sketched by Mr. Wirt nearly a quarter of a century after, he certainly possessed the more striking outlines of it. Strength, cogency of reasoning, was the characteristic excellence of all his intellectual displays. His maxim seems always to have been, 'aim exclusively at strength.' Of eloquence, in the usual sense, he evidently was not emulous, and, perhaps, not capable. His object was to convince, and he sought to do this in the most direct and simple manner. It was always remarkable of him, says Wirt, 'that he almost invariably seized one strong point only, the pivot of the controversy; this point he would enforce with all his powers, never permitting his own mind to waver, nor obscuring those of his hearers by a cloud of inferior, unimportant considerations.'[1] This 'convincing eloquence,' which he so pre-eminently possessed, 'is infinitely more serviceable to its possessor than the most florid harangue, or the most pathetic tones that can be imagined; and the man who is thoroughly convinced himself, who understands his subject, and the language he speaks in, will be more apt to silence opposition, than he who studies the force of his periods, and fills our ears with sounds, while our minds are destitute of conviction.'[2]

The period succeeding the Revolutionary War witnessed a great accession of business in the Courts. Outstanding debts, unfulfilled contracts, together with the mutations property had undergone amid the conflicts of a long war, were fruitful sources of litigation. 'Does not every gentleman here know' demanded Marshall in the Virginia Convention of 1788, when

---

[1] The British Spy, p. 211.

[2] The Bee, No. VI.

maintaining the necessity of a Federal Judiciary, 'that the causes in our Courts are more numerous than they can decide, according to their present construction? Look at the dockets. You will find them crowded with suits, which the life of man will not see determined. If some of these suits be carried to other Courts, will it be wrong? They will still have business enough.'

It was a period not only of profitable employment to the Bar, but a period calculated to stimulate the highest energies of their minds. The fair fabric of American jurisprudence was yet unreared. The law was in an unsettled state. Questions of novel character occupied the attention of the Courts; questions to be settled, not by the weight of authority, but by the light of reason. It was in the investigation and argument of causes like these, where the advocate was neither aided nor impeded by precedents; where he was compelled to rely on the unassisted powers of his own mind; to support his own thoughts, rather than quote the thoughts of others, that the great abilities of Marshall found an adequate theatre for their employment and display.

When the Federal Judiciary was established, the sphere of his practice was enlarged. Several of the causes in which he was engaged possessed great public interest, and attracted universal attention. The fame of his arguments spread through the Union. Ware *versus* Hylton, familiarly known as the British debt case, was one of the causes in which he particularly distinguished himself. It came on for trial at the Circuit Court of the United States at Richmond, in 1793; Chief Justice Jay, Judge Iredell, and Griffin, the Judge of the District Court, holding the term. Patrick Henry, Marshall, Alexander Campbell, and James

Innis, appeared for the American debtors; and Andrew Ronald, John Wickham, 'the eloquent, the witty, and the graceful," and Starke, and Baker, for the English creditors.

The question was, whether the treaty of peace, which provided that creditors on either side should meet with no *lawful impediment* to the recovery of the full value of all *bona fide* debts theretofore contracted, revived debts which had been sequestered during the war by an act of the Virginia Legislature.

The eminence of the counsel, as well as the extensive interests to be affected by the decision of the Court, brought together an eager and expectant audience. The Countess of Huntington, then in this country, was present during the trial, and remarked, after hearing the several speakers, 'that if every one of them had spoken in Westminster Hall, they would have been honored with a peerage.'[1] 'The cause,' said Judge Iredell, 'has been spoken to, at the Bar, with a degree of ability equal to any occasion. However painfully I may at any time reflect on the inadequacy of my own talents, I shall, as long as I live, remember with pleasure and respect the arguments which I have heard in this case. They have discovered an ingenuity, a depth of investigation, and a power of reasoning fully equal to any thing I have ever witnessed, and some of them have been adorned with a splendor of eloquence surpassing what I have ever felt before. Fatigue has given way under its influence, and the heart has been warmed, while the understanding has been instructed.'[2]

Patrick Henry shone, on this occasion, with unsur-

---

[1] Howe's Virginia Historical Collections, p. 221.

[2] Dallas' Reports, vol. iii., p. 257.

passed splendor. His vivid feelings, that irresistible charm of his eloquence, were fully aroused, and enlisted in the cause. He made unwonted preparation for the trial; shutting himself up in his office for three days, during which time he did not see even his family; his food being handed by a servant through the office-door.[1] His argument occupied the attention of the Court during three days. He had a diamond ring on his finger, and, while he was speaking, the Countess of Huntington exclaimed to Judge Iredell, who had never before heard him, 'The diamond is *blazing!*' 'Gracious God!' replied he, 'he is an orator indeed.' In this cause he injured his voice so that it never recovered its original power.[2]

We have no abstract of Marshall's argument on this occasion, and shall not attempt to supply its place by resorting to conjecture. Its character, however, may be surmised by his subsequent argument before the Supreme Court of the United States, whither the cause was carried by writ of error. His colleague in the trial before the latter tribunal was Alexander Campbell. It was, doubtless, to the arguments on this occasion to which Wirt refers in the following extract of a letter to his friend Gilmer. He speaks of them, however, as having been made in the cause which turned on the constitutionality of the carriage tax, a cause, indeed, which was heard at the same term of the Court; but Marshall was not one of the counsel.

'From what I have heard of Campbell,' says Wirt, 'I believe that, for mere eloquence, his equal has never been seen in the United States. He and the

[1] Virginia Historical Collections, *supra*.

[2] Ibid. See also Wirt's Patrick Henry, for abstract of his argument

Chief Justice went to Philadelphia to argue a cause which turned on the constitutionality of the carriage tax. It was somewhere about 1795 or 1796. They were opposed by Hamilton, Lewis, and others. Campbell played off his Appollonian airs; but they were lost. Marshall spoke, as he always does, to the judgment merely, and for the simple purpose of convincing. Marshall was justly pronounced one of the greatest men of the country. He was followed by crowds, looked upon, and courted with every evidence of admiration and respect for the great powers of his mind. Campbell was neglected and slighted, and came home in disgust. Marshall's maxim seems always to have been, "aim exclusively at strength;" and from his eminent success, I say, if I had my life to go over again, I would practice on his maxim with the most rigorous severity, until the character of my mind was established.'[1]

Marshall's argument, as preserved in the report of the case, will now claim our attention: —

'The case resolves itself,' said he, 'into two general propositions. First, That the Act of Assembly of Virginia is a bar to the recovery of the debt, independent of the treaty. Secondly, That the treaty does not remove the bar.

'That the Act of Assembly of Virginia is a bar to the recovery of the debt, introduces two subjects for consideration: —

'First, Whether the Legislature had power to extinguish the debt? Secondly, Whether the Legislature had exercised that power?

---

[1] Kennedy's Wirt, vol. ii., p. 83.

'First. It has been conceded, that independent nations have, in general, the right of confiscation; and that Virginia, at the time of passing her law, was an independent nation. But, it is contended, that, from the peculiar circumstances of the war, the citizens of each of the contending nations having been members of the same government, the general right of confiscation did not apply, and ought not to be exercised. It is not, however, necessary for the defendant in error to show a parallel case in history; since it is incumbent on those who wish to impair the sovereignty of Virginia, to establish, on principle, or precedent, the justice of their exception. That State being engaged in a war, necessarily possessed the powers of war; and confiscation is one of those powers, weakening the party against whom it is employed, and strengthening the party that employs it. War, indeed, is a state of force; and no tribunal can decide between the belligerent powers. But did not Virginia hazard as much by the war, as if she had never been a member of the British empire? Did she not hazard more, from the very circumstance of its being a civil war? It will be allowed, that nations have equal powers; and that America, in her own tribunals at least, must, from the 4th of July, 1776, be considered as independent a nation as Great Britain. Then, what would have been the situation of American property, had Great Britain been triumphant in the conflict? Sequestration, confiscation, and proscription would have followed in the train of that event; and why should the confiscation of British property be deemed less just in the event of the American triumph? The rights of war clearly exist between members of the same empire, engaged in a civil war.

'But, suppose a suit had been brought, during the

war, by a British subject against an American citizen, it could not have been supported; and, if there was a power to suspend the recovery, there must have been a power to extinguish the debt. They are, indeed, portions of the same power, emanating from the same source. The legislative authority of any country can only be restrained by its own municipal constitution. This is a principle that springs from the very nature of society; and the judicial authority can have no right to question the validity of a law, unless such a jurisdiction is expressly given by the Constitution. It is not necessary to inquire how the judicial authority should act, if the Legislature were evidently to violate any of the laws of God; but property is the creature of civil society, and subject, in all respects, to the disposition and control of civil institutions. . . . .

'But it is now to be considered, whether, if the Legislature of Virginia had the power of confiscation, they have exercised it? The third section of the Act of Assembly discharges the debtor; and, on the plain import of the term, it may be asked, if he is discharged, how can he remain charged? The expression is, he shall be discharged from the debt; and yet, it is contended he shall remain liable to the debt. Suppose the law had said, that the debtor should be discharged from the Commonwealth, but not from his creditor, would not the Legislature have betrayed the extremest folly in such a proposition? and what man in his senses would have paid a farthing into the treasury under such a law? Yet, in violation of the expressions of the Act, this is the construction which is now attempted.

'It is, likewise, contended, that the Act of Assembly does not amount to a confiscation of the debts paid into the treasury; and that the Legislature had no power, as between creditors and debtors, to make a substitution, or commutation, in the mode of payment. But, what is a confiscation? The substance, and not the form, is to be regarded. The State had a right either to make the confiscation absolute, or to modify it as she pleased. If she had ordered the debtor to pay the money into the treasury, to be applied to public uses, would it not have been, in the eye of reason, a perfect confiscation? She has thought proper, however, only to authorize the payment, to exonerate the debtor from his creditor, and to retain the money in the treasury, subject to her own discretion, as to its future appropriation. As far as the arrangement has been made, it is confiscatory in its nature, and must be binding on the parties; though, in the exercise of her discretion, the State might choose to restore the whole, or any part, of the money to the original creditor. Nor is it sufficient to say, that the payment was voluntary, in order to defeat the confiscation. A law is an expression of the public will; which, when expressed, is not the less obligatory, because it imposes no penalty. . . .

'Having thus, then, establised that, at the time of entering into the treaty of 1783, the defendant owed nothing to the plaintiff, it is next to be inquired, whether that treaty revived the debt in favor of the plaintiff, and removed the bar to a recovery, which the law of Virginia had interposed? The words of the fourth article of the treaty are, "that creditors on either side shall meet with no lawful impediment to the recovery of the full value, in sterling money, of all *bona fide* debts heretofore contracted." Now, it may be asked, who are creditors? There cannot be a creditor where there is not a debt; and British debts were extinguished by the act of confiscation. The articles, therefore, must be construed with reference to those creditors who had *bona fide* debts subsisting, in legal force, at the time of making the treaty; and the word recovery can have no effect to create a debt, where none previously existed. Without discussing the power of Congress to take away a vested right by treaty, the fair and rational construction of the instrument itself is sufficient for the defendant's cause. The words ought, surely, to be very plain, that shall work so evident a hardship, as to compel a man to pay a debt which he had before extinguished. The treaty itself does not point out any particular description of persons who were to be deemed debtors; and it must be expounded in relation to the existing state of things.

'It is not true, that the fourth article can have no meaning, unless it applies to cases like the present. For instance — there was a law of Virginia, which prohibited the recovery of British debts, that had not been paid into the treasury. These were *bona fide* subsisting debts; and the prohibition was a legal impediment to the recovery, which the treaty was intended to remove. So, likewise, in several other States, laws had been passed authorizing a discharge of British debts in paper money, or by a tender of property at a valuation, and the treaty was calculated to guard against such impediments to the recovery of the sterling value of those debts. It appears, therefore, that, at the time of making the treaty, the state of things was such, that Virginia had exercised her sovereign right of confiscation, and had actually received the money from the British debtors. If debts thus paid were within the scope of the fourth article, those who framed the article knew of the payment; and, upon every principle of equity and law, it ought to be presumed, that the recovery, which they contemplated, was intended against the receiving State, not against the paying debtor. Virginia possessing the right of compelling a payment for her own use, the payment to her, upon her requisition, ought to be considered as a payment to the attorney, or agent, of the British creditor. Nor is such a substitution a novelty in legal proceedings; a foreign attachment is founded upon the same principle. . . .

'This Act of Virginia must have been known to the American and British Commissioners; and, therefore, cannot be repealed without plain and explicit expressions directed to that object. Besides, the public faith ought to be preserved. The public faith was plighted by the Act of Virginia; and, as a revival of the debt in question would be a shameful violation of the faith of the State to her own citizens, the treaty should receive any possible interpretation to avoid so dishonorable and so pernicious a consequence. It is evident, that the power of the Government to take away a vested right, was questionable in the minds of the American Commissioners, since they would not exercise that power in restoring confiscated real estate; and confiscated debts, or other personal estate, must come within the same rule,' &c.

The abstract of an argument like this of Marshall's, must necessarily give the reader an imperfect idea of its power. Nevertheless, he cannot fail to be impressed with the vigor, rigorous analysis, and close reasoning that mark every sentence of it. We have seen that it elicited great admiration at the time of its delivery, and enlarged the circle of his reputation. His practice, for several years before his final withdrawal from the Bar, was more extensive than that of any other lawyer in Virginia. The Duke de Liancourt, who was in Richmond, in 1797, speaking of Edmund Randolph, the ex-Secretary of State, says that 'he has great practice, and stands, in that respect, nearly on a par with Mr. J. Marshall, the most esteemed and celebrated counsellor in this town. The profession of a lawyer is here, as in every other part of America, one of the most profitable. But, though the employment be here more constant than in Carolina, the practitioner's emoluments are very far from being equally considerable. Mr. Marshall does not, from his practice, derive above four or five thousand dollars *per annum*, and not even that sum every year.'[1]

'Mr. J. Marshall,' says the Duke, after a more familiar acquaintance with the public characters at the capital of Virginia, 'conspicuously eminent as a professor of the law, is, beyond all doubt, one of those who rank highest in the public opinion at Richmond. He is what is termed a Federalist, and perhaps, at times, somewhat warm in support of his opinions, but never exceeding the bounds of propriety, which a man of his goodness, and prudence, and knowledge, is incable of transgressing. He may be considered as a distinguished character in the United States. His political enemies allow him to possess great talents, but accuse him of ambition. I know not whether the charge be well or ill-grounded, or whether that ambition might ever be able to impel him to a dereliction of his principles — a conduct of which I am inclined to disbelieve the possibility on his part. He has already refused several employments under the General Government, preferring the income derived from his professional labors (which is more than sufficient

---

[1] Travels, vol. ii., p. 38.

for his moderate system of economy), together with a life of tranquil ease in the midst of his family, and in his native town.[1] Even by his friends he is taxed with some little propensity to indolence; but, even if this reproach were well-founded, he, nevertheless, displays great superiority in his profession when he applies his mind to business.'[2]

We shall see, in the following chapters, that Marshall never sought office; that, in most instances, he accepted it with reluctance, and always returned to his profession with renewed interest, and a determination to pursue it with undivided attention. His ambition, if that sentiment held any place in his mind at all, sought its gratification in the triumphs of the Bar. Though warmly and earnestly attached to the political principles of the Federal party, he seems to have had a repugnance to a political career. His nature was not sufficiently eager and aspiring to seek or covet its honors. When he engaged in the public service, it was, for the most part, for some special purpose, and on some special occasion. In truth, the insinuation that selfish ambition influenced either his sentiments or conduct finds no support in any act of his life.

'Even by his friends he is taxed with some little propensity to indolence,' says the Duke de Liancourt; and his friends, we suspect, were not unjust to him. In truth, he was something of a truant. But such were the vigor and comprehension of his mind, that he could better afford, than most men, to indulge a fondness for social, and even convivial enjoyment.

---

[1] This is a mistake; Marshall being a native of Fauquier County.

[2] Travels, vol. ii., p. 62.

It was hardly possible for a lawyer of Marshall's conceded abilities, and great personal popularity, to keep aloof from public life during the eventful period in which he lived. Having, therefore, seen what success crowned his exertions at the Bar, we shall now proceed to trace his various services to the public, at home and abroad.

CHAPTER V.

1782–1788.

MEMBER OF THE VIRGINIA LEGISLATURE.

THE political career of John Marshall is prominently distinguished for his devotion to the Union of the States, and a government competent to maintain it. He early perceived the inadequacy of the Confederation, and the absolute necessity of a more comprehensive and vigorous central authority. He belonged, from the outset, to the party who would strengthen the General Government, and enable it to execute the powers with which it might be invested, independently of the several States. Virginia was the State of his birth, and the home of his affections; but the *United* States constituted his country — a country dearer and more comprehensive than the local limits within which he was born. His attachment to the Union was formed early, and fostered by the circumstances that attended his outset in life.

'When I recollect,' thus he wrote long after to a friend, 'the wild and enthusiastic notions with which my political opinions of that day were tinctured, I am disposed to ascribe my devotion to the Union, and to a government competent to its preservation, at least, as much to casual circumstances as to judgment. I had grown up at a time when the love of the Union, and the resistance to the claims of Great Britain, were the inseparable inmates of the same bosom; when patriotism and a strong fellow-feeling with our suffering fellow-citizens of Boston were identical; when the maxim, "United we stand; divided we fall," was the maxim of every orthodox American. And I had imbibed these sentiments so thoroughly, that they constituted a part of my being. I carried them with me into the army, where I found myself associated with brave men from different States, who were risking life and everything valuable, in a common cause, believed by all to be most precious; and where I was in the habit of considering America as my country, and Congress as my government.'[1]

These sentiments were confirmed by the progress of events, and his experience in the Assembly of Virginia. He was elected a member of that body in the spring of 1782, and in the autumn a member of the Executive Council. He knew what hardships the army had endured; he had partaken their sufferings, and 'my immediate entrance into the State Legislature,' said he in the letter from which the preceding extract is taken, 'opened to my view the causes which had been chiefly instrumental in augmenting those sufferings; and the general tendency of State politics convinced me, that no safe and permanent remedy could be found, but in a more efficient and better organized General Government.'[2]

At this time, the Federal treasury was destitute of money, and the army without pay, provisions or clothing. The non-compliance of the States with the requisitions of Congress threatened the most disastrous con-

[1] Story's Discourse on the Life, &c., of John Marshall. [2] Ibid.

sequences. We have seen, in the Life of Rutledge, that that body sent a deputation to the Eastern and Southern States, to explain the condition of public affairs, and the danger to which the country was exposed by the delinquency of the several members of the Confederacy.[1] Rutledge and Clymer, who were deputed to visit the Southern States, were permitted to make a personal address to the Virginia Assembly.[2] Of this Assembly Marshall was a member; and a steady advocate of all measures that tended to strengthen the Federal authority, and enable it to perform its obligations to the army, and the public creditors. His vindications of the claims of the army upon the country were constant and earnest, and awakened their gratitude. But so feeble was the Confederacy, and so languid and exhausted the States, that he clearly perceived the impossibility of reviving the public spirit, and restoring the public credit, without the establishment of a more vigorous and comprehensive system of government. This was the leading idea of his scheme of politics.

On the 3d of January, 1783, he was married to Mary Willis Ambler, a daughter of Jacqueline Ambler, then Treasurer of Virginia. He had become attached to this lady before he left the army; an attachment which continued with unabated fervor to the end of his days. She died several years before him; but he cherished her memory with unaffected tenderness, and in his will described her as a sainted spirit that had fled from the sufferings of life.

About the time of his marriage, he fixed his residence in Richmond. Desirous of devoting himself more closely to his profession, he resigned his seat in

---

[1] Vol. i., p. 591. [2] On the 14th of June, 1782.

the Executive Council. But he was not permitted thus to withdraw from public life. His old friends, neighbors, and former constituents of Fauquier County, immediately after his resignation, namely, in the spring of 1784, again elected him a member of the Assembly. Three years later, Henrico, his adopted county, paid him the same tribute of respect.

At the time of this last election, the affairs of the United States were fast sinking into utter disorder and confusion. Reflecting minds beheld the progress of events with the most gloomy forebodings. They saw that immediate and effectual reform alone could arrest the downward tendency of things. To accomplish that object they now earnestly addressed themselves. Shall the arm of the Federal Government be strengthened; shall it be invested with larger and more effectual powers over the commerce, the money, the foreign and mutual relations of the States; shall it have a revenue independent of them, and authority to carry into effect its measures without their instrumentality? These were the questions that now awakened and agitated the public mind. Marshall's judgment, reflection, and experience, alike concurred in giving them an affirmative answer. But in all the States, and particularly in Virginia, there was a party who were actuated by an extreme jealousy of national sovereignty. Although it was notorious that the Articles of Confederation had proved totally inadequate to all the purposes of a government, they insisted that, with some slight modifications, they conferred on the central authority all the power with which it was either prudent or safe to invest it. Rather than give it more, they would risk a dissolution of the Union; believing that a consolidated government was more to be dreaded, than the possible separation of the States.[1]

Against notions like these, Marshall earnestly protested. He believed that the salvation of his country depended on the prevalence of more enlarged views, and more solid principles. In the Assembly, in popular meetings, he maintained the necessity of a more vigorous scheme of government, not only to preserve the Union, but to insure its benefits. The doctrines he now advocated formed the basis of his political creed through life. He adhered to them when they were in the ascendant, and after they had fallen into disfavor. From first to last, he was a Federalist.

'Among innumerable false, unmov'd,
Unshaken, unseduc'd, unterrified;
His loyalty he kept, his love, his zeal.'

He hailed the call of the Federal Convention as an auspicious event; and, without hesitation, vindicated the result of its labors.

---

[1] Judge Story has said that 'the question, whether the Union ought to be continued, or dissolved by a total separation of the States, was freely discussed,' in the halls of the Virginia Legislature; 'and either side of it was maintained, not only without reproach, but with an uncompromising fearlessness of consequences.' Discourse on Marshall, p. 25. In this the learned Judge is, probably, in error. There were in Virginia, as in every other State, enemies of the Union; but they were not to be found, we apprehend, among her public men. Many of these, indeed, protested against conferring on the General Government what they considered dangerous powers; but they professed great attachment to the Union of the States. Said George Mason in the Virginia Convention, 'I have never, in my whole life, heard one single man deny the necessity and propriety of the Union.' And Governor Randolph, on the same occasion, spoke of a dissolution of the Union, as that deplorable thing 'which no man yet has dared openly to advocate.'

'In the course of the session of 1788,' he says, 'the increasing efforts of the enemies of the Constitution made a deep impression; and before its close, a great majority showed a decided hostility to it. I took an active part in the debates on this question, and was uniform in support of the proposed Constitution.'

With these sentiments, he was elected a member of the Virginia Convention, and in the next chapter we shall see the part he took in its deliberations.

CHAPTER VI.

1788.

MEMBER OF THE VIRGINIA CONVENTION.

Personally, Marshall was the most popular of men. His serene and joyous temper, his kind and generous heart, his exemption from pride and affectation, his moderation, candor, and integrity, attracted and fixed the regards of men. Though party spirit might run high, and the principles he espoused be little in favor, he never failed, when a candidate, to secure his election. A conspicuous instance of this personal weight and influence was his election as a member of the Virginia Convention, which met to decide on the ratification of the Federal Constitution. The current of opinion had set strongly against that instrument throughout Virginia. A majority of the voters of Henrico County were supposed to be hostile to it. Nevertheless, Marshall, with his well-known opinions, came forward as a candidate for the Convention.

'The questions,' he said afterwards, 'which were perpetually recurring in the State Legislatures; and which brought annually into doubt principles which I thought most sacred; which proved, that everything was afloat, and that we had no safe anchorage ground; gave a high value, in my estimation, to that article in the Constitution which imposes restrictions on the

States. I was, consequently, a determined advocate for its adoption, and became a candidate for the Convention.'[1] His opinions constituted the only obstacle to his election; and the determined effort that was made, on that ground, to defeat him, signally failed. 'Parties,' as he subsequently said, 'had not yet become so bitter as to extinguish the private affections;' and he was elected by a considerable majority.

The Convention assembled at Richmond on the 2d day of June, 1788. It was composed of the best abilities of Virginia. The fame of the speakers, and the magnitude of the question that was to engage their powers, created a vast expectation.

'Industry deserted its pursuits, and even dissipation gave up its objects, for the superior enjoyments which were presented by the hall of the Convention. Not only the people of the town and neighborhood, but gentlemen from every quarter of the State, were seen thronging to the metropolis, and speeding their eager way to the building in which the Convention held its meetings. Day after day, from morning till night, the galleries of the house were continually filled with an anxious crowd, who forgot the inconvenience of their situation in the excess of their enjoyment; and far from giving any interruption to the course of the debate, increased its interest and solemnity by their silence and attention. No bustle, no motion, no sound, was heard among them, save only a slight movement, when some new speaker arose, whom they were all eager to see as well as to hear; or when some masterstroke of eloquence shot thrilling along their nerves, and extorted an involuntary and inarticulate murmur.

[1] Story's Discourse, p. 28.

Day after day was this banquet of the mind and of the heart spread before them, with a delicacy and variety which could never cloy.'[1]

Conspicuous among those who opposed the ratification of the Constitution were Patrick Henry, George Mason, and William Grayson; a combination of eloquence, vigor, and genius, not often surpassed, and seldom equalled. Foremost among those who supported it were James Madison and Edmund Randolph. On the same side were arrayed, among other distinguished names, the venerable Edmund Pendleton, who presided over the deliberations of the Convention; James Innis, the Attorney-General of Virginia, a gentleman of great eloquence, 'eloquence,' said Patrick Henry, 'splendid, magnificent, and sufficient to shake the human mind,' George and William Nicholas, and John Marshall.

The after-acquired renown of the latter gives a sort of retroactive interest to his efforts on this occasion; but, even disconnected with his subsequent career, they will be found to possess sufficient merit to foreshow great reputation as a debater. That perfect exemption from needless incumbrance of matter or ornament, which has been pointed out as characteristic of all his intellectual displays, and as the effect, in some degree, of an aversion to the labor of thinking, is equally evinced in the speeches we are about to lay before the reader. We could wish, at the same time, to give him an accurate idea of the speaker's manner in public debate. That manner was peculiar, but effective. In nothing, perhaps, did it emulate the unrivalled oratorical qualities of Patrick Henry. Indeed,

---

[1] Life of Patrick Henry, p. 293.

a greater contrast could hardly be conceived than between these two men. The one had passion, fire, impetuosity, and, as shown by these debates, vigorous conceptions and clear ideas. The other depended on reason alone, and yet, when in full career, held the attention of his audience with as firm a grasp as his more eloquent opponent. His exordium, however, was little calculated to create expectation, or awaken sympathy.

'So great a mind, perhaps, like large bodies in the physical world, is with difficulty set in motion. That this is the case with Mr. Marshall's is manifest, from his mode of entering on an argument, both in conversation and in public debate. It is difficult to rouse his faculties: he begins with reluctance, hesitation, and vacancy of eye: presently, his articulation becomes less broken, his eye more fixed, until, finally, his voice is full, clear, and rapid, his manner bold, and his whole face lighted up with the mingled fires of genius and passion: and he pours forth the unbroken stream of eloquence in a current deep, majestic, smooth, and strong. He reminds one of some great bird, which flounders and flounces on the earth for awhile, before it acquires *impetus* to sustain its soaring flight.'[1]

Marshall's first speech in the Convention was on the power of taxation; but as the debate had been discursive, he did not confine his attention exclusively to that topic, and replied to many of the objections

[1] 'Sketches and Essays of Public Characters,' by Francis W. Gilmer.

that had been urged against the Constitution as a whole.

'I conceive,' said he, 'that the object of the discussion now before us is, whether democracy or despotism be most eligible. I am sure that those who framed the system submitted to our investigation, and those who now support it, intend the establishment and security of the former. The supporters of the Constitution claim the title of being firm friends of the liberty and the rights of mankind. They say that they consider it as the best means of protecting liberty. We, Sir, idolize democracy. Those who oppose it have bestowed eulogiums on monarchy. We prefer this system to any monarchy, because we are convinced that it has a greater tendency to secure our liberty, and promote our happiness. We admire it, because we think it a well-regulated democracy. It is recommended to the good people of this country; they are, through us, to declare whether it be such a plan of government as will establish and secure their freedom.

'Permit me to attend to what the honorable gentleman [Patrick Henry] has said. He has expatiated on the necessity of a due attention to certain maxims; to certain fundamental principles, from which a free people ought never to depart. I concur with him in the propriety of the observance of such maxims. They are necessary in any government, but more essential to a democracy than to any other. What are the favorite maxims of democracy? A strict observance of justice and public faith, and a steady adherence to virtue. These, Sir, are the principles of a good government. No mischief, no misfortune, ought to deter us from a strict observance of justice and public faith. Would to Heaven that these principles had been observed under the present government! Had this been the case, the friends of liberty would not be so willing now to part with it. Can we boast that our government is founded on these maxims? Can we pretend to the enjoyment of political freedom or security, when we are told that a man has been, by an Act of Assembly, struck out of existence without a trial by jury, without examination, without being confronted with his accusers and witnesses, without the benefits of the law of the land? Where is our safety, when we are told that this act was justifiable, because the person was not a Socrates? What has become of the worthy member's maxims? Is this one of them? Shall it be a maxim, that a man shall be deprived of his life without the benefit of law? Shall such a deprivation of life be justified by answering, that the man's life was not taken *secundum artem* because he was a bad man? [1] Shall it be a maxim, that government ought not to be empowered to protect virtue?'

---

[1] Marshall here refers to the case of Josiah Phillips, which had been adduced by Governor Randolph as an instance of gross departure from national principles, as well as a violation of the Constitution of Virginia. The facts of the case were thus stated by Randolph:— 'From mere reliance on general reports, a gentleman in the House of Delegates informed the House, that a certain man (Phillips) had committed several crimes, and was running at large, perpetrating other crimes. He, therefore, moved for leave to attaint him; he obtained that leave instantly; no sooner did he obtain it, than he drew from his pocket a bill ready written for that effect; it was read three times in one day, and carried to the Senate. I will not say that it passed the same day through the Senate; but he was attainted very speedily and precipitately, without any proof better than vague reports. Without being confronted with his accusers and witnesses, without the privilege of calling for evidence in his behalf, he was sentenced to death, and was afterwards actually executed. Was this arbitrary deprivation of life, the dearest gift of God to man, consistent with the genius of a republican government? Is this compatible with the

'He says, we wish to have a strong, energetic, powerful government. We contend for a well-regulated democracy. He insinuates that the power of the government has been enlarged by the Convention, and that we may apprehend it will be enlarged by others. The Convention did not, in fact, assume any power.

---

spirit of freedom? This, Sir, has made the deepest impression on my heart, and I cannot contemplate it without horror.' —*Elliott's Debates*, vol. iii., p. 66.

Patrick Henry thus replied: —'The honorable gentleman has given you an elaborate account of what he judges tyrannical legislation, and an *ex post facto law*, in the case of Josiah Phillips. He has misrepresented the facts. That man was not executed by a tyrannical stroke of power. Nor was he a Socrates. He was a fugitive murderer, and an outlaw; a man who commanded an infamous banditti, and at a time when the war was at the most perilous stage. He committed the most cruel and shocking barbarities. He was an enemy to the human name. Those who declare war against the human race may be struck out of existence as soon as they are apprehended. He was not executed according to those beautiful legal ceremonies which are pointed out by the laws in criminal cases. The enormity of his crimes did not entitle him to it. I am truly a friend to legal forms and methods; but, Sir, in this case the occasion warranted the measure. A pirate, an outlaw, or a common enemy to all mankind, may be put to death at any time. It is justified by the laws of nature and nations.' —*Ibid.*, p. 140.

When this act of attainder passed, Henry was the Governor of Virginia, and Jefferson a member of the Assembly. Randolph, who had been hard pressed by Henry in debate, and arraigned for inconsistency in now supporting the Constitution, when, as a member of the Federal Convention, he had refused to sign it, brought forward the case of Phillips as a means of retaliation. But Jefferson says that Phillips was not executed under the act of attainder; that he was indicted at common law for either robbery or murder; was regularly tried, convicted, and executed. No use, he says, was ever made of the act of attainder. Governor Randolph acted for the Commonwealth in the prosecution; he being, at that time, Attorney-General. Jefferson supposes that there must have been some mistake in the report of Randolph's statement of the case in the Convention, as well as in Henry's reply.—*See Jefferson's Works*, vol. vi., pp. 369, 440.

They have proposed to our consideration a scheme of government which they thought advisable. We are not bound to adopt it, if we disapprove of it. Had not every individual in this community a right to tender that scheme which he thought most conducive to the welfare of his country? Have not several gentlemen already demonstrated that the Convention did not exceed their powers? But the Congress have the power of making bad laws, it seems. The Senate, with the President, he informs us, may make a treaty which shall be disadvantageous to us; and that, if they be not good men, it will not be a good Constitution. I shall ask the worthy member only, if the people at large, and they alone, ought to make laws and treaties? Has any man this in contemplation? You cannot exercise the powers of government personally yourselves. You must trust to agents. If so, will you dispute giving them the power of acting for you, from an existing possibility that they may abuse it? As long as it is impossible for you to transact your business in person, if you repose no confidence in delegates, because there is a possibility of their abusing it, you can have no government; for the power of doing good is inseparable from that of doing some evil.'

'Let me pay attention to the observation of the gentleman who was last up [Mr. Monroe], that the power of taxation ought not to be given to Congress. This subject requires the undivided attention of this House. This power I think essentially necessary; for, without it, there will be no efficiency in the government. We have had a sufficient demonstration of the vanity of depending on requisitions. How, then, can the General Government exist without this power? The possibility of its being abused is urged as an argument against its expediency. To very little purpose did

Virginia discover the defects in the old system; to little purpose, indeed, did she propose improvements; and to no purpose is this plan constructed for the promotion of our happiness, if we refuse it now, because it is possible it may be abused. The Confederation has nominal powers, but no means to carry them into effect. If a system of government were devised by more than human intelligence, it would not be effectual if the means were not adequate to the power. All delegated powers are liable to be abused. Arguments drawn from this source go in direct opposition to the government, and in recommendation of anarchy. The friends of the Constitution are as tenacious of liberty as its enemies. They wish to give no power that will endanger it. They wish to give the government powers to secure and protect it. Our inquiry here must be, whether the power of taxation be necessary to perform the objects of the Constitution, and whether it be safe, and as well guarded as human wisdom can do it? What are the objects of the national government? To protect the United States, and to promote the general welfare. Protection, in time of war, is one of its principal objects. Until mankind shall cease to have ambition and avarice, wars will arise.'

'There must be men and money to protect us. How are armies to be raised? Must we not have money for that purpose? But the honorable gentleman says that we need not be afraid of war. Look at history, which has been so often quoted. Look at the great volume of human nature. They will foretell you that a defenceless country cannot be secure. The nature of man forbids us to conclude that we are in no danger from war. The passions of men stimulate them to avail themselves of the weakness of others. The Powers of Europe are jealous of us. It is our interest to watch their conduct, and guard against them. They must be pleased with our disunion. If we invite them, by our weakness, to attack us, will they not do it? If we add debility to our present situation, a partition of America may take place. It is, then, necessary to give the government that power, in time of peace, which the necessity of war will render indispensable, or else we shall be attacked unprepared. The experience of the world, a knowledge of human nature, and our own particular experience, will confirm this truth. When danger shall come upon us, may we not do what we were on the point of doing once already; that is, appoint a dictator. . . . . We may now regulate and frame a plan that will enable us to repel attacks, and render a recurrence to dangerous expedients unnecessary. If we be prepared to defend ourselves, there will be little inducement to attack us. But, if we defer giving the necessary power to the General Government till the moment of danger arrives, we shall give it then, and with an *unsparing hand.*'

'I defy you to produce a single instance where requisitions on several individual States, composing a Confederacy, have been honestly complied with. Did gentlemen expect to see such punctuality complied with in America? If they did, our own experience shows the contrary.' 'A bare sense of duty, or a regard to propriety, is too feeble to induce men to comply with obligations. We deceive ourselves, if we expect any efficacy from these. If requisitions will not avail, the government must have the sinews of war some other way. Requisitions cannot be effectual. They will be productive of delay, and will ultimately be inefficient. By direct taxation, the necessities of the government will be supplied in a peaceable manner, without irritating the minds of the people. But requisitions cannot be rendered efficient without a civil war; without great expense of money, and the blood of our citizens.'

'Is the system so organized as to make taxation dangerous? . . . I conceive its organization to be sufficiently satisfactory to the warmest friend of freedom. No tax can be laid without the consent of the House of Representatives. If there be no impropriety in the mode of electing the Representative, can any danger be apprehended? They are elected by those who can elect Representatives in the State Legislature. How can the votes of the electors be influenced? By nothing but the character and conduct of the men they vote for.' 'If they are to be chosen for their wisdom, virtue and integrity, what inducement have they to infringe on our freedom? We are told that they may abuse their power. Are there strong motives to prompt them to abuse it? Will not such abuse militate against their own interest? Will not they, and their friends, feel the effects of iniquitous measures? Does the Representative remain in office for life? Does he transmit his title of Representative to his son? Is he secured from the burden imposed on the community? To procure their re-election, it will be necessary for them to confer with the people at large, and convince them that the taxes laid are for their good. If I am able to judge on the subject, the power of taxation now before us is wisely conceded, and the Representatives wisely elected.'

'The extent of the country is urged as another objection, as being too great for a republican government. This objection has been handed from author to author, and has been certainly misunderstood and misapplied. To what does it owe its source? To observations and criticisms on governments, where representation did not exist. As to the legislative power, was it ever supposed inadequate to any extent? Extent of country may render it difficult to execute the laws, but not to legislate. Extent of country does not extend the power. What will be sufficiently energetic and operative in a small territory, will be feeble when extended over a wide-extended country. The gentleman tells us there are no checks in this plan. What has become of his enthusiastic eulogium on the American spirit. We should find a check and control, when oppressed, from that source. In this country, there is no exclusive personal stock of interest. The interest of the community is blended and inseparably connected with that of the individual. When he promotes his own, he promotes that of the community. When we consult the common good, we consult our own. When he desires such checks as these, he will find them abundantly here. They are the best checks. What has become of his eulogium on the Virginia Constitution? Do the checks in this plan appear less excellent than those of the Constitution of Virginia? If the checks in the Constitution be compared to the checks in the Virginia Constitution, he will find the best security in the former.'

'The worthy member [Patrick Henry] has concluded his observations by many eulogiums on the British Constitution. It matters not to us whether it be a wise one or not. I think that, for America at least, the government on your table is very much superior to it. I ask you, if your House of Representatives would be better than it is, if a hundredth part of the people were to elect a majority of them, if your Senators were for life, would they be more agreeable to you? If your President were not accountable to you for his conduct — if it were a constitutional maxim, that he could do no wrong — would you be safer than you are now? If you can answer, Yes, to these questions, then adopt the British Constitution. If not, then, good as that government may be, this is better.

'The worthy gentleman who was last up [Monroe], said the confederacies of ancient and modern times were not similar to ours, and that, consequently, reasons which applied against them could not be urged against it. Do they not hold out one lesson very useful to us? However unlike in other respects, they resemble it in its total inefficacy. They warn us to shun their calamities, and place in our government those necessary powers, the want of which destroyed them. I hope we shall avail ourselves of their misfortunes, without experiencing them. There was something peculiar in one observation he made. He said that those who governed the cantons of Switzerland were purchased by foreign powers, which was the cause of their uneasiness and trouble. How does this apply to us? If we adopt such a government as theirs, will it not be subject to the same inconvenience? Will not the same cause produce the same effect? What shall protect us from it? What is our security? He then proceeded to say, the causes of war are removed from us; that we are separated by the sea from the powers of Europe, and need not be alarmed. Sir, the sea makes them neighbors to us. Though an immense ocean divides us, we may speedily see them with us. What dangers may we not apprehend to our commerce? Does not our naval weakness invite an attack on our commerce? May not the Algerines seize our vessels? Cannot they, and every other predatory or maritime nation, pillage our ships, and destroy our commerce, without subjecting themselves to any inconvenience? He would, he said, give the General Government all necessary powers. If anything be necessary, it must be so to call forth the strength of the Union when we may be attacked, or when the general purposes of America require it. The worthy gentleman then proceeded to show, that our present exigencies are greater than they ever will be again. Who can penetrate into futurity? How can any man pretend to say that our future exigencies will be less than our present? The exigencies of nations have been generally commensurate to their resources. It would be the utmost impolicy to trust to a mere possibility of not being attacked, or obliged to exert the strength of the community.'

'He then told you that your continental government will call forth the virtue and talents of America. This being the case, will they encroach on the power of the State governments? Will our most virtuous and able citizens wantonly attempt to destroy the liberty of the people? Will the most virtuous act the most wickedly? I differ in opinion from the worthy gentleman. I think the virtue and talents of the members of the General Government will tend to the security, instead of the destruction, of our liberty. I think that the power of direct taxation is essential to the existence of the General Government, and that it is safe to grant it. If this power be not necessary, and as safe from abuse as any delegated power can possibly be, then, I say that the plan before you is unnecessary; for it imports not what system we have, unless it have the power of protecting us in time of peace and war.'

Marshall next addressed the Convention in support of that clause of the Constitution which gives Congress power to provide for arming, organizing, and disciplining the militia, and governing those in the actual service of the Union. It had been attacked by Patrick Henry as a very alarming power. He declared that, as the clause expressly vested the General Government with power to call out the militia to suppress insurrections, &c., it appeared to him, most decidedly, that the power of suppressing insurrections was *exclusively* given to Congress. If it remained in the States, it was by implication.

Marshall asked, in reply, if gentlemen were serious when they asserted that, if the State governments had power to interfere with the militia, it was by implication. 'If they were, he asked the Committee whether the least attention would not show that they were mistaken. The State governments did not derive their powers from the General Government; but each government derived its powers from the people, and each was to act according to the powers given to it. Would any gentleman deny this? He demanded if powers not given were retained by implication. Could any man say so? Could any man say that this power was not retained by the States, as they had not given it away? For, says he, does not a power remain until it is given away? The State Legislatures had power to command and govern their militia before, and have it still, undeniably, unless there be something in this Constitution that takes it away.' 'The truth is, that when power is given to the General Legislature, if it was in the State Legislature before, both shall exercise it; unless there be an incompatibility in the exercise by one to that by the other, or negative words precluding the State governments from it. But there are no negative words here. It rests, therefore, with the States. To me it appears, then, unquestionable that the State governments can call forth the militia, in case the Constitution should be adopted, in the same manner as they would have done before its adoption.

'When the government is drawn from the people, and depending on the people for its continuance, oppressive measures will not be attempted, as they will certainly draw on their authors the resentment of those on whom they depend. On this government, thus depending on ourselves for its existence, I will rest my safety, notwithstanding the danger depicted by the honorable gentleman. I cannot help being surprised that the worthy member thought this power so dangerous. What government is able to protect you in time of war? Will any State depend on its own exertions? The consequence of such dependence, and withholding this power from Congress, will be, that State will fall after State, and be a sacrifice to the want of power in the General Government. United we are strong, divided we fall. Will you preveut the General Government from drawing the militia of one State to another, when the consequence would be, that every State must depend on itself? The enemy, possessing the water, can quickly go from one State to another. No State will spare to another its militia, which it conceives necessary for itself. It requires a superintending power in order to call forth the resources of all to protect all. If this be not done, each State will fall a sacrifice. This system merits the highest applause in this respect. The honorable gentleman said that a general regulation may be made to inflict punishments. Does he imagine that a militia law is to be ingrafted on the scheme of government, so as to render it incapable of being changed? The idea of the worthy member supposes that men renounce their own interests. This would produce general inconveniences throughout the Union, and would be equally opposed by all the States. But the worthy member fears, that in one part of the Union they will be regulated and disciplined, and in another neglected. This danger is enhanced by leaving this power to each State; for some States may attend to their militia, and others may neglect them. If Congress neglect our militia, we can arm them ourselves. Cannot Virginia import arms? Cannot she put them into the hands of her militia men?'

The judicial power bestowed on the General Government by the Constitution, was denounced by the opponents of that instrument with great earnestness. It was said that its exercise might destroy the dearest rights of the community; that the effect and operation of the Federal Courts would go to the destruction of the State governments. To arguments like these, and of a similar strain, Marshall thus replied:—

'Mr. Chairman, this part of the plan before us is a great improvement on that instrument from which we are now departing. Here are tribunals appointed for the decision of controversies, which were before either not at all, or improperly, provided for. That many benefits will result from this to the members of the collective society, every one confesses. Unless its organization be defective, and so constructed as to injure, instead of accommodating, the convenience of the people, it merits our approbation. After such a candid and fair discussion by those gentlemen who support it—after the very able manner in which they have investigated and examined it—I conceived it would be no longer considered as so very defective, and that those who opposed it would be convinced of the impropriety of some of their objections. But I perceive that they still continue the same opposition. Gentlemen have gone on an idea that the Federal Courts will not determine the causes which may come before them, with the same fairness and impartiality with which other Courts decide. What are the reasons of this supposition? Do they draw them from the manner in which the judges are chosen, or the tenure of their office? What is it that makes us trust our judges? Their independence in office, and manner of appointment. Are not the judges of the Federal Court chosen with as much wisdom as the judges of the State governments? Are they not equally, if not more independent? If so, shall we not conclude that they will decide with equal impartiality and candor? If there be as much wisdom and knowledge in the United States as in a particular State, shall we conclude that that wisdom and knowledge will not be equally exercised in the selection of judges?'

'With respect to its cognizance [the cognizance of the Federal judiciary] in all cases arising under the Constitution and the laws of the United States, he [George Mason] says that the laws of the United States being paramount to the laws of the particular State, there is no case, but what this will extend to. Has the Government of the United States power to make laws on every subject? Does he understand it so? Can they make laws affecting the mode of transferring property, or contracts, or claims, between citizens of the same State? Can they go beyond the delegated powers? If they were to make a law not warranted by any of the powers enumerated, it would be considered by the judges as an infringement of the Constitution which they are to guard. They would not consider such a law as coming under their jurisdiction. They would declare it void.'

'How disgraceful is it, that the State Courts cannot be trusted, says the honorable gentleman. What is the language of the Constitution? Does it take away their jurisdiction? Is it not necessary that the Federal Courts should have cognizance of cases arising under the Constitution and the laws of the United States? What is the service or purpose of a judiciary, but to execute the laws in a peaceable, orderly manner, without shedding blood, or creating a contest, or availing yourselves of force? If this be the case, where can its jurisdiction be more necessary than here?'

'With respect to disputes between a State, and the citizens of another State, its jurisdiction has been decried with unusual vehemence. I hope that no gentleman will think that a State will be called at the bar of the Federal Court.[1] Is there no such case at present? Are there not many cases in which the Legislature of Virginia is a party, and yet the State is not sued? It is not rational to suppose that the sovereign power should be dragged before a court. The intent is, to enable States to recover claims of individuals residing in other States. I contend that this construction is warranted by the words; but, say they, there will be partiality in it, if a State cannot be defendant — if an individual cannot proceed to obtain judgment against a State, though he may be sued by a State. It is necessary to be so, and cannot be avoided. I see a difficulty in making a State defendant, which does not prevent its being plaintiff. If this be only what cannot be avoided, why object to the system on that

[1] This, however, was actually done in the case of Chisholm *v.* Georgia. See vol. i., p. 385 *et seq.* The decision of the Court in that case led to an amendment of the Constitution, forbidding such an excise of authority.

account? If an individual has a just claim against any particular State, is it to be presumed that, on application, he will not obtain satisfaction? But how could a State recover any claim from a citizen of another State, without the establishment of these tribunals?

'The honorable member objects to suits being instituted in the Federal Courts, by the citizens of one State, against the citizens of another State. Were I to contend that this was necessary in all cases, and that the government, without it, would be defective, I should not use my own judgment. But are not the objections to it carried too far? Though it may not, in general, be absolutely necessary, a case may happen, as has been observed, in which a citizen of one State ought to be able to recur to this tribunal, to recover a claim from the citizen of another State. What is the evil which this can produce? Will he get more than justice there? The independence of the judges forbids it. What has he to get? Justice. Shall we object to this, because the citizen of another State can obtain justice without applying to our State Courts? It may be necessary, with respect to the laws and regulations of commerce, which Congress may make. It may be necessary in cases of debt, and some other controversies. In claims for land, it is not necessary, but it is not dangerous. In the Court of which State will it be instituted? said the honorable gentleman. It will be instituted in the Court of the State where the defendant resides, where the law can come at him, and no where else. By the laws of which State will it be determined? said he. By the laws of the State where the contract was made. According to those laws, and those only, can it be decided. Is this a novelty? No; it is a principle in the jurisprudence of this Commonwealth. If a man contracted a debt in the East Indies, and it was sued for here, the decision must be consonant to the laws of that country.'

Such was the line of argument adopted by Marshall in support of the Federal Constitution. His speeches were evidently not premeditated; but made on the spur of the occasion, and in reply to objections brought forward by his opponents. If not as comprehensive in their scope as the speeches of Madison, they were, nevertheless, vigorous, pointed, and adapted to the end he had in view. They were, chiefly, in answer to the arguments of Patrick Henry and George Mason. How they were estimated by the former may be inferred from his brief, but generous eulogium. 'I have,' said he, 'the highest veneration and respect for the honorable gentleman, and I have experienced his candor on all occasions.'

After an earnest debate of twenty-five days, a debate illustrated by an extraordinary display of eloquence and ability, the Convention accepted the Constitution by a majority of ten votes. The result, it has been thought, would have been different, had not the news arrived, while the Convention was yet in session, that nine States had already given their voice in its favor, and thus insured its success.

The Constitution adopted, we shall see, in the following chapters, that Marshall gave an earnest support to the government organized in accordance with its provisions, and to the principles on which that government was conducted by the Administrations of Washington and Adams.

CHAPTER VII.

1788-1797.

MEMBER OF THE VIRGINIA LEGISLATURE.

THE high professional reputation to which Marshall had attained, seemed naturally to invite an exclusive devotion of his talents to the labors of the Bar. A narrow fortune and growing family were impelling motives to that line of conduct. Accordingly, he now determined to relinquish public life, and adhere, for the future, to his profession. But the opposition the Constitution had already encountered in Virginia, and the hostility that still existed against that instrument, indicated that the government which was now to be organized in pursuance of its provisions, would be likely to meet with very lukewarm support from the State Legislature, if the anti-Federalists should secure an ascendency in that body. It was, therefore, the obvious policy of the Federalists to effect, if possible, a different result; under such circumstances Marshall was prevailed upon to forego his determination to quit public life, and become a candidate for the Legislature.

He was elected, and continued to serve in that body until the spring of 1791. The anti-Federalists, however, had the majority, and sent to the Senate of the United States, William Grayson and Richard Henry Lee, who had opposed the Constitution, in preference to Madison and Pendleton, who had supported it. All the leading measures of the Administration were freely criticised and discussed in the Virginia Legislature, and their tendency regarded with a jealous watchfulness.

Marshall, who had the greatest confidence in the wisdom of Washington, and naturally inclined to favor a line of policy that would impart vigor and efficiency to the new system, supported with all his powers those measures which most excited the animadversion, and aroused the hostility, of the party who had originally opposed the Constitution as fraught with danger to liberty, and now thought they perceived, in the action of the government, the approaching realization of their fears. The funding system, the assumption of the State debts, and the creation of a national bank, were regarded as violative of the powers conferred on the General Government, and leading directly to consolidation. These grave questions were reviewed, criticised, and discussed in the halls of the Virginia Legislature, with abilities equal to the topics, and the occasion. Marshall participated in these debates, and asserted the constitutionality as well as the policy of the measures thus assailed; but the current was too strong to be resisted. The predominant party in Virginia were opposed to nearly every important measure of Washington's Administration, and took no pains to conceal their disapprobation and disgust.

In 1792, Marshall declined a re-election, and for the next three years was immersed in the business of his profession. He was engaged, on one side or the other, in nearly all the important causes in the State and Federal Courts. These were, probably, the most active years of his professional life. But, extensive as were his engagements at the Bar, it was impossible for a man of his abilities, and avowed opinions, in the stirring times in which he lived, to withdraw himself entirely from politics. Assailed as was the domestic policy of the government, its foreign policy was even more fiercely denounced. The President's celebrated Proclamation of Neutrality[1] inflamed the elements of discontent, stimulated the zeal, and increased the strength of the opposition. On this occasion, Marshall came forward in support of the President's course, and at a meeting of the citizens of Richmond obtained a considerable majority in favor of resolutions approving it. But he paid the usual penalty, rigorously inflicted upon all who, with whatever purity of motive, actively participate in political discussions; he was assailed by the opposite party with great bitterness. Bold reproaches and witty malice were studiously employed to weaken his influence, and detract from the merit of his arguments. He was denounced as an advocate of aristocratic principles; as a loyalist and an enemy of republicanism. But these attacks failed of their aim. In Richmond, where his character, political sentiments, and manner of life were well understood, the assaults upon him proved perfectly harmless.

In 1795, he was again elected a member of the State Legislature; but against his wishes, and without his consent. The circumstances, however, seemed to justify this step. It was doubtful, so nearly equally were parties divided, whether the regular candidate of the Federalists, an intimate personal friend of Marshall's, could be elected. Accordingly, a poll was opened for Marshall, while he was engaged in one of the Courts, (notwithstanding he had declined being a candidate, and declared that his feelings and honor were engaged

---

[1] Ante, vol. i., p. 390; and vol. ii., p. 168.

for his friend,) and he was again returned as a member of the Legislature.

The Jay treaty, as we have elsewhere seen, had, at this time, created throughout the country an unparalelled ferment and excitement.[1] In Virginia, it was attacked with unsparing zeal and bitterness. At a meeting of the citizens of Richmond, at which the venerable Chancellor Wythe presided, resolutions were adopted, denouncing it 'as insulting to the dignity, injurious to the interest, dangerous to the security, and repugnant to the Constitution of the United States.' At a subsequent meeting of the same citizens, Marshall introduced resolutions of a contrary tenor, and supported them in a speech of great power. His resolutions were adopted; but, marked as was his success on this occasion, it was in the Legislature that he received the most gratifying proofs of the vigor and effect of his arguments. There, both the expediency and constitutionality of the treaty were warmly denied. Inasmuch as the power to regulate commerce was bestowed on Congress, it was maintained, with great confidence, that the Executive had no constitutional right to negotiate a commercial treaty. Marshall's reply to this position has been considered as one of the most memorable displays of his genius. His speech, however, was not reported; but the traditional account is, that, for cogency of reasoning, and comprehensive knowledge of the whole subject matter of the debate, it was altogether admirable. He demonstrated so clearly the competency of the Executive to make the treaty, that all objection to it on constitutional grounds was abandoned. And even the resolution of the House approving the conduct of the Vir-

[1] Vol. i., pp. 412, 633.

ginia Senators in voting against the treaty, expressed confidence in the patriotism and wisdom of the President, and declared that it was not intended to censure his motives in ratifying it. The fame of this great argument of Marshall's extended beyond the limits of Virginia. It made his name familiar throughout the country. When he visited Philadelphia a few months after, to argue the British debt case,[1] he was an object of marked attention.

'I then became acquainted,' he says, in a letter to a friend, 'with Mr. Cabot, Mr. Ames, Mr. Dexter, and Mr. Sedgwick of Massachusetts, Mr. Wadsworth of Connecticut, and Mr. King of New York. I was delighted with these gentlemen. The particular subject [the British treaty] which introduced me to their notice, was at that time so interesting, and a Virginian, who supported, with any sort of reputation, the measures of the Government, was such a *rara avis*, that I was received by them all with a degree of kindness, which I had not anticipated. I was particularly intimate with Mr. Ames, and could scarcely gain credit with him, when I assured him that the appropriations would be seriously opposed in Congress.'[2]

The death of Mr. Bradford, the Attorney-General, in the summer of 1795, gave Washington an opportunity to mark his appreciation of the character and abilities of Marshall, by tendering him the vacant post.

---

[1] Ante, p. 310.

[2] Story's Discourse, p. 40. See Marshall's Letter to Hamilton, of April 25th, 1796, (Hamilton's Works, vol. vi.,) giving an account of a public meeting in Richmond, at which a resolution was carried declaring the validity of the treaty, and its binding effect on Congress.

'The salary annexed thereto,' said the President's letter, 'and the prospect of a lucrative practice in this city [Philadelphia], the present seat of the General Government, must be as well known to you, better, perhaps, than they are to me, and, therefore, I shall say nothing concerning them.'[1] This offer he declined upon the ground that it would interfere with his engagements at the Bar in Virginia.

In the following summer, Washington again called upon Marshall to enter the public service, as successor of Monroe at Paris; but he declined, on the ground that the crisis of his affairs rendered it impossible for him to leave the United States. 'Otherwise,' he added, 'such is my conviction of the importance of that duty which you would confide to me, and, pardon me if I add, of the fidelity with which I should attempt to perform it, that I would certainly forego any consideration not decisive with respect to future fortunes, and would surmount that just diffidence I have ever entertained of myself, to make an effort to convey truly and faithfully to the Government of France those sentiments which I have ever believed to be entertained by that of the United States.'[2] At this time, he thought his determination to remain at the Bar unalterable. 'My situation at the Bar,' said he, 'appeared to me to be more independent, and not less honorable, than any other; and my preference for it was decided.'[3] In the next chapter, we shall see the occasion that induced him to change his determination, and first engaged him in the service of the General Government.

In the meantime he continued a member of the Virginia Legislature; but rarely participated in the de-

[1] Washington's Writings, vol. xi., p. 62. August 25th, 1796.

[2] Ibid., p. 143. July 11th, 1796.

[3] Story's Discourse, p. 41.

bates, except to vindicate the measures of the Federal Administration. One of these debates he has thus described: — 'It was, I think,' says the Chief Justice, 'in the session of 1796, that I was engaged in a debate, which called forth all the strength and violence of party. Some Federalist moved a resolution, expressing the high confidence of the House in the virtue, patriotism, and wisdom of the President of the United States. A motion was made to strike out the word *wisdom*. In the debate the whole course of the Administration was reviewed, and the whole talent of each party was brought into action. Will it be believed, that the word was retained by a very small majority? A very small majority of the Legislature of Virginia acknowledged the wisdom of General Washington!'[1]

In the next chapter we shall view the course of Marshall and his colleagues in their endeavors to adjust the difficulties with France, and witness the admirable temper which marked his conduct throughout his disagreeable stay at Paris.

---

[1] Story's Discourse, p. 41.

CHAPTER VIII.

1797—1798.

ENVOY EXTRAORDINARY TO FRANCE.

We have seen, in the preceding chapter, that when Monroe was recalled from France, for causes which we have elsewhere explained,[1] the vacant post was offered to Marshall. When he declined it, the appointment was conferred on Charles Cotesworth Pinckney. The result of his mission we have already seen; the French Government not only refused to receive him, but finally ordered him to leave the country. He then proceeded to Amsterdam, and awaited instructions from home. In this conjuncture, the Administration determined to send out an Extraordinary Commission to renew negotiations with France, and thus, if possible, avoid the alternative of war. Accordingly, on the 31st of May, 1797, President Adams nominated, as Envoys Extraordinary to that country, Charles Cotesworth Pinckney, John Marshall, and Francis Dana. The latter declining the appointment, it was conferred on Elbridge Gerry.

Marshall accepted the post which was thus assigned him with reluctance; but the occasion was so interesting, and the exigency so great, that he did not feel at liberty to decline it. He arranged his affairs at home

---

[1] Ante, Life of Ellsworth, p. 213.

with all convenient despatch, and by July was ready to embark for Europe. On his departure from Richmond, he was attended, for several miles, by a large cavalcade of his fellow-citizens, who, on this, as on all occasions, invariably evinced the greatest attachment to his person, and respect for his character. However assailed he might be by political opponents, and however his political sentiments might be questioned, that attachment and respect were never wanting.

He embarked at Philadelphia for Amsterdam, in the ship Grace, Captain Willis, on the 17th of July, 1797. On the same day, the President, in a letter to Gerry, thus describes him: — 'He is a plain man, very sensible, cautious, guarded, and learned in the law of nations. I think you will be pleased with him.'[1]

Naturally, very great solicitude was felt as to the reception that awaited him and his colleagues at Paris; and that solicitude was increased by the long interval which elapsed before any communication was received from them. Owing to the delays incident to a winter's voyage, their first official letter did not reach the Secretary of State until the 4th of March, 1798. That letter dissipated all hope that they would be officially recognized, or the objects of their mission be accomplished.

This mission constitutes a curious chapter in the history of diplomacy, and the circumstances that marked its progress and result are full of interest.

The Envoys arrived at Paris on the evening of October 4th, 1797. The next day, verbally and unofficially, they informed M. Talleyrand, the Minister of Foreign Affairs, of their arrival, and desired to know when he would be at leisure to receive one of their

---

[1] Adams' Works, vol. viii., p. 549.

Secretaries with the official notification. He appointed the next day at two o'clock; when their letter of credence was duly presented to him. On the 8th, they waited upon him at his house, where he kept his office. He informed them that the Directory had required him to make a report relative to the situation of the United States with regard to France, which he was then about, and which would be furnished in a few days, when he would let them know what steps were to follow. They asked if cards of hospitality were, in the meantime, necessary. He said they were, and should be delivered to them. The next day they were sent, and in a style suitable to their official character.

Thus far appearances indicated that they would be received, and the negotiation proceed; but on the 14th, Major Mountflorence, Chancellor of the American Consulate at Paris, informed General Pinckney that he had had a conversation with Talleyrand's private and confidential Secretary, who told him that the Directory were greatly exasperated at some parts of the President's speech at the opening of the late session of Congress, and would require an explanation of them from the American Ministers. In another conversation, the Secretary informed Mountflorence that M. Talleyrand had told him that it was probable they would not have a public audience of the Directory till their negotiation was finished; that, in the meantime, persons might be appointed to treat with them, but they would report to Talleyrand, who would have the direction of the negotiation.

On the 18th, M. Hottinguer, who had been described to General Pinckney, as a gentleman of considerable credit and reputation, called on the General, and informed him that he had a message from M. Talleyrand to communicate; that he was sure M. Talleyrand had a great regard for America and its citizens; and was very desirous that there should be a reconciliation between the two countries. To accomplish this, he was ready, if it was thought proper, to suggest a plan, confidentially, which M. Talleyrand expected would answer the purpose. General Pinckney said he should be glad to hear it. M. Hottinguer replied, that the Directory, and particularly two of them, were exceedingly irritated at some passages of the President's speech, and desired that they should be softened; that this step would be necessary previous to their reception; and besides this, a sum of money was required for the pocket of the Directory, which would be at the disposal of M. Talleyrand, and that a loan would also be insisted on. M. Hottinguer said, these measures acceded to, M. Talleyrand had no doubt that the differences with France might be accommodated. The particular passages of the President's speech that had given offence he could not point out, nor the quantum of the loan, but the *douceur* for the Directory, he said, was twelve hundred thousand livres, about £50,000 sterling.

General Pinckney told him, that he and his colleagues, from their arrival in Paris, had been treated with great slight and disrespect; that they wished for peace with France, and had been entrusted with great powers to accomplish it, on honorable terms; but with regard to the propositions communicated by M. Hottinguer, he would not consider them before he had disclosed them to his colleagues; that having done so, M. Hottinguer should hear from him.

On communicating to his colleagues the purport of M. Hottinguer's visit, it was agreed, that General Pinckney should request him to make his propositions to them all, and, to avoid mistakes or misapprehension, reduce the heads of them to writing. Accordingly, on the next day, General Pinckney called on M. Hottinguer, who consented to see the Envoys in the evening. He came at the appointed time, and left with them a set of propositions in writing. He had informed General Pinckney, however, that his communication was not directly with M. Talleyrand, but through another gentleman, in whom M. Talleyrand had great confidence. This afterwards proved to be M. Bellamy, of Hamburg.

On the morning of the 20th, M. Hottinguer called, and informed the Envoys, that M. Bellamy, the confidential friend of M. Talleyrand, would see them himself, and make the necessary explanations. He came in the evening, and was received in General Marshall's room. He mentioned the favorable impressions of M. Talleyrand towards the United States, impressions which were made by the kindness and civilities he had personally received while there; and that he was solicitous to repay those kindnesses, and was willing to aid the Envoys in their negotiatiation by his good offices with the Directory, who were extremely irritated on account of passages in the President's speech, and who had neither acknowledged nor received them, and, consequently, had not authorized M. Talleyrand to have any communications with them. In consequence, he could not see them himself, but had authorized M. Bellamy to communicate to them certain propositions, and receive their answers. But, in the same breath, as it were, he declared that he was no diplomatic character, was clothed with no authority, and was merely the friend of M. Talleyrand, and trusted by him. He then pointed out the objectionable passages of the President's speech, and made a series of propositions as the basis of the negotiation. These propositions referred to certain disavowals and reparations which were to be preliminary to a treaty. The treaty itself was to place France, with respect to the United States, on the same footing as they stood with England in consequence of the Jay Treaty. It was also to contain a secret article stipulating a loan to France.

M. Bellamy dilated very much on the keenness of the resentment the President's speech had produced, and expatiated largely on the satisfaction indispensably necessary as a preliminary to negotiation. 'But,' said he, 'gentlemen, I will not disguise from you, that this satisfaction being made, the essential part of the treaty remains to be adjusted. *Il faut de l'argent—il faut beaucoup d'argent;* you must pay money, you must pay a great deal of money.' The next morning M. Bellamy and M. Hottinguer breakfasted with the Envoys at Mr. Gerry's. The former did not come until ten o'clock, having passed the morning with M. Talleyrand. He represented that both M. Talleyrand and himself were extremely sensible of the pain the Envoys must feel in disavowing the obnoxious passages of the President's speech; but that they must consider such disavowal as an indispensable preliminary to their reception, unless they could find means to change the determination of the Directory. He said he was not authorised to suggest those means; but, as a private individual, he would express the opinion that, with money, they would be able to succeed. He stated the sum which he believed would be satisfactory, and an eligible mode of giving it. There were, he said, thirty-two millions of Dutch rescriptions, worth ten shillings in the pound, which might be assigned to the United States at twenty shillings in the pound. In the end they would lose nothing, for, after a peace, the Dutch Government would certainly repay them the amount. Hence, he said, the only operation of the measure would be an advance to France of thirty-two millions, on the credit of the Government of Holland. When asked if the *douceur* to the Directory must be in addition to this sum, he answered in the affirmative.

The Envoys told him that their powers were ample to negotiate a treaty; but the proposition of a loan in any form exceeded the limits of their instructions. That one of their number would return to the United States in order to consult the Government respecting it, provided the Directory would suspend further captures of American vessels, and proceedings on those already captured, &c. At this offer M. Bellamy was evidently disappointed. He said they treated the proposition of a loan as if it came from the Directory, whereas it did not proceed from them, nor even from M. Talleyrand, but was only a suggestion from himself, as a substitute to be proposed by the Envoys, in lieu of the painful disavowal that the Directory had determined to demand of them. They replied that they understood the matter perfectly; that the proposition in form was to come from them, but, substantially, it proceeded from the Minister. M. Bellamy expressed himself vehemently on the resentment of France; complained that the Envoys, instead of proposing a substitute for the reparations demanded of them, were stipulating conditions to be performed by the Directory itself; that he could not take charge of their offers, and that the Directory would persist in demanding a disavowal of the offensive passages of the President's speech. They replied, that they could not help it; that the Directory must determine what the honor and interests of France required them to do; but for themselves they must guard the honor and interests of the United States. That the idea of disavowing the President's speech could not be treated by them in a serious light; that an attempt to do it would merely make them ridiculous to the Government and people they represented. M. Bellamy said, they certainly would not be received, and seemed to shudder at the consequences.

About the 27th of October, news reached Paris that the definitive articles of peace between France and Austria had been signed, and on that day the Envoys received another visit from M. Hottinguer. He said some proposals had been expected from them; that the Directory were becoming impatient, and would take a decided course towards America, unless they could be softened. He spoke of the different position France occupied in consequence of the peace, as warranting the expectation of a change in the system of the Envoys. They replied that that position they had anticipated, and it would not in any degree affect their conduct. He urged that, since the peace, the Directory had taken a higher and more decided tone with respect to the United States and all other neutral nations than ever before, and were determined that all nations should aid them or be treated as enemies. They answered, that they had anticipated as much when they refused the propositions that had been made to them. M. Hottinguer, after expatiating on the power and violence of France, returned once more to the subject of money. Said he, 'Gentlemen, you do not speak to the point; it is money. It is expected that you will offer money.' They said they had already given a very explicit answer to that point. 'No,' said he, 'you have not. What is your answer?' They replied, *'It is no; no; not a sixpence.'* The conversation continued for nearly two hours; and the public and private advance of money was pressed and repressed in a variety of forms. M. Hottinguer then said he would communicate, as nearly as he could, the substance of what had passed, either to the Minister, or to M. Bellamy, who would make the communication.

Thus far the Envoys had no proof whatever that M. Hottinguer and M. Bellamy were acting by direction of M. Talleyrand, except their own assertions to that effect, the nature of their propositions, and the respectability of their characters. These left no doubt on their minds that they were authorised to confer with them. With M. Talleyrand himself they had held no direct communication, and had seen him but once, and that only on a formal occasion, and for a few moments. We shall now see that M. Talleyrand directly committed himself, and furnished conclusive evidence that the propositions and suggestions, which had been made to the Envoys, proceeded directly from himself.

On the 22d of October, M. Hautval, a French gentleman of respectable character, informed Mr. Gerry that M. Talleyrand had expected to have seen the American Ministers frequently in their private capacities, and to have conferred with them individually on the objects of their mission; and had authorised him to make this communication to Mr. Gerry. The latter sent for his colleagues, and a conference was held with M. Hautval on the subject. Pinckney and Marshall said, as they were not acquainted with M. Talleyrand, they could not, with propriety, call on him; but, according to the custom of France, he might expect this of Gerry from a previous acquaintance in the

United States. The next day Gerry, with great reluctance, however, called on M. Talleyrand, in company with M. Hautval; but the Minister not being at his office, appointed the 28th for the interview. On that occasion, after the first introduction, M. Talleyrand began the conference. He said the Directory had passed an arrête, in which they demanded of the Envoys an explanation of some parts of the President's speech at the opening of the extra session of Congress, and a reparation for other parts. He said he was sensible that difficulties would exist on the part of the Envoys relative to this demand; but on their offering money he thought he could prevent the effect of the arrête. Mr. Gerry requested M. Hautval to inform the Minister that the Envoys had no power to offer money. In that case, replied M. Talleyrand, they can take a power on themselves; and proposed that they should make a loan. Mr. Gerry, in answer to the observations of M. Talleyrand, said, that the uneasiness of the Directory respecting the President's speech was unconnected with the object of the mission; that they had no instructions with regard to it, and no powers whatever to make a loan. If it was deemed expedient, however, one of their number could return for instructions on that point, provided the other objects of the negotiation could be discussed and adjusted. Mr. Gerry then expressed his wish that M. Talleyrand would confer with his colleagues. M. Talleyrand, in answer, said, he should be glad to confer with the other Envoys individually, *but that this matter about the money must be settled directly, without sending to America;* that he would not communicate the arrête for a week; and that, if they could adjust the difficulty respecting the speech, an application would, nevertheless, go to the United States for a loan.

The reader will not fail to observe the complete correspondence between M. Talleyrand's propositions to Mr. Gerry, and the propositions made by M. Hottinguer and M. Bellamy. The money which M. Talleyrand said must be settled directly, referred to the *douceur* of £50,000, and he knew full well that the credit of the Envoys could command it. Indeed, a mercantile house, one of whose members introduced M. Hottinguer to General Pinckney, had offered to answer their draughts; a circumstance, doubtless, well known to M. Talleyrand.

Another visit from M. Hottinguer and M. Bellamy succeeded Mr. Gerry's interview with Talleyrand. The same propositions that had hitherto formed the burden of their communications, were substantially repeated, and enforced by high and threatening language. If the offers of Talleyrand were rejected, and war ensued, the fate of Venice might befall the United States, &c. 'Perhaps,' said M. Bellamy, 'you believe that, in returning, and exposing to your countrymen the unreasonableness of the demands of this Government, you will unite them in their resistance to those demands. You are mistaken. You ought to know that the diplomatic skill of France, and the means she possesses in your country, are sufficient to enable her, with the French party in America, to throw the blame which will attend the rupture of the negotiations on the Federalists, as you term yourselves, but on the British party, as France terms you; and you may assure yourselves this will be done.'

Such was the haughty style adopted by these unofficial agents, and it produced its natural result. The Envoys now determined to hold no more indirect intercourse with the French Government; and nothing but an anxious solicitude to preserve peace with

France induced them to remain longer at Paris, unreceived as they were, and treated with personal neglect and contempt. They informed the agents of M. Talleyrand that they would receive no more propositions from persons without acknowledged authority to treat with them; but, notwithstanding this, frequent and urgent attempts were made to inveigle them into an unofficial negotiation.

Beaumarchais, through John A. Chevallie, his agent at Richmond, had employed Marshall as his advocate in a suit against the State of Virginia for military stores, &c., furnished during the Revolution. Very naturally, Beaumarchais invited Marshall and his colleagues to dine with him, and they reciprocated the attention. Beaumarchais was an intriguer, almost by profession, and an exceedingly clever one. The sort of intimacy existing between him and the Envoys was a source of hope to M. Bellamy. M. de Beaumarchais entered into his views at once. He had obtained a judgment for one hundred and forty-five thousand pounds sterling in his suit against Virginia; but from this judgment an appeal was pending, and the final result was very uncertain.

On the 17th of December, M. Bellamy informed Marshall that Beaumarchais had consented, provided his claim could be established, to sacrifice £50,000 sterling of it, as the private gratification which had been required of the Envoys, so that the payment of that sum would not be any actual loss to the American Government. But the Envoys considered this proposition as a renewal of the old system of indirect, unauthorized negotiation, and would not entertain it.

'Having been originally the counsel of M. de Beaumarchais,' says Marshall, 'I had determined, and so I had informed General Pinckney, that I would not, by my voice, establish any agreement in his favor; but that I would positively oppose any admission of the claim of any French citizen, if not accompanied with the admission of the claims of the American citizens for property captured and condemned for want of a *rôle d'equipage*.'[1]

On the 17th of December, Mr. Gerry accompanied M. Bellamy on a visit to Talleyrand, who received them politely. Mr. Gerry observed to him, that M. Bellamy had stated to him that morning some propositions as coming from M. Talleyrand (referring to the gratuity of £50,000 sterling, and the purchase of the Dutch rescriptions, as the means of restoring friendship between the two countries), respecting which he could give no opinion. M. Talleyrand said the information M. Bellamy had given him was just, and might always be relied on; but that he would reduce to writing his propositions, which he did, and after showing them to Mr. Gerry, he burnt the paper. His propositions related to the purchase of the Dutch rescriptions; but M. Talleyrand, on this occasion, did not mention the gratuity. That he left to the management of his agents.

In this stage of the business, the Envoys came to the determination to prepare a letter to M. Talleyrand, stating the object of their mission, and discussing the subjects of difference between the two nations, in the same manner as if they had actually been received; and to close the letter with requesting the Government to open the negotiation with them, or grant them their

[1] Marshall's Journal. Wait's American State Papers, vol. iii., p. 214. We should observe that the despatches of the Envoys detailing the history of their mission were prepared, for the most part, by Marshall; and from them the narrative in the text is chiefly derived.

passports. This letter was prepared by Marshall, and has always been regarded as one of the most admirable of our State papers. For clearness of statement, cogency of argument, and dignified moderation, it deserves unqualified praise.[1] Talleyrand, in his reply of the 18th of March, complained that it reversed the known order of facts, 'so that it would appear,' he said, 'from that exposition, as partial as unfaithful, that the French Republic has no real grievance to substantiate, no legitimate reparation to demand, whilst the United States should alone have a right to complain, should alone be entitled to claim satisfaction.' This testimony to the ability with which the vindication of the United States was conducted, was rather enhanced by the failure of Talleyrand to substantiate the demerits which he attributed to it. Indeed, if the United States had the right, consistently with their treaty of alliance with France, to observe a fair and honest neutrality, and that right, said Marshall, 'is not recollected ever to have been questioned, and is believed not to admit of doubt,' then all the general charges of an unfriendly disposition, made against them by M. Talleyrand, really amounted to nothing, because the facts which he adduced to support them grew inevitably out of that situation.

On the 18th of January, 1798, the French Government passed a decree subjecting to capture all neutral vessels laden in part or whole with the manufactures or productions of England or its possessions. This decree convinced the Envoys that it was entirely impracticable to effect the objects of their mission. They determined, therefore, to write Talleyrand another let-

[1] See this letter in Wait's State Papers, vol. iii., p. 219. We regret that our space forbids us to make extracts from it. It was dated January 17th, 1798.

ter, state their objections to the decree, and announce their purpose to return to the United States. This letter was prepared, but, before sending it, and demanding their passports, they deemed it expedient to know of Talleyrand if he had any reply to make to their previous letter, which thus far remained unnoticed. He informed their Secretary, on the 19th of February, that he had no answer to make, as the Directory had taken no order on the subject; but when they did, the Envoys should be informed of it. Anxious to hear explicitly from Talleyrand before sending their final letter, whether they possessed the means to accommodate the differences with France, they solicited a personal interview with him. He appointed a day to receive them. Accordingly, they waited upon him. The particulars of this interview it is unnecessary to state.

The substance of what M. Talleyrand said was, that the Directory would require some proof of a friendly disposition on the part of the United States previous to a treaty, and he alluded very intelligibly to a loan as the means of furnishing that proof. To this it was replied that they had no power to make a loan; that such an act would violate the neutrality of the United States, and involve them in war with Great Britain. Talleyrand, in answer, said that persons in their situation must often use their discretion, and exceed their powers for the public good. That a loan could be so disguised, as effectually to prevent any interference with the neutral position of the United States; that if they desired to effect the thing, they would have no difficulty in finding the means.

Mr. Gerry had already received a proposition from Talleyrand's Secretary, to stipulate a loan to the French Government now, payable after the war, in supplies of American produce for St. Domingo, and the French islands. He was in favor, it would seem, of negotiating a treaty on the basis of such a loan, which he thought might be so guarded, as not to violate our neutrality.[1]

Accordingly, he now observed, that Dutrimond had suggested a loan of this character, and Talleyrand signified that the proposed mode of payment was a means of covering it. If they were only sincere in their wish, said he, it would be easy to bring about the end. Marshall told Talleyrand, among other things, that for the United States to furnish money to France was, in fact, to make war; which they could not consent to do; that they could not make a stipulation of the kind, because it would absolutely transcend their powers; that, with respect to supplies to St. Domingo, no doubt could be entertained that American merchants would furnish them very abundantly, if France would permit the commerce; and a loan really payable after the war might then be negotiated.[2] But

---

[1] Federal Administrations, vol. ii., p. 35.

[2] As the commerce would be a perfectly lawful one with respect to the belligerents, Marshall's idea seems to have been, although not very clearly expressed, that a loan to France, payable after the war, and limited to a specific object, namely, to pay for these very supplies, might be negotiated with perfect propriety. It was not furnishing France with the means of raising money for immediate use, but enabling her at a definite time, viz., after the war, to pay for supplies which it was lawful for the merchants of a neutral nation to send to her ports.

Gerry, on the contrary, as it would appear, was in favor of stipulating a loan to France, subject only to two conditions, namely, that it should be payable after the war, and in supplies. If France could raise money on such a loan for present use, she was at liberty to do so. However disguised such a stipulation might be, it would, without doubt, have violated the neutral position of the United States. The only difference between furnishing the loan in money

Talleyrand insisted that, to prove the friendship of the United States, there must be some immediate aid, or something which might avail France.

He complained that the Envoys had not visited him, and said that, because the Directory had not given them an audience, was no reason why they should not have seen him often, and endeavored to remove the obstacles to a mutual approach. Marshall told him that their seeing the Directory, or not, was an object of no sort of concern to them; that they were perfectly independent with regard to it; but they conceived that, until their public character was in some degree recognized, and they were treated as the Ministers and representatives of their Government, they could not take upon themselves to act as Ministers; because, by doing so, they might subject themselves to some injurious circumstance to which they could not submit.

At a subsequent interview, General Pinckney told him that the Envoys considered the propositions he had suggested to them when they had previously seen him, as substantially the same as had been made to them by M. Hottinguer and M. Bellamy, and they had no power to accede to them. M. Talleyrand, without at all disavowing M. Hottinguer and M. Bellamy, proceeded to argue that it would be no departure from neutrality, to stipulate a loan after the war; but Marshall replied that any act of the American Government, on which one of the belligerent powers could raise money for immediate use, would be furnishing aid to that power, and would be taking part in the war; that he could not say what his Government

---

and in supplies, so far as it might affect France, would be, that she could raise money more readily and advantageously in the former case than in the latter.

would do if on the spot, but he was perfectly clear that, without additional orders, they could not do what France desired.

About two weeks after this last interview, namely, on the 18th of March, M. Talleyrand transmitted to the Envoys his answer to their letter of the 17th of January, which we have described on a previous page. He said it was disagreeable to be obliged to think that the instructions, under which they acted, had not been drawn up with the sincere intention of attaining pacific results; 'because, far from proceeding, in their memorial, upon some avowed principles and acknowledged facts, they have inverted and confounded both, so as to be enabled to impute to the Republic all the misfortunes of a rupture, which they seem willing to produce by such a course of proceedings. It is evident that the desire, plainly declared, of supporting, at every hazard, the treaty of London, which is the principal grievance of the Republic, of adhering to the spirit in which this treaty was formed and executed, and of not granting to the Republic any of the means of reparation, which she has proposed, through the medium of the undersigned, have dictated those instructions.' 'The undersigned does not hesitate to believe, that the American nation, like the French nation, sees this state of things with regret, and does not consider its consequences without sorrow.' 'It is, therefore, only in order to smooth the way of discussions, that he declares to the Commissioners and Envoys Extraordinary, that, notwithstanding the kind of prejudice which has been entertained with respect to them, the Executive Directory is disposed to treat with that one of the three, whose opinions, presumed to be more impartial, promise, in the course of the explanations, more of that reciprocal confidence, which is indispensable.' The Minister intended, by this language, to designate Gerry, whose views respecting a loan were supposed to be more favorable to France than those of his colleagues.

To this letter of M. Talleyrand, the Envoys presented a reply on the 3d of April. It proceeded from the pen of Marshall, and is characterized by the same ability, candor, and moderation, that distinguished his first letter. 'You contend, citizen Minister,' say the Envoys, 'that the priority of complaint is on the side of France, and that those measures, which have so injured and oppressed the people of the United States, have been produced by the previous conduct of their Government. To this the undersigned will now only observe, that if France can justly complain of any act of the Government of the United States, whether that act be prior or subsequent to the wrongs received by that Government, a disposition and a wish to do in the case what justice and friendship may require, is openly avowed, and will continue to be manifested.'

A full and searching reply to all the complaints urged against the United States by M. Talleyrand, demonstrates how insubstantial was the basis upon which they rested. The reply to two of Talleyrand's specifications of an unfriendly disposition on the part of the United States, we shall venture, at the risk of some little prolixity, to quote at length. M. Talleyrand, in pointing out the Jay Treaty as an object of complaint on the part of France, said, that the small majority by which it was sanctioned in the two Houses of Congress, and the number of respectable voices raised against it in the nation, deposed honorably in favor of the opinion which the French Government entertained of it.

'You must be sensible, citizen Minister,' was the reply, 'that the criterion by which you ascertain the merits of the instrument in question, is by no means infallible, nor can it warrant the inference you draw from it. In a republic like that of the United States, where no individual fears to utter what his judgment or his passions may dictate, where an unrestrained press conveys alike to the public eye the labors of virtue, and the efforts of particular interests, no subject which agitates and interests the public mind can unite the public voice, or entirely escape public censure. In pursuit of the same objects a difference of opinion will arise in the purest minds, from the different manner in which those objects are viewed; and there are situations in which a variety of passions combine to silence the voice of reason, and to betray the soundest judgments. In such situations, if the merit of an instrument is to be decided, not by itself, but by the approbation or disapprobation it may experience, it would surely be a safer rule to take as a guide the decision of a majority, however small that majority may be, than to follow the minority. A treaty, too, may be opposed as injurious to the United States, though it should not contain a single clause which could prejudice the interests of France. It ought not to be supposed that a treaty would, for that reason, be offensive to this Republic. . . . It is considered as having been demonstrated, that this treaty leaves the neutrality of the United States, with respect both to France and England, precisely in its former situation, and that it contains no concessions which are either unusual, or derogatory, from their alliance with this Republic. But if, in forming this judgment, the American Government has deceived itself, still it ought to be remembered that it has ever manifested a readiness to place

France on the footing of England, with respect to the articles complained of.'

Another allegation of M. Talleyrand was, 'that the journals known to be indirectly under the control of the Cabinet, have redoubled their invectives and calumnies against the Republic, its magistrates and its Envoys; and that pamphlets openly paid for by the Minister of Great Britain have reproduced, under every form, those insults and calumnies, without having ever drawn the attention of the Government to a state of things so scandalous, and which it might have repressed.' The Envoys replied thus: —

'The genius of the Constitution, and the opinions of the people of the United States, cannot be overruled by those who administer the Government. Among those principles deemed sacred in America — among those sacred rights considered as forming the bulwark of their liberty, which the Government contemplates with awful reverence, and would approach only with the most cautious circumspection, there is no one, of which the importance is more deeply impressed on the public mind, than the liberty of the press. That this liberty is often carried to excess, that it has sometimes degenerated into licentiousness, is seen and lamented; but the remedy has not yet been discovered. Perhaps it is an evil inseparable from the good with which it is allied; perhaps it is a shoot which cannot be stripped from the stalk, without wounding vitally the plant from which it is torn. However desirable those measures might be, which might correct without enslaving the press, they have never yet been devised in America. No regulations exist which enable the Government to suppress whatever calumnies and invectives any individual may choose to offer to the public eye; or to punish such calumnies and invectives, otherwise than by a legal prosecution in courts, which are alike open to all who consider themselves as injured. Without doubt, this abuse of a valuable privilege is matter of peculiar regret when it is extended to the Government of a foreign nation. The undersigned are persuaded, it never has been so extended with the approbation of the Government of the United States. Discussions respecting the conduct of foreign powers, especially in prints respecting the rights and interests of America, are unavoidably made in a nation where public measures are the results of public opinion, and certainly do not furnish cause for reproach; but it is believed that calumny and invective have never been substituted for the manly reasoning of an enlightened and injured people, without giving pain to those who administer the affairs of the Union. Certainly this offence, if it be deemed by France of sufficient magnitude to be worthy of notice, has not been confined to this Republic. It has been still more profusely lavished on its enemies, and has even been bestowed with an unsparing hand on the Federal Government itself. Nothing can be more notorious than the calumnies and invectives with which the wisest measures, and the most virtuous characters of the United States, have been pursued and traduced. It is a calamity occasioned by, and incident to, the nature of liberty, and which can produce no serious evil to France. It is a calamity occasioned neither by the direct nor indirect influence of the American Government. In fact, that Government is believed to exercise no influence over any press.

'You must be sensible, citizen Minister, with how

much truth the same complaint might be urged on the part of the United States. You must know well, what degrading and unworthy calumnies against their Government, its principles and its officers, have been published to the world by French journalists and in French pamphlets. That Government has even been charged with betraying the best interests of the nation, with having put itself under the guidance, nay, more, with having sold itself to a foreign court. But these calumnies, atrocious as they are, have never constituted a subject of complaint against France. Had not other causes, infinitely more serious and weighty, interrupted the harmony of the two republics, it would still have remained unimpaired, and the mission of the undersigned would never have been rendered necessary.'

To the suggestion of M. Talleyrand that the Executive Directory was disposed to treat with one of the Envoys, they answered that no one of them was authorized to take upon himself a negotiation evidently intrusted, by the tenor of their powers and instructions, to the whole; nor could any two of them propose to withdraw themselves from the task committed to them by their Government, whilst a possibility remained of their performing it. They concluded their letter by requesting that, if they had failed to dissipate the prejudices which had been conceived against them, and it should be the will of the Directory to order passports for the whole, or any number of them, M. Talleyrand would accompany such passports with letters of safe conduct, which would protect the vessels in which they might respectively sail, from French cruisers.

It was, doubtless, the hope and expectation of M.

Talleyrand that Pinckney and Marshall would voluntarily leave France, upon receiving his letter of the 18th of March, in which he made the offensive distinction between them and their colleague Gerry, on the ground that the 'opinions' of the latter were more 'impartial' than theirs. In a letter to Gerry, of April 3d, he said, 'I suppose, Sir, that Messrs. Pinckney and Marshall have thought it useful and proper, in consequence of the intimations which the end of my note of the 18th of March last presents, to quit the territory of the Republic.' As the Envoys, however, had previously made a conditional application for their passports, this hint to them was quite unnecessary. The truth is, the Directory wished to get rid of Pinckney and Marshall, but, at the same time, to avoid the odium of sending them away. Having done all they could, consistently with self-respect and the honor of their country, to accomplish the objects of their mission, and having failed, without any fault on their part, they were anxious to return to the United States. But they would not leave Paris on the mere intimation of the French Minister, nor without those protections which the law of nations entitled them to demand.

Marshall told Talleyrand that this was not the manner in which a foreign Minister ought to be treated. He replied that Marshall was not a foreign Minister, but was to be considered as a private American citizen; and must obtain his passports, like others, through the Consul. To this it was answered, that he was a foreign Minister, and that the French Government could not deprive him of that character, which was conferred on him, not by Talleyrand, but by the United States; and, though the Directory might refuse to receive or to treat with him, still his country had clothed him with the requisite powers, which he held independently of France; that if he was not acceptable to the French Government, and, in consequence, they determined to send him away, still he ought to be sent away like a Minister; that he ought to have his passports, with letters of safe conduct, which would protect him from the cruisers of France. Talleyrand replied, that, if Marshall wished for a passport, he must give in his name, stature, age, complexion, &c., to the American Consul, who would obtain one for him; that, with respect to a letter of safe conduct, it was unnecessary, as no risk from the cruisers would be incurred.[1]

Treated with studied indignities, Pinckney and Marshall, nevertheless, persisted in their demands, and passports were finally sent to them. The latter left Paris on the 12th of April, and France on the 16th; but General Pinckney obtained permission, with great difficulty, however, to remain for two or three months, on account of the critical state of his daughter's health. Gerry, who, according to Talleyrand, had manifested 'himself more disposed to lend a favorable ear to everything which might reconcile the two Republics,' was induced, by threats of immediate war against the United States, to separate from his colleagues, and stay in Paris. He steadily refused, however, to enter into a formal negotiation, and in August sailed for the United States. With fair intentions, doubtless, his conduct, nevertheless, was marked by several instances of weakness, and provoked severe criticisms.

The despatches of the Envoys, containing the facts narrated in this chapter, were published in the United

---

[1] Marshall's Journal. Wait's American State Papers, vol. iii., p. 394.

States, and republished in England. They reached Paris the latter part of May, and, naturally enough, attracted eager attention. Talleyrand hastened to dissipate the impressions they were calculated to make. Col. Pickering, the Secretary of State, had substituted the initials X. Y. Z. for the names of M. Hottinguer, M. Bellamy, and M. Hautval, in consequence of a promise by the Envoys that they should, in no event, be made public. Talleyrand affected an entire ignorance of the persons thus designated, and, with cool effrontery, addressed a note to Mr. Gerry, requesting their names. 'I cannot observe without surprise,' he said, 'that intriguers have profited of the insulated condition in which the Envoys of the United States have kept themselves, to make proposals and hold conversations, the object of which was evidently to deceive you.' And this was addressed to Mr. Gerry, who had Talleyrand's own assurance, that M. Bellamy *might always be relied on;* to Mr. Gerry, who had heard the propositions of the agents substantially repeated by the Minister, and was present when General Pinckney told him that his suggestions were considered by the Envoys as, in effect, the same that had been made by M. Hottinguer and M. Bellamy, the men he now styled intriguers, but then did not venture to disavow.[1]

On the 7th of June, *The Redacteur*, the official gazette, contained Talleyrand's observations on the despatches of the Envoys. They were drawn up with infinite art; and were calculated to produce an impression favorable to the purity of the French Directory. He described the despatches as a 'deplorable monument of credulity and contradictions,' and a pro-

---

[1] Ante, pp. 370.

vocation 'visibly suggested by the British Government.' Pinckney and Marshall, he said, manifested against France prejudices brought from America, or imbibed from the nature of the connections which they lost no time in forming at Paris; but Gerry had announced more impartiality. 'From this ill-suited union, which disclosed dispositions not very conciliatory, there must needs result, and there has, in fact, resulted a crooked and embarrassed career on the part of those Commissioners; hence their constant aversion to do what might reconcile, their eagerness to write what might disgust.' 'To come at some accommodation, some friendly explanation, frequent communications with the Minister of the Exterior were necessary. The latter complained publicly that he did not see them, and they avowed that he caused them to be often informed of this reproach; but two of the Commissioners, shielding themselves under ceremony, refused to comply with the desire. Mr. Gerry, at length, resolved to go, spoke twice with the Minister; . . . . said but little; and did not venture to decide on any thing.' In the meantime, says Talleyrand, they thought themselves bound to transmit to the President a very voluminous account of their negotiation; an account necessarily filled 'with the despicable manœuvres of all the intriguers.' 'It will be for ever inconceivable, that men, authorized to represent the United States near the French Republic, could have been for an instant deceived by manœuvres so evidently counterfeit, and that there should exist a temptation to convert the error in this respect into bad faith.'

We have not space to follow the ingenious turns and cool assurance of Talleyrand, through this curious performance. So disguised are his artifices, and so bold his criminations, that one is almost inclined to believe that that the Envoys had been 'most strangely deceived' by 'the incoherent prating of two intriguers.' It is only by again recurring to the facts that the reader is disabused of the impression that M. Talleyrand is a martyr in the cause of honor and innocence.

Apprehensions were entertained that the Envoys might remain in France until after the arrival there of their despatches. 'In that case,' wrote Cabot to Wolcott, 'they must give up their lives, or contradict their communications, or, according to the order of the day, pay a deal of money.'[1] But Pinckney had left Paris on the 19th of April, Gerry it suited the Directory to treat with a show of civility, and Marshall arrived at New York on the 17th of June. He found a high and general indignation among the people at the treatment himself and colleagues had received at Paris. He was received, wherever he appeared, with warmth and enthusiasm. These demonstrations Jefferson, naturally enough, viewed with extreme jealousy. The late events had visibly increased the strength of the Federalists, and diminished that of the Republicans. In a letter to Madison, he mentions the arrival of Marshall at New York, says that he has postponed his own departure from Philadelphia, in order to see if that circumstance would produce any new projects, and thus proceeds:—'No doubt he there received more than hints from Hamilton as to the tone required to be assumed, yet I apprehend he is not hot enough for his friends. Livingston came with him from New York. Marshall told him they had no idea, in France, of a war with us. That Talleyrand sent passports to him and Pinckney, but none to Gerry. Upon this Gerry staid, without explaining to

[1] Federal Administrations, vol. ii., pp 47, 48.

them the reason.[1] He wrote, however, to the President by Marshall, who knew nothing of the contents of the letter. So that there must have been a previous understanding between Talleyrand and Gerry.

'Marshall was received here [Philadelphia] with the utmost eclat. The Secretary of State and many carriages, with all the city cavalry, went to Frankford to meet him, and, on his arrival here in the evening, the bells rung till late in the night, and immense crowds were collected to see and make part of the show, which was circuitously paraded through the streets before he was set down at the city tavern.

'All this,' Jefferson characteristically adds, 'was to secure him to their views, that he might say nothing which would oppose the game they have been playing. Since his arrival, I can hear nothing directly from him, while they are disseminating through the town things, as from him, diametrically opposite to what he said to Livingston.'[2]

Congress being at this time in session, a public dinner was given to him by members of both Houses, 'as an evidence of affection for his person, and of their grateful approbation of the patriotic firmness with which he sustained the dignity of his country during his important mission.'

Marshall now returned to Virginia, (where he was received with every demonstration of respect,) and re-

---

[1] Marshall could not have told Livingston this, because Gerry had agreed with Talleyrand to remain, had told his colleagues that he intended to remain, and this, too, before the passports were sent. His not receiving a passport had nothing to do with his staying. It would have been sent, had he demanded it.

[2] Jefferson's Works, vol. iv., p. 249. June 21st, 1798. We have quoted Jefferson's letter for the facts which it contains; his conjectures are not so important.

sumed his labors at the Bar. But his determination to withdraw from political life was overcome by the clouded state of affairs, and the earnest appeals that were made to him, to come forward, at such a juncture, and engage in the public service. In the next chapter we shall view him as a member of Congress.

CHAPTER IX.

1799—1800.

MEMBER OF CONGRESS.

It was the good fortune of Marshall, as we have already had occasion to observe, to enjoy the unqualified respect and esteem of Washington; and it was a circumstance creditable to Washington's successor in the Presidency, that he invariably manifested similar sentiments towards him, and, at last, placed him in that exalted judicial position where, for so long a period, he rendered such signal services, and achieved such lasting and honorable fame.

On the death of Judge Wilson, in the summer of 1798, Mr. Adams fixed upon Marshall as his successor. 'General Marshall or Bushrod Washington,' thus he wrote the Secretary of State, 'will succeed Judge Wilson, if you have not some other gentleman to propose, who, in your opinion, can better promote the public honor and interest. Marshall is first in age, rank, and public services, probably not second in talents.'[1] In a subsequent letter to the Secretary, he says, 'The name, the connections, the character, the merit, and abilities of Mr. Washington are greatly respected. But I still think General Marshall ought to be preferred. Of the three Envoys, the conduct of

[1] Adams' Works, vol. viii., p. 596. September 14th, 1798.

Marshall alone has been entirely satisfactory, and ought to be marked by the most decided approbation of the public.[1] He has raised the American people in their own esteem, and if the influence of truth and justice, reason and argument, is not lost in Europe, he has raised the consideration of the United States in that quarter. He is older at the Bar than Mr. Washington; and you and I know by experience that seniority at the Bar is nearly as much regarded as it is in the army. If Mr. Marshall should decline, I should next think of Mr. Washington.'[2] The post was accordingly offered Marshall; but insurmountable considerations, he wrote the Secretary of State, obliged him to decline it. Subsequently, it was conferred on Bushrod Washington.

One of the reasons, and, perhaps, the chief reason, that probably induced Marshall to decline the office thus tendered him, was the resolution he had reluctantly formed to become a candidate for Congress. It was at the earnest instance of Washington that he thus consented to forego his determination to remain at the Bar, and embark on the angry sea of politics. 'I learnt with much pleasure,' wrote the former to his nephew, Bushrod Washington, 'from the postscript to your letter, of General Marshall's intention to make me a visit. I wish it of all things; and it is from the ardent desire I have to see him, that I have not delayed a moment to express it, lest, if he should have intended it on his way to Frederic, and hear of my indisposition, he might change his route. I can add, with sincerity and truth, that, if you can make it comport

---

[1] Compare letter to Cunningham, of November 7th, 1808.

[2] Adams' Works, vol. viii., p. 597. Sept. 26th, 1798. Adams, at this time, was at Quincy.

with your business, I should be exceedingly happy to see you along with him. The crisis is important. The temper of the people in this State, at least, in some places, is so violent and outrageous, that I wish to converse with General Marshall and yourself on the elections, which must soon come.'[1]

Marshall and Bushrod Washington accordingly visited Mount Vernon, and, while there, the former was induced, by the urgent wishes of General Washington, to come forward as a candidate for Congress. The following anecdote concerning this visit, though erroneous as to the time when it occurred, shows that there were personal incidents connected with it, apart from public considerations, that gave Washington much pleasure. 'He was accustomed sometimes to tell the following story:—On one occasion, during a visit he paid to Mount Vernon while President, he had invited the company of two distinguished lawyers, each of whom afterwards attained to the highest judicial situations in this country. They came on horseback, and, for convenience, or some other purpose, had bestowed their wardrobe in the same pair of saddle-bags, each one occupying his side. On their arrival, wet to the skin by a shower of rain, they were shown into a chamber to change their garments. One unlocked his side of the bag, and the first thing he drew forth was a black bottle of whiskey. He insisted that this was his companion's repository; but, on unlocking the other, there was found a huge twist of tobacco, a few pieces of corn-bread, and the complete equipment of a wagoner's pack-saddle. They had exchanged saddle-bags with some traveller on the way, and finally made their appearance in borrowed clothes, that fitted them

---

[1] Washington's Writings, vol. xi., p. 292. August 27th, 1798.

most ludicrously. The General was highly diverted, and amused himself with anticipating the dismay of the wagoner when he discovered this oversight of the men of law. It was during this visit that Washington prevailed on one of his guests to enter into public life, and thus secured to his country the services of one of the most distinguished magistrates of this or any other age.'[1]

The election contest upon which Marshall now entered was a very severe one. The public feeling was in a peculiarly inflamed state, and nowhere more so than in Virginia. Attacks on private character, imputation of unworthy motives, suspicions and conjectures, were freely employed as instruments of party warfare; and fortunate was that public character who was not more or less assailed by them. Marshall no sooner announced himself as a candidate, than he became a mark for all the shafts of party calumny. One of the means used to procure his defeat was the circulation of a malicious report through the district, that Patrick Henry was unfriendly to his election. When Mr. Henry was informed of the use that was being made of his name, he addressed a letter to his friend Archibald Blair; and the following extract will show the estimation in which he held the future Chief Justice: —

'General Marshall and his colleagues,' thus he wrote, 'exhibited the American character as respectable. France, in the period of her most triumphant fortune, beheld them as unappalled. Her threats left them as she found them, mild, temperate, firm. Can it be thought, that, with these sentiments, I should

[1] Paulding's Life of Washington, vol. ii., p. 191.

utter anything tending to prejudice General Marshall's election. Very far from it, indeed. Independently of the high gratification I felt from his public Ministry, he ever stood high in my esteem as a private citizen. His temper and disposition were always pleasant, his talents and integrity unquestioned. These things are sufficient to place that gentleman far above any competition in the district for Congress. But when you add the particular information and insight which he has gained, and is able to communicate to our public councils, it is really astonishing that even blindness itself should hesitate in the choice. But it is to be observed, that the efforts of France are to loosen the confidence of the people everywhere in the public functionaries, and to blacken characters most eminently distinguished for virtue, talents, and public confidence; thus smoothing the way to conquest, or those claims of superiority as abhorrent to my mind as conquest, from whatever quarter they may come.

'Tell Marshall I love him, because he felt and acted as a republican, as an American. The story of the Scotch merchants and old tories voting for him is too stale, childish, and foolish, and is a French *finesse;* an appeal to prejudice, not to reason and good sense. . . . As to the particular words stated by you, and said to come from me, I do not recollect saying them. But, certain I am, I never said anything derogatory to General Marshall; but, on the contrary, I really should give him my vote for Congress, preferably to any citizen in the State at this juncture, one only excepted, and that one is in another line.'[1]

---

[1] Washington's Writings, vol. xi., p. 558, January 8th, 1799. General Washington is supposed to be the citizen whom alone Mr. Henry would prefer to Marshall, and he, at that time, was in command of the army.

Another calumny employed to defeat his election is disclosed in the following letter from Marshall to Washington: —

'You may possibly have seen,' he says, 'a paragraph in a late publication, stating that several important offices in the gift of the Executive, and among others, that of Secretary of State, had been attainable by me. Few of the unpleasant occurrences produced by my declaration as a candidate for Congress (and they have been very abundant) have given me more real chagrin than this. To make a parade of proffered offices is a vanity, which I trust I do not possess; but to boast of one never in my power would argue a littleness of mind at which I ought to blush. I know not how the author may have acquired his information, but I beg leave to assure you that he never received it directly nor indirectly from me. I had no previous knowledge that such a publication was designed, or I would certainly have suppressed so much of it as relates to this subject. The writer was unquestionably actuated by a wish to serve me, and by resentment at the various malignant calumnies which have been so profusely bestowed on me. One of these was, that I only wished a seat in Congress for the purpose of obtaining some office, which my devotion to the Administration might procure. To repel this was obviously the motive of the indiscreet publication I so much regret.

'A wish to rescue myself, in your opinion, from the imputation of an idle vanity, which forms, if I know myself, no part of my character, will, I trust, apologize for the trouble this explanation may give you.'[1] But

[1] Writings of Washington, vol. xi., p. 424. May 1st, 1799.

to Washington, who knew him, this explanation was unnecessary. 'I am sorry to find,' thus he wrote in reply, 'that the publication you allude to should have given you a moment's disquietude. I can assure you, it made no impression on my mind, of the tendency apprehended by you.'[1]

Notwithstanding the persevering and systematic efforts that were made to effect a different result; notwithstanding the 'gleam of Federalism in Virginia' was fast expiring, Marshall, to the honor of the Richmond district, be it said, was elected. His majority, however, was small; and that was the only drawback to the gratification of his friends. 'The election of General Lee and Marshall,' wrote Washington, 'is grateful to my feelings. I wish, however, both of them had been elected by greater majorities; but they are elected, and that alone is pleasing. As the tide is turned, I hope it will come in with a full flow; but this will not happen, if there is any relaxation on the part of the Federalists.'[2]

Marshall took his seat in Congress at the opening of the session, in December, 1799. The state of parties in the public councils, and the part Marshall was thought likely to play there, are thus described in a letter from Wolcott to Fisher Ames:—

'The Federal party,' he says, 'is composed of the old members who were generally re-elected in the Northern, with new members from the Southern States. New York has sent an anti-Federal majority; Pennsylvania has done the same; opposition princi-

[1] Writings of Washington, vol. xi., p. 424. May 5th, 1799.

[2] Ibid., p. 425. May 5th, 1799. Letter to Bushrod Washington. The election took place in April, 1799.

ples are gaining ground in New Jersey and Maryland, and, in the present Congress, the votes of these States will be fluctuating and undecided. A number of distinguished men appear from the southward, who are not pledged by any act to support the system of the last Congress; these men will pay great respect to the opinions of General Marshall. He is, doubtless, a man of virtue and distinguished talents; but he will think much of the State of Virginia, and is too much disposed to govern the world according to rules of logic. He will read and expound the Constitution as if it were a penal statute, and will sometimes be embarrassed with doubts, of which his friends will not perceive the importance.'[1]

The opinion Wolcott thus expressed of Marshall was also professed by his political adversaries. They 'allege that he is a mere lawyer; that his mind has been so long trammelled by judicial precedent, so long habituated to the quart and tierce of forensic digladiation, (as Doctor Johnson would probably have called it,) as to be unequal to the discussion of a great question of State.'[2] This sort of criticism will be deemed less singular, when we reflect that it has been employed with respect to almost all distinguished lawyers who have entered political life; that in England, especially, the habits and learning of the Bar have been regarded as inconsistent with those bold, unfettered, comprehensive views that mark the character of the great statesman; and that, besides the evident motive which his political opponents had to depreciate his statesmanship, Wolcott and the majority of the Cabinet were equally

---

[1] Federal Administrations, vol. ii., p. 314.

[2] The British Spy, p. 183,

liable to undervalue his political sagacity, from the fact that he differed with them on a question of policy which they deemed of capital importance, namely, the mission to France; he approving, and they strongly disapproving it. Nevertheless, when it is considered that Marshall, throughout his long judicial career, invariably maintained what has been termed the liberal construction of the Constitution, and that the bias of his mind was to general principles rather than to technical distinctions, it must strike the reader as a little odd that he should have been thought, at any period of his public life to have brought to the exposition of that instrument narrow rules, or limited views. At the same time, it may be admitted that his peculiar excellence was judicial rather than political; that he was better fitted to explore the mazes of ingenious argument, to pronounce clear, impartial judgment on the systems and measures of others, than to devise systems and measures himself; and that the forming hand of nature intended him for a great magistrate, rather than a great political leader.

The answer to the President's speech was drafted by Marshall, who was Chairman of the Committee appointed for that purpose. It was a delicate task. The Federalists were divided in sentiment as to the propriety of the mission to France; those from the Northern States, for the most part, denouncing it, while the new members from the South, coming from a region of country where the anti-Federalists were rapidly gaining the ascendency, and where they had been beset by the popular cry, that the country was being hurried into war with France in consequence of British influence, and that peace was attainable, if right steps were taken, approved it. In this contrariety of opinion, Marshall had a difficult duty to perform, and that he failed to please all is not singular. In guarded, moderate language, the address expressed approbation of the mission, and, in that form, 'passed with silent dissent.'[1]

When we reflect how solicitous Washington was, that Marshall should enter Congress, and how gratified he was at his election, we cannot fail to be struck with the circumstance, that it was among the first of his Congressional duties, to announce the death of that great man, whose loss the whole nation deplored. The rumor of Washington's decease reached Philadelphia on the 18th of December. On that day, Marshall, 'in a voice that bespoke the anguish of his mind, and a countenance expressive of the deepest regret,' rose, and after stating the calamity that had probably befallen the country, moved an adjournment of the House. The next day, with 'suppressed voice, and deep emotion,' he addressed the Chair as follows: —

'Mr. Speaker: — The melancholy event which was yesterday announced with doubt, has been rendered but too certain. Our Washington is no more! The Hero, the Sage, and the Patriot of America—the man on whom, in times of danger, every eye was turned, and all hopes were placed—lives now only in his own great actions, and in the hearts of an affectionate and afflicted people.

'If, Sir, it had not been usual openly to testify respect for the memory of those whom Heaven had selected as its instruments for dispensing good to men, yet such has been the uncommon worth, and such the extraordinary incidents which have marked the life

---

[1] Federal Administrations, vol. ii., p. 314. See this address in Benton's Debates of Congress, vol. ii., p. 431.

of him whose loss we all deplore, that the whole American nation, impelled by the same feelings, would call with one voice for a public manifestation of that sorrow which is so deep and so universal.

'More than any other individual, and as much as to any one individual was possible, has he contributed to found this, our wide-spreading empire, and to give to the Western world its independence and freedom. Having effected the great object for which he was placed at the head of our armies, we have seen him converting the sword into the ploughshare, and voluntarily sinking the soldier in the citizen.'

'Having been twice unanimously chosen the Chief Magistrate of a free people, we see him, at a time when his re-election, with the universal suffrage, could not have been doubted, affording to the world a rare instance of moderation, by withdrawing from his high station to the peaceful walks of private life.

'However the public confidence may change, and the public affections fluctuate with respect to others, yet, with respect to him, they have in war and in peace, in public and private life, been as steady as his own firm mind, and as constant as his own exalted virtues.

'Let us then, Mr. Speaker, pay the last tribute of respect and affection to our departed friend — let the Grand Council of the nation display those sentiments which the nation feels.

'For this purpose, I hold in my hand some resolutions, which I will take the liberty to offer to the House.'[1]

---

[1] These were the resolutions drafted by General Lee; the last of which described Washington as 'first in war, first in peace, and first in the hearts of his countrymen.'

To every capital measure of Washington's Administration, Marshall, both in public and private life, had given an ardent and able support; to the Administration of John Adams he gave a similar support, unless, indeed, we except his approval of the mission to France, which was a measure of the President's, a measure disapproved by his Cabinet, and the leading Federal members of Congress, and, also, his vote to repeal the obnoxious clause of the sedition act.[1] This act had everywhere, and particularly in Virginia, encountered the most violent hostility. It was an exceedingly impolitic measure, and Marshall, during the canvass that resulted in his election, had announced his purpose to vote for its repeal; not because it was unconstitutional, but because it was inexpedient.[1] That pledge, he now redeemed.

He did not often mingle in the debates, while he remained a member of the House; but when he did, he made an impression upon his auditors, not easily effaced. His career in Congress was especially marked by his speech in the celebrated case of Jonathan Robbins; a speech which forever settled the questions of constitutional law involved in it. Thomas Nash, who assumed the name of Jonathan Robbins, and claimed to be a citizen of the United States, impressed by the British, was committed to jail, in Charleston, South Carolina, at the instance of the British Consul, on suspicion of having been an accomplice in piracy and murder on board the British frigate Hermione. The English Minister having made a requisition to the President for the delivery of Nash as a fugitive from justice, under a provision of the Jay treaty, the latter advised and requested the Federal judge at Charleston

[1] We refer to the clause relating to seditious libels.

to deliver him up, provided such evidence of his criminality was produced as, by the laws of the United States, or of South Carolina, would justify his commitment for trial, if the offence had been committed within the jurisdiction of the United States. Nash was accordingly delivered to the British Consul, was afterwards tried by a court-martial, found guilty of mutiny and murder, and executed. He acknowledged, before his death, that he was an Irishman.

The delivery of Nash to the British authorities occasioned a great outcry. Before the people, it was asserted that he was an American citizen, had been impressed, and was now surrendered as a murderer, for having committed a homicide in the attempt to liberate himself from illegal confinement. But, in Congress, it was admitted that he was an Irishman, and guilty of the crimes for which he suffered death. The ground of complaint was, that the question whether he should be given up, belonged exclusively to the courts, and, consequently, the advice and request of the President to have him delivered up, upon the conditions we have stated, was a dangerous interference of Executive with judicial authority.

In opposition to this view of the matter, and in defence of the course pursued by the President, Marshall addressed the House. His speech is strictly argumentative, and clearly demonstrates three propositions.

First. That the case of Nash, as stated to the President, was completely within the meaning of the rendition clause of the Jay Treaty.

Secondly. That it constituted a question for Executive and not judicial decision.

Thirdly. That, in deciding it, the President was not chargeable with an interference with judicial functions.

The train of reasoning that led him to these results elicited, at the time, the highest admiration, and has, ever since, been equally applauded. We have space for only a single extract. It relates, however, to an observation which had been made in the course of the debate, and is not directly connected with the line of his argument. But it contains sentiments which were so well calculated to interest the public feelings; sentiments, too, so worthy of him, that we have selected it for quotation.

'The gentleman from Pennsylvania [Mr. Gallatin] has said that an impressed American seaman, who should commit homicide for the purpose of liberating himself from the vessel in which he was confined, ought not to be given up as a murderer. In this I concur entirely with that gentleman. I believe the opinion to be unquestionably correct, as are the reasons he has given in support of it. I never heard any American avow a contrary sentiment, nor do I believe a contrary sentiment can find a place in the bosom of an American. I cannot pretend, and do not pretend to know the opinion of the Executive on this subject, because I have never heard the opinions of that department; but I feel the most perfect conviction, founded on the general conduct of the Government, that it could never surrender an impressed American to the nation which, in making the impressment, committed a national injury. This belief is in no degree shaken by the conduct of the Executive in this particular case. . . .

'The President has decided that a murder committed on board a British frigate on the high seas, is within the jurisdiction of that nation, and, consequently, within the twenty-seventh article of its treaty with the United States. He therefore directed Thomas Nash to be delivered to the British Minister, if satisfactory evidence of the murder should be adduced. The sufficiency of the evidence was submitted entirely to the Judge. If Thomas Nash had committed a murder, the decision was that he should be surrendered to the British Minister; but if he had not committed a murder, he was not to be surrendered. Had Thomas Nash been an impressed American, the homicide on board the Hermione would, most certainly, not have been a murder.

'The act of impressing an American, is an act of lawless violence. The confinement on board a vessel is a continuation of the violence, and an additional outrage. Death committed within the United States, in resisting such violence, is not murder, and the person giving the wound cannot be treated as a murderer. Thomas Nash was only to be delivered up to justice on such evidence as, had the fact been committed within the United States, would be sufficient to have induced his commitment and trial for murder. Of consequence, the decision of the President was so expressed, as to exclude the case of an impressed American liberating himself by homicide.'

Though the case of Nash had been made a party question, so conclusive was the argument in support of the President's course, that many of the Democratic members voted in its justification, and the resolutions censuring it were lost by a vote of sixty-one to thirty-five. Out of doors, too, the fierce invective and denunciation that had been called forth by a misapprehension of the case, were silenced, and the public opinion was rescued from the prejudices that had surrounded it.

Congress adjourned on the 14th of May, and Marshall having been appointed Secretary of State, resigned his seat in that body. We have seen with what difficulty he was elected; and, as an evidence of the strength of the current that was setting against the Federalists, we may mention that, at the subsequent election, his place was supplied by a Republican. 'Mr. Mayo, who was proposed to succeed General Marshall, lost his election by an immense majority, was grossly insulted in public by a brother-in-law of the late Senator Taylor, and was afterwards wounded by him in a duel.'[1]

---

[1] Wolcott to Ames, August 10th, 1800. Federal Administrations, vol. ii., pp. 400, 404.

CHAPTER X.

1800-1801.

SECRETARY OF STATE.

THE Cabinet of President Adams, as described at the time, was an exceedingly disjointed one. They were, as he afterwards said, 'a legacy of Secretaries left him by General Washington.' The Secretary of State was Timothy Pickering; of the Treasury, Oliver Wolcott; of War, James M'Henry; of the Navy, Benjamin Stoddart;[1] and the Attorney-General was Charles Lee.

The first, Mr. Adams has described with characteristic point, and in terms which, it has been observed, would be equally applicable to himself. 'He [Mr. Pickering] is, for anything I know, a good son, husband, father, grandfather, brother, uncle, and cousin; but he is a man in a mask, sometimes of silk, sometimes of iron, and sometimes of brass; and he can change them very suddenly, and with some dexterity.' 'He is extremely susceptible of violent and inveterate prejudices; and yet, such are the contradictions to be found in human characters, he is capable of very sudden and violent transitions from one extreme to an opposite extreme. Under the simple appearance of a

[1] Stoddart was appointed by Mr. Adams; the Navy Department being created after his accession to the Presidency.

bald head and *straight hair*, and under professions of profound republicanism, he conceals an ardent ambition, envious of every superior, and impatient of obscurity. I always think of a coal-pit, covered over with red earth, glowing within, but unable to conceal its internal heat, for the interstices which let out the smoke, and now and then a flash of flame.'

Wolcott, though not belonging to the highest grade of public character, was a man of abilities; energetic, ardent, and sagacious. He administered the affairs of the Treasury with great prudence, and graced the position he occupied.

M'Henry, though 'sensible, judicious, well-informed, of an integrity never questioned, of a temper which, though firm in the support of principles, had too much moderation and amenity to offend by the manner of doing it,'[1] did not possess the peculiar qualifications required for the duties of the War Department. He wanted skill in the details of administration. 'The diffidence which he feels,' wrote Wolcott, 'exposes his business to delays, and he sometimes commits mistakes which his enemies employ to impair his influence.'[2]

The Secretary of the Navy, and the Attorney-General, are thus described, and by the same hand: —

'Mr. Stoddart,' he says, 'is a man of great sagacity, and conducts the business of his Department with success and energy; he means to be popular; he has more of the confidence of the President than any offi-

[1] Thus described by Hamilton.

[2] Wolcott to Ames, December 29th, 1799. Federal Administrations, vol. ii., p. 315.

cer of the Government. He professes to know less than he really knows, and to be unequal to the task of forming or understanding a political system. He will have much influence in the Government, and avoid taking his share of the responsibility.

'Mr. Lee is a sensible man, and I think a candid man, who thinks much of Virginia. He fears disorders and a dissolution of the Union. He frequently dissents to what is proposed by others, and approves the sentiments of the President; but, with respect to *measures*, will rarely take an active part'.[1]

The differences between the President and his three principal Secretaries, Pickering, M'Henry, and Wolcott, respecting the mission to France, and the acrimonious feelings growing out of those differences, led to important changes in the Cabinet. M'Henry was forced to resign, and Pickering, refusing to resign, was dismissed. Wolcott was retained, it was said, because the President feared derangements in the affairs of the Treasury;[2] but the more probable cause is, that he was not informed as to the extent of his hostility. Wolcott, however, voluntarily resigned before the close of the year.

M'Henry resigned on the 6th of May, 1800; the re-

[1] Wolcott to Ames, December 29th, 1799. Federal Administrations, vol. ii., p. 315.

[2] M'Henry to M'Henry, May 20th, 1800. Ibid., pp. 346, 348. It must be admitted that Adams had just cause for the removal of his obnoxious Secretaries. He certainly was entitled to the aid of a Cabinet who sympathized with his views. But Pickering, Wolcott, and M'Henry not only condemned his policy, but were personally opposed to him. Pickering hated him, openly denounced him, and all desired to get rid of him. Mutual confidence was gone. The wonder is, considering Adams' impetuous temperament, that they were not dismissed at an earlier moment.

signation to take effect on the 1st of June. On the 7th, Marshall was nominated as his successor. 'He was never consulted, and had no intimation that M'Henry was to retire.'[1] This appointment he declined; but, on the 13th, accepted the Department of State, from which Pickering had been removed the day before. The War Department was filled by Mr. Dexter.

The accession of Marshall to the Cabinet, under the circumstances we have described, caused not the slightest diminution of friendship between Pickering and himself, nor the least abatement of confidence and respect on the part of those who sympathized with the discarded Secretaries. Even Wolcott applauds his acceptance of the post assigned him, and bears testimony to the importance of his services. 'Let me not be suspected,' thus he writes, 'of entertaining the harsh opinion that the gentlemen lately appointed to office are not independent men. I highly respect and esteem them both, and consider their acceptance of their offices as the best evidence of their patriotism. . . I consider General Marshall and Mr. Dexter as more than Secretaries — as State Conservators — the value of whose services ought to be estimated, not only by the good they do, but by the mischief they have prevented. If I am not mistaken, however, General Marshall will find himself out of his proper element.'[2]

'But,' says Mr. Adams, 'my new Minister, Marshall, did all to my entire satisfaction,' and he might have added, to the public satisfaction also. His instructions to Mr. King, our Minister at the Court of St. James,

---

[1] Wolcott to Ames, August 10th, 1800. Federal Administrations, vol. ii., pp. 400, 402.

[2] Ibid.

respecting the claims of British creditors, and neutral rights, have always, deservedly, held high rank in the roll of American State papers. The pending negotiations with France threatened to compromit us with England, as the negotiations with England six years before had threatened to involve us in war with France. But this pretension, that one nation may interfere with the concerns of another nation, equally independent and sovereign as itself, was never submitted to by the United States. The Jay treaty was ratified in spite of the clamors and threats of France, and the negotiations with France were prosecuted to a successful conclusion, notwithstanding the jealousy of England. 'The United States,' said Marshall, in a despatch to Mr. King, 'do not hold themselves in any degree responsible to France or to Great Britain for their negotiations with the one or the other of those Powers; but they are ready to make amicable and reasonable explanations with either. The aggressions sometimes of one and sometimes of another belligerent Power, have forced us to contemplate and prepare for war as a probable event. We have repelled, and we will continue to repel, injuries not doubtful in their nature, and hostilities not to be misunderstood. But this is a situation of necessity, not of choice. It is one in which we are placed, not by our own acts, but by the acts of others, and which we change as soon as the conduct of others will permit us to change it.

The Presidential election in 1800 was conducted with great violence, and resulted, as is well known, in the defeat of Mr. Adams. His competitor was the only public character, it is believed, towards whom Marshall ever imbibed and retained feelings of personal hostility. He had no confidence either in his politics or morals. When, therefore, it was ascertained that the

House of Representatives would be compelled to choose between Jefferson and Burr for President, he inclined to the opinion that the Federalists should support the latter. A letter from Hamilton, however, portraying the character of Burr, presented the matter in a different light. 'Being no longer in the House of Representatives,' thus he wrote Hamilton, 'and, consequently, compelled by no duty to decide between them, my own mind had scarcely determined to which of these gentlemen the preference was due. To Mr. Jefferson, whose political character is better known than that of Mr. Burr, I have felt almost insuperable objections. His foreign prejudices seem to me totally to unfit him for the Chief Magistracy of a nation, which cannot indulge those prejudices without sustaining deep and permanent injury. In addition to this solid and immovable objection, Mr. Jefferson appears to me to be a man who will embody himself with the House of Representatives. By weakening the office of President, he will increase his personal power. He will diminish his responsibility, sap the fundamental principles of the Government, and become the leader of that party which is about to constitute the majority of the Legislature. The morals of the author of the letter to Mazzei cannot be pure.[1] With these impressions concerning Mr. Jefferson, I was, in some degree, disposed to view with less apprehension any other characters, and to consider the alternative now offered us as a circumstance not to be entirely neglected.

'Your representation of Mr. Burr, with whom I am entirely unacquainted, shows that from him still greater danger than even from Mr. Jefferson may be apprehended. Such a man as you describe is more to

---

[1] Compare Ellsworth's opinion, ante, p. 177.

be feared, and may do more immediate, if not greater, mischief. Believing that you know him well, and are impartial, my preference would certainly not be for him; but I can take no part in this business. I cannot bring myself to aid Mr. Jefferson. Perhaps respect for myself should, in my present situation, deter me from using any influence (if, indeed, I possess any) in support of either gentleman. Although no consideration could induce me to be the Secretary of State while there was a President whose political system I believed to be at variance with my own, yet this cannot be so well known to others, and it might be suspected that a desire to be well with the successful candidate had, in some degree, governed my conduct.'[1]

With such sentiments, and a line of conduct, uniform and consistent, in support of Federal measures, unless his concurrence with the President respecting the mission to France, and his opposition to the sedition act, be exceptions, it was yet reported, before the result of the election was known, that, whatever the event, he would not voluntarily retire from his post. 'I have been told,' wrote M'Henry, that 'Mr. Marshall has signified that he does not mean to resign in the event of Mr. Jefferson being elected President, but to wait most patiently the development of his politics. Will there, my friend, be so great an antipathy between the politics of the two gentlemen, that one of them must fly off from the other?'[2] To this Wolcott thus replied:— 'The issue of the election is uncertain, but if Mr. Jefferson should be chosen, Mr. Marshall will certainly

[1] Marshall to Hamilton, January 1st, 1801. Hamilton's Works, vol. vi., p. 501.

[2] M'Henry to Wolcott, November 9th, 1800. Federal Administrations, vol. ii., p. 445.

retire. The opposition of sentiment between these men appears to be decided, and, I believe, is unchangeable; what you have heard is, therefore, a mistake.'[1]

Marshall continued to discharge the duties of the State Department until the close of Mr. Adams' Administration, on the 4th of March, 1801. He had, however, in the meantime, as we shall see in the next chapter, been appointed Chief Justice of the United States.

---

[1] November 26th, 1800. Ibid., p. 447.

CHAPTER XI.

1801—1835.

CHIEF JUSTICE OF THE UNITED STATES.

Upon the resignation of Chief Justice Ellsworth, Jay was nominated as his successor; but he declined the appointment. A very general expectation was then entertained that the vacant post would be tendered to Judge Patterson. He stood high in the estimation of the Bar for learning and abilities; nor was the President insensible to his merits. But Mr. Adams objected to his nomination, it is said, lest it might wound the feelings of Judge Cushing, an old friend, and the senior member of the Court. Looking, therefore, beyond the bench for a suitable person to fill the office, his 'prompt and spontaneous choice' fell upon John Marshall. Accordingly, on the 31st of January, 1801, he received the appointment of Chief Justice of the United States.

He had now attained the age of forty-five. His personal appearance at this period of his life has been thus described—'The Chief Justice of the United States is, in his person, tall, meagre, emaciated: his muscles relaxed, and his joints so loosely connected, as not only to disqualify him, apparently, for any vigorous exertion of body, but to destroy everything like harmony in his air and movements. Indeed, in his whole appearance and demeanor; dress, attitudes, gesture; sitting, standing, or walking; he is as far removed from the idolized graces of Lord Chesterfield, as any other gentleman on earth. His head and face are small, in proportion to his height; his complexion swarthy; the muscles of his face, being relaxed, make him appear to be fifty years of age, nor can he be much younger. His countenance has a faithful expression of great good humor and hilarity; while his black eyes, that unerring index, possess an irradiating spirit which proclaims the imperial powers of the mind that sits enthroned within.'[1]

Several years later, Judge Story, then a young man of thirty, who had gone to Washington to argue the case of Fletcher *v.* Peck,[2] communicated to a friend the following description of the Chief Justice: —

'Marshall,' he says, 'is of a tall, slender figure, not graceful nor imposing, but erect and steady. His hair is black, his eyes small and twinkling, his forehead rather low, but his features are, in general, harmonious. His manners are plain, yet dignified; and an unaffected modesty diffuses itself through all his actions. His dress is very simple, yet neat; his language chaste, but hardly elegant; it does not flow rapidly, but it seldom wants precision. In conversation, he is quite familiar, but is occasionally embarrassed by a hesitancy and drawling. His thoughts are always clear and ingenious, sometimes striking, and not often inconclusive; he possesses great subtlety of mind, but it is only occasionally exhibited. I love his laugh — it is too hearty for an intriguer — and his good tem-

---

[1] The British Spy, p. 178.

[2] Cranch, vol. vi., p. 137.

per and unwearied patience are equally agreeable on the Bench and in the study. His genius is, in my opinion, vigorous and powerful, less rapid than discriminating, and less vivid than uniform in its light. He examines the intricacies of a subject with calm and persevering circumspection, and unravels the mysteries with irresistible acuteness. He has not the majesty and compactness of thought of Dr. Johnson; but, in subtle logic, he is no unworthy disciple of David Hume.'[1]

'There is no man in the Court that strikes me like Marshall,' wrote Daniel Webster when serving as a member of Congress from New Hampshire. 'He is a plain man, looking very much like Col. Adams, and about three inches taller. I have never seen a man of whose intellect I had a higher opinion.'[2] And the impression thus early made upon Mr. Webster was confirmed and strengthened by his subsequent practice in the Supreme Court. Alluding to the common expression of the Chief Justice, 'it is admitted,' he once remarked to Judge Story, 'when Judge Marshall says, it is admitted, Sir, I am preparing for a bomb to burst over my head, and demolish all my points.'[3]

When Marshall first came to the Bench, his distinguished talents were known and recognized; but as time advanced, and his abilities were more conspicu-

---

[1] Story's Life and Letters, vol. i., p. 166. Letter to Fay, February 25th, 1808.

[2] Private Correspondence of Daniel Webster, vol. i., p. 243. Letter to Ezekiel Webster, March 28th, 1814.

[3] Story's Life and Letters, vol. ii., p. 505.

ously exhibited, and the winning graces of his daily life more generally observed, he came to be regarded by the Bar and the country with reverence and affection. If we except Washington, it may be safely asserted, that no American citizen, either in public or private life, has been so universally beloved and esteemed. He occupied the post of Chief Justice during the long period of thirty-four years, and thirty-two volumes of reports, in which his decisions are collected and preserved, attest the extent, variety, and importance of his labors. In all coming time, the student of international and constitutional jurisprudence will there discover that intellectual power, that depth of investigation, and wisdom of decision, which gave him such a commanding position among the jurists of his time.

He combined, in a remarkable degree, the qualities that constitute a great magistrate; a mind which no sophistry or subtlety could mislead; a firmness that nothing could shake, untiring patience, and spotless integrity. In legal acquirements, indeed, he has been surpassed by others. He was more familiar with principles than cases, and more 'knowing' than 'learned.' 'His mind,' said a gifted cotemporary, 'is not very richly stored with knowledge; but it is so creative, so well organized by nature, or disciplined by early education, and constant habits of systematic thinking, that he embraces every subject with the clearness and facility of one prepared by previous study to comprehend and explain it. So perfect is his analysis, that he extracts the whole matter, the kernel of inquiry, unbroken, clean, and entire. In this process, such are the instinctive neatness and precision of his mind, that no superfluous thought, or even word, ever presents itself, and still he says everything that seems appropriate to the subject.'[1] It was the rare faculty which he possessed, of detecting intuitively, as it were, the decisive point of a case, that particularly distinguished him. 'It was matter of surprise,' says Judge Story, 'to see how easily he grasped the leading principles of a case, and cleared it of all its accidental incumbrances; how readily he evolved the true points of the controversy, even when it was manifest, that he never before had caught even a glimpse of the learning, upon which it depended.'[2]

It has been said of Fox, that, owing to his want of extensive information, his conversation degenerated into argument. He challenged propositions, and discussed facts, in order to fix and satisfy his own mind. For a similar reason, perhaps, Marshall courted and delighted in the discussions of the Bar. 'He was solicitous,' says the authority we have just quoted, 'to hear arguments; and not to decide causes without them. And no Judge ever profited more by them. No matter whether the subject was new or old; familiar to his thoughts, or remote from them; buried under a mass of obsolete learning, or developed for the first time yesterday; whatever was its nature, he courted argument, nay, he demanded it.'[3] And, says Mr. Binney, 'whether the argument was animated or dull, instructive or superficial, the regard of his expressive eye was an assurance that nothing that ought to affect the cause was lost by inattention or indifference; and the courtesy of his general manner was only so far restrained on the Bench, as was necessary for the dignity of office, and for the suppression of familiarity.'[4]

[1] Sketches and Essays of Public Characters, by Francis W. Gilmer.

[2] Discourse on Marshall, p. 70.

[3] Ibid.

[4] Eulogy on John Marshall, p. 58.

He never evaded, nor attempted to evade the force of an opposing argument. He met it fairly, gave it its due weight, and then exposed its fallacy, or inapplicability, with irresistible cogency. 'Perhaps no judge ever excelled him in the capacity to hold a legal proposition before the eyes of others in such various forms and colors. It seemed a pleasure to him to cast the darkest shades of objection over it, that he might show how they could be dissipated by a single glance of light. He would, by the most subtle analysis, resolve every argument into its ultimate principles, and then, with a marvellous facility, apply them to the decision of the cause.'[1]

It has been remarked, that no judge ever profited more from argument; and it is not, perhaps, diverging into the circle of exaggeration, to say, that no Bar was ever more capable of aiding the mind of the Bench, than the Bar of the Supreme Court, in the time of Chief Justice Marshall.

Massachusetts was there represented by Dexter, a man of original power, who brought to the discussions of the forum something more than the learning of the lawyer; a comprehension that grasped the very foundations of all law, and a force of argument and illustration that riveted all minds;[2] and Webster, eminent for his powers of argument and eloquence, learned in

---

[1] Story's Discourse, p. 69.

[2] Mr. Dexter depended much more upon the suggestions and deductions of his own mind than upon the learning of the books. It has been said, that he 'often found himself sustained by the authority of a Scott or a Mansfield, when he was not aware that he was treading in the footsteps of those great jurists.' He was, undoubtedly, one of the ablest advocates that has ever appeared at the American Bar.

the principles of the common law, strong, compact, and massive.[1]

New York sent there, along with Hoffman, Wells, and Ogden,—Emmett and Oakly; the one possessing a mind of great activity, vigor, and resource, and a heart full of the springs of an affecting eloquence; and the other, with an intellect so naturally logical, and so adapted to reasoning upon legal subjects, that, without the aid of profound learning, he rose to a high grade of distinction as a lawyer, and discharged the duties of Chief Justice of New York with an ability that adorned even the seat that had been so long and eminently filled by a Kent.

Pennsylvania supplied a Tilghman, 'strong, clear, pointed, and logical;'[2] a Rawle, precise, perspicuous, and accurate, but with a mind better adapted, perhaps, to explore the niceties of the law than firmly to grasp its more enlarged principles; an Ingersoll, learned and laborious, but diffuse and tedious; a Duponceau, diligent, acute, and ingenious; a Hopkinson, an able lawyer, and a man of liberal principles and culture; a Sergeant, distinguished for the vigor and grasp of his mind; together with another and living name, whose merits and abilities the voice of future eulogy cannot fail to distinguish and record.[3]

Maryland asserted a high, and, probably, a pre-eminent place at that Bar, in the persons of Luther Martin, William Pinkney, and Robert G. Harper. Jefferson termed the former, during the progress of Burr's

[1] A very comprehensive and candid estimate of 'Daniel Webster as a jurist,' will be found in a pamphlet, under that title, which contains an Address to the Law Students at Cambridge, by the Hon. Joel Parker, LL.D.

[2] Judge Story. See also a notice of Tilghman, by Judge Duncan, in Lyle *v.* Richards, in Sergeant & Rawle's Reports, vol. ix.

[3] It is scarcely necessary to say, that reference is here made to Horace Binney.

trial, 'an impudent Federal bull-dog,' a description suggestive of the pluck, vigor, and strength, that distinguished him. Nature had given him a mind of great force; and deep study had stored it with profound learning. His uncommon powers, however, were not always at command, and, before he could concentrate them upon his objects, he was desultory, wandering, and inaccurate.

Pinkney was vain, artificial, arrogant, and overbearing; but, in those qualities that constitute the great lawyer and advocate, he was unequalled, certainly not surpassed by any of his cotemporaries. His talents, powerful from nature, and cultivated by learning, were stimulated and excited by an ambition that never paused in the pursuit of professional fame. Chief Justice Marshall said, that he never knew his equal as a reasoner — so clear and luminous was his method of argumentation.[1] With a harsh and feeble voice, with a manner vehement, nay, almost boisterous; 'yet, notwithstanding these defects,' says Judge Story, 'such is his strong and cogent logic, his elegant and perspicuous language, his flowing graces, and rhetorical touches, his pointed and persevering arguments, that he enchants, interests, and almost irresistibly leads away the understanding.'[2]

Harper was an able lawyer, a graceful orator, and united, in his forensic efforts, argument and eloquence with admirable felicity.

Virginia furnished fit representatives of her genius in Wickham, Leigh, Nicholas, and the buoyant and gifted Wirt, who combined, not, perhaps, in exact proportions, the great and the graceful, and enforced his

---

[1] Story's Life and Letters, vol. ii., p. 494.

[2] Ibid., vol. i., p. 217. Letter to Mrs. Story, March 5th, 1812.

carefully prepared arguments with an attractive and persuasive oratory.

These were the men, with others, among the living and the dead, who graced the Bar, and enlightened the wisdom of the Court over which presided Chief Justice Marshall. Assisted by their learning, their investigations, and arguments, his judicial career furnishes a series of closely reasoned decisions which stand, and will forever stand, enduring monuments of his intellectual power. His conclusions may not always command assent, but the force of his reasoning cannot fail to be felt. Several of these decisions, of a more interesting character, perhaps, than the others, though the ability they display is characteristic of them all, will now claim our attention. It should be observed, however, that it was more particularly in the department of constitutional law that the influence of Chief Justice Marshall, in the decisions of the Supreme Court, was most marked and observable. When it came to the exposition of the Constitution, his colleagues on the Bench, learned, able, and distinguished as they were, submitted to his superior wisdom, and the impress of his mind is indelibly stamped on their adjudications. His opinions as to the scope of that instrument, the extent of the powers conferred by it, and the ends contemplated by its framers, were not the growth of a day, nor formed after he came to the Bench. He had borne a part in the deliberations of the Virginia Convention; he had participated in the discussions that had shaken the halls of the Virginia Legislature respecting the rights of the States, as well as the rights and powers of the General Government; and his experience, studies, and reflection had led him to adopt what has been called the liberal interpretation of the Constitution; an interpretation which he believed necessary to secure its benefits, and promote the intentions of its framers. Hence his decisions as a judge, in cases involving questions of constitutional law, were the natural fruit of the system of construction which he had previously and maturely adopted. What he thought of the opposing system may be seen from his opinion in the case of Gibbons *v.* Ogden.[1]

'This instrument,' said he, 'contains an enumeration of powers expressly granted by the people to their Government. It has been said that these powers ought to be construed strictly. But why ought they to be so construed? Is there one sentence in the Constitution which gives countenance to this rule? In the last of the enumerated powers, that which grants expressly the means for carrying all others into execution, Congress is authorized "to make all laws which shall be necessary and proper" for the purpose. But this limitation on the means which may be used is not extended to the powers which are conferred; nor is there one sentence in the Constitution, which has been pointed out by the gentlemen of the Bar, or which we have been able to discern, that prescribes this rule. We do not, therefore, think ourselves justified in adopting it. What do gentlemen mean by a strict construction? If they contend only against that enlarged construction which would extend words beyond their natural and obvious import, we might question the application of the term, but should not controvert the principle. If they contend for that narrow construction which, in support of some theory not to be found in the Constitution, would deny to the Government those powers which the words of the grant, as usually understood,

---

[1] Wheaton, vol. ix., p. 187.

import, and which are consistent with the general views and objects of the instrument; for that narrow construction which would cripple the Government, and render it unequal to the objects for which it is declared to be instituted, and to which the powers given, as fairly understood, render it competent; then we cannot perceive the propriety of this strict construction, nor adopt it as the rule by which the Constitution is to be expounded.'

And again:—'Powerful and ingenious minds taking, as postulates, that the powers expressly granted to the Government of the Union are to be contracted, by construction, into the narrowest possible compass, and that the original powers of the States are retained, if any possible construction will retain them, may, by a course of well-digested, but refined and metaphysical reasoning, founded on these premises, explain away the Constitution of our country, and leave it, a magnificent structure, indeed, to look at, but totally unfit for use. They may so entangle and perplex the understanding as to obscure principles which were before thought quite plain, and induce doubts where, if the mind were to pursue its own course, none would be perceived. In such a case it is peculiarly necessary to recur to safe and fundamental principles, to sustain those principles, and, when sustained, to make them the tests of the arguments to be examined.'[1]

And, in his dissenting opinion in the case of Ogden *v.* Saunders,[2] the Chief Justice incidentally remarked upon the principles which he thought ought to be applied to to the construction of the Constitution. 'To say,' he observed, 'that the intention of the instru-

[1] Wheaton, vol. ix., p. 221. [2] Ibid., vol. xii., p. 332.

ment must prevail; that this intention must be collected from its words; that its words are to be understood in that sense in which they are generally used by those for whom the instrument was intended; that its provisions are neither to be restricted into insignificance, nor extended to objects not comprehended in them, nor contemplated by its framers — is to repeat what has been already said more at large, and is all that can be necessary.'

Before proceeding to notice the cases in which the principles, as thus explained, were applied to the interpretation of the Constitution, we shall invite the reader's attention to several of those criminal and prize causes which constitute marked features of Marshall's judicial career. Of the former class, the treason trials growing out of the enterprizes of Col. Burr will necessarily find a place here.

Aaron Burr, whether viewed in the worst or best aspects of his character, was an extraordinary man. He was distinguished as a soldier, and, if judged by the standard of success, had but few superiors as a lawyer. He was aptly termed 'the subtlest practitioner of the times.'[1] In public life he was remarked for his commanding dignity and impressive oratory; and, in private, for an ease and grace, and charm of manner, which won the regards of men, and dazzled and captivated women. 'He was brave, affable, munificent, of indomitable energy, of signal perseverance. In his own person, he combined two opposite natures. He was studious, but insinuating; dignified, yet seduc-

[1] His definition of law, however, namely, 'whatever is boldly asserted and plausibly maintained,' shows the estimate in which he held his profession, and the ethics he applied to its practice.

tive. Success did not intoxicate, nor reverse dismay him.'[1] On the other hand, he is represented as 'profligate in morals, public and private; selfish and artful; a master in dissimulation, treacherous, cold-hearted, subtle, intriguing, full of promise, a sceptic in honesty, a scorner of all things noble and good,' from whom the people shrank, 'in mistrust, as from a cold and glittering serpent.'[2]

Suspected, and separated, in great measure, from his own party, by reason of his contest with Jefferson, and anathematized by the other in consequence of his duel with Hamilton, Burr found himself, in the maturity of his years and talents, cut off, apparently, from the very source of political honors. Being thus debarred from a career, in his own country, that could give employment to his abilities, and scope to his ambition, he naturally looked abroad for an appropriate field of action. At this time, namely, in the spring of 1805, and at the close of his term as Vice-President of the United States, the imminence of war with Spain held out to him a prospect of power and aggrandizement.

It was well known that there was great dissatisfaction throughout Mexico with the mother country; that the priesthood were very generally disaffected, and ready to lend their powerful aid in throwing off the yoke of Spain, provided their privileges were asserted and secured. The times seemed eminently favorable for the prosecution of a successful enterprize against that country; an enterprize, it is stated, which, in the event of war, and as a means of inflicting a blow upon Spain, was favored by Mr. Jefferson. 'Burr saw the glittering prize, and resolved to seize it. He

---

[1] Safford's Life of Blennerhassett, p. 182. [2] Ibid.

would conquer this gorgeous realm, and realize, in this new world, as Napoleon did in the old, a dream of romance.'[1] That he also anticipated a separation of the Western from the Atlantic States, and hoped to profit by such an event, is probable; but that it constituted any part of his project to accomplish, or attempt to accomplish such separation, is very improbable. 'That a man of sense and ability should entertain such a notion, relying for aid on associates whom he knew would countenance no treason, is a preposterous and insane supposition. As he said on his death-bed, he might as well have attempted to seize the moon, and parcel it out among his followers.'[2] There are some circumstances, however, that seemingly justify the suspicion that he intended to avail himself of the discontents existing in the Mississippi and Louisiana territories, and, if the people were ready for such a movement, to detach them from the Union.

In the spring of 1805, he visited the Western country, with the view to make arrangements for the conquest of Mexico, and subordinately to engage in a land speculation. Through the summer and autumn of that year, everything seemed to favor his project. War with Spain appeared to be inevitable. The men of the West, under the impression that Burr's enterprise was favored by the Administration, were eager and impatient to enlist under his banner. But, in the winter of 1805–6, the idea of war with Spain, unless the United States were actually invaded, was abandoned by the Administration. Burr, therefore, no longer had the benefit of that pretext in prosecuting his designs; but, nevertheless, he pressed forward to their accomplishment. During his tour through the

---

[1] Safford's Life of Blennerhassett, p. 71. [2] Ibid., p. 182.

West, in 1805, he had an interview with General Wilkinson, who was then in command of the Western forces, and, without question, Wilkinson promised to co-operate with him. With the expectation of such powerful support, Burr prosecuted his arrangements with great vigor, and on the 29th of July, 1806, being then at Philadelphia, he despatched Samuel Swartwout to Wilkinson with a letter in *cypher;* a letter which, it is hardly conceivable, so cautious and astute a person would write, unless a previous understanding existed with the party to whom it was addressed. The letter, however, related to an enterprise against the Spanish territories, and had no necessary or natural reference to any other.

Trusting to Wilkinson's co-operation, Burr proceeded to the West in August, and commenced active preparations for his projected enterprise. Boats and stores of various kinds were collected, and an unusual number of strange faces made their appearance on the Ohio and its tributary waters. Rumors now began to circulate that these circumstances boded no good to the country; that a conspiracy had been set on foot to dismember the Union; and that designs were meditated which were masked from the public eye. Wilkinson, too, on receiving Burr's communication by Swartwout, proved, according to Burr, 'a perfidious villain.' He denounced the enterprise, and adopted very vigorous measures to defeat it. Burr's letter he forwarded to the President; arrested Swartwout, Bollman, and others, whom he refused to deliver to the civil authorities, and proceeded to erect works for the defence of New Orleans.

On the 27th of November, 1806, the President issued a proclamation against Burr's proceedings, and enjoined the arrest of all persons concerned in them.

The result was, that the expedition was broken up, and Burr arrested, while attempting to escape across the country to Pensacola, and sent under guard to Richmond, Virginia, for trial. Swartwout and Bollman had already been sent to Washington, where they were committed to prison on a charge of treason against the United States.

Their counsel moved the Supreme Court, then in session[1] at Washington, for a writ of *habeas corpus*, to bring them before that tribunal, that the cause of their commitment might be inquired into. This motion was granted. It was then moved that the prisoners be either discharged or admitted to bail.[2]

The evidence against Swartwout consisted chiefly of an affidavit made by General Wilkinson, which comprehended the substance of Burr's letter, of which we have seen Swartwout was the bearer, and also Swartwout's declarations to General Wilkinson.[3] The Court held that Burr's enterprise, as disclosed in his letter, related to a foreign power, and, consequently, was not treasonable; that Swartwout's declarations, even though they might show a treasonable intention, afforded no sufficient proof that there was an open assemblage of men to carry it into execution, without which the crime of treason had not been consummated;

---

[1] February term, 1807. [2] Cranch, vol. iv., pp. 75–137.

[3] Swartwout, on an inquiry from Wilkinson, said, 'This territory, (meaning, probably, the Louisiana territory, though this is not altogether clear,) 'would be revolutionized where the people were ready to join them, and that there would be some seizing, he supposed, at New Orleans.' He also stated that 'Col. Burr, with the support of a powerful association extending from New York to New Orleans, was levying an armed body of seven thousand men from the State of New York and the Western States and territories, with a view to carry an expedition to the Mexican territories.'

and, consequently, that he could not be held on that charge. Against Bollman there was no evidence, whatever, to support a charge of treason, and he was likewise discharged.

Marshall, *Chief Justice.* 'The specific charge brought against the prisoners is treason in levying war against the United States.' 'To constitute that specific crime for which the prisoners now before the Court have been committed, war must be actually levied against the United States. However flagitious may be the crime of conspiring to subvert, by force, the Government of our country, such conspiracy is not treason. To conspire to levy war, and actually to levy war, are distinct offences. The first must be brought into operation by the assemblage of men for a purpose treasonable in itself, or the fact of levying war cannot have been committed.' 'It is not the intention of the Court to say that no individual can be guilty of this crime who has not appeared in arms against his country. On the contrary, if war be actually levied, that is, if a body of men be actually assembled for the purpose of effecting by force a treasonable purpose, all those who perform any part, however minute, or however remote from the scene of action, and who are actually leagued in the general conspiracy, are to be considered as traitors. But there must be an actual assembling of men for the treasonable purpose to constitute a levying of war.' 'The application of these general principles to the particular case before the Court will depend on the testimony which has been exhibited against the accused.' 'Although, in making a commitment, the magistrate does not decide on the guilt of the prisoner, yet he does decide on the probable cause, and a long and painful imprisonment may be the consequence of his decision. This probable cause, therefore, ought to be proved by testimony in itself legal, and which, though, from the nature of the case, it must be *ex parte,* ought, in most other respects, to be such as a court and jury might hear.'

Marshall held the May term of the Circuit Court for the district of Virginia, at which indictments were found against Burr and others for treason, and misdemeanor. The proceedings on the trial, the various motions that were made, and the various discussions that took place, were minutely reported, and subsequently published in two large volumes. We shall reproduce here, however, only the points that proved decisive of the cause. The trial, in every respect, was an interesting one. The nature of the charge against the prisoner, his acknowledged talents, and the high positions he had hitherto held, the number and eminence of the counsel employed, as well as the consequences involved, excited an extraordinary interest in the community. The indictments were brought in by the grand jury on the 24th of June, and the trial was then postponed until the 3d of August.

On that day the Court again assembled; but it was not until the 17th of the month that a jury was obtained, so general were the prepossessions against the prisoner and his cause. But, however strongly the current had set against him elsewhere, he could confidently rely on the Court for impartiality and candor; for a firm and faithful administration of the law, uninfluenced by the wishes of the Government, and unawed by popular clamor. Burr knew this, and, as the private memoranda of Blennerhassett show, strongly expressed it.

'Burr did not,' says Blennerhassett, 'infer that Chief J. will, on the present occasion, shrink from his duty, as an able judge or a virtuous patriot, to avert the revenge of an unprincipled Government, or avoid other trials menaced and preparing for himself, by its wretched partizans. . . . I am certain, whatever insects may have sought the judge's robes, whilst off his back, none will venture to appear upon the ermine which bedecks his person.'[1]

'Burr's forensic army' consisted of Edmund Randolph, John Wickham, Benjamin Botts, John Baker, Luther Martin, and Charles Lee, the late Attorney-General of the United States. Burr, too, was a host in himself, and discovered great acumen and ability in conducting his defence. 'The vivacity of his wits,' says Blennerhassett, 'and the exercise of his proper talents, now constantly solicited here, in private and public exhibition, . . . display him, to the eager eyes of the multitude, like a favorite gladiator, measuring over the arena of his fame, with firm step and manly grace, the pledges of easy victory.'[2] The Government was represented by George Hay, Alexander M'Rae, and William Wirt.

The indictment contained two counts; one charging that the prisoner, with a number of persons unknown, levied war on Blennerhassett's island, in Wood County, Virginia; and the other adding the circumstance of their proceeding from that island down the river, for the purpose of seizing New Orleans by force. The testimony adduced by the prosecution to prove the overt act laid in the indictment, showed, and the prosecuting

[1] 'Private Memoranda' of Blennerhassett, kept while confined at Richmond. American Review for 1845, p. 146.

[2] Davis's Life of Burr, vol. ii., p. 393.

Attorney admitted, that Burr was not present when the alleged act was committed. The defence, therefore, insisted that any testimony that connected him with those who committed the overt act was irrelevant, because, conformably to the Constitution of the United States, no man can be convicted of treason who was not present when the war was levied; and because, even if it were otherwise, no testimony could be received, to charge one man with the overt acts of others, until those overt acts, as laid in the indictment, be proved to the satisfaction of the Court. Besides, it was contended that the indictment, having charged the prisoner with levying war on Blennerhassett's island, and containing no other overt act, could not be supported by proof that war was levied at that place by other persons, in his absence, even though he was connected with such persons in one common treasonable conspiracy; but, even if this were not the case, the previous conviction of some person who committed the act, supposed to constitute a levying of war, was indispensable to the conviction of a person who advised or procured such act. On the part of the prosecution it was contended that, although the accused was not actually present with the party assembled at Blennerhassett's island, he was yet legally present, and, therefore, might properly be charged in the indictment as being present in fact. And the opinion of the Court in *ex parte* Bollman and Swartwout was relied upon to sustain this position. The questions thus presented to the Court were most important; for, if the testimony objected to was arrested, the prosecution was at an end. The discussions at the Bar lasted a week, and 'a degree of eloquence seldom displayed on any occasion embellished a solidity of argument, and a depth of research,' which the Chief Justice gracefully acknowledged had greatly aided him in the opinion he delivered. He knew and appreciated the responsibility that rested upon him. He knew that a decision favorable to the prisoner would subject him to the severest criticisms; that his motives would be impeached; that the press would assail him; and that the public mind, excited and prejudiced, was liable to be poisoned and misled. But the fear of consequences did not for a moment influence him.

'That this Court,' said he, 'dares not usurp power is most true. That this Court dares not shrink from its duty is not less true. No man is desirous of placing himself in a disagreeable situation. No man is desirous of becoming the peculiar subject of calumny. No man, might he let the bitter cup pass from him without self-reproach, would drain it to the bottom. But if he has no choice in the case; if there is no alternative presented to him but a derilection of duty, or the opprobrium of those who are denominated the world, he merits the contempt, as well as the indignation of his country, who can hesitate which to embrace.'

As the prosecution relied on the opinion in *ex parte* Bollman and Swartwout, to sustain the positions they had assumed, the Chief Justice entered into an explanation of the general expressions employed by the Court in that case, in order to show that they did not warrant the interpretation which had been put upon them. In that case, the Court had said, 'if war be actually levied, that is, if a body of men be actually assembled for the purpose of effecting, by force, a treasonable object, all those who perform any part, however minute, or however remote from the scene of action, and who are actually leagued in the general conspiracy, are to be considered as traitors.' But, as the

Chief Justice remarked, this opinion did not touch the case of a person who advised or procured an assemblage, and did nothing further. It had reference to the person who performs a part in the actual levying of war; and this part, however minute or remote, constitutes the overt act on which alone the person who performs it can be convicted. He must be indicted for the part actually performed by him, and not for a part which was, in truth, performed by others. If, therefore, the assemblage on Blennerhassett's island, was an assemblage in force, was a military assemblage in a condition to make war,[1] and having a treasonable object, it was, in fact, a levying of war, and, consequently, treason. But, as the accused was not present, and performing a part, as charged, evidence of his acts elsewhere was irrelevant. In other words, the indictment charged him with actually levying war on Blennerhassett's island, and, therefore, could not be supported by evidence which showed that he was actually absent from the scene of action. In short, that the Government could not state one case, and prove a very different one; or charge the prisoner with aiding in one transaction, and prove him to be actually employed in another. If the prisoner advised, procured, or commanded the treasonable act, though this might not

[1] Marshall, *Chief Justice*. 'An assemblage to constitute an actual levying of war, should be an assemblage with such force as would justify the opinion that they met for the purpose.' 'Why is an assemblage absolutely required? Is it not to judge, in some measure, of the end by the proportion which the means bear to the end? Why is it that a single armed individual, entering a boat and sailing down the Ohio, for the avowed purpose of attacking New Orleans, could not be said to levy war? Is it not that he is apparently not in a condition to levy war? If this be so, ought not the assemblage to furnish some evidence of its intention and capacity to levy war, before it can amount to levying war?'

amount to treason, under the Constitution of the United States, yet the indictment should have charged him with what he actually did, and the evidence should conform to the charge.

Marshall, *Chief Justice*. 'The whole treason laid in this indictment is the levying of war on Blennerhassett's island, and the whole question to which the inquiry of the Court is now directed is, whether the prisoner was legally present at that fact. I say this is the whole question, because the prisoner can only be convicted on the overt act laid in the indictment. With respect to this prosecution, it is as if no other overt act existed. If other overt acts can be inquired into, it is for the sole purpose of proving the particular fact charged; it is as evidence of the crime consisting of this particular fact, not as establishing the general crime by a distinct fact.' 'It is, then, the opinion of the Court that this indictment can be supported only by testimony which proves the accused to have been actually or constructively[1] present when the assemblage took place on Blennerhassett's island, or by the admission of the doctrine that he who procures an act may be indicted as having performed that act. It is, further, the opinion of the Court that there is no testimony whatever which tends to prove that the accused was actually or constructively present when that assemblage did take place. Indeed, the contrary is most apparent. With respect to admitting proof of procure-

[1] If the accused, though he had not arrived in the island, had taken a position near enough to co-operate with those on the island, to assist them in any act of hostility, or to aid them if attacked, he, then, might have been *constructively* present, and this would have been a mixed question of law and fact, for the jury, with the aid of the Court, to decide.

ment to establish a charge of actual presence, the Court is of opinion that, if this be admissible in England on an indictment for levying war, which is far from being conceded, it is admissible only by virtue of the operation of the common law upon the statute, and, therefore, is not admissible in this country unless by virtue of a similar operation; a point far from being established, but on which, for the present, no opinion is given. If however, this point be established, still the procurement must be proved in the same manner, and by the same kind of testimony, which would be required to prove actual presence.' 'If those who perpetrated the fact be not traitors, he who advised the fact cannot be a traitor. . . . His guilt, therefore, depends on theirs, and their guilt cannot be legally established in a prosecution against him.' 'Now an assemblage on Blennerhassett's island is proved by the requisite number of witnesses, and the Court might submit it to the jury, whether that assemblage amounted to a levying of war; but the presence of the accused at that assemblage being nowhere alleged, except in the indictment, the overt act is not proved by a single witness, and, of consequence, all other testimony must be irrelevant.'

The jury having heard the opinion of the Court on the law of the case, brought in a verdict of 'Not Guilty.' On the 9th of September, Burr was again arraigned, upon an indictment for a misdemeanor; but the evidence failed to support the charge, and again the verdict of the jury was 'not guilty.'

The published correspondence of Jefferson shows how keen was his disappointment at the result of these prosecutions, and how warm his resentment against the Chief Justice, to whom he deemed that result was attributable. 'Federalism in the Judiciary Department'[1] had always been a subject of annoyance to the President, and the acquittal of Burr was not likely to mollify the sentiment. At the next session of Congress his personal friend, and one of the warmest among the supporters of his Administration, namely, Mr. Giles, introduced a bill into the Senate to define treason. He made a speech in support of it, and 'attacked Chief Justice Marshall with insidious warmth.' Amongst other things he said, 'I have learned that judicial opinions on this subject are like changeable silks, which vary their colors as they are held up in political sunshine.'[2] It is easier, however, to impute motives than to answer arguments; and as neither the reasoning of the Chief Justice, nor the conclusions to which it led, have yet been refuted, we may safely conclude that the principles by which he was guided were entirely correct.

Having failed to convict Burr upon either of the indictments, the prosecution now moved to commit him for trial in Ohio; and, after hearing the arguments of the respective parties, the Chief Justice finally held him to bail in the sum of three thousand dollars to answer in that State for a misdemeanor, in setting on foot a military expedition against the Spanish territories. This decision, naturally enough, was very annoying to Burr, and he commented upon it with no little bitterness. 'I found Burr,' says Blennerhassett, before the decision was pronounced, but when it had been foreshadowed, 'after a consultation with his counsel,

[1] Jefferson's Works, vol. v., p. 63. Letter to Bowdoin, April 2d, 1807. See also his letters to George Hay during the progress of the trial, and at its conclusion, in the same volume.

[2] Story's Letters, vol. i., p. 157. Letter to Fay, February 13th, 1808.

secretly writhing under much irritation at the conduct of Judge Marshall, but affecting an air of contempt for his alleged inconsistencies, as Burr asserted he [the Judge] did not, for the last two days, understand either the questions or himself; that he had wavered in his opinions before yesterday's adjournment, and should, in future, be put right by *strong language.* I am afraid to say *abuse,* though I think I could swear to that word.'[1] As the Chief Justice was not 'put right,' according to Burr's conception of that phrase, we might safely conclude, even in the absence of any proof as to the propriety of his conduct, that he did not employ the 'strong language' which he threatened. To his daughter he wrote, that 'the opinion was a matter of regret and surprise to the friends of the Chief Justice, and of ridicule to his enemies; all believing that it was a sacrifice of principle to conciliate Jack Cade.'[2] If the decision was a proper one, if it was legal, even though the firmness and integrity of the Chief Justice were unknown to us, we might justly infer that it proceeded from good motives; and upon the question of law, the opinion of the Chief Justice will have more weight, perhaps, than the opinion of Col. Burr.

It would be impossible, and, if possible, improper, in a work of this character, to go into an examination of the multitude of prize, commercial, insurance, patent, and land cases that were pronounced upon by the Supreme Court in the time of Chief Justice Marshall. We shall only venture to select from them one or two prize cases, which will be more likely, perhaps, than others, to interest the reader. All the leading doctrines

---

[1] Davis's Burr, vol. ii., p. 397. September 20th, 1807.
[2] Ibid., p. 411. October 23d, 1807.

of prize law were discussed and confirmed by the Court, and its decisions on this subject constitute an elaborate and imperishable code. Among the more celebrated judgments of the Chief Justice, in this branch of the law, may be mentioned Rose *v.* Himely;[1] the Exchange,[2] in which it was held that the capture of an American vessel, and her subsequent commission in the service of the capturing Power, stamped her with the character of foreign nationality, and that the American owner must look to his Government for redress; the vessel in such a case, though coming within the territorial jurisdiction of the American courts, not being amenable to judicial process; and the Nereide,[3] which involved the question whether a hostile force added to a hostile flag infects with a hostile character the goods of a friend. The facts in the latter case were as follows: —

The Nereide, a British vessel, mounting sixteen guns, was hired by Manuel Pinto, a merchant of Buenos Ayres, to transport a cargo belonging to himself and some of his countrymen from London to Buenos Ayres. On her passage she was captured by an American privateer, brought into the port of New York, and both vessel and cargo condemned as lawful prize. From this decree Mr. Pinto appealed to the Supreme Court. He was there represented by Emmett and Hoffman; the captors by Pinkney and Dallas. Emmett and Pinkney were the opposing champions who attracted most attention, and whose efforts elicited most applause. Their arguments were among the best displays of their forensic abilities.

---

[1] Cranch, vol. iv., p. 241.

[2] Ibid., vol. vii., p. 116.

[3] Ibid., vol. ix., p. 430. Compare with this case the decision of Lord Stowell in Dodson's Adm. Rep., vol. i., p. 443. See also The Atalanta, in Wheaton's Reports, vol. iii., p. 409

Of course it was conceded that the goods of a neutral on board an unarmed enemy vessel were exempt from condemnation as prize; but it was contended that the neutral character was forfeited, if they were placed on board an armed enemy vessel, inasmuch as the neutral thereby set in motion an agent of hostility. If it were otherwise, if the contrary idea were personified, said Pinkney, 'we shall have neutrality, soft and gentle, and defenceless in herself, yet clad in the panoply of her warlike neighbors, with the frown of defiance upon her brow, and the smile of conciliation upon her lip; with the spear of Achilles in one hand, and a lying protestation of innocence and helplessness enfolded in the other. Nay, if I may be allowed so bold a figure in a mere legal discussion, we shall have the branch of olive entwined around the bolt of Jove, and neutrality in the act of hurling the latter under the deceitful cover of the former.'

'Call you that neutrality which thus conceals beneath its appropriate vestments the giant limbs of war, and converts the charter-party of the counting-house into a commission of marque and reprisals, which makes of neutral trade a laboratory of belligerent annoyance; which, with a perverse and pernicious industry, warms a torpid serpent into life, and places it beneath the footsteps of a friend with a more appalling lustre on its crest, and added venom in its sting; which, for its selfish purposes, feeds the fire of international discord, which it should rather labor to extinguish, and, in a contest between the feeble and the strong, enhances those inequalities that give encouragement to ambition, and triumph to injustice?'[1]

But the Court viewed the subject in a different light.

[1] Wheaton's Life of Pinkney.

Marshall, *Chief Justice.* 'The Nereide was armed, governed, and conducted by belligerents. With her force, or her conduct, the neutral shippers had no concern; they deposited their goods on board the vessel, and stipulated for their direct transportation to Buenos Ayres. It is true that, on her passage, she had a right to defend herself, and might have captured an assailing vessel; but to search for the enemy would have been a violation of the charter-party and of her duty.

'With a pencil dipped in the most vivid colors, and guided by the hand of a master, a splendid portrait has been drawn, exhibiting this vessel and her freighter as forming a single figure, composed of the most discordant materials of peace and war. So exquisite was the skill of the artist, so dazzling the garb in which the figure was presented, that it required the exercise of that cold investigating faculty which ought always to belong to those who sit on this Bench, to discover its only imperfection — its want of resemblance.

'The Nereide has not that centaur-like appearance which has been ascribed to her. She does not rove over the ocean, hurling the thunders of war, while sheltered by the olive-branch of peace. She is not composed in part of the neutral character of Mr. Pinto, and in part of the hostile character of her owner. She is an open and declared belligerent; claiming all the rights, and subject to all the dangers of the belligerent character. She conveys neutral property which does not engage in her warlike equipments, or in any employment she may make of them; which is put on board solely for the purpose of transportation, and which encounters the hazard incident to its situation— the hazard of being taken into port, and obliged to seek another conveyance, should its carrier be captured. In this, it is the opinion of the majority of the

Court, there is nothing unlawful. The character of the vessel and the cargo remain as distinct in this as in any other case.'

Marbury *v.* Madison[1] was the first case involving a constitutional question of any importance, that came before Chief Justice Marshall. The facts of the case were these: — Mr. Adams, before the expiration of his term of office, nominated Marbury to the Senate as Justice of the Peace for the District of Columbia, and the Senate approved the nomination. A commission was then drawn up, signed by the President, and sealed with the seal of the United States; but it had not been delivered when Mr. Jefferson succeeded to the Presidency. He, thinking the appointment incomplete until delivery of the commission, countermanded its delivery. A *mandamus* was then moved for, commanding Mr. Madison, the Secretary of State, to deliver it.

The interposition of the Court was invoked, on the ground that they were authorized by an act of Congress 'to issue writs of mandamus, in cases warranted by the principles and usages of law, to any courts appointed, or persons holding office, under the authority of the United States.' The first question, then, that naturally presented itself was, whether the authority thus given to the Supreme Court, to issue writs of mandamus to public officers, was warranted by the Constitution, and, if not, whether the Court was competent to declare the act void which conferred the authority; or, in other words, whether the Supreme Court possessed the power to declare void an act of Congress which they deemed repugnant to the Constitution? The order, however, in which the Court

---

[1] Cranch's Reports, vol. i., p. 158.

viewed the subject reversed the objects of inquiry. They first considered whether Marbury had a right to the commission which he claimed? And they decided that he had; that an appointment is complete when the commission is signed by the President; that the commission is complete when the seal of the United States has been affixed to it; and to withhold such commission from an officer not removable at the will of the Executive, is violating a vested legal right.

As the legality of his conduct, in directing the Secretary of State to withhold the commission from Marbury, was involved in this part of the decision, it was natural, perhaps, that Jefferson should be somewhat restive under the conclusions at which the Chief Justice arrived. His view of the matter was, that the validity of a commission, like that of a deed, depends on delivery; and as the Court held that they had no cognizance of the case, he considered their opinion as to the legality of Marbury's claim 'gratuitous,' 'an *obiter* dissertation of the Chief Justice,' and, at all events, a 'perversion of the law.'[1] Whether it be an irregular and censurable practice, as he termed it, for a court to express an opinion on the merits of a case in which they have no jurisdiction, they may, nevertheless, do it with very good motives, however those motives may be questioned. As to the real decision of the Court, namely, on the question of jurisdiction, and its power to declare void an unconstitutional act of Congress, the reasoning and conclusions of the Chief Justice have commanded universal assent.

Marshall, *Chief Justice*. 'The Constitution vests the whole political power of the United States in one

[1] Jefferson's Works, vol. vii., p. 290. Letter to Judge Johnson, June 12th, 1823. See also vol. v., p. 84.

Supreme Court, and such inferior Courts as Congress shall from time to time ordain and establish.' 'In the distribution of this power it is declared that "the Supreme Court shall have original jurisdiction in all cases affecting Ambassadors, other public Ministers, and Consuls, and those in which a State shall be a party. In all other cases the Supreme Court shall have appellate jurisdiction.' 'To enable this Court, then, to issue a mandamus, it must be shown to be an exercise of appellate jurisdiction, or to be necessary to enable them to exercise appellate jurisdiction.' 'It is the essential criterion of appellate jurisdiction that it revises and corrects the proceedings in a cause already instituted, and does not create that cause. Although, therefore, a mandamus may be directed to Courts, yet to issue such a writ to an officer for the delivery of a paper is, in effect, the same as to sustain an original action for that paper, and, therefore, seems not to belong to appellate, but to original jurisdiction. Neither is it necessary, in such a case as this, to enable the Court to exercise its appellate jurisdiction. The authority, therefore, given to the Supreme Court, by the act establishing the Judicial Courts of the United States, to issue writs of mandamus to public officers, appears not to be warranted by the Constitution; and it becomes necessary to inquire whether a jurisdiction so conferred can be exercised.

'The question, whether an act repugnant to the Constitution can become the law of the land, is a question deeply interesting to the United States; but, happily, not of an intricacy proportioned to its interest.' 'If an act of the Legislature repugnant to the Constitution is void, does it, notwithstanding its invalidity, bind the courts, and oblige them to give it effect? Or, in other words, though it be not law, does it constitute a rule as operative as if it was a law? This would be to overthrow in fact what was established in theory; and would seem, at first view, an absurdity too gross to be insisted on. It shall, however, receive a more attentive consideration. It is emphatically the province and duty of the judicial department to say what the law is. Those who apply the rule to particular cases must of necessity expound and interpret that rule. If two laws conflict with each other, the courts must decide on the operation of each. So, if a law be in opposition to the Constitution; if both the law and the Constitution apply to a particular case, so that the court must either decide that case conformably to the law, disregarding the Constitution; or, conformably to the Constitution, disregarding the law; the court must determine which of these conflicting rules governs the case. This is of the very essence of judicial duty. If, then, the courts are to regard the Constitution, and the Constitution is superior to any ordinary act of the Legislature, the Constitution, and not such ordinary act, must govern the case to which they both apply.'

As in the case of Marbury *v.* Madison, the Supreme Court declared void an act of Congress which they deemed repugnant to the Constitution, so in the case of Fletcher *v.* Peck,[1] they declared void, for the same reason, an act of a State Legislature.[2] The Legislature of Georgia passed an act authorizing a patent to issue, granting a tract of land within the limits of that State. After the patent had been granted, a succeeding Legislature repealed the act which authorized it. It was contended that the original act was repugnant to the Constitution of Georgia; that the Legislature which

[1] Cranch's Reports, vol. vi. p. 87.

[2] This was also done in twenty-six subsequent instances.

passed it was corrupted; and that one Legislature cannot restrain a succeeding Legislature from repealing its acts.

Marshall, *Chief Justice.* 'The question whether a law be void for its repugnancy to the Constitution is, at all times, a question of much delicacy, which ought seldom, if ever, to be decided in the affirmative in a doubtful case. The Court, when impelled by duty to render such a judgment, would be unworthy of its station, could it be unmindful of the solemn obligations which that station imposes. But it is not on slight implication and vague conjecture that the Legislature is to be pronounced to have transcended its powers, and its acts to be considered as void. The opposition between the Constitution and the law should be such that the judge feels a clear and strong conviction of their incompatibility with each other. In this case the Court can perceive no such opposition. In the Constitution of Georgia, adopted in the year 1789, the Court can perceive no restriction on the Legislative powers which inhibits the passage of the act of 1795. The Court cannot say that, in passing that act, the Legislature has transcended its powers and violated the Constitution.'

'The case, as made out in the pleadings, is simply this. An individual who holds lands in the State of Georgia, under a deed covenanting that the title of Georgia was in the grantor, brings an action of covenant upon this deed, and assigns as a breach that some of the members of the Legislature were induced to vote in favor of the law which constituted the contract, by being promised an interest in it; and that, therefore, the act is a mere nullity. This solemn question cannot be brought thus collaterally and incidentally before the Court. It would be indecent in the extreme, upon a private contract between two individuals, to enter into an inquiry respecting the corruption of the sovereign power of a State. If the title be plainly deduced from a Legislative act which the Legislature might constitutionally pass, if the act be clothed with all the requisite forms of law, a court, sitting as a court of law, cannot sustain a suit brought by one individual against another, founded on the allegation that the act is a nullity in consequence of the impure motives which influenced certain members of the Legislature which passed the law.'

'The principle asserted is, that one Legislature is competent to repeal any act which a former Legislature was competent to pass, and that one Legislature cannot abridge the powers of a succeeding Legislature. The correctness of this principle, so far as it respects general legislation, can never be controverted. But, if an act be done under a law, a succeeding Legislature cannot undo it. The past cannot be recalled by the most absolute power. Conveyances have been made, those conveyances have vested legal estates, and if those estates may be seized by the sovereign authority, still that they originally vested is a fact, and cannot cease to be a fact. When, then, a law is in its nature a contract, when absolute rights have vested under that contract, a repeal of the law cannot divest those rights.' 'The validity of this rescinding act, then, might be doubted, were Georgia a single sovereign power. But Georgia cannot be viewed as a single, unconnected, sovereign power, on whose Legislature no other restrictions are imposed than may be found in its own Constitution. She is a part of a large empire; she is a member of the American Union; and that Union has a Constitution, the supremacy of which all acknowledge, and which imposes limits to the Legislatures of the several States, which none claim a right to pass. The Constitution of the United States declares that "no State shall pass any bill of attainder, *ex post facto* law, or law impairing the obligation of contracts."

'Does the case now under consideration come within this prohibitory section of the Constitution? In considering this very interesting question we immediately ask ourselves, What is a contract? Is a grant a contract?' 'A contract executed is one in which the object of contract is performed; and this, says Blackstone, differs in nothing from a grant. The contract between Georgia and the purchasers was executed by the grant. A contract executed, as well as one which is executory, contains obligations binding on the parties. A grant, in its own nature, amounts to an extinguishment of the right of the grantor, and implies a contract not to reassert that right. A party is, therefore, always estopped by his own grant.' 'If, under a fair construction of the Constitution, grants are comprehended under the term "contracts," is a grant from a State excluded from the operation of the provision? Is the clause to be considered as inhibiting the State from impairing the obligation of contracts between two individuals, but as excluding from that inhibition contracts made with itself? The words themselves contain no such distinction. They are general, and are applicable to contracts of every description.' 'Why, then, should violence be done to the natural meaning of words for the purpose of leaving to the Legislature the power of seizing, for public use, the estate of an individual, in the form of a law annulling the title in which he holds that estate? The Court can perceive no sufficient grounds for making this distinction.'

The case of Dartmouth College,[1] from some accidental circumstances connected with it, and from the importance of the principle which it established, namely, that a grant of corporate powers is a contract, the obligation of which the States are inhibited to impair, attracted great attention at the time, and has lost but little of its interest since.

The facts of the case were as follows: — A charter was granted to Dartmouth College, in 1769, by the Crown, on the representation that property would be given the College, if chartered; and, after the charter was granted, property was actually given. In 1816, the Legislature of New Hampshire passed three acts, amending the charter, which amendment the trustees would not accept. They invoked the aid of the State Courts; but judgment being given against them, they carried their case to the Supreme Court. There they were represented by Mr. Hopkinson and Mr. Webster; and the other side by Mr. Wirt, then Attorney-General of the United States, and Mr. Holmes.

The chief interest of the argument consisted in the speeches of Webster and Wirt. The former had argued the case in the State Courts, was familiar with the whole field of controversy, was a graduate of the College, and his feelings as a man combined with his ambition as an advocate to urge him to the utmost exertion of his powers. He addressed the Court for more than four hours, in an argument marked by his usual characteristics — clearness of statement, force and precision of reasoning.

'The argument ended,' says an eye-witness,[2] 'Mr.

---

[1] Wheaton, vol. iv., p. 518.

[2] Prof. Goodrich, of Yale College. Vide Choate's Eulogy on Webster.

Webster stood, for some moments, silent before the Court, while every eye was fixed intently upon him. At length, addressing the Chief Justice, Marshall, he proceeded thus: —

'This, Sir, is my case! It is the case not merely of that humble institution — it is the case of every college in our land. It is more. It is the case of every eleemosynary institution throughout our country — of all those great charities founded by the piety of our ancestry to alleviate human misery, and scatter blessings along the pathway of life. It is more! It is, in some sense, the case of every man among us, who has property of which he may be stripped; for the question is simply this: "Shall our State Legislatures be allowed to take that which is not their own, to turn it from its original use, and apply it to such ends or purposes as they, in their discretions, shall see fit?" Sir, you may destroy this little institution; it is weak; it is in your hands! I know it is one of the lesser lights in the literary horizon of our country. You may put it out. But if you do so, you must carry through your work. You must extinguish, one after another, all those great lights of science which, for more than a century, have thrown their radiance over our land! It is, Sir, as I have said, a small college. And yet there are those who love it. [Here the feelings which he had thus far succeeded in keeping down, broke forth; his lips quivered; his firm cheeks trembled with emotion; his eyes were filled with tears; his voice choked; and he seemed struggling to the utmost simply to gain that mastery over himself which might save him from an unmanly burst of feeling. I will not attempt to give you the few broken words of tenderness in which he went on to speak of his attachment to the college; the whole seemed to be mingled throughout with the recollections of father, mother, brother, and all the trials and privations through which he had made his way into life. Every one saw that it was wholly unpremeditated, a pressure on his heart, which sought relief in words and tears.]

'The court-room, during these two or three minutes, presented an extraordinary spectacle. Chief Justice Marshall, with his tall and gaunt figure bent over, as if to catch the slightest whisper, the deep furrows of his cheek expanded with emotion, and eyes suffused with tears; Mr. Justice Washington, at his side, with his small and emaciated frame, and a countenance more like marble than I ever saw on any other human being, leaning forward with an eager, troubled look; and the remainder of the Court, at the two extremities, pressing, as it were, towards a single point, while the audience below were wrapping themselves around in closer folds beneath the bench, to catch every look and every movement of the Speaker's face. If a painter could give us the scene on canvass — those forms and countenances, and Daniel Webster as he then stood — it would be one of the most touching pictures in the history of eloquence.' 'Mr. Webster had now recovered his composure, and, fixing his keen eye on the Chief Justice, said, in that deep tone with which he sometimes thrilled the heart of an audience: —

'Sir, I know not how others may feel,' (glancing at the opponents of the college before him,) 'but, for myself, when I see my *alma mater* surrounded, like Cæsar in the Senate House, by those who are reiterating stab upon stab, I would not, for this right hand, have her turn to me and say, "*et tu quoque mi fili.*" And thou, too, my son! He sat down. There was a death-like stillness throughout the room for some moments; every one seemed to be slowly recovering himself, and coming gradually back to his ordinary range of thought and feeling.'

The argument of Mr. Wirt in support of the acts of the Legislature amendatory of the College charter, though overshadowed by Mr. Webster's, 'was a full, able, and most eloquent exposition of the rights of the defendant.' [1]

The opinion of the Court was delivered by

Marshall, *Chief Justice*. 'This is plainly a contract, to which the donors, the trustees, and the Crown (to whose rights and obligations New Hampshire succeeds), were the original parties. It is a contract made on a valuable consideration. It is a contract for the security and disposition of property. It is a contract, on the faith of which real and personal estate has been conveyed to the corporation. It is, then, a con-

---

[1] Webster to Wirt. Kennedy's Wirt, vol. ii., p. 82. It detracts somewhat from the value of Mr. Webster's commendation, when we find him, at the same time, writing thus to his friend, Jeremiah Mason:—'Wirt followed. He is a good deal of a lawyer, and has very quick perceptions, and handsome power of argument; but he seemed to treat this case as if his side could furnish nothing but declamation.' Private Correspondence, vol. i., p. 275. March 13th, 1818.

Again, in writing to Chief Justice Smith, he says:—'Wirt has talents, is a competent lawyer, and argues a good cause well. In this case he said more nonsensical things than became him.' Ibid., p. 276. March 14th, 1818.

Nevertheless, and notwithstanding Mr. Pinkney, who desired to have the argument reopened, in order that he might address the Court in support of the assumed right of the State to amend the College charter, declared that Wirt's back was not strong enough for such a case, his argument must be considered as one of very great merit.

tract within the letter of the Constitution, and within its spirit, also, unless the fact, that the property is invested by the donors in trustees for the promotion of religion and education, for the benefit of persons who are perpetually changing, though the objects remain the same, shall create a particular exception, taking this case out of the prohibition contained in the Constitution. . . . On what safe and intelligible ground can this exception stand? There is no expression in the Constitution, no sentiment delivered by its cotemporaneous expounders, which would justify us in making it. In the absence of all authority of this kind, is there, in the nature and reason of the case itself, that which would sustain a construction of the Constitution not warranted by its words? Are contracts of this description of a character to excite so little interest, that we must exclude them from the provisions of the Constitution, as being unworthy of the attention of those who framed the instrument? Or does public policy so imperiously demand their remaining exposed to Legislative alteration, as to compel us, or rather permit us, to say that these words, which were introduced to give stability to contracts, and which, in their plain import, comprehend this contract, must yet be so construed as to exclude it?'

An examination of the subject induces a negative answer to these queries; and, hence, the opinion of the Court being, that the charter constituted a contract, whose obligation had been impaired by the Legislature of New Hampshire, it followed that the action of the Legislature was repugnant to the Constitution of the United States, and consequently void.

At the same term of the Court that the case of Dartmouth College was argued, was also argued the case of M'Culloch *v.* The State of Maryland.[1] It involved the question as to the constitutionality of the act incorporating the Bank of the United States. It had been a vexed question from the foundation of the Government. The opponents of the Bank insisted that no clause of the Constitution authorized Congress to create a corporation; that, though they were empowered to make all laws 'necessary and proper' to carry into effect the powers conferred on the Government, yet such laws were only 'necessary and proper,' as were absolutely indispensable, and without which the powers conferred would be nugatory. On the other hand, it was contended, that, to carry on its operations, the Government must employ persons, and that their acting in an artificial capacity was not material, as the Government must be authorized to exercise a discretion in the choice of agents, and that the power to make all 'necessary and proper' laws to carry into execution the enumerated powers, did not restrict Congress to the passage of only such laws as were *absolutely* necessary, but to such as were 'necessary' in the ordinary and usual meaning of the word. The case presented for the decision of the Court arose as follows: —

In April, 1816, Congress incorporated the Bank of the United States. In 1817, a branch of this Bank was placed at Baltimore, Maryland. In 1818, the Legislature of Maryland passed a law to tax all banks, or branches thereof, located in that State, and not chartered by its Legislature. The branch Bank refused to pay this tax, and M'Culloch, the cashier, was sued for it. Judgment being given against him in the Maryland Courts, he carried it before the Supreme

[1] Wheaton, vol. iv., p. 316.

Court. Naturally enough, the decision of this tribunal was looked for with eager interest.

The counsel employed on either side were of the highest professional eminence. Pinkney, Wirt, and Webster appeared for the Bank; and Martin, Hopkinson, and Jones for the State. Pinkney shone, on this occasion, with unrivalled splendor. He made the closing argument. 'I never, in my whole life,' says Judge Story, 'heard a greater speech. It was worth a journey from Salem to hear it; his elocution was excessively vehement, but his eloquence was overwhelming. His language, his style, his figures, his arguments, were most brilliant and sparkling. He spoke like a great statesman and patriot, and a sound constitutional lawyer. All the cobwebs of sophistry and metaphysics about State rights and State sovereignty, he brushed away as with a mighty besom. . . . . Mr. Pinkney possesses, beyond any man I ever saw, the power of elegant and illustrative amplification.'[1]

The opinion of the Court was, that the act incorporating the Bank was constitutional; that the Bank might properly establish a branch in the State of Maryland; and that Maryland could not, without violating the Constitution, tax that branch.

Marshall, *Chief Justice.* 'Although, among the enumerated powers of Government, we do not find the word "bank," or "incorporation," we find the great powers to lay and collect taxes, to borrow money, to regulate commerce, to declare and conduct a war, and to raise and support armies and navies. The sword and the purse, all the external relations, and no inconsiderable portion of the industry of the nation, are

---

[1] Story's Life and Letters, vol. i., p. 325. Story to White, March 3d, 1819.

entrusted to its government.' 'The power being given, it is the interest of the nation to facilitate its execution. It can never be their interest, and cannot be presumed to have been their intention, to clog and embarrass its execution by withholding the most appropriate means. Throughout this vast Republic, from the St. Croix to the Gulf of Mexico, from the Atlantic to the Pacific, revenue is to be collected and expended, armies are to be marched and supported. . . . Is that construction of the Constitution to be preferred which would render these operations difficult, hazardous, and expensive? Can we adopt that construction (unless the words imperiously require it) which would impute to the framers of that instrument, when granting these powers for the public good, the intention of impeding their exercise by withholding a choice of means?' 'The Government which has a right to do an act, and has imposed on it the duty of performing that act, must, according to the dictates of reason, be allowed to select the means; and those who contend that it may not select any appropriate means, that one particular mode of effecting the object is excepted, take upon themselves to prove the exception. . . . But the Constitution of the United States has not left the right of Congress to employ the necessary means for the execution of the powers conferred on the Government to general reasoning. To its enumeration of powers is added that of making "all laws which shall be necessary and proper for carrying into execution the foregoing powers, and all other powers vested by this Constitution in the Government of the United States, or in any department thereof." To employ the means necessary to an end is generally understood as employing any means calculated to produce the end, and not as being confined to those single means without which the end would be entirely unattainable. . . . The good sense of the public has pronounced, without hesitation, that the power of punishment appertains to sovereignty, and may be exercised whenever the sovereign has a right to act, as incidental to his constitutional powers. It is a means for carrying into execution all sovereign powers, and may be used, although not indispensably necessary. It is a right incidental to the power, and conducive to its beneficial exercise.' 'If the word *necessary* means *needful, essential, requisite, conducive to*, in order to let in the power of punishment for the infraction of law,[1] why is it not equally comprehensive when required to authorize the use of means which facilitate the execution of the powers of government without the infliction of punishment?'

Having thus arrived at the conclusion that the creation of a bank is warranted by the Constitution, the Chief Justice proceeds to inquire whether it or its branches may be taxed by the States.

'That the power to tax,' said he, 'involves the power to destroy; that the power to destroy may defeat and render useless the power to create; that there is a plain repugnance in conferring on one government a power to control the constitutional measures of another, which other, with respect to those very measures, is declared to be supreme over that which exerts the control, are propositions not to be denied.' 'If the

[1] As in the case of the power 'to establish post-offices and post-roads.' From this has been inferred, without question or denial, the power to carry the mail along the post-road, from one post-office to another; and from this *inferred* power has again been *inferred* the right to punish those who steal letters from the post-office, or rob the mail.

States may tax one instrument employed by the Government in the execution of its powers, they may tax any and every other instrument. They may tax the mail; they may tax the mint; they may tax patent-rights; they may tax the papers of the custom-house; they may tax judicial process; they may tax all the means employed by the Government, to an excess which would defeat all the ends of government. This was not intended by the American people. They did not design to make their Government dependent on the States.[1]

In the case of Cohens *v.* State of Virginia,[2] two very important questions were presented for adjudication, namely, whether the Court could exercise jurisdiction, one of the parties being a State, and the other a citizen of that State; and, secondly, whether, in the exercise of its appellate jurisdiction, it could revise the judgment of a State Court, in a case arising under the Constitution, laws, and treaties of the United States. The Court held that it had jurisdiction in both instances.

The facts involved in the case were these:—An act of Congress authorized the city of Washington to establish a lottery, and, by virtue of the act, the lottery was established. Cohen was indicted, at Norfolk, Virginia, for selling tickets of this lottery, contrary to a law of Virginia, prohibiting such sale. In the State Court, he claimed the protection of the act of Congress under which the lottery was established; but judgment being given against him, he sued out a writ of error to

---

[1] Weston *v.* City of Charleston (Peters, vol. ii., p. 449) was decided on similar principles; the Court holding that stock issued for loans to the Government cannot be taxed by States and corporations.

[2] Wheaton, vol. vi., p. 264.

the Supreme Court of the United States. There the judgment of the State Court was sustained; it being held that the lottery law did not control the laws of the States prohibiting the sale of the tickets. The chief interest of the case, however, depended on the question, whether the Supreme Court could take cognizance of it. And it is with reference to that point that the opinion of the Court is quoted.

Marshall, *Chief Justice.* 'It [the Supreme Court] is authorized to decide all cases, of every description, arising under the Constitution or laws of the United States. From this general grant of jurisdiction no exception is made of those cases in which a State may be a party. When we consider the situation of the Government of the Union and of a State in relation to each other, the nature of our Constitution, the subordination of the State Governments to that Constitution, the great purpose for which jurisdiction over all cases arising under the Constitution and laws of the United States is confided to the Judicial Department, are we at liberty to insert in this general grant an exception of those cases in which a State may be a party? Will the spirit of the Constitution justify this attempt to control its words? We think it will not. We think a case arising under the Constitution or laws of the United States is cognizable in the Courts of the Union, whoever may be the parties to that case.' 'The laws must be executed by individuals acting within the several States. If these individuals may be exposed to penalties, and if the Courts of the Union cannot correct the judgments by which these penalties may be enforced, the course of the Government may be, at any time, arrested by the will of one of its members. Each member will possess a veto on the will of the whole.'

'That the United States form, for many and for most important purposes, a single nation has not yet been denied.' 'These States are constituent parts of the United States. They are members of one great empire — for some purposes sovereign, for some purposes subordinate. In a government so constituted, is it unreasonable that the judicial power should be competent to give efficacy to the constitutional laws of the Legislature? That department can decide on the validity of the Constitution or law of a State, if it be repugnant to the Constitution or to a law of the United States Is it unreasonable that it should also be empowered to decide on the judgment of a State tribunal enforcing such unconstitutional law? Is it so very unreasonable as to furnish a justification for controlling the words of the Constitution? We think not. . . . The exercise of the appellate power over those judgments of the State tribunals which may contravene the Constitution or laws of the United States is, we believe, essential to the attainment of those objects.'

In the case of Johnson *v.* M'Intosh,[1] the Court held, that the Indians have only a right of occupancy to their lands, and are incapable to convey a title to them in fee. The plaintiff claimed certain lands under a private purchase from the Indians; the defendant held under the United States.

Marshall, *Chief Justice.* 'We will not enter into the controversy, whether agriculturists, merchants, and manufacturers have a right, on abstract principles, to expel hunters from the territory they possess, or to contract their limits. Conquest gives a title which

---

[1] Wheaton, vol. viii., p. 543.

the courts of the conqueror cannot deny, whatever the private and speculative opinions of individuals may be, respecting the original justice of the claim which has been successfully asserted.' 'However extravagant the pretension of converting the discovery of an inhabited country into conquest may appear; if the principle has been asserted in the first instance, and afterwards sustained; if a country has been acquired and held under it; if the property of the great mass of the community originates in it, it becomes the law of the land, and cannot be questioned. So, too, with respect to the concomitant principle, that the Indian inhabitants are to be considered merely as occupants, to be protected, indeed, while in peace, in the possession of their lands, but to be deemed incapable of transferring the absolute title to others. However this restriction may be opposed to natural right, and to the usages of civilized nations, yet, if it be indispensable to that system under which the country has been settled, and be adapted to the actual condition of the two people, it may, perhaps, be supported by reason, and certainly cannot be rejected by courts of justice.'

Gibbons *v.* Ogden[1] was a case of great celebrity, and involved considerations of the most important character. New York granted to Robert R. Livingston and Robert Fulton, for a term of years, the exclusive right to navigate the waters of that State with boats moved by steam. From them Ogden derived the right to use such boats in the waters between Elizabethtown, New Jersey, and the city of New York. Gibbons put two steamboats on that route, and claimed that he had a right to do so, inasmuch as his boats were regularly

[1] Wheaton, vol. ix., pp. 1–240.

licensed under the laws of Congress. The rights of the parties were litigated in the Courts of New York, and both the Court of Chancery and the Court of Errors sustained the validity of the State laws. Gibbons now brought his case before the Supreme Court of the United States. It had attracted universal attention, and the opinion of the tribunal of last resort was awaited with eager interest.

Webster and Wirt appeared for Gibbons, and Emmet and Oakly for Ogden. 'To-morrow begin my toils in the Supreme Court,' wrote Wirt to his friend Judge Carr, 'and about to-morrow week will come on the great steamboat question from New York. Emmet and Oakly on one side, Webster and myself on the other. Come down and hear it. Emmet's whole soul is in the cause, and he will stretch all his powers. Oakly is said to be one of the first logicians of the age; as much a Phocion as Emmet is a Themistocles; and Webster is as ambitious as Cæsar. He will not be outdone by any man, if it is within the compass of his power to avoid it. It will be a combat worth witnessing.'[1]

The argument on both sides was conducted with consummate ability, but to Mr. Webster belongs the credit of suggesting the ground which constituted the basis of the reasoning and conclusions of the Court. The proposition he maintained was, that Congress has the *exclusive* authority to regulate commerce in all its forms, on all the navigable waters of the United States, their bays, rivers, and harbors, without any monopoly, restraint, or interference created by State legislation. It is said that 'Mr. Webster having stated his positions to the Court, Judge Marshall laid down his pen,

---

[1] Kennedy's Wirt, vol. ii., p. 142. Letter to Carr, February 1st, 1824

turned up his coat-cuffs, dropped back upon his chair, and looked sharply upon him; that Mr. Webster continued to state his propositions in varied terms, until he saw his eyes sparkle, and his doubts giving way; that he then gave full scope to his argument; and that he never felt the occasion of putting forth his powers as when he was arguing a question before Judge Marshall.'[1]

Marshall, *Chief Justice.* 'The word [commerce] used in the Constitution comprehends, and has been always understood to comprehend, navigation, within its meaning; and a power to regulate navigation is as expressly granted as if that term had been added to the word "commerce."[2] To what commerce does this power extend? The Constitution informs us, to commerce "with foreign nations, and among the several States, and with the Indian tribes." "It has been truly said that commerce, as the word is used in the Constitution, is a unit, every part of which is indicated by the term. If this be the admitted meaning of the word, in its application to foreign nations, it must carry the same meaning throughout the sentence, and remain a unit, unless there be some plain, intelligible cause which alters it. The subject to which the power is most applied is to commerce "among the several States." The word "among" means intermingled with. A thing which is among others is intermingled with them. Commerce among the States cannot stop at the external boundary line of each State, but may be introduced into the interior. It is not intended to say that these words comprehend that commerce which

---

[1] 'Daniel Webster as a Jurist,' by Joel Parker, LL.D.

[2] See Marshall's opinion to the same effect in the case of the Brig Wilson, Brockenbrough's C. C. R., vol. i., p. 423.

is completely internal, which is carried on between man and man in a State, or between different parts of the same State, and which does not extend to or affect other States. Such a power would be inconvenient, and is certainly unnecessary. Comprehensive as the word "among" is, it may very properly be restricted to that commerce which concerns more States than one.'

'What is commerce "among" them? [the States,] and how is it to be conducted?' 'Commerce among the States must, of necessity, be commerce with the States. . . . The power of Congress, then, whatever it may be, must be exercised within the territorial jurisdiction of the several States.' 'What is this power? It is the power to regulate; that is, to prescribe the rule by which commerce is to be governed. This power, like all others vested in Congress, is complete in itself, may be exercised to its utmost extent, and acknowledges no limitations other than are prescribed in the Constitution.' 'It has been contended by the counsel for the appellant, that, as the word "to regulate" implies in its nature full power over the thing to be regulated, it excludes, necessarily, the action of all others that would perform the same operation on the same thing. That regulation is designed for the entire result, applying to those parts which remain as they were, as well as to those which are altered. It produces a uniform whole, which is as much disturbed and deranged by changing what the regulating power designs to leave untouched, as that on which it has operated. There is great force in this argument, and the Court is not satisfied that it has been refuted. Since, however, in exercising the power of regulating their own purely internal affairs, whether of trading or police, the States may sometimes enact laws, the validity of which depends on their interfering with, and being contrary to, an act of Congress passed in pursuance of the Constitution, the Court will enter upon the inquiry, whether the laws of New York, as expounded by the highest tribunal of that State, have, in their application to this case, come into collision with an act of Congress, and deprived a citizen of a right to which that act entitles him.'

The result of the inquiry was, that the acts of New York were in collision with the act of Congress under which Gibbons derived his coasting license, and consequently, must yield to it; the Constitution and the laws made in pursuance of it being supreme.

In the case of Osborn *v.* The United States Bank,[1] among other questions presented for the decision of the Court was the very difficult one, whether, since the Constitution has exempted a State from the suits of citizens of other States, the Supreme Court may act upon the agents employed by the State, and on the property in their hands? Or, in other words, though the Court has no jurisdiction where the suit is against the State directly, has it such jurisdiction where the State, though not directly a party, is so indirectly, in consequence of her agents, acting by her order, and executing her mandates, being substituted in her place?

Marshall, *Chief Justice.* 'A denial of jurisdiction forbids an inquiry into the nature of the case. It applies to cases perfectly clear in themselves; to cases where the Government is in the exercise of its best established and most essential powers, as well as to those which may be deemed questionable. It asserts

[1] Wheaton, vol. ix., p. 738.

that the agents of a State, alleging the authority of a law void in itself, because repugnant to the Constitution, may arrest the execution of any law of the United States. It maintains that, if a State shall impose a fine or penalty on any person employed in the execution of any law of the United States, it may levy that fine or penalty by a ministerial officer, without the sanction even of its own courts; and that the individual, though he perceives the approaching danger, can obtain no protection from the judicial department of the Government. The carrier of the mail, the collector of the revenue, the marshal of a district, the recruiting officer, may all be inhibited, under ruinous penalties, from the performance of their respective duties; the warrant of a ministerial officer may authorize the collection of these penalties, and the person thus obstructed in the performance of his duty may, indeed, resort to his action for damages, after the infliction of the injury, but cannot avail himself of the primitive justice of the nation to protect him in the performance of his duties. Each member of the Union is capable, at its will, of attacking the nation, of arresting its progress at every step, of acting vigorously and effectually in the execution of its designs; while the nation stands naked, stripped of its defensive armor, and incapable of shielding its agent or executing its laws, otherwise than by proceedings which are to take place after the mischief is perpetrated, and which must often be ineffectual, from the inability of the agents to make compensation.'

'The question, then, is, whether the Constitution of the United States has provided a tribunal which can peacefully and rightfully protect those who are employed in carrying into execution the laws of the Union, from the attempts of a particular State to resist the execution of those laws. The State of Ohio denies the existence of this power, and contends that no preventive proceedings whatever, or proceedings against the very property which may have been seized by the agent of a State, can be sustained against such agent, because they would be substantially against the State itself, in violation of the eleventh amendment of the Constitution.' 'Do the provisions, then, of the American Constitution, respecting controversies to which a State may be a party, extend, on a fair construction of that instrument, to cases in which the State is not a party on the record?' 'It may, we think, be laid down, as a rule which admits of no exception, that, in all cases where jurisdiction depends on the party, it is the party named on the record. Consequently, the eleventh amendment, which restrains the jurisdiction granted by the Constitution over suits against States, is, of necessity, limited to those suits in which a State is a party on the record. The amendment has its full effect, if the Constitution be construed as it would have been construed, had the jurisdiction of the Court never been extended to suits brought against a State by the citizens of another State, or by aliens.'

In the case of Brown *v.* The State of Maryland,[1] the interesting question came before the Court, whether a State can constitutionally require the importer of foreign articles to take out a license from the State, before being permitted to sell a bale or package so imported?

Marshall, *Chief Justice.* 'There is no difference, in effect, between a power to prohibit the sale of an arti-

---

[1] Wheaton, vol. xii., p. 419.

cle and a power to prohibit its introduction into the country. The one would be a necessary consequence of the other. No goods would be imported, if none could be sold. No object of any description can be accomplished by laying a duty on importation, which may not be accomplished with equal certainty by laying a duty on the thing imported in the hands of the importer. It is obvious that the same power which imposes a light duty can impose a very heavy one, one which amounts to a prohibition. Questions of power do not depend on the degree to which it may be exercised. If it may be exercised at all, it must be exercised at the will of those in whose hands it is placed. If the tax may be levied in this form by a State, it may be levied to an extent which will defeat the revenue by import, so far as it is drawn from importations into the particular State.' 'It is sufficient, for the present, to say, generally, that, when the importer has so acted upon the thing imported that it has become incorporated and mixed up with the mass of property in the country, it has, perhaps, lost its distinctive character as an import, and has become subject to the taxing power of the State; but while remaining the property of the importer, in his warehouse, in the original form or package in which it was imported, a tax upon it is too plainly a duty on imports to escape the prohibition in the Constitution.' 'It may be proper to add, that we suppose the principles laid down in this case to apply equally to importations from a sister State. We do not mean to give any opinion on a tax discriminating between foreign and domestic articles.'[1]

---

[1] In connection with this case the reader will do well to read the cases of Thurlow *v.* Massachusetts; Fletcher *v.* Rhode Island; and Pierce *v.* New Hampshire; Howard's Reports, vol. v., p. 504.

In the case of Craig *v.* The State of Missouri,[1] an act of that State establishing loan offices, and authorizing the issue of certificates of stock, was declared void, as being repugnant to that clause of the Constitution which prohibits the States from emitting bills of credit.

Marshall, *Chief Justice.* 'What is the character of the certificates issued by authority of the act under consideration? What office are they to perform? Certificates, signed by the auditor and treasurer of the State, are to be issued by those officers, to the amount of two hundred thousand dollars, of denominations not exceeding ten dollars, nor less than fifty cents. The paper purports, on its face, to be receivable at the treasury, or at any loan office of the State of Missouri, in discharge of taxes or debts due to the State.' 'Had they been termed "bills of credit," instead of "certificates," nothing would have been wanting to bring them within the prohibitory words of the Constitution. And can this make any real difference? Is the proposition to be maintained, that the Constitution meant to prohibit names and not things? That a very important act, big with great and ruinous mischief, which is expressly forbidden by words most appropriate for its description, may be performed by the substitution of a name? That the Constitution, in one of its most important provisions, may be openly evaded by giving a new name to an old thing? We cannot think so. We think the certificates emitted under the authority of this act are as entirely bills of credit as if they had been so denominated in the act itself.'[2]

[1] Peters' Reports, vol. iv., p. 411.

[2] Compare Byrne *v.* The State of Missouri, Peters' Rep., vol. viii., p. 40; and Briscoe *v.* The Bank of Kentucky, ibid., vol. xi., p. 257.

The case of The Cherokee Nation *v.* The State of Georgia,[1] which came before the Court at the January term, 1831, attracted universal attention, and was well calculated to enlist the sympathies of the American people in behalf of the unfortunate Indians, whose clear and undeniable rights had been wrested from them by Georgia, without reference to the obligations the Government of the United States owed to them, and without any other consideration than to get rid of them and possession of their lands. But, while the conduct of Georgia is without justification, when viewed solely with reference to the Indians, it must be admitted, we think, that there was much in the policy of the General Government to provoke it, as the following brief statement of the case will show.

By treaty with the Indians in 1791, the Government guaranteed to them their lands. By agreement with Georgia, in 1802, the Government, in consideration of the cession to the United States by Georgia of the territory now included within the limits of Alabama and Mississippi, undertook to extinguish the title of the Indians to their lands within the limits of Georgia, 'as soon as it could be done peaceably, and on reasonble terms.' The lands, moreover, were not to be taken from the Indians without their consent, and the utmost good faith was to be observed towards them. But the Government, though having the means to extinguish the Indian title, and bound to do it within a reasonable time, failed to do so. In 1817, it is true, one-half of the tribe were induced to remove; but it is believed that the whole nation might, at that time, have been persuaded to leave, had the Government used the appropriate means. Instead, however, of this being done,

---

[1] Peters' Reports, vol. v., pp. 1–80.

the policy of the Government tended directly to make the Indians permanent residents of the soil. They were encouraged to become civilized, and, under the influence of this encouragement, were happily becoming so. Cultivated farms, schools, and churches, were seen among them; — admirable instruments for their elevation, but calculated to attach them more strongly to the soil, and render them averse to removal. Georgia complained that the policy of the Government in thus civilizing the Indians, however beneficial to them, was inconsistent with the obligations it owed to her. And we cannot help thinking that there was force in this complaint.

In 1824, the Indians took a step which indicated very clearly that they never intended to leave their territory in Georgia for the wild hunting-grounds beyond the Mississippi. They formed and adopted a constitution for a permanent government. Great excitement thereupon ensued throughout Georgia, and the Legislature passed a series of laws which went directly to annihilate the Cherokees as a political society, and to seize their lands for the use of the State; lands which the United States had assured to them by the most solemn treaties. All this was flagrantly unjust to the Indians, who were innocent of any offence to Georgia, and were entitled, if they desired it, to hold their lands forever, and be governed by their own laws and regulations, as a distinct community. But, on applying to the Administration of General Jackson for aid in their troubles, they were told that the Government would not interfere. They then employed counsel, and a bill was brought before the Supreme Court, praying an injunction to restrain the State from the execution of the obnoxious laws. The State paid no attention to the proceeding, was not represented at the hearing, and did not intend to respect an adverse decision. The argument on behalf of the Cherokees was conducted with uncommon ability and eloquence by Mr. Wirt, and John Sergeant of Philadelphia. The Court held, however, that they had no jurisdiction of the case.

Marshall, *Chief Justice.* 'If courts were permitted to indulge their sympathies, a case better calculated to excite them can scarcely be imagined. A people once numerous, powerful, and truly independent, found by our ancestors in the quiet and uncontrolled possession of an ample domain, gradually sinking beneath our superior policy, our arts, and our arms, have yielded their lands by successive treaties, each of which contains a solemn guarantee of the residue, until they retain no more of their former extensive territory than is deemed necessary to their comfortable subsistence. To preserve this remnant, the present application is made.'

'Has this Court jurisdiction of the cause? The third article of the Constitution describes the extent of the judicial power. The second section closes an enumeration of the cases to which it is extended, with "controversies" "between a State, or the citizens thereof, and foreign States, citizens, or subjects." A subsequent clause of the same section gives the Supreme Court original jurisdiction in all cases in which a State shall be a party. The party defendant may, then, unquestionably, be sued in this Court. May the plaintiff sue in it? Is the Cherokee nation a foreign State in the sense in which that term is used in the Constitution?'

'Though the Indians are acknowledged to have an unquestionable, and heretofore unquestioned, right to the lands they occupy, until that right shall be extinguished by a voluntary cession to our Government; yet it may well be doubted whether those tribes which reside within the acknowledged boundaries of the United States can, with strict accuracy, be denominated foreign nations. They may, more correctly, perhaps, be denominated domestic dependent nations.' 'They and their country are considered by foreign nations, as well as by ourselves, as being so completely under the sovereignty and dominion of the United States, that any attempt to acquire their lands, or to form a political connection with them, would be considered by all as an invasion of our territory, and an act of hostility.' 'The Court has bestowed its best attention on this question, and, after mature deliberation, the majority is of opinion that an Indian tribe or nation is not a foreign State in the sense of the Constitution, and cannot maintain an action in the Courts of the United States.'

One of the laws of Georgia relating to the Cherokees, prohibited any white person from residing within the limits of the Indian territory without a license from the Governor, and without taking an oath to support and defend the Constitution and laws of the State. This law was aimed at the missionaries residing among the Indians, and who were supposed to be inimical to the policy of Georgia with regard to them. Samuel A. Worcester, a citizen of Vermont, was one of these missionaries. He had been sent out in that capacity by the American Board of Foreign Missions, and with the sanction of the President of the United States. Refusing to comply with the law of Georgia, he and six others, who occupied the same position with himself, were arrested, tried, and convicted for its violation, and each sentenced to four years' imprisonment at hard labor in the penitentiary. A pardon was then offered them on condition that, in the future, they would conform to the policy of the State. Five of the missionaries accepted the pardon; but Worcester, and another, the Rev. Elizur Butler, refused it. The interposition of the Supreme Court was now invoked in their behalf, and their cause was argued by the same counsel who had appeared for the Indians. The Court held that the law under which they were convicted was void, as being repugnant to the Constitution, laws, and treaties of the United States, and that the judgment of the Georgia Court ought to be reversed and annulled.

Marshall, *Chief Justice*. 'The treaties and laws of the United States contemplate the Indian territory as completely separated from that of the States; and provide that all intercourse with them shall be carried on exclusively by the Government of the Union.' 'The Cherokee nation, then, is a distinct community, occupying its own territory, with boundaries accurately described, in which the laws of Georgia can have no force, and which the citizens of Georgia have no right to enter, but with the assent of the Cherokees themselves, or in conformity with treaties, and with the acts of Congress. The whole intercourse between the United States and this nation is, by our Constitution and laws, vested in the Government of the United States. The act of the State of Georgia, under which the plaintiff in error was prosecuted, is, consequently, void, and the judgment a nullity.'[1]

---

[1] Worcester *v.* Georgia, Peters' Reports, vol. vi., pp. 515–597. The Georgia authorities paid no attention to this decision of the

The judicial opinions of the Chief Justice which we have cited in the preceding pages will give the general reader an idea of his style and mode of reasoning. The march of his mind was in a direct line. He proceeded straight onward to his conclusions. He did not encumber himself, nor embarrass others with a mass of authorities. Discerning, as if by intuition, the principle upon which the decision must depend, he did not look far for cases either to illustrate or support it. Witness his judgment in the Dartmouth College case. In truth, however, on questions of constitutional law, there were no precedents to guide him. He was necessarily obliged to rely on the native strength of his mind; and it is here that his unrivalled penetration, his powers of analysis and combination, are most conspicuously displayed. In the decisions of what other jurist do we find such simple, connected, compacted, demonstrative reasoning? In acquisitions, in various legal knowledge, he has been surpassed by others; but for grasp of intellect, and profoundness of judgment, where shall we look for his equal? He was less dependent on mere learning than others; for, so distinguishing were his faculties, and so exquisite his penetration, that he unfolded the original principles which lie at the very foundations of the law. By the clear light of his reason he could

'—— sit in the centre and enjoy bright day.'

He had the 'liberal heart' and 'judging eye,' the clear head, and sound, good sense that insure wisdom of decision. By strict adherence to recognised autho-

---

Supreme Court, kept the missionaries in the penitentiary a year and a half under the judgment which that Court had declared utterly void, and only released them, at last, when the State had accomplished its objects with regard to the Indians.

rities, an industrious and conscientious, though inferior man, may make a good judge; he will not be likely to go very far wrong, or give much occasion for complaint. But when 'a new and troubled scene is opened, and the file affords no precedent,' then mediocrity is placed in a situation of infinite difficulty, and may do infinite mischief. Precisely in such a situation did the extraordinary abilities of Marshall find their most fitting theatre for display. Then was seen with what ease he could disentangle the complicated web which had vainly taxed the skill of others; with what rare facility he could 'penetrate, resolve, combine,' and with what an irradiating spirit he advanced to his conclusions.

'Enter but that hall,' says Judge Story, 'and you saw him listening with a quiet, easy dignity to the discussions at the Bar; silent, serious, searching; with a keenness of thought which sophistry could not mislead, or error confuse, or ingenuity delude; with a benignity of aspect which invited the modest to move on with confidence; with a conscious firmness of purpose which repressed arrogance, and overawed declamation. You heard him pronounce the opinion of the Court in a low, but modulated voice, unfolding in luminous order every topic of argument, trying its strength, and measuring its value, until you felt yourself in the presence of the very oracle of the law.'[1]

In forming his opinions, he depended more upon general principles than cases, though he yielded all proper respect to authority. 'He seized,' says Judge Story, 'as it were by intuition, the very spirit of juri-

[1] Story's Discourse, p. 68.

dical doctrines, though cased up in the armor of centuries; and he discussed authorities, as if the very minds of the judges themselves stood disembodied before him.'[1]

No judge, perhaps, was ever regarded with more veneration and affection than Chief Justice Marshall. The Bar and the country appreciated, and with pride and pleasure did homage to his extraordinary merits. In the discharge of his high duties there was so much gentleness, modesty, and simplicity, united with such depth and compass of mind, that the profession loved him quite as much as they admired and respected him. His demeanor on the Bench was a model of judicial dignity and courtesy. Whether the counsel was eminent, or comparatively little known, he listened with the same attention, patience, and respect. 'He was endowed by nature,' says Mr. Binney, 'with a patience that was never surpassed — patience to hear that which he knew already, that which he disapproved, that which questioned himself. When he ceased to hear, it was not because his patience was exhausted, but because it ceased to be a virtue.'[2] An illustration of this latter remark may be found in the following anecdote, as related by Judge Story. He used to tell with glee, that Chief Justice Marshall, on one occa-

---

[1] Story's Discourse, p. 70. The criticism of Lord Stowell, however, was hardly applicable to him. 'I rather think,' says that renowned magistrate, 'we are too fond of cases; when a matter is to be argued, we look immediately for the cases, and by them we are determined more than, perhaps, by the real justice that belongs to the question; this may enforce the uniformity of the law, which is certainly a very desirable purpose, but is by no means the first purpose that ought to be considered; for, if the judgment be erroneous, it is but an indifferent exposition of the law.' Story's Life and Letters, vol. i., p. 554. May 17th, 1828.

[2] Eulogy on John Marshall, p. 58.

sion, when a very pompous and tedious advocate was arguing a case before the Supreme Court, and going back to the undisputed and preadamite rules of the law, interrupted the course of his argument by saying:—'Mr. C——, I think this is unnecessary. There are some things which a Court constituted as this is may be presumed to know.'[1]

The Supreme Court, in his day, was an object of great attraction, and he the most interesting figure of the scene. 'At some moments,' says Miss Martineau, who was at Washington in the winter of 1835, 'this Court presents a singular spectacle. I have watched the assemblage while the Chief Justice was delivering a judgment; — the three judges on either hand gazing at him more like learners than associates; Webster standing firm as a rock, his large, deep-set eyes wide awake, his lips compressed, and his whole countenance in that intent stillness which instantly fixes the eye of the stranger; — Clay leaning against the desk in an attitude whose grace contrasts strangely with the slovenly make of his dress, his snuff-box for the moment unopened in his hand, his small, gray eye and placid half-smile conveying an expression of pleasure, which redeems his face from its usual unaccountable commonness; — the Attorney-General,[2] his fingers playing among his papers, his quick black eye, and thin tremulous lips for once fixed, his small face, pale with thought, contrasting remarkably with the other two; — these men, absorbed in what they are listening to, thinking neither of themselves, nor of each other, while they are watched by the groups of idlers and listeners around them,—the newspaper corps, the dark Cherokee

---

[1] Story's Life and Letters, vol. ii., p. 596.

[2] Benjamin F. Butler.

chiefs, the stragglers from the far west, the gay ladies in their waving plumes, and the members of either House that have stepped in to listen,—all these have I seen at one moment constitute one silent assemblage, while the mild voice of the aged Chief Justice sounded through the Court.'[1]

Having now contemplated Chief Justice Marshall as a magistrate, we shall proceed to trace his footsteps in other scenes of labor and public service.

---

[1] Martineau's Western Travel, vol. i., p. 275, English ed.

CHAPTER XII.

1800 – 1806.

HIS BIOGRAPHY OF WASHINGTON.

General Washington, as is well known, bequeathed all his valuable public and private papers to his favorite nephew, Mr. Justice Washington. When this circumstance came to the knowledge of the public, a Life of that eminent person, prepared from materials so copious and authentic, was eagerly anticipated. The publishers, too, foreseeing a large demand for such a work, early applied to Judge Washington to purchase the copy-right. In reply to a letter of this kind from Mr. Caleb P. Wayne, at that time editor and proprietor of the United States Gazette, he says: — 'With General Marshall, who is to write the history, I consulted, when I saw him in February last, respecting the proposition which you and others had made to purchase the copyright, with a view to making some estimate of its value; but being ignorant of such matters, we were unable to form even an opinion on the subject, particularly at this early stage of the work. We shall, therefore, decline any negotiation upon the subject for the present, but will keep in remembrance your two propositions, and will write you again when the work is more advanced.'[1]

[1] MS., April 11th, 1800. Washington died December 14th, 1799.

The agreement between Judge Washington and the Chief Justice seems to have been a very equitable one; the former was to furnish the papers, and the latter to prepare the biography, and the amount obtained for the copyright was to be divided equally between them. What estimate they placed upon this will be seen from the following extract of a letter written by Judge Washington to Wayne, at a time when the advanced condition of the work enabled them to form an opinion upon the subject: —

'Great exertions,' thus he writes, 'will be made to finish it in the course of the next year; and we are not without hopes of success, if the present order of the Courts be not disturbed, or very materially changed. At any rate, many of the volumes will be ready in that time, and may be put to press. . . . We have endeavored to form some estimate of the value of this work, with a view to a reasonable price at which to dispose of it. We suppose that less than a dollar a volume cannot be thought of; and, upon the calculation of thirty thousand subscribers in America, this would amount to $150,000, supposing there to be five volumes. This, that is, a dollar a volume, would content us, whilst it would leave a very large profit to the purchaser, and a still larger profit should he be also the printer. But the subscriptions may exceed or fall short of the number mentioned, and, to escape the trouble of that part of the business, we will consent to receive $100,000 for the copyright in the United States; less than this sum we will not take. . . . . . Should you wish to purchase the entire right to this work, to dispose of in Europe as well as in the United States, you will say so; and, knowing the grounds upon which we calculate the value in the United

States, I could wish you to make an offer for the whole. We have received propositions for the purchase of the right to sell in Great Britain, upon which we have not yet decided.'[1]

In a subsequent letter to Wayne, he says: — 'To your ideas upon this subject I have given the fullest consideration; and I cannot help thinking that, however I may have exceeded or fallen short of the precise value of the work in question, the grounds of calculation which you assume must be erroneous. In asking for the author one dollar per volume, I think it impossible that I can be charged with demanding too much. The profit which this will leave to the printer and purchaser of the copyright is immense, and I choose it should be so. If I miscalculated then, in anything, it was in overrating the number of subscribers to be obtained in this country. I certainly believe that I was not very inaccurate as to this part of the subject. . . . As to the number you speak of, I can have no doubt but that it could be obtained in either of the four large towns in the United States.' 'Upon the whole, although I sincerely think that the sum mentioned in my former letter is a moderate estimate of the value of the American copyright, yet I acknowledge myself very little acquainted with the subject, and as apt as other men to be deceived. If you prefer a total abandonment of this right for a gross sum, and will state the highest sum which you think it prudent to offer, I will consider it, and give you both a speedy and candid answer. After having disclosed the ground upon which I made my calculation, and assured you of the sincerity with which it was made,

[1] MS., December 11th, 1801.

I should be at a loss for some principle upon which to name a smaller sum. Your superior information upon subjects of this kind may suggest reasons not perceived by me at this time. My wish is, that the purchaser may be not only safe, but liberally rewarded for the trouble he must encounter.'[1]

Soon after receiving this letter, Wayne made Judge Washington a visit at his place in Virginia, and, while there, agreed to buy the American copyright for seventy thousand dollars, provided he could furnish satisfactory security for the payment of the money. But his friends were unwilling to become liable for so large an amount, though ready to be bound for any sum which he might actually receive. In the latter case, as he wrote the Judge, 'the security would be for my integrity, and nothing would be involved in the success of the work.'[2] He therefore proposed, in place of a gross sum, to pay one dollar a volume for each copy of the work subscribed for, and to encounter all the trouble and expense of obtaining subscribers. After consulting with Judge Marshall upon the subject, Judge Washington, though still preferring a gross sum, acceded to Wayne's proposal. 'We cannot gratify the desire we feel to conform to your situation,' thus he writes, 'without yielding that point, and we shall do so. A prospectus will be prepared and forwarded shortly, for I agree with you that the sooner you set on foot the subscription the better.'[3]

---

[1] MS., Washington to Wayne, January 22d, 1802.

[2] MS., Wayne to Washington, March 17th, 1802.

[3] MS., May 9th, 1802. The contract was executed September 22d, 1802. 'The said Wayne,' so it was expressed, 'agrees to pay to the said Washington, his executors, administrators, and assigns, one dollar for every volume of the aforesaid work which may be sub-

Although Marshall had not been announced as the author of the proposed Life of Washington, yet the fact soon became generally known, and awakened no little jealousy and apprehension on the part of the Republicans. His politics were so decided, that it was assumed that he would give a party bias to the work. Two years before the first volume was published, Jefferson, with his usual facility in stating conjectures as facts, thus wrote his friend Joel Barlow, the author of the Columbiad, who was then residing at Paris: —

'Mr. Madison and myself,' he says, 'have cut out a piece of work for you, which is, to write the history of the United States, from the close of the war downwards. We are rich ourselves in materials, and can open all the public archives to you; but your residence here is essential, because a great deal of the knowledge of things is not on paper, but only within ourselves, for verbal communication. John Marshall is writing the Life of General Washington from his papers. It is intended to come out just in time to influence the next Presidential election. It is written, therefore, principally with a view to electioneering purposes. But it will, consequently, be out in time to aid you with information, as well as to point out the perversions of truth necessary to be rectified. Think of this, and agree to it.'[1]

The assertions thus hazarded by Jefferson as to the character and designs of the work were totally unfounded. 'The Democrats may say what they please,' wrote Judge Washington, 'and I have expected they

---

scribed for, or which may be sold and paid for at any time during the continuance of the copyright.'

[1] Jefferson's Works, vol. iv., p. 437. May 3d, 1802.

would say a great deal; but this is, at least, not intended to be a party work, nor will any candid man have cause to make this charge.'[1] The contrary impression, nevertheless, had an unfavorable influence in the canvass for subscribers. Weems, who had been rector of Mount Vernon parish, was one of the soliciting agents for the work. In a letter to the publisher from Baltimore, he says:—'The people are very fearful that it will be prostituted to party purposes. I mean, of course, the Life of Washington. For Heaven's sake, drop now and then a cautionary hint to John Marshall, Esq.'[2] This sort of impression respecting the

---

[1] MS., Washington to Wayne, November 19th, 1802.

[2] MS., Mason L. Weems to C. P. Wayne, December 14th, 1802. As a book agent, Weems displayed unrivalled tact and activity. The following extract from one of his letters to Wayne, dated Annapolis, Md., December 22d, 1802, will show his mode of procedure. On his arrival there he found the Legislature in session. 'I instantly determined,' he says, 'the House still in session, to congregate them. Next morning I threw in a note to the Chair, soliciting the honor of uttering before them a *patriotic oration.* They came together. They were pleased, and have begun to subscribe.' 'Patriotic orations! Gazette puffs! Washingtonian anecdotes! sentimental, moral, military, and wonderful!—all should be tried, and every exertion made to push into every family, into every hand, so very interesting and highly moralizing a work as yours; but, alas! I am not able to do it on my present allowance.' It was on this idea of creating a sensation that Weems wrote his Lives of Washington, Marion, Franklin, and Penn; and the extraordinary success of those books shows that he possessed a profitable knowledge of human nature.

In a letter to Wayne from Frederick, Md., April 8th, 1803, he says:—'Give old Washington fair play, and all will be well. I mean, let but the *interior* of the work be *liberal,* and the *exterior elegant,* and a town house and a country house, a coach, and sideboard of massy plate, shall all be thine. I sicken when I think how much may be marr'd. . . . God! I pray him, grant this work may bring moral blessings on our country, and honor and wealth on C. P. W. and M. L. W.

work, coupled with the more serious objection to its cost, soon proved the fallaciousness of the expectations that had been entertained with regard to the demand for it. Instead of thirty thousand subscribers, as Judge Washington had anticipated, the number actually obtained fell short of eight thousand.

Owing to the pressure of his judicial duties, and the time and labor required to examine many trunks of papers, Marshall was unable to hasten the work as rapidly as the impatience of the subscribers demanded. They clamored loudly at the delay, but it was unavoidable. It was not until the winter of 1803–4, that the first volume was placed in the hands of the printer. It was Marshall's intention that his name should not appear as the author of the work; and he only yielded the point to the wishes of others.

Unless there be some law,' thus he wrote his son, 'which I have not seen, the Clerk of the District Court, in my opinion, transcends his duty, and requires more than the act of Congress requires, when he demands the name of the author. If he persists in the demand, I wish Mr. Wayne to inform me of it, and I will then consult with Mr. Washington on the course to be pursued. But I wish Mr. Wayne, when he receives the title-page, which was sent some time since with the preface to Mr. Washington, to present it to the Clerk, and to call his attention to the law. I do not wish to give in my name as the author, and will only do so if it be unavoidable. The book is expressed to be written under the inspection of Judge Washington, and that, in my opinion, is more than sufficient.

'I wish Mr. Wayne to write freely to me on this subject, and to suggest, without difficulty, anything which occurs to him. I am not among those who feel wounded at a criticism on my writings, and in the present instance, at least, would much rather it should be directly made, than felt and suppressed. I am much inclined to believe that the first part of the work is too minute in its details, and have often regretted that I did not abridge it.'[1]

In a subsequent letter to Wayne he says:—'My repugnance to permitting my name to appear in the title still continues; but it shall yield to your right to make the best use you can of the copy. I do not myself imagine that the name of the author being given or withheld can produce any difference in the number of subscribers; but if you think differently, I should be very unwilling, by a pertinacious adherence to what may be deemed a mere prejudice, to leave you in the opinion that a real injury has been sustained. I have written to Mr. Washington on this subject, and shall submit my scruples to you and him, only requesting that my name may not be given but on mature consideration and conviction of its propriety. If this shall be ultimately resolved on, I wish not my title in the Judiciary of the United States to be annexed to it. Mr. Washington will probably write to you; but I have requested that no decision be made, unless it shall be necessary, till I see him, which will be at Washington, early in February.'[2]

The question thus referred to Judge Washington was promptly decided. 'The Chief Justice,' he says, in a letter to Wayne, 'with great reluctance consents

---

[1] MS., December 23d, 1803. Letter to Thomas Marshall. Young Marshall, at this time, was in college at Princeton; but, at the date of his father's letter, staying for a few days in Philadelphia.

[2] MS., Marshall to C. P. Wayne, January 10th, 1804.

that his name as author may be inserted in the title-page, provided I insist upon it. It gives me pain to decide against his wishes; but I really think it necessary, for many reasons. He requests, however, that his name may be modestly introduced, without any addition of the title he bears as a member of the Judiciary. It will, I presume, be sufficient to say, "By John Marshall." He is of opinion that there is no necessity for inserting the number of volumes in the title-page, and in this I concur with him. It would be very embarrassing in this instance if it were otherwise, for it is next to impossible, at this time, to say whether there will be four or five volumes.'[1]

That innate modesty which pervaded Marshall's character, and diffused itself through all his actions, is very conspicuous in the letters addressed to his publisher during the progress of his work. 'If Mr. Short is in Philadelphia,' thus he wrote Wayne, 'present, with my compliments, my thanks for the aid he has been so good as to give you, and tell him the obligation would have been much greater, if he would more freely have corrected the inaccuracies which must have presented themselves to him as well as you. Indeed, my dear Sir, I am persuaded that I have reason to complain of you. I feared that you would not censure and alter freely, and, therefore, particularly requested that you would do so. I do not think you can have complied with my wishes. You mistake me very much, if you think I rank the corrections of a friend with the bitter sarcasms of a foe, or that I should feel either wounded or chagrined at my inattentions and inaccuracies being pointed out by another. I know there are many and

---

[1] MS., January 24th, 1804.

great defects in the composition — defects which I shall lament sincerely, and feel sensibly, when I shall see the work in print. The hurried manner in which it is pressed forward renders this inevitable.'[1]

Owing to his other engagements, and the urgency of the publisher for the manuscript, he was unable to give the work that thorough revision and retrenchment which were required; and, from another cause, was prevented from even correcting the proof-sheets. 'Although I ought to have known,' he says, 'that I was too far from Philadelphia to inspect the proof-sheets, I had still unaccountably considered the corrections I had made as to find a place in the first impression, and am not a little mortified to discover my mistake. There are, however, some very few inaccuracies which you will readily perceive ought to be mentioned in the *errata*. These are, where some word is obviously omitted, or has been mistaken for another. . . . I regret your determination to print a second edition immediately. I have not time to correct the first at present, nor can I have time till the work shall be completed. The employment of finishing the fourth volume, and of superintending the copying, added to my various other avocations, absolutely disable me from giving the sheets you send me such a reading as I can be satisfied with. The third volume has been, for some time, in Mr. Washington's hands, and I should hope has been forwarded to you before this time. . . . If you make an additional impression, I hope it will be a very small one, and I cannot consent to its being stated to be revised and corrected by the author. It would, perhaps, be as well to make the

[1] MS., April, 1804.

amendments which I have suggested, and to add to the number of the first edition so much as there may be an absolute demand for. I am anxious, before the books shall be very much multiplied, to give them a very serious reading at perfect leisure, and prepare them for a second edition. There are really errors in the present publication which manifest a greater degree of carelessness than I had suspected when I had only seen the manuscript.'

'My state of health requires that I should pass the residue of the summer in the mountain country. As I cannot take the papers with me to prosecute the work, I had proposed to retain the first volume, and to read it while in the country. Perhaps the transmission of the third to you will enable you to leave the first with me. I wish to know your situation in this respect.'[1]

The following letter was written after the first volume of the work had been published: —

'Sir: — I have received your letter with part of the sheets of the second volume, and your resolution to postpone the second edition of the first. I am just setting out for the upper country, where I shall give the first volume one considerate reading, and then forward it to you by the post. You will please to direct to me at Front Royal, Frederick County, Virginia. . . . I have no doubt that the errors noticed are principally, if not entirely, in the manuscript. Some very few, I believe, are not; but they are very few. I am confident of the care you have bestowed on the subject, and wish every other person could have performed

[1] MS. Letter to Wayne, July 4th, 1804.

his part with as much attention and exactness as you have done. I thank you for the two papers you sent me. I take the Gazette of the United States, and shall, of course, see anything which may appear in that paper. The very handsome critique in the Political and Commercial Register was new to me. I could only regret that there was in it more of panegyric than was merited. The editor of that paper, if the author of the critique, manifests himself to be master of a style of a very superior order, and to be, of course, a very correct judge of the compositions of others.

'Having, Heaven knows how reluctantly, consented against my judgment to be known as the author of the work in question, I cannot be insensible to the opinions entertained of it; but I am much more solicitous to hear the strictures upon it, than to know what parts may be thought exempt from censure. As I am about to give a reading to the first volume, and as not much time can be employed upon it, the strictures of those who are either friendly or hostile to the work may be useful, if communicated to me, because they may direct my attention to defects which might otherwise escape a single reading, however careful that reading may be. I will, therefore, thank you to convey to me at Front Royal every condemnatory criticism which may reach you. It would be impossible, and I shall not attempt to polish every sentence. That would require repeated readings, and a long course of time; but I wish to correct obvious imperfections, and the animadversions of others would aid me very much in doing so.'[1]

In reply to this letter Wayne thus writes:—'Every

[1] MS., Marshall to Wayne, July 20th, 1804.

review of the work which I can lay my hand on shall be forwarded to you. The editor of the Commercial and Political Register is William Jackson, Esq., formerly, I believe, an aid to General Washington, and recently dismissed from a situation in the custom-house. He bears the title of Major. You will pardon me for mentioning what I have heard spoken of as a fault in the work; it is where the *enemy* is spoken of. It has been suggested that an author ought not to write as an American, but assume an independent ground. I understand the volume will be reviewed in a magazine published here. I shall send it.'[1]

'I have the pleasure of being acquainted with Major Jackson,' says Marshall in answer to the above, 'and have a high opinion of his taste and judgment. I heard him deliver a very excellent oration on the death of General Washington — one of the best which that melancholy occasion produced. You need make no apology for mentioning to me the criticism on the word "enemy." I am glad you have done so. I will endeavor to avoid it where it can be avoided. It has, probably, been used improperly, and unnecessarily, but may, I think, be occasionally employed without censure. A historian, it is true, is of no nation, but the person whose history he writes is; and the word is used to denote, not the enemy of the author, but of the person or army whose actions the historian is relating. I wish, however, if it can be done, that the third volume may be corrected in this respect, when, without repetition, the term may be changed. For the first and second the correction can only be made for the second edition.

---

[1] MS., Wayne to Marshall, July 25th, 1804.

'I am just finishing a review of the first volume, and am mortified beyond measure to find that it has been so carelessly written. Its inelegancies are more numerous than I had supposed could have appeared in it. I have thought it necessary to reconstruct very many of the sentences, and am sorry to impose on you the task of changing your types so materially. I hope you have not printed a greater number of the second volume than you have of the first, and that you will not print a greater number of the third. I lament that the first edition is so large as you have made it. . . . I have directed my son to make a present to the Whig Society in Princeton of a copy of the work. I could wish it to be of the second edition.'[1]

The criticism of Major Jackson's upon the first volume bestows merited praise upon the author, and more reservedly, perhaps, applause upon his work.

'The first volume of the Life of Washington,' he says, 'has now been some time before the public. The author of this work, Mr. Marshall, has every claim to stand in the foremost rank of our distinguished men. To the merit which belongs to professional exaltation he has added that of an able ambassador, and an eloquent legislator. Passing from these characters, he

---

[1] MS. Letter to Wayne, August 10th, 1804. In the following year he requests Wayne to send a copy of the work, so far as completed, to his friend, the late President of the United States. 'I will thank you,' he writes, 'to take some opportunity of sending three volumes to Mr. Adams, with the following words written on a blank leaf in each: — "Mr. Adams is requested to accept a copy of the Life of Washington, as a small mark of the respect and attachment of his obliged and obedient servant,

'"THE AUTHOR."

'"June 7th, 1805.

now fills, with acknowledged ability, the office of first judicial magistrate of our nation. If he succeeds as an author and historian, it can only be from that variety of excellence which belongs to minds of the highest order. . . . Seldom, if ever, has any book gone into the world under the circumstances which mark the appearance of Mr. Marshall's. He cannot be entirely regarded as the voluntary author of it. The Abbe Barthelimie spent thirty years in writing the travels of Anacharsis; and the historian of The Decline and Fall of the Roman Empire employed the labor of a life upon his work. But the biographer of the Life of Washington tells us, "that the public were already looking for his work before the writer was fixed on, or the documents from which it was to be composed, placed in his hands." Since the writer was fixed on, and the materials furnished, not three years have elapsed, and four octavo volumes are prepared for the press. It must be added, that, during this very short period, the labors of the author have been mixed with a regular attention to the duties of an office of the highest importance and difficulty.

'Under this great disadvantage has the first volume of the Life of Washington been placed in our hands, and yet we hope there will not be that disappointment the author has anticipated. Whoever expects to see, in a work thus rapidly written, every sentence highly polished, who looks in every page for the splendid ornament of Gibbon, or the continued elegance of Hume, may not have his expectations answered; but it has, nevertheless, conspicuous merit. The style is chaste, energetic, and elevated. A narrative interesting, because it is our own history, but deficient in striking incident, is conducted with ease and perspicuity, and every proof afforded of a mind vigorous, comprehensive, and discriminating. We highly applaud Mr. Marshall's plan of presenting, under one view, the history of the first settlement and early progress of the different colonies. It is a proper introduction to his work, and forms a valuable accession to American literature. In the latter part of the volume, where events of a higher interest are described than those on which the earlier pages of it are occupied, we mark in Mr. Marshall's style a corresponding elevation.'[1]

Major Jackson's criticism, unhappily, did not speak the public voice. The first volume of the work occasioned general disappointment. Neither in matter nor manner did it meet the public expectations. It contained nothing new, and the style was not more attractive than the annals and histories from which it was compiled. The critics exposed its infelicities of expression, and everybody pronounced it dull. It certainly, for a time, detracted from Marshall's reputation for ability. Nevertheless, there are passages in that volume which indicate talents for historical composition, of no common order. His portraiture of Pitt may be cited as an example: —

'Mr. Pitt,' he says, 'had long been distinguished in the House of Commons for the boldness and splendor of his eloquence. His parliamentary talents, and the independent grandeur of his character, had given him a vast ascendency in that body, and had made him the idol of the nation. In 1756 he had been introduced into the councils of his sovereign; but dissenting essentially from the system adopted for the prosecution of

---

[1] Political and Commercial Register, July 9th, 1804.

the war, he retained his station for a very short time. The public affection followed him out of office, and the national disasters continuing, it was found impracticable to conduct the complicated machine of government without his aid. In the summer of 1757, an Administration was formed so as to conciliate the great contending interests in Parliament, and Mr. Pitt was placed at its head. The controlling superiority of his character gave him, in the Cabinet, the same ascendency which he had obtained in the House of Commons, and he seemed to dictate the measures of the nation. But a very short time was necessary to show that, in this extraordinary man, were combined qualities seldom united in the same person. His talents for action seemed even to eclipse those he had displayed in debate; and in directing the vast and complicated movements of a war, extending on both elements over every quarter of the world, he unfolded a vigor of mind, a clearness of judgment, and a decision of character, surpassing the expectations even of those who had been long accustomed to admire the firmness with which he had pursued his political course. His plans, partaking of the proud elevation of his own mind, and the exalted opinion he entertained of his countrymen, were always grand; and the means he employed for their execution never failed to be adequate to the object. Possessing without limitation the public confidence, he commanded all the resources of the nation, and drew liberally from the public purse; but the money was, at all times, faithfully and judiciously applied in the public service. Too great in his spirit, too sublime in his views, to become the instrument of faction, when placed at the head of the nation, he regarded only the interest of the nation, and overlooking the country, or the party which had given birth to merit, he searched for merit only, and employed it wherever it could be found. From the elevation of the house of Brunswick to the British throne, a very considerable portion of the people, under the denomination of tories, had been degraded, persecuted, and oppressed. Superior to this narrow and short-sighted policy, Mr. Pitt sought to level these enfeebling and irritating distinctions, and to engage every British subject in the cause of his country. Thus, equally commanding the strength and the wealth of the kingdom, with perhaps greater talents, he possessed certainly greater means than any of his predecessors.'[1]

Marshall felt very keenly the strictures of the press. 'I wish very sincerely,' he writes Wayne, 'that some of those objections which are now made to the plan of the work had been heard when the proposals for subscription were first published. I should very readily have relinquished my opinion respecting it, if I had perceived that the public taste required a different course. I ought, indeed, to have foreseen that the same impatience which precipitated the publication would require that the life and transactions of Washington should be immediately entered upon; and, if my original ideas of the subject had been preserved in the main, yet I ought to have departed from them, so far as to have composed the introductory volume at leisure, after the principal work was finished.

'I have also to sustain increased mortification on account of the careless manner in which the work has been executed. I had to learn that, under the pressure of constant application, the spring of the mind loses its elasticity, and that the style will be insensibly

[1] Vol. i., p. 423, *et seq.*

influenced by that of the authors we have been perusing. That compositions thus formed require constant revisals when the impression under which they were written has worn off. But regrets for the past are unavailing. It is of more service to do what is best under existing circumstances. There will be great difficulty in retrieving the reputation of the first volume, because there is a minuteness and a want of interest in details of the transactions of infant settlements, which will always affect the book containing them, however it may be executed. I have, therefore, some doubts whether it may not be as well to drop the first volume for the present, that is, not to speak of a republication of it, and to proceed with the others. I shall, at all events, conform to your request, and be silent respecting the corrections I have prepared.'[1]

On receiving a printed copy of the second volume, the Chief Justice wrote the publisher as follows: —

'I have been critically examining the second volume since my return, and am sorry to find that, especially in the first chapter, there is much to correct. The third I hope will not be so defective, and it shall be my care to render the fourth more fit for the public eye. I wish it was possible for me to receive the proof-sheets. But I suppose it is not. . . . . Should there be a second edition, the volumes will all be reduced within the compass you propose, and will, of course, receive very material corrections. On this subject, however, I remain silent. Perhaps a free expression of my thoughts respecting the inaccuracies of the present edition may add to the current which

[1] MS. Letter to Wayne, September 3d, 1804.

seems to set against it, and may, therefore, be for the present indiscreet. . . . The first edition should be completely in possession of the public before a second is spoken of.'[1]

The three first volumes of the work were published in the course of the year 1804, the fourth in the ensuing year,[2] and the fifth in 1807. This latter volume, relating to Washington's administration of the Government, was a work of great labor.

'The unavoidable delays,' he says, 'the immense researches among volumes of manuscripts, and chests of letters and gazettes, which I am compelled to make, will impede my progress so much, that it is absolutely impossible to get the residue of the work completed in the short time which remains to be devoted to it. I regret this at least as much as you do, but cannot prevent it. I hope you will be able to employ yourself profitably on some other work until the succeeding volume shall be ready for you, which will be, I hope, next spring, as I shall apply to it again the instant I return from the Supreme Court. I flatter myself the numbers of the first edition will not be multiplied. I would not be understood to think humbly of it as re-

---

[1] MS., September 8th, 1804.

[2] 'I believe,' he writes, 'the fourth volume to be much less inaccurate than those which preceded it, as I have bestowed much more attention on the style than was given to them. Yet I cannot flatter myself that it will not need a considerable reform. I am confident that I shall perceive, when I read it in print, many defects that escape me in manuscript. I should, therefore, wish it were possible to see the proof-sheets, or to correct a copy as I have done the three first, before the additional number of copies shall be printed. But if this would occasion you additional expense, I would not wish it.' MS. Letter to Wayne, February 27th, 1805.

vised. I have not read more than one hundred pages of the revised copy; but I am persuaded that, had the whole work come out originally in that form, it would have been better received. Yet the revisal given to the first impression was not only hasty, but pursued so unremittingly, that many inaccuracies, and still more inelegancies, must have escaped me. For the sake of giving to the world a more careful correction of the work, and for the sake of some essential alterations which I contemplate, I wish a second edition; and I am confident that every volume added to the first must tend to prevent any demand for a second edition.'[1]

The anxious wish of the Chief Justice, that there should be a revised and improved edition of the Life of Washington, was not gratified. A second edition of the original work was never called for. He prepared,

[1] MS. Letter to Wayne, October 5th, 1805. At the date of this letter, he was just recovering from a bilious fever. Two weeks later, October 19th, 1805, he wrote as follows:—'Immediately after writing to you, my fever returned, and I am not yet recovered. My ill-health is not more unwelcome on its own account, than on account of the additional delays it will create in the business in which I am engaged. That these delays should affect you in any degree I sincerely lament. They are occasioned by several accidents which concur, with the nature of the work (which requires researches beyond measure laborious), to protract the time of its completion. But you may be assured that your interest is still more concerned in having time taken to digest the materials properly, than in the celerity with which they are thrown together. Be this as it may, my health has compelled me to take refuge in the mountains from the sultry heats of our climate; and the continuing fever under which I have labored since my return, and which is only stopped to-day, and still threatens me with a visit, admonishes me that my return was premature, and has prevented my deriving, from the time I counted on employing in this important business, the benefits I expected.'

however, an abridged edition, which preserved all the essential information of the larger work, without its prolixity, and proved much more acceptable to the public. It was published in two volumes, in 1831.[1] He also prepared an edition of the latter for the use of schools, which, however, did not make its appearance until after his death. The candor that pervades these productions has been remarked as among their characteristic excellences. Jefferson, it is true, took exception to the note in the fifth volume of the original work, respecting his letter to Mazzei. That letter, written in April, 1796, was published at Florence, and afterwards at Paris, in the Moniteur. It attributed monarchical designs to the leaders of the Federal party, and asserted that they wished to introduce into the United States the substance, as they had already done the forms,[2] of the British Government. The editor of the Moniteur accompanied the letter with very severe strictures on the conduct of the United States, and it was supposed that our difficulties with France were complicated in consequence of it. In a letter to Martin Van Buren, in 1824, Jefferson, after declaring that an entire paragraph had been interpolated into his letter to Mazzei, (and, as he surmised, by the persons in power at Paris,) by which he was made to charge his own country with ingratitude and injustice to France, proceeds to say, 'And even Judge Marshall makes history descend from its dignity, and the ermine from its sanctity, to exaggerate, to record, and to sanction this forgery.'[3]

---

[1] The introductory part of the work had been previously published as a distinct work, called the 'History of the Colonies.'

[2] It was printed 'form' in the foreign papers; but Jefferson says he wrote 'forms,' referring to the President's levees, birth-days, &c.

[3] Jefferson's Works, vol. vii., p. 366. It is curious that Jefferson,

In the abridged edition of his work, the Chief Justice replies to this charge of Mr. Jefferson, and vindicates himself with irresistible cogency.[1] This, we believe, is the only instance in which he was called upon to assert his candor and impartiality.

We have seen how unfavorable were the circumstances under which the Life of Washington was written and submitted to the public eye. It, nevertheless, possesses great and undeniable merit. It is full, impartial, and accurate. It has always ranked as a standard authority. It is, however, the work of a jurist, and not of an artist. The style is something jejune. It lacks spirit, picturesqueness, and warmth of coloring. It has nothing of 'the long-resounding march, and energy divine;' nothing of the glow, the *ardentia verba*, that distinguish the more celebrated productions of Chief Justice Jay. At the same time, as we have before remarked, the work evinces talents for literary labor, which, with a more exclusive devotion to that object, would have joined to the praise of solid merit the attractions of grace and elegance. His delineation of the person and character of Washington may serve as an illustration of this latter observation.

'General Washington,' he says, 'was rather above the common size, his frame was robust, and his constitution vigorous, capable of enduring great fatigue, and requiring a considerable degree of exercise for the preservation of his health. His exterior created in the

in a letter to Mr. Madison, just after the publication of the Mazzei letter in this country, while giving very politic reasons for not publicly noticing it, does not insinuate that the paragraph in question was an interpolation; but admits that the letter, in substance, was his. Vide Letter to James Madison, August, 1797.

[1] His reply is contained in a note.

beholder the idea of strength united with manly gracefulness. His manners were rather reserved than free, though they partook nothing of that dryness and sternness which accompany reserve when carried to an extreme; and, on all proper occasions, he could relax sufficiently to show how highly he was gratified by the charms of conversation, and the pleasures of society. His person and whole deportment exhibited an unaffected and indescribable dignity, unmingled with haughtiness, of which all who approached him were sensible; and the attachment of those who possessed his friendship, and enjoyed his intimacy, was ardent, but always respectful. His temper was humane, benevolent, and conciliatory; but there was a quickness in his sensibility to anything apparently offensive, which experience had taught him to watch and to correct. . . . He made no pretensions to that vivacity which fascinates, or to that wit which dazzles, and frequently imposes on the understanding. More solid than brilliant, judgment rather than genius constituted the most prominent feature of his character.

'As a military man, he was brave, enterprizing, and cautious. That malignity which has sought to strip him of all the higher qualities of a general, has conceded to him personal courage, and a firmness of resolution which neither dangers nor difficulties could shake. But candor will allow him other great and valuable endowments. If his military course does not abound with splendid achievements, it exhibits a series of judicious measures, adapted to circumstances, which probably saved his country. . . .

'No man has ever appeared upon the theatre of public action, whose integrity was more incorruptible, or whose principles were more perfectly free from the contamination of those selfish and unworthy passions which find their nourishment in the conflicts of party. Having no views which required concealment, his real and avowed motives were the same; and his whole correspondence does not furnish a single case, from which even an enemy would infer that he was capable, under any circumstances, of stooping to the employment of duplicity. No truth can be uttered with more confidence, than that his ends were always upright, and his means always pure. He exhibited the rare example of a politician, to whom wiles were absolutely unknown, and whose professions to foreign governments, and to his own countrymen, were always sincere. In him was fully exemplified the real distinction which forever exists between wisdom and cunning, and the importance as well as truth of the maxim, that 'honesty is the best policy.'

CHAPTER XIII.

1829.

VIRGINIA STATE CONVENTION.

THE original Constitution of Virginia was formed in 1776. It continued in existence for more than half a century; but, at the session of the Virginia Legislature, in 1827–8, the question was submitted to the people of the State whether a convention should be called to revise it. It was carried in the affirmative. The subject was viewed throughout the State with absorbing interest. A party, powerful in wealth, talents, and social position, were invincibly opposed to any important innovation in the fundamental law. Another, and more numerous party, with champions of acknowledged character and abilities, were, in some essential particulars, for laying the axe at the root of the tree. They would extend the right of suffrage, readjust the basis of representation, reform the judiciary, and make other and important changes. The discussion of these opposing sentiments produced great excitement throughout Virginia. Both parties naturally selected their ablest advocates to represent them in the Convention. The result was, that a body of men were brought together, scarcely inferior to the renowned Convention of 1788.

Chief Justice Marshall was elected a member, as were also the ex-Presidents Madison and Monroe. The

Convention assembled at the Capitol, in Richmond, October 5th, 1829. A gentleman, who attended their debates a fortnight, has given a very graphic description of several of the more eminent members. 'Mr. Madison,' he says, 'sat on the left of the Speaker, Mr. Monroe on the right.[1] Mr. Madison spoke once for half an hour; but, although a pin might have been heard to drop, so low was his tone, that from the gallery I could distinguish only one word, and that was, "Constitution." He stood not more than six feet from the Speaker. When he rose, a great part of the members left their seats, and clustered around the aged statesman, thick as a swarm of bees. Mr. Madison was a small man, of ample forehead, and some obliquity of vision, (I thought the effect probably of age,) his eyes appearing to be slightly introverted. His dress was plain; his overcoat a faded brown surtout. Mr. Monroe was very wrinkled and weather-beaten; ungraceful in attitude and gesture, and his speeches only common-place. Mr. Giles wore a crutch — was then Governor of the State. His style of delivery was perfectly conversational — no gesture, no effort; but in ease, fluency, and tact, surely he had not there his equal; his words were like honey pouring from an eastern rock.

'Judge Marshall, whenever he spoke, which was seldom, and only for a short time, attracted great attention. His appearance was revolutionary and patriarchal. Tall, in a long surtout of blue, with a face of genius, and an eye of fire, his mind possessed the rare faculty of condensation; he distilled an argument down to its essence. There were two parties in the

---

[1] Mr. Monroe was chosen President of the Convention; but, owing to his indisposition, the chair was chiefly occupied by Mr. Powell and P. P. Barbour.

House; the Western, or radical, and the Eastern, or conservative. Judge Marshall proposed something in the nature of a compromise.

'John Randolph was remarkably deliberate, distinct, and emphatic. He articulated excellently, and gave the happiest effect to all he said. His person was frail and uncommon; his face pale and withered; but his eye radiant as a diamond. He owed, perhaps, more to his manner than to his matter; and his mind was rather poetical than logical. Yet, in his own particular vein, he was superior to any of his cotemporaries. Benjamin Watkins Leigh cut a distinguished figure in the Convention, as the leader of the lowland party. His diction is clear, correct, elegant, and might be safely committed to print just as spoken. Yet, high as he stands, he is not, perhaps, in the highest rank of speakers. He never lightens, never thunders; he can charm, he can convince, but he can hardly overwhelm. Mr. Tazewell I never saw up but once, for a moment, on a point of order; a tall, fine-looking man. P. P. Barbour presided over the body with great dignity and ease.'[1]

The question which excited most feeling, both in the Convention and out of it; the question which threatened to produce the most fatal results, putting in jeopardy the union and integrity of the State, related to the basis of representation. The Western districts contended for an equal representation of the free white population; the Eastern, or rather, as John Randolph said, 'the great slave-holding and tobacco-planting districts,' would found representation upon a combination

[1] Howe's Virginia Historical Collections, page 313. This sketch of the Convention was originally printed in a newspaper, under the signature of C. C.

of persons and property. The debate upon this subject was conducted with great ability and earnestness, and extended through several weeks.

Much irritation prevailed, and great apprehensions began to be entertained that the Convention would separate without adopting any plan to allay the divisions, and restore the tranquillity of the State. At this portentous moment, however, several propositions for a compromise were introduced. It was now that the Chief Justice rose, and addressed the Convention. His voice was feeble, and those who sat far off could not hear him. Whenever, therefore, he spoke, 'the members would press towards him, and strain, with outstretched necks and eager ears, to catch his words.'[1] His candor, and courtesy of manner, attracted and conciliated all parties.

'No person in the House,' said he, 'can be more truly gratified than I am, at seeing the spirit that has been manifested here to-day; and it is my earnest wish that this spirit of conciliation may be acted upon in a fair, equal, and honest manner, adapted to the situation of the different parts of the Commonwealth which are to be affected. As to the general propositions which have been offered, there is no essential difference between them. That the Federal numbers and the plan of the white basis shall be blended together, so as to allow each an equal portion of power, seems very generally agreed to. The difference is, that one party applies these two principles separately, the one to the Senate, the other to the House of Delegates; while the other party proposes to unite the two principles, and to carry them in their blended form

[1] Southern Literary Messenger, vol. ii., p. 188.

through the whole Legislature. One gentleman differs in the whole outline of his plan. He seems to imagine that we claim nothing of republican principles, when we claim a representation for property. Permit me to set him right. I do not say that I hope to satisfy him, or others, who say that republican government depends on adopting the naked principle of numbers, that we are right; but I think I can satisfy him that we do entertain a different opinion. I think the soundest principles of republicanism do sanction some relation between representation and taxation. Certainly no opinion has received the sanction of wiser statesmen and patriots. I think the two ought to be connected. I think this was the principle of the Revolution; the ground on which the colonies were torn from the mother country, and made independent States.

'I shall not, however, go into that discussion now. The House has already heard much said about it. I would observe, that this basis of representation is a matter so important to Virginia, that the subject was reviewed by every thinking individual before this Convention assembled. Several different plans were contemplated. The basis of white population alone; the basis of free population alone; a basis of population alone; a basis compounded of taxation and white population (or, which is the same thing, a basis of Federal numbers); two other bases were also proposed, one referring to the total population of the State, the other to taxation alone. Now, of these various propositions, the basis of white population, and the basis of taxation, alone are the two extremes. Between the free population, and the white population, there is almost no difference. Between the basis of total population and the basis of taxation, there is but little difference. The people of the East thought that they offered a fair compromise, when they proposed the compound basis of population and taxation, or the basis of the Federal numbers. We thought that we had republican precedent for this — a precedent given us by the wisest and truest patriots that ever were assembled; but that is now past. We are now willing to meet on a new middle ground, beyond what we thought was a middle ground, and the extreme on the other side. We considered the Federal numbers as middle ground, and we may, perhaps, now carry that proposition. The gentleman assumed too much when he said that question was decided. It cannot be considered as decided, till it has come before the House. The majority is too small to calculate upon it as certain in the final decision. We are all uncertain as to the issue. But all know this, that if either extreme is carried, it must leave a wound in the breast of the opposite party, which will fester and rankle, and produce I know not what mischief. The majority, also, are now content once more to divide the ground, and to take a new middle ground. The only difficulty is, whether the compromise shall be affected by applying one principle to the House of Delegates, and the other to the Senate, or by mingling the two principles, and applying them in the same form to both branches of the Legislature? I incline to the latter opinion. I do not know, and have not heard, any sufficient reason assigned for adopting different principles in the two branches. Both are the Legislature of Virginia, and if they are to be organized on different principles, there will be just the same divisions between the two, as appears in this Convention. It can produce no good, and may, I fear, produce some mischief. It will be said, that one branch is the representation of one division of the State, and the other branch of another division of it. Ought they not both to represent the whole? Yet I am ready to submit to such an arrangement, if it shall be the opinion of a majority of this House. If this Convention shall think it best that the House of Delegates shall be organized in one way, and the Senate in another, I shall not withhold my assent. Give me a Constitution that shall be received by the people; a Constitution in which I can consider their different interests to be duly represented, and I will take it, though it may not be that which I most approve. . . .

'The principle, then, which I propose as a compromise is, that the apportionment of representation shall be made according to an exact compound of the two principles, of the white basis and of the Federal numbers, according to the census of 1820.'

This 'exact compound' would have given, as the basis of representation, the whole white population, and three-tenths of the colored, whether bond or free. After considerable discussion, the Chief Justice again addressed the Convention, and his speech, though short, 'was at the time regarded as an unrivalled specimen of lucid and conclusive reasoning.'[1]

'Two propositions,' he said, 'respecting the basis of representation, have divided this Convention almost equally. One party has supported the basis of white population alone, the other has supported a basis compounded of white population and taxation; or, which is the same thing in its results, the basis of Federal numbers. The question has been discussed, until discussion has become useless. It has been argued, until

[1] Southern Literary Messenger, vol. ii., p. 188.

argument is exhausted. We have now met on the ground of compromise. . . . One party proposes that the House of Delegates shall be formed on the basis of white population exclusively, and the Senate on the mixed basis of white population and taxation, or on the Federal numbers. The other party proposes that the white population shall be combined with Federal numbers, and shall, mixed in equal proportions, form the basis of representation in both Houses. This last proposition must be equal. All feel it to be equal. If the two principles are combined exactly, and, thus combined, form the basis of both Houses, the compromise must be perfectly equal. . . .

'After the warm language (to use the mildest phrase) which has been mingled with argument on both sides, I heard, with inexpressible satisfaction, propositions for compromise proposed by both parties, in the language of conciliation. I hail these auspicious appearances with as much joy as the inhabitant of the polar regions hails the reappearance of the sun after his long absence of six tedious months. Can these appearances prove fallacious? Is it a meteor we have seen, and mistaken for that splendid luminary which dispenses light and gladness throughout creation? It must be so, if we cannot meet on equal ground. If we cannot meet on the line that divides us equally, then take the hand of friendship, and make an *equal* compromise; it is vain to hope that *any* compromise can be made.'

A gentleman from Augusta County, who had taken a prominent part in the debate, and certainly displayed a good deal of ability, replied to the Chief Justice. One of his friends pronounced his argument to be unanswerable. This called up John Randolph, whose esteem and admiration for Judge Marshall, we are told (though they differed widely on Federal politics) amounted almost to idolatry.[1]

'The statement of the argument,' said he, 'by the gentleman from Richmond, the Chief Justice of the United States, had been such, as to put at defiance all that gentleman had said, or all that any man on earth could say. Where was the necessity of defending the fortress of Gibraltar against the abortive and puny attacks of the gentleman from Augusta? The Chief Justice had put the argument on ground which never could be shaken; and which had no more been impugned, than the fortress of Gibraltar could be affected, by attacking it with a pocket pistol. He had put it in a light — I do not mean any compliment — in which he puts everything that he attempts to place in a clear light. He had shown that the weak and helpless government proposed in the plan of the gentleman from Frederick was not what it was represented to be, and had shown them what *was* a compromise.'

On the various questions relating to the Judiciary, the Chief Justice manifested great interest. He was particularly anxious to preserve the county court system; a system, by the bye, which Mr. Jefferson regarded with the utmost aversion. The justices of these courts, said the latter, 'are self-chosen, are for life, and perpetuate their own body in succession forever, so that a faction once possessing themselves of the Bench of a county, can never be broken up, but hold their county in chains forever indissoluble. Yet these justices are the real Executive, as well as Judi-

[1] Southern Literary Messenger, vol. ii., p. 188.

ciary, in all our minor and most ordinary concerns. They tax us at will; fill the office of sheriff . . . name nearly all our military leaders, which leaders, once named, are removable but by themselves. The juries, our judges of all fact, and of law when they choose it, are not selected by the people, nor amenable to them. They are chosen by an officer named by the Court and Executive.'[1] Judge Marshall, on the contrary, adverting to the practical operation of these courts, would preserve them, and preserve, too, the mode in which the justices were appointed.

'I am not in the habit,' he said, 'of bestowing extravagant eulogies upon my countrymen; I would rather hear them pronounced by others; but it is a truth, that no State in the Union has hitherto enjoyed more complete internal quiet than Virginia. There is no part of America, where less disquiet, and less of ill-feeling between man and man is to be found, than in this Commonwealth; and I believe, most firmly, that this state of things is mainly to be ascribed to the practical operation of our county courts. The magistrates who compose those courts consist, in general, of the best men in their respective counties. They act in the spirit of peace-makers, and allay, rather than excite, the small disputes and differences which will sometimes arise among neighbors. It is certainly much owing to this, that so much harmony prevails amongst us. These courts must be preserved: if we part with them, can we be sure that we shall retain among our justices of the peace the same respectability and weight of character as are now to be found? I think not.'

---

[1] Jefferson's Works. Letter to Samuel Kerchival, July 12th, 1816.

John Randolph declared that he had long considered the county court system as one of the main pillars 'in the ancient edifice of our State Constitution.' In the course of the discussion upon this subject, 'the Chief Justice, thinking that some remark of his had been understood by Mr. Randolph as personally unkind, arose with earnestness to assure him it was not so intended. Mr. R. as earnestly strove to quiet Judge M.'s uneasiness, by assuring him that he had not understood the remark as offensive. In their eagerness, the one to apologize, and the other to show that no apology was necessary, they interrupted each other two or three times: at length Mr. R. effectually silenced his friend by saying, "I know the goodness of his heart too well to have supposed it possible that he could have intended to give me pain. Sir, I believe that, like My Uncle Toby, *he would not even hurt a fly!*"'[1]

One clause of the proposed Constitution provided that no modification or abolition of any court should be construed to deprive any judge thereof of his office; but such judge should perform any judicial duties which the Legislature might assign him. It met with great opposition; but was supported with equal earnestness by Judge Marshall. He contended that the independence of the judges was absolutely essential. 'I have grown old in the opinion,' said he, 'that there is nothing more dear to Virginia, or ought to be dearer to her statesmen, and that the best interests of our country are secured by it. Advert, Sir, to the duties of a judge. He has to pass between the Government and the man whom that Government is prosecuting:

[1] Southern Literary Messenger, vol. ii., p. 188.

between the most powerful individual in the community, and the poorest and most unpopular. It is of the last importance that, in the exercise of these duties, he should observe the utmost fairness. Need I press the necessity of this? Does not every man feel that his own personal security, and the security of his property, depends on that fairness? The judicial department comes home, in its effects, to every man's fireside: it passes on his property, his reputation, his life, his all. Is it not, to the last degree, important, that he should be rendered perfectly and completely independent, with nothing to influence or control him but God and his conscience?' 'We have heard about sinecures and judicial pensioners. Sir, the weight of such terms is well known here. To avoid creating a sinecure, you take away a man's duties, when he wishes them to remain; you take away the duty of one man, and give it to another: and this is a sinecure. What is this, in substance, but saying, that there is no such thing as judicial independence? You may take a judge's duties away, and then discard him. What is this but saying, that there is, and can be, and ought to be, no such thing as judicial independence?' 'I have always thought, from my earliest youth till now, that the greatest scourge an angry Heaven ever inflicted upon an ungrateful and a sinning people, was an ignorant, a corrupt, or a dependent judiciary. Will you draw down this curse upon Virginia? Our ancestors thought so; we thought so till very lately; and I trust the vote of this day will show that we think so still.'

Judge Marshall objected to that clause of the proposed Constitution which inhibited the Senate from altering a money bill, and confined their action simply to its approval or rejection. 'He never could conceive,' he said, 'the reason in favor of this part of the old Constitution. It had always appeared to him to have been introduced into it, from an assimilation of the Senate to the House of Lords. . . . But nothing could be more dissimilar than our Senate and the House of Lords, which was a paramount body, hereditary in its structure, sitting in its own right, and naturally apt to be much under the influence of the Crown.' 'But there was nothing of this sort in Virginia. The members of the Senate were as much the representatives of the people as those of the House of Delegates. They were elected in the same manner, by the same persons, and they receive the same pay as members of the other House.' On his motion, the clause was struck out.

Among the noticeable votes of the Chief Justice was one against empowering the Legislature to declare, by law, the disqualification of any person to hold office under the Government of Virginia, who should fight a duel, or send or accept a challenge, or act as second to either party, or knowingly be the bearer of a challenge.[1] As he did not explain the reasons that in-

[1] This provision was incorporated into the Constitution by a large majority; by a vote of more than two-thirds of the members in its favor. As Virginia, in the previous Presidential election, had voted for General Jackson, who had been engaged in several duels and rencontres, it gave John Randolph an opportunity to make one of his characteristic retorts. 'You will vote for a man,' said he, 'who has fought a duel, for President of the United States, and then you come back here, and gravely declare that no such man shall be a member of that august and illustrious assembly, the House of Burgesses! Sir, it is over-shooting the mark. . . It is a sanctimonious sort of republicanism not to my taste, not at all.'

duced him to give this vote, it may be idle to conjecture them. We are persuaded, however, that he was favorable to the object sought to be attained, that is, the suppression of duelling; and only objected to the means employed to effect it. He might object to giving the Legislature a power of disfranchisement. A general power of that kind would be extremely dangerous, and such as no legislative body ought to be entrusted with. It might, in times of excitement, be exercised so as to disqualify an opposing party in politics, or an obnoxious sect in religion. The Chief Justice might be opposed to recognising a principle of that nature, however modified or restricted it might be, lest in the future an enlarged application of it should be demanded.

The respect and affection with which all parties in the Convention regarded him was very marked and observable. Any dissent from his opinions was almost invariably accompanied by some expression of veneration for his character, or attachment to his person. Indeed, it was said that there was some little inconsistency on the part of certain members, between their warm professions of respect for his wisdom and gratitude for his spirit of conciliation, and their votes, which by no means conformed to his. 'Up gets the gentleman from Loudon,' said B. Watkins Leigh, when discussing the question as to the basis of representation, 'and thanks his honored, and venerable, and venerated friend from Richmond (Judge Marshall), for saying that he will vote for their proposition; and immediately after, another gentleman from Loudon *made* an occasion to say that his highly venerated friend was his political father — that he took delight in following his lessons — and that it was gratifying to his heart to find, that his very venerable friend from Richmond was willing to take what they proposed to give, if he could not get what he preferred. But, Sir, have we heard one word like a purpose to meet the generous spirit of that gentleman with a like generous spirit? Any, the least intimation, that if their proposition failed, they would accede to his? Not one word. . . . The generous and affectionate disposition of the gentleman from Richmond they applaud and countenance; but they — they will yield nothing! They were called upon to stand firm, and firm they stand.'

The Constitution finally adopted by the Convention was the result of mutual concession and compromise. Many of its features, considered separately, the Chief Justice could not approve. We have seen what opinions he entertained with regard to the question of suffrage, the basis of representation, and the independence of the Judiciary. His politics were conservative; but he was too wise not to know that it is an eternal law of political society, that concession and compromise are essential to its existence. 'All government, indeed every human benefit and enjoyment, every virtue, and every prudent act, is founded on compromise and barter. We balance inconveniences; we give and take; we remit some rights, that we may enjoy others; and we choose rather to be happy citizens, than subtle disputants.'[1] On these principles, the Chief Justice gave his cordial assent to the Constitution of Virginia, though, in several of its provisions, it ran counter to his opinions.

He was now in the seventy-fifth year of his age, and, apart from his duties as Chief Justice, he did not

[1] Burke. Speech on Conciliation with America.

again mingle in public life. Indeed, with the exception of this Convention, and the Convention which assembled at Charlottesville in the previous year, to devise a system of internal improvements for the State, and of which he was a member, he had not done so since his accession to the Bench.

In the following chapter we shall trace his footsteps through the brief, remaining period of his life, and view him more closely as a man and a citizen.

CHAPTER XIV.

1829—1835.

CONCLUSION.

THE residence of the Chief Justice in Richmond was built by himself, and situated on Shockhoe Hill.[1]

---

[1] 'Among the oldest and most respectable of the occupants of Shockhoe Hill was the Ambler family, of which the *Treasurer, Jaquelin Ambler* was the head. His own residence yet stands, between Marshall and Clay streets, and is occupied by one of his sons-in-law. His daughters were married to gentlemen who built their dwellings not far from the paternal mansion, and a distinguished circle they formed.

'*Chief Justice* (*then* General) *Marshall* is entitled to priority. His residence yet stands on the street named in his honor, but the grounds have been reduced one-half, and a number of fine dwellings erected on them, between Eighth and Ninth streets.

'*Col. Edward Carrington*, also a soldier of the Revolution, married another of the Misses Ambler, a most excellent lady, as was each of her sisters. He was a member of the old Congress in 1785–6. The high estimation in which Col. Carrington was held by his personal friend, General Washington, is shown by his selection of him to be Quarter-Master General, when, in 1798, war with France was expected, and an organization of officers formed for the crisis. Under John Adams's Administration, Col. Carrington held the office of Commissioner of the Revenue of the United States for Virginia — direct taxes being then resorted to, in consequence of the depredations on our commerce. . . . Col. Carrington was a man of dignified deportment, which was well sustained by his tall and massive figure. He was a pure patriot, and pure in all the relations of life. He died October 28th, 1810, aged 61.

Though without the slightest architectural pretensions, it was commodious, and the grounds were ample.[1] No man was more attached to his home, and his judicial labors were so distributed, that he was enabled to spend the most of each year in the midst of his family. The session of the Supreme Court at Washington, and the Circuit Courts for Virginia and North Carolina, completed the annual round of his judicial duties.

Having considerable leisure, and being fond of agriculture, he purchased a farm three or four miles from Richmond, which he visited frequently, often on foot. He also owned a farm in Fauquier, his native county, to which he made an annual visit. His family and social attachments were warm and constant, and his periodical visits to Fauquier were always highly enjoyed both by himself and his numerous relatives and friends.

He took great delight in social, and even convivial pleasures. He was a member of The Barbacue, or Quoit Club, at Richmond, for more than forty years; and no one participated in the exercise and recreation that took place at their meetings with more zest and enthusiasm than himself. The Club was formed in 1788, and consisted of thirty members. They met once a fortnight, from May until October, at a place near 'Buchanan's Spring,' about a mile from the town. A

'*Daniel Call*, a distinguished lawyer, married another of the sisters Ambler, and his residence on the square between the Capitol and Broad street was taken down a few years ago, to be substituted by Mr. Valentine's large store.

'*George Fisher* married a fourth sister, and he, a retired merchant, and one of our oldest citizens, is the survivor of all that I have mentioned, and is the occupant of the patriarchal mansion of Treasurer Ambler.' — *Richmond in By-gone Days*, p. 64 *et seq.*

[1] About two acres.

visitor, who was present at a meeting of the Club, in the life-time of the Chief Justice, has given the following account of it: —

'The Club consists,' he says, 'of judges, lawyers, doctors, and merchants, and the Governor of the Commonwealth has a general invitation when he enters into office. What gave additional interest to this body, some years ago, was the constant attendance (as honorary members) of two venerable clergymen — one of the Episcopal, and the other of the Presbyterian Church — who joined in the innocent pastime of the day. They were pious and exemplary men, who discerned no sin in harmless gaiety. Quoits and backgammon are the only games indulged in, and one of the clergyman was, for many years, "cock of the walk' in throwing the *discus*. They are gone to their account, and have left a chasm that has not been filled.[1]

'Some years ago an amendment was made to the constitution, which admits the use of porter. Great opposition was made to this innovation, and the destruction of the Club was predicted as the consequence. The oppositionists, however, soon became as great consumers of malt and hops as their associates; and now they even consent to the introduction of wine at the last meeting of every year, provided there be "a shot in the locker." The members each advance ten dol-

[1] One of these clergymen was the Rev. Mr. Buchanan, an Episcopalian, and the other the Rev. Mr. Blair, a Presbyterian. 'These two clergymen were beloved throughout the community, for their many virtues. They were not ascetics, but liked to see their flocks gay and happy, and to promote and partake of such feelings within proper bounds. Each possessed a fund of wit, and was liberal in expending it.' — *Richmond in By-gone Days*, p. 120.

lars to the treasurer at the beginning of the season, and every member is entitled to invite any strangers as guests, on paying into the general fund one dollar for each; while the caterers of the day, consisting of two members in rotation, provide, and have the privilege of bringing each a guest (either citizen or non-resident) at free cost.

'On the day I was present, dinner was ready at half-past three o'clock, and consisted of excellent meats and fish, well-prepared and well-served, with the vegetables of the season. Your veritable gourmand never fails to regale himself on his favorite *barbecue*, which is a fine fat pig, called "shoot," cooked on the coals, and highly-seasoned with cayenne; a dessert of melons and fruits follows, and punch, porter, and toddy, are the table liquors; but with the fruits comes on the favorite beverage of the Virginians, mint julep, in place of wine. I never witnessed more festivity and good humor than prevail at this Club. By the constitution, the subject of politics is forbidden, and each man strives to make the time pleasant to his companions. The members think they can offer no higher compliment to a distinguished stranger, than to introduce him to the Club; and all feel it a duty to contribute to his entertainment. It was refreshing to see such a man as Chief Justice Marshall laying aside the reserve of his dignified station, and contending with the young men at a game of quoits, with all the emulation of a youth.

'Many anecdotes are told of occurrences at these meetings. Such is the partiality for the Chief Justice, that it is said the greatest anxiety is felt for his success in the game by the bystanders; and, on one occasion, an old Scotch gentleman was called on to decide between his quoit and that of another member, who, after seemingly careful measurement, announced, "*Mister Mareshall has it a leattle,*" when it was visible to all that the contrary was the fact. A French gentleman (Baron Quenet) was at one time a guest, when the Governor, the Chief Justice, and several of the Judges of the High Court of Appeals, were engaged with others, *with coats off*, in a well-contested game. He asked, "if it was possible that the dignitaries of the land could thus intermix with private citizens;" and, when assured of the fact, he observed, with true gallican enthusiasm, that "he had never before seen the real beauty of republicanism."'[1]

Not one of the members, it is stated, was more punctual in his attendance at the meetings of the Club, than the Chief Justice, and not one who contributed more to their pleasantness. Even in advanced years, he was 'among the most skilful in throwing the *discus* as he was in discussion, . . . and it delighted his competitors as much as himself, to see him "ring the meg."'[2] 'He would hurl his iron ring of two pounds weight, with rarely erring aim, fifty-five or sixty feet; and, at some *chef d'œuvre* of skill in himself or his *partner*, would spring up and clap his hands, with all the light-hearted enthusiasm of boyhood.'[3] In his yearly visits to Fauquier, 'where the proper implements of his sport were not to be had, he still practised it among his rustic friends, with *flat stones* for quoits. A casual guest at a *barbacue* in that county — one of those rural entertainments so frequent among the country people of Virginia — soon after his arrival at the spot, saw an old man emerge from a

[1] American Turf Register for 1829.

[2] Richmond in By-gone Days, p. 189.

[3] Southern Literary Messenger, vol. ii., p. 188.

thicket which bordered the neighboring brook, carrying as large a pile of these flat stones as he could hold between his right arm and his chin: he stepped briskly up to the company, and threw down his load among them, exclaiming, "There! Here are quoits enough us for all!" The stranger's surprise may be imagined, when he found that this plain and cheerful old man was the Chief Justice of the United States.'[1] In all his actions, there was the same winning simplicity, the same forgetfulness of self; 'his native humility, modesty, and candor never forsook him, even on surprise or provocation; nor was the least degree of assumption visible to the most scrutinizing eye, in any part of his conduct or discourse.'[2]

'He was a most conscientious man,' says Bishop Meade, 'in regard to some things which others might regard as too trivial to be observed. It was my privilege, more than once, to travel with him between Fauquier and Fredericksburgh, when we were both going to the lower country. On one occasion, the roads being in their worst condition, when we came to that most miry part called the "Black Jack," we found that the travellers through it had taken a nearer and better road through a plantation. The fence being down, or very low, I was proceeding to pass over, but he said we had better go round, although each step was a plunge, adding, that it was his duty, as one in office, to be very particular in regard to such things. As to some other matters, however, he was not so particular. Although myself never much given to dress or equipage, yet I was not at all ashamed to compare

[1] Southern Literary Messenger, vol. ii., p. 189.

[2] Burke of Sir Joshua Reynolds, and eminently true of Marshall.

with him during these travels, whether as to clothing, horse, saddle, or bridle. Servant he had none. Federalist as he was in politics, in his manners and habits he was truly republican. Would that all republicans were like him in this respect. . . . On one of my visits to Richmond, being in a street near his house, between daybreak and sunrise one morning, I met him on horseback, with a bag of clover-seed lying before him, which he was carrying to his farm, it being the time of sowing such seed.'[1]

The dress of the Chief Justice was always plain, and worn very carelessly. He usually wore blue-mixed woollen stockings, and a suit of black, of rather ordinary quality. He adhered to the mode of the last century, but his body was so ill-compacted, that it balked and marred the utmost skill of the shears. He was an early riser; 'and nothing was more usual, than to see him returning from market at sunrise, with poultry in one hand, and a basket of vegetables in the other.'[2] It is related that, while at the market on one occasion, a young man, who had recently removed to Richmond, was swearing violently because he could hire no one to take home his turkey. Marshall stepped up, and, ascertaining of him where he lived, replied, 'That is in my way, and I will take it for you.' When arrived at his dwelling, the young man inquired, 'What shall I pay you?' 'Oh, nothing,' was the rejoinder, 'you are welcome; it was on my way, and no trouble.' 'Who is that polite old gentleman who brought home my turkey for me?' inquired the other of a bystander, as Marshall stepped away.

---

[1] Old Churches and Families of Virginia, vol. ii., p. 222.

[2] Southern Literary Messenger, vol. ii., p. 188.

'That,' replied he, 'is John Marshall, Chief Justice of the United States.'[1] The mortification of the young man may be imagined.

As we have already remarked, he held the Circuit Courts for Virginia and North Carolina, and nothing could present a greater contrast than the Lord Chancellor of England going in state to Westminster Hall, and the Chief Justice of the United States making his annual journey to Raleigh, in the latter State, to preside at the Federal Court held there. His style of travelling to and from that place, about 175 miles each way, 'was, for many years, in that primitive sort of vehicle, a stick gig (or chair, as it was then called), with one horse, and with no attendant.'[2]

His equipage, dress, and unpretending manner never would have suggested to a stranger the remotest idea of his position in life. He was once travelling in the northern part of Virginia, and about night-fall arrived at the village of Winchester, in Frederick County. He drove to what was then known as M'Guire's hotel. What occurred there has been thus related:—

'It is not long since a gentleman was travelling in one of the counties of Virginia, and, about the close of the day, stopped at a public house to obtain refreshment, and spend the night. He had been there but a short time, before an old man alighted from his gig, with the apparent intention of becoming his fellow-guest at the same house. As the old man drove up, he observed that both the shafts of his gig were

---

[1] Howe's Virginia Historical Collections, page 266.

[2] Richmond in By-gone Days, p. 64.

broken, and that they were held together by withes formed from the bark of a hickory sapling. Our traveller observed further, that he was plainly clad, that his knee-buckles were loosened, and that something like negligence pervaded his dress. Conceiving him to be one of the honest yeomanry of our land, the courtesies of strangers passed between them, and they entered the tavern. It was about the same time that an addition of three or four young gentlemen was made to their number — most, if not all of them, of the legal profession. As soon as they became conveniently accommodated, the conversation was turned by the latter upon an eloquent harangue which had that day been displayed at the Bar. It was replied by the other, that he had witnessed, the same day, a degree of eloquence no doubt equal, but that it was from the pulpit. Something like a sarcastic rejoinder was made to the eloquence of the pulpit; and a warm and able altercation ensued, in which the merits of the Christian religion became the subject of discussion. From six o'clock until eleven, the young champions wielded the sword of argument, adducing, with ingenuity and ability, everything that could be said pro and con. During this protracted period, the old gentleman listened with all the meekness and modesty of a child; as if he was adding new information to the stores of his own mind; or perhaps he was observing, with philosophic eye, the faculties of the youthful mind, and how new energies are evolved by repeated action; or, perhaps, with patriotic emotion, he was reflecting upon the future destinies of his country, and on the rising generation upon whom these future destinies must devolve; or, most probably, with a sentiment of moral and religious feeling, he was collecting an argument which — characteristic of himself — no art would be "able to elude, and no force resist." Our traveller remained a spectator, and took no part in what was said.

'At last one of the young men, remarking that it was impossible to combat with long established prejudices, wheeled around, and with some familiarity exclaimed, "Well, my old gentleman, what think you of these things?" If, said the traveller, a streak of vivid lightning had at that moment crossed the room, their amazement could not have been greater than it was with what followed. The most eloquent and unanswerable appeal was made for nearly an hour, by the old gentleman, that he ever heard or read. So perfect was his recollection, that every argument urged against the Christian religion was met in the order in which it was advanced. Hume's sophistry on the subject of miracles was, if possible, more perfectly answered than it had already been done by Campbell. And in the whole lecture there was so much simplicity and energy, pathos and sublimity, that not another word was uttered. An attempt to describe it, said the traveller, would be an attempt to paint the sunbeams. It was now a matter of curiosity and inquiry who the old gentleman was. The traveller concluded it was the preacher from whom the pulpit eloquence was heard; but no, it was the *Chief Justice of the United States*.'[1]

If a stranger might not infer Marshall's greatness from his personal appearance, he could not long be in his company without perceiving his goodness, his un-

---

[1] This anecdote was originally published in the Winchester Republican, but preserved in durable form by being printed in Howe's Virginia Historical Collections, p. 275.

affected kindness, and genial nature. 'Meet him in a stage-coach, as a stranger, and travel with him a whole day, and you would only be struck with his readiness to administer to the accommodations of others, and his anxiety to appropriate the least to himself. Be with him, the unknown guest at an inn, and he seemed adjusted to the very scene, partaking of the warm welcome of its comforts, whenever found, and, if not found, resigning himself without complaint to its meanest arrangements. You would never suspect, in either case, that he was a great man; far less, that he was the Chief Justice of the United States. But if, perchance, invited by the occasion, you drew him into familiar conversation, you would never forget that you had seen and heard that "old man eloquent."'[1]

He was fond of the young, and they found in him a cheerful and most agreeable companion. 'One, whose first recollection of him referred to his triumphal entry (for such it was) into Richmond, on his return from France, and who, as a printer's boy, afterwards, for several years, was carrier of a newspaper to him, describes him as "remarkably fond of boys' company—always chatty—and always pleasant."[2] The same printer's boy having been transferred to Washington, in 1800, while Marshall was Secretary of State, renewed his acquaintance with him. 'Again,' he says, 'did the pleasing office of serving him with the "Washington Federalist" devolve on me. He resided in a brick building hardly larger than most of the kitchens now in use. I found him still the same plain, unostentatious John Marshall: always accessi-

[1] Story's Discourse, p. 52.

[2] Southern Literary Messenger, vol. ii., p. 189.

ble, and always with a smile on his countenance when I handed him the "Federalist." His kindness of manner won my affections; and I became devotedly attached to him.'[1]

No man was more just or more generous. In his dealings he was so scrupulous, as always to prefer his own loss to the possibility of his wronging another.[2] In his practice at the Bar, he never knowingly argued in defence of injustice, or took a legal advantage at the expense of moral honesty. He once endorsed a bond amounting to several thousand dollars; and the drawer having failed, he was called upon to pay it. He knew the bond could be avoided, because the holder had advanced the money at usurious interest; but he was utterly incapable of throwing off the moral obligation in that way, and he paid it.[3] His generosity was 'as large as his mind, and as unostentatious as his life.' We shall cite a single example. 'In passing through Culpepper, on his way to Fauquier, he fell in company with Mr. S., an old fellow-officer in the army of the Revolution. In the course of conversation, Marshall learned that there was a lien upon the estate of his friend to the amount of $3000, about due, and he was greatly distressed at the prospect of impending ruin. On bidding farewell, Marshall privately left a check for the amount, which being presented to Mr. S., after his departure, he, impelled by a chivalrous independence, mounted, and spurred his horse until he overtook his friend. He thanked him for his generosity, but refused to accept it.

---

[1] Southern Literary Messenger, vol. ii., p. 189.

[2] Ibid.

[3] Howe's Virginia Historical Collections, p. 266.

Marshall strenuously persisted in its acceptance, and the other as strongly persisted in not accepting. Finally, it resulted in a compromise, by which Marshall took security on the lien, but never called for pay.'[1] He was a member, for nearly half a century, of the Amicable Society at Richmond, which was formed to relieve strangers and wayfarers in distress, for whom the law made no provision. In short, his unobtrusive acts of generosity were innumerable, and flowed from the spontaneous goodness of his heart.

Upon the vexed and disagreeable, but important subject of slavery, his opinions were well known. He belonged to the Colonization Society, and manifested much interest in its objects. Though a slaveholder himself, he, nevertheless, regarded the institution as an incubus upon the prosperity of a State; an incubus whose effects the Colonization Society might palliate, but could not remove. Until the British emancipation in the West Indies, he always maintained that the abolition of slavery by legal enactment was impracticable; and that the evil was incurable, except by convulsion. After the experiment was actually made, he is said to have expressed hope as to the future of his beloved Virginia. Possibly, if he had lived to see the result in the West Indies, he might have anticipated less good from a similar experiment elsewhere. To promote the objects of the Colonization Society, he was in favor of an application to the several States for permanent aids; but his chief reliance was upon the General Government. 'It is undoubtedly of great importance,' he said, 'to retain the countenance and protection of the General Government. Some of our cruisers stationed on the coast of Africa

---

[1] Howe's Virginia Historical Collections, p. 266.

would, at the same time, interrupt the slave-trade — a horrid traffic, detested by all good men — and would protect the vessels and commerce of the colony from pirates who infest those seas. The power of the Government to afford this aid is not, I believe, contested. I regret that its power to grant pecuniary aid is not equally free from question. On this subject I have always thought, and still think, that the proposition made by Mr. King, in the Senate, is the most unexceptionable, and the most effective, that can be devised. . . . . The lands are the property of the United States, and have hitherto been disposed of by the Government under the idea of absolute ownership.'[1]

Though taking no part in the political controversies of the day, Marshall manifested to the last a warm interest in them. To the prevailing politics of his native State he was invincibly opposed. Towards the latter part of his life, he viewed, with something of gloom and despondency, the future prospects of his country, from the ascendency of principles which he believed would destroy the efficiency and perpetuity of the General Government. In a letter to Judge Story, two years before his death, he says, 'I have just finished reading your great work,[2] and wish it could be read by every statesman, and every would-be statesman in the United States. It is a comprehensive and an accurate commentary on our Constitution, formed in the spirit of the original text. In the South,

[1] Fifteenth Annual Report of the Colonization Society, p. 32. Letter from Marshall, December 14th, 1831.

[2] Commentaries on the Constitution; which were dedicated to Judge Marshall.

we are so far gone in political metaphysics, that I fear no demonstration can restore us to common sense. The word "State Rights," as expounded by the resolutions of 1798, and the report of 1799, construed by our Legislature, has a charm against which all reasoning is vain. Those resolutions, and that report, constitute the creed of every politician who hopes to rise in Virginia; and to question them, or even to adopt the construction given by their author, is deemed political sacrilege. The solemn and interesting admonitions of your concluding remarks will not, I fear, avail as they ought to avail against this popular frenzy. I am grateful for the very flattering terms in which you speak of your friend in many parts of this valuable work, as well as in the dedication. In despite of my vanity, I cannot suppress the fear, that you will be supposed by others, as well as myself, to have consulted a partial friendship farther than your deliberate judgment will approve. Others may not contemplate this partiality with as much gratification as its object.'[1]

In a subsequent letter to Judge Story, he says:— 'On my return, a day or two past, from an annual visit to our mountains, I had the real gratification of receiving a number of the New England Magazine for August last, containing an Essay, entitled "Statesmen: their Rareness and Importance," forwarded to me by yourself, and thank you truly for the real pleasure afforded by its perusal. The justness and solidity of its sentiments, the distinguished individual who is selected as an example of the real statesman,[2] and the

[1] Story's Life and Letters, vol. ii., p. 135. July 31st, 1833.

[2] Daniel Webster.

kind notice taken of an old friend who is under so many obligations to you, designate the author as certainly as if his name had been affixed to the work.

'It is in vain to lament, that the portrait which the author has drawn of our political and party men is, in the general, true. Lament it as we may, much as it may wound our vanity or our pride, it is still, in the main, true; and will, I fear, so remain. . . . . In the South, political prejudice is too strong to yield to any degree of merit; and the great body of the nation contains, at least appears to me to contain, too much of the same ingredient. To men who think as you and I do, the present is gloomy enough; and the future presents no cheering prospect. The struggle now maintained in every State in the Union seems to me to be of doubtful issue; but should it terminate contrary to the wishes of those who support the enormous pretensions of the Executive, should victory crown the exertions of the champions of constitutional law, what serious and lasting advantage is to be expected from this result? In the South (things may be less gloomy with you) those who support the Executive do not support the Government. They sustain the personal power of the President, but labor incessantly to impair the legitimate powers of the Government. Those who oppose the violent and rash measures of the Executive (many of them nullifiers, many of them seceders) are generally the bitter enemies of a constitutional government. Many of them are the avowed advocates of a league; and those who do not go the whole length, go great part of the way. What can we hope for in such circumstances? As far as I can judge, the Government is weakened, whatever party may prevail. Such is the impression I receive from the language of those around me.'[1]

Though strongly opposed to the general policy of Jackson's Administration, and the principles upon which it was conducted, the Chief Justice warmly approved his proclamation and message against nullification. Secession and nullification he regarded as political heresies of the most dangerous character; as theories utterly subversive of all stability in our Government, and at war with its fundamental principles. Speaking of a dinner at the President's, about the time of the debate on the Force bill, Judge Story says, 'I forgot to say, that, notwithstanding I am "the most dangerous man in America,"[2] the President specially invited me to drink a glass of wine with him. But, what is more remarkable, since his last proclamation and message, the Chief Justice and myself have become his warmest supporters, and shall continue so just as long as he maintains the principles contained in them. Who would have dreamed of such an occurrence.'[3]

Marshall was fond of books, which, in his intervals of leisure, he read 'for delight.' His familiarity with general literature was extensive. The great masters of English letters were his favorite companions. He read novels with intense interest, and would spend the night over their alluring pages. He had formed a very high estimate of female genius, and the productions of female authors he read with an interest in

---

[1] Story's Life and Letters, vol. ii., p. 172. October 6th, 1834.

[2] So styled by General Jackson.

[3] Story's Life and Letters, vol. ii., p. 117. January 27th, 1833.

some sort proportioned to his admiration of their sex. Acknowledging the receipt of a discourse by Judge Story, he says, 'I have read it with real pleasure, and am particularly gratified with your eulogy on the ladies. It is matter of great satisfaction to me to find another judge who, though not as old as myself, thinks justly of the fair sex, and commits his sentiments to print. I was a little mortified, however, to find that you had not admitted the name of Miss Austin into your list of favorites. I had just finished reading her novels when I received your discourse, and was so much pleased with them, that I looked in it for her name, and was rather disappointed at not finding it. Her flights are not lofty, she does not soar on eagles' wings, but she is pleasing, interesting, equable, and yet amusing. I count on your making some apology for this omission.'[1]

The Chief Justice had imbibed, in his youth, a love of poetry; and the 'sweetly uttered wisdom' of song he found a solace and delight in his age. No doubt these studies contributed very much to preserve his intellect in that vigor and freshness which it exhibited down to the very close of his life. His mind was not suffered to grow rigid by dwelling only on professional topics; but was variously exercised, which is 'healthful and sovereign for the understanding.'

The constitution of the Chief Justice was robust, and his health good. From youth to age, he suffered but little from sickness. In his latter years, however, he was afflicted with that most excruciating malady, the stone. In October, 1831, he visited Philadelphia, and submitted to an operation by Dr. Physick,

[1] Story's Life and Letters, vol. i., p. 506. November 26th, 1826.

which gave him relief. 'This case,' says Dr. Randolph, 'was attended with singular interest, in consequence of the exalted position of the patient, his advanced age, and the circumstance of there being upwards of one thousand calculi taken from his bladder. . . . . It will be readily admitted that, in consequence of Judge Marshall's very advanced age, the hazard attending the operation, however skilfully performed, was considerably increased. I consider it but an act of justice, due to the memory of that good and great man, to state that, in my opinion, his recovery was, in a great degree, owing to his extraordinary self-possession, and to the calm and philosophical views which he took of his case, and the various circumstances attending it. It fell to my lot to make the necessary preparations. In the discharge of this duty, I visited him on the morning of the day fixed on for the operation, two hours previously to that at which it was to be performed. Upon entering his room, I found him engaged in eating his breakfast. He received me with a pleasant smile upon his countenance, and said, "Well, Doctor, you find me taking breakfast, and I assure you I have had a good one. I thought it very probable that this might be my last chance, and therefore I was determined to enjoy it, and eat heartily." I expressed the great pleasure which I felt at seeing him so cheerful, and said that I hoped all would soon be happily over. He replied to this, that he did not feel the least anxiety or uneasiness respecting the operation or its result. He said that he had not the slightest desire to live, laboring under the sufferings to which he was then subjected; that he was perfectly ready to take all the chances of an operation, and he knew there were many against him; and that, if he could be relieved by it, he was willing to live out his appointed time, but if not, would rather die, than hold existence accompanied with the pain and misery which he then endured. After he had finished his breakfast, I administered to him some medicine: he then inquired at what hour the operation would be performed. I mentioned the hour of eleven. He said, "Very well; do you wish me now for any other purpose, or may I lie down and go to sleep?" I was a good deal surprised at this question, but told him that if he could sleep it would be very desirable. He immediately placed himself upon the bed and fell into a profound sleep, and continued so until I was obliged to rouse him in order to undergo the operation. He exhibited the same fortitude, scarcely uttering a murmur throughout the whole procedure, which, from the peculiar nature of his complaint, was necessarily tedious.'[1]

His situation had been considered dangerous, and, throughout the country, caused much anxiety: his happy recovery occasioned corresponding joy. 'Pray tell the Chief Justice,' wrote Judge Story to his friend Peters, 'how deeply every one here has been interested in his situation. He is beloved and reverenced here beyond all measure, though not beyond his merits. Next to Washington, he stands the idol of all good men. And who so well deserves it? I look upon his judicial life as good now for at least six years longer?'[2]

Though recovering himself, he received, soon after,

---

[1] Memoir of Dr. P. S. Physick, by J. Randolph, M. D., p. 96, *et seq.*

[2] Story's Life and Letters, vol. ii., p. 70. Letter to Richard Peters, October 29th, 1831.

a severe blow in the death of his wife, to whom he was ardently attached. She had suffered much from ill-health, and the tender and assiduous attention he paid to her, says Bishop Meade, was the most interesting and striking feature in his domestic character. 'Mrs. Marshall was nervous in the extreme. The least noise was sometimes agony to her whole frame, and his perpetual endeavor was to keep the house, and yard, and outhouses, as free as possible from the slightest cause of distressing her; walking himself, at times, about the house and yard without shoes. On one occasion, when she was in her most distressing state, the town authorities of Richmond manifested their great respect for him, and sympathy for her, by having either the town-clock or town-bell muffled.'[1]

Marshall first met his future wife at York, while on a visit to his father, Colonel Marshall, who was the commanding officer at that place. She was but fourteen years of age at the time, and it is stated to have been a case of love at first sight. It is also said, that he endeared himself to her family, 'notwithstanding his slouched hat, and negligent and awkward dress, by his amiable manners, fine talents, and especially his love for poetry, which he read to them with deep pathos.' In proof of the ardor of his character, and the tenderness of his attachment to his intended wife, his sister-in-law, Mrs. Carrington, remarks, that he often said to her, 'that he looked with astonishment on the present race of lovers,' so totally unlike what he had been himself. On his marriage, after paying the minister his fee, his sole remaining fortune was a guinea.[2]

---

[1] Old Churches and Families of Virginia, vol. ii., p. 222.

[2] Ibid., vol. i., p. 99, note.

Mrs. Marshall died on the 25th of December, 1831. Her loss weighed heavily on his spirits. 'On going into the Chief Justice's room this morning,' says his friend, and brother judge, 'I found him in tears. He had just finished writing out for me some lines of General Burgoyne, of which he spoke to me last evening as eminently beautiful and affecting. I asked him to change the purpose, and address them to you, which he instantly did, and you will find them accompanying this. I saw at once that he had been shedding tears over the memory of his own wife; and he has said to me several times during the term, that the moment he relaxes from business he feels exceedingly depressed, and rarely goes through a night without weeping over his departed wife. She must have been a very extraordinary woman, so to have attached him, and I think he is the most extraordinary man I ever saw, for the depth and tenderness of his feelings.'[1]

The following affecting tribute to her memory was written by himself, December 25th, 1832:—

'This day of joy and festivity to the whole Christian world is, to my sad heart, the anniversary of the keenest affliction which humanity can sustain. While all around is gladness, my mind dwells on the silent tomb, and cherishes the remembrance of the beloved object which it contains.

'On the 25th of December, 1831, it was the will of Heaven to take to itself the companion who had

---

[1] Story's Life and Letters, vol. ii., p. 86. Letter to Mrs. Story, March 4th, 1832.

sweetened the choicest part of my life, had rendered toil a pleasure, had partaken of all my feelings, and was enthroned in the inmost recess of my heart. Never can I cease to feel the loss, and to deplore it. Grief for her is too sacred ever to be profaned on this day, which shall be, during my existence, marked by a recollection of her virtues.

'On the 3d of January, 1783, I was united by the holiest bonds to the woman I adored. From the moment of our union to that of our separation, I never ceased to thank Heaven for this, its best gift. Not a moment passed in which I did not consider her as a blessing from which the chief happiness of my life was derived. This never-dying sentiment, originating in love, was cherished by a long and close observation of as amiable and estimable qualities as ever adorned the female bosom. To a person which, in youth, was very attractive, to manners uncommonly pleasing, she added a fine understanding, and the sweetest temper which can accompany a just and modest sense of what was due to herself. She was educated with a profound reverence for religion, which she preserved to her last moments. This sentiment, among her earliest and deepest impressions, gave a coloring to her whole life. Hers was the religion taught by the Saviour of man. She was a firm believer in the faith inculcated by the Church [Episcopal] in which she was bred.

'I have lost her, and with her have lost the solace of my life! Yet she remains still the companion of my retired hours, still occupies my inmost bosom. When alone, and unemployed, my mind still recurs to her. More than a thousand times, since the 25th of December, 1831, have I repeated to myself the beautiful lines written by General Burgoyne, under a similar affliction, substituting "Mary" for "Anna:"

'"Encompassed in an angel's frame,
An angel's virtues lay;
Too soon did Heaven assert its claim,
And take its own away!
My Mary's worth, My Mary's charms,
Can never more return!
What now shall fill these widowed arms?
Ah me! My Mary's urn!
Ah me! Ah me! My Mary's urn!"'[1]

At the ensuing term of the Supreme Court (January, 1833), the Chief Justice was at his post, and, though he had now attained the seventy-eighth year of his age, his health seemed fully re-established. 'The Court opened on Monday last,' says Judge Story, 'and all the Judges were present, except Judge Baldwin. They were in good health, and the Chief Justice especially looked more vigorous than usual. He seemed to revive, and enjoy anew his green old age. He brought with him, and presented to each of us, a copy of the new edition of his Life of Washington, inscribing in the fly-page of mine a very kind remark. . . Having some leisure on our hands, the Chief Justice and myself have devoted some of it to attendance upon the theatre, to hear Miss Fanny Kemble, who has been in the city the past week. We attended on Monday night, and, on the Chief Justice's entrance into the box, he was cheered in a marked manner. He behaved as he always does, with extreme modesty, and seemed not to know that the compliment was designed for him. We have seen Miss Kemble as Julia,

---

[1] Old Churches and Families of Virginia, vol. ii., p. 223, note.

in the Hunchback, and as Mrs. Haller, in the Stranger. . . . I have never seen any female acting at all comparable to hers. She is so graceful, that you forget that she is not very handsome. In Mrs. Haller, she threw the whole audience into tears. The Chief Justice shed them in common with younger eyes.'[1]

The celebrity of Marshall, the reverence and affection with which he was regarded by his own countrymen, naturally made him an object of interest to strangers visiting the United States. And he inspired in them, as in every one who knew him, and became acquainted with his character, sentiments of veneration and esteem. Miss Martineau was in Washington the winter preceding his death, and she has thus recorded her impressions of his appearance and conversation: —

'With Judge Story,' she says, 'sometimes came the man to whom he looked up with feelings little short of adoration; the aged Chief-Justice Marshall. There was almost too much mutual respect in our first meeting; we knew something of his individual merits and services; and he maintained through life, and carried to his grave, a reverence for woman as rare in its kind as in its degree. It had all the theoretical fervour and magnificence of Uncle Toby's, with the advantage of being grounded upon an extensive knowledge of the sex. He was the father and the grandfather of woman; and out of this experience he brought, not only the love and pity which their offices and position command, and the awe of purity which they excite in the

---

[1] Story's Life and Letters, vol. ii., p. 116. Letter to Mrs. Story, January 2d, 1833.

minds of the pure, but a steady conviction of their intellectual equality with men; and, with this, a deep sense of their social injuries. Throughout life he so invariably sustained their cause, that no indulgent libertine dared to flatter and humor, no sceptic, secure in the possession of power, dared to scoff at the claims of woman in the presence of Marshall, who, made clear-sighted by his purity, knew the sex far better than either.

'How delighted we were to see Judge Story bring in the tall, majestic, bright-eyed old man! — old by chronology, by the lines on his composed face, and by his services to the republic; but so dignified, so fresh, so present to the time, that no feeling of compassionate consideration for age dared to mix with the contemplation of him.

'The first evening, he asked me much about English politics, and especially whether the people were not fast ripening for the abolition of our religious establishment — an institution which, after a long study of it, he considered so monstrous in principle, and so injurious to true religion in practice, that he could not imagine that it could be upheld for anything but political purposes. There was no prejudice here, on account of American modes being different; for he observed that the clergy were there, as elsewhere, far from being in the van of society, and lamented the existence of much fanaticism in the United States: but he saw the evils of an establishment the more clearly, not the less, from being aware of the faults in the administration of religion at home. The most animated moment of our conversation was when I told him I was going to visit Mr. Madison, on leaving Washington. He instantly sat upright in his chair, and with beaming eyes began to praise Mr. Madison. Madison received the mention of Marshall's name in just the same manner: yet these men were strongly opposed in politics, and their magnanimous appreciation of each other underwent no slight or brief trial.'[1]

In the spring of this year (1835), and after the return of the Chief Justice to Virginia, another English traveller spent a week at Richmond, enjoying the hospitality of its inhabitants; and to his pen we are indebted for the following sketch of the Chief Justice:

'Judge Marshall, who is Chief Justice of the Supreme Court, and, in fact, Lord Chancellor of the United States, is one of the most remarkable and distinguished men that has adorned the Legislature of either shore of the Atlantic. He began life as a soldier; and, during the American war, served in the militia, where he rose to the rank of General:[2] after which he came to the Bar, and passed through all its gradations to his present high position, which is, in my opinion, the proudest that an American can enjoy, not excepting that of President; inasmuch as it is less subject *arbitrio popularis auræ;* and as the Court over which he presides can affirm and decide what is and what is not the Constitution of the United States.

'The Judge is a tall, venerable man, about eighty years of age, his hair tied in a cue, according to olden custom, and with a countenance indicating that simplicity of mind and benignity which so eminently distinguish his character. As a judge he has no rival, his knowledge being profound, his judgment clear and

---

[1] Martineau's Western Travel, vol. i., p. 247, English ed.

[2] This is erroneous. *After* the war, and not *during* the war, he served in the militia, and was appointed a militia general.

just, and his quickness in apprehending either the fallacy or truth of an argument as surprising. I had the pleasure of several long conversations with him, and was struck with admiration at the extraordinary union of modesty and power, gentleness and force, which his mind displays. What he knows he communicates without reserve; he speaks with a clearness of expression, and in a tone of simple truth, which compel conviction; and on all subjects on which his knowledge is not *certain*, or which admit of doubt or argument, he delivers his opinion with a candid diffidence, and with a deference for that of others, amounting almost to timidity: still, it is a timidity which would disarm the most violent opponent, and win respect and credence from any auditor. I remember having often observed a similar characteristic attributed to the immortal Newton. The simplicity of his character is not more singular than that of his life; pride, ostentation, and hypocrisy are "Greek to him;" and he really lives up to the letter and spirit of republicanism, while he maintains all the dignity due to his age and office.

'His house is small, and more humble in appearance than those of the average of successful lawyers or merchants. I called three times upon him; there is no bell to the door: once I turned the handle of it, and walked in unannounced; on the other two occasions he had seen me coming, and had lifted the latch and received me at the door, although he was at the time suffering from some severe contusions received in the stage while travelling on that road from Fredericksburgh to Richmond, which I have before described. I verily believe there is not a particle of vanity in his composition, unless it be of that venial and hospitable nature which induces him to pride himself on giving to his friends the best glass of Madeira in Virginia. In short, blending, as he does, the simplicity of a child and the plainness of a republican with the learning and ability of a lawyer, the venerable dignity of his appearance would not suffer in comparison with that of the most respected and distinguished-looking peer in the British House of Lords.'[1]

This absence of vanity, this childlike simplicity, this unpretending manner, that distinguished Marshall, and which every one remarked, often induced a feeling of disappointment on a first introduction to him. He used no tricks 'to maintain the credit of his sufficiency;" and never talked to display his knowledge or ability, or 'to get opinion,' as Bacon expresses it. There was an utter unconsciousness of self in his manner; all was simple, natural, and unaffected. He presumed nothing upon his age or station, and his ordinary conversation, though agreeable, sensible, and suitable to the occasion, did not betoken the depth of his mind. It was only in the company of his intimate friends, and when the conversation was directed to some subject that elicited discussion, that the powers of his mind were displayed. The following anecdote may be cited as an example: —

'Mr. Dexter,' says Judge Story, 'was once in company with Fisher Ames and Chief Justice Marshall. The latter commenced a conversation, or rather an opinion (for he was almost solus in the dialogue), which lasted some three hours. On breaking up, the

---

[1] Travels in North America, by the Honorable Charles Augustus Murray, vol. i., p. 158. Murray, by the bye, was a grandson of Lord Dunmore.

two former commenced, on their way homeward, praising the depth and learning of their noble host. Said Ames, after a short talk, "to confess the truth, Dexter, I have not understood a word of his argument for half an hour." "And I," good-humoredly rejoined Dexter, "have been out of my depth for an hour and a half."'[1]

The Chief Justice fearing the effects of age upon his mind, and anxious that, 'in life's last scenes,' he might not exhibit another instance of the 'follies of the wise,' had charged his confidential friends to let him know whenever they perceived the slightest abatement in his intellectual vigor, and he would at once retire from the Bench. But they never had occasion to perform that delicate office. His intellect remained unclouded and undimmed to the last moment. At the session of the Supreme Court, however, in the winter of 1835, it was apparent that his health was rapidly declining. His complaints were very much aggravated by the injuries received while travelling in the stage between Fredericksburgh and Richmond, on his return home at the close of the term. He suffered great pain through the spring; but, early in June, experienced a delusive interval of convalescence. It did not last long, and, at the earnest solicitation of friends, he revisited Philadelphia to seek that relief which the medical skill of that city had formerly afforded him. He was accompanied by three of his sons,[2] and through-

[1] Story's Life and Letters, vol. ii., p. 404.

[2] His eldest son, Mr. Thomas Marshall, who was 'highly esteemed for his talents, his many virtues, and his exemplary and useful life,' was killed at Baltimore by the fall of a chimney, while on his way to attend the death-bed of his father. He died June 28th. This melancholy calamity was considerately concealed from the dying parent.

out his illness had every consolation from filial attention, and from the kindness and attention of his numerous friends at Philadelphia, who manifested the deepest interest in his situation, and did all in their power to alleviate it. But it was evident, from the moment of his arrival in the city, that the sands of his life had nearly run out. The cause of his death was a very diseased condition of the liver, which was enormously enlarged, and contained several tuberculous abscesses of great size; its pressure upon the stomach had the effect of dislodging this organ from its natural situation, and compressing it in such a manner, that, for some time previous to his death, it would not retain the smallest quantity of nutriment.[1] He was conscious of his approaching end, and viewed it with perfect composure. Two days before his death, and in full view of it, with a modesty characteristic of himself, he wrote the following inscription for his monumental tablet: — 'John Marshall, son of Thomas and Mary Marshall, was born on the 24th of September, 1755, intermarried with Mary Willis Ambler the 3d of January, 1783, departed this life the —— day of ——, 18—.'

He expired without a struggle, on Monday, the 6th of July, 1835, about six o'clock in the evening. The news of his death elicited everywhere manifestations of sorrow and respect. The citizens of Philadelphia assembled in town meeting to express their sentiments on the occasion. The venerable Bishop White, then in the 88th year of his age, presided. Suitable resolutions were adopted, and the whole proceedings evinced the respect and reverence with which his character was regarded.

---

[1] Randolph's Memoir of Dr. Physick, p. 101.

His remains were conveyed to Richmond, accompanied by a committee of the Philadelphia Bar. On their arrival at that place they were met by an imposing procession composed of the military, the Masonic brethren, the civil authorities, and citizens, and escorted to his residence, where the funeral service was performed by the Right Reverend Bishop Moore, in a most fervent and feeling manner. He was buried near the ashes of his wife, in what was called the New Burying-ground. It is said that his statue, representing Justice, will occupy one of the six pedestals that surround the main column of the Washington Monument now being erected in the Capitol square at Richmond. Certainly nothing could be more appropriate.

Judge Marshall was a sincere friend to religion, and a constant attendant upon its ministrations. Brought up in the Episcopal Church, he adhered to it through life, though not until a short time before his death a believer in its fundamental doctrines.

'I often visited,' says the Rev. Mr. Norwood, 'Mrs. General Harvey during her last sickness. From her I received this statement. She was much with her father [Judge Marshall] during the last months of his life, and told me that the reason why he never communed was, that he was a Unitarian in opinion, though he never joined their society. He told her that he believed in the truth of the Christian revelation, but not in the divinity of Christ; therefore he could not commune in the Episcopal Church. But, during the last months of his life, he read Keith on Prophecy, where our Saviour's divinity is incidentally treated, and was convinced by his work, and the fuller investigation to which it led, of the supreme divinity of the Saviour. He determined to apply for admission to the communion of our Church—objected to communion in private, because he thought it his duty to make a public confession of the Saviour; and, while waiting for improved health to enable him to go to the Church for that purpose, he grew worse, and died, without ever communing. Mrs. Harvey was a lady of the strictest probity, the most humble piety, and of a clear, discriminating mind; and her statement, the substance of which I give you accurately (having reduced it to writing), may be entirely relied on.

I remember to have heard Bishop Moore repeatedly express his surprise (when speaking of Judge Marshall), that, though he was so punctual in his attendance at church, and reproved Mr. ——, and Mr. ——, and Mr. ——, when they were absent, and knelt during the prayers and responded fervently, yet he never communed. The reason was that he gave to his daughter, Mrs. Harvey. She said he died an humble, penitent believer in Christ, according to the orthodox creed of the Church. . . .

'P. S.—Another fact, illustrating the lasting influence of maternal instruction, was mentioned by Mrs. Harvey. Her father told her that he never went to bed without concluding his prayers with those which his mother taught him when a child, viz., the Lord's Prayer, and the prayer beginning, "Now I lay me down to sleep."'[1]

I can never forget,' says Bishop Meade, 'how he would prostrate his tall form before the rude low

---

[1] Old Churches and Families of Virginia, vol. ii., p. 223, note. Letter from Rev. William Norwood to Bishop Meade.

benches without backs, at Cool Spring Meeting-house, in the midst of his children, and grandchildren, and his old neighbors. In Richmond he always set an example to the gentlemen of the same conformity, though many of them did not follow it. At the building of the Monumental Church he was much incommoded by the narrowness of the pews, which partook too much of the modern fashion. Not finding room for his whole body within the pew, he used to take his seat nearest the door of his pew, and throwing it open, let his legs stretch a little into the aisle.' [1]

He not only conformed to the ceremonies of religion, but his whole life evinced virtuous principles and affections. 'He had no frays in his boyhood. He had no quarrels or outbreakings in manhood. He was the composer of strifes. He spoke ill of no man. He meddled not with their affairs. He viewed their worst deeds through the medium of charity. He had eight sisters and six brothers, with all of whom, from youth to age, his intercourse was marked by the utmost kindness and affection; and although his eminent talents, high public character, and acknowledged usefulness, could not fail to be a subject of pride and admiration to all of them, there is no one of his numerous relations, who has had the happiness of a personal association with him, in whom his purity, simplicity, and affectionate benevolence, did not produce a deeper and more cherished impression, than all the achievements of his powerful intellect.' 'In private life he was upright, and scrupulously just in all his transactions. His friendships were ardent, sincere, and constant — his charity and benevolence unbounded. He was fond

[1] Old Churches and Families of Virginia, vol. ii., p. 221, note.

of society, and, in the social circle, cheerful and unassuming. He participated freely in conversation, but, from modesty, rather followed than led. Magnanimous and forgiving, he never bore malice, of which illustrious instances might be given. A republican from feeling and judgment, he loved equality, abhorred all distinctions founded upon rank instead of merit, and had no preference for the rich over the poor. Religious from sentiment and reflection, he was a Christian, believed in the Gospel, and practised its tenets.' [1]

Such was John Marshall in his youth and in his age. We need add no more. The circle is complete. We have recorded his services, and furnished the evidence of his virtues.

---

[1] The testimony of a kinsman and of a friend. Vide, Binney's Eulogy on John Marshall, p. 68.

INDEX.

THE END.